Problems
of
National
Strategy

This book was compiled
under the auspices of
The Center for International Affairs
Harvard University

Problems
of
National
Strategy

A BOOK OF READINGS

EDITED BY

Henry A. Kissinger

FREDERICK A. PRAEGER, *Publishers*

New York   Washington   London

FREDERICK A. PRAEGER, PUBLISHERS
111 Fourth Avenue, New York, N.Y. 10003, U.S.A.
5, Cromwell Place, London S.W.7, England

Published in the United States of America in 1965
by Frederick A. Praeger, Inc., Publishers
Third printing, 1968

© 1965, by Frederick A. Praeger, Inc.

Library of Congress Catalog Card Number: 65–24933

Printed in the United States of America

Acknowledgments

In preparing this book, the assistance of Maury Feld, Librarian of the Center for International Affairs, Harvard University, has been invaluable. His advice regarding selections and introductory notes has been crucial. Elisabeth Sifton, of the Praeger editorial department, has been patient and enormously efficient.

HENRY A. KISSINGER

Contents

Contents

Problems
of
National
Strategy

Editor's Introduction

THE NATURE OF MODERN POWER

It has been a commonplace to say that we are living in an age of technological, strategic, and political upheaval. In order to understand the nature of the changed relationship between power and policy, a few definitions are required:

1. *Offensive* power is the ability of a political unit to impose its will on another.

2. *Defensive* power is the ability of a state to avoid coercion by another.

Defensive power may be further subdivided into purely defensive policy and precautionary policy. Power has a purely defensive use when a country waits for a threat to materialize before dealing with it. It is used in a precautionary manner when policy is directed toward preventing potential and not actual challengers. The policy of the United States before World War II was purely defensive. The tendency was to allow threats to become unambiguous and then to muster every effort to overcome them. The United States could afford such a course because its wide margin of survival guaranteed that no conceivable early reverse could menace the national interest.

Great Britain's policy in the eighteenth and nineteenth centuries illustrates the precautionary mode of action. Britain acted on the principle that Antwerp must not fall into the hands of a modern power. This was not because of any certainty that a major power would use Antwerp with hostile intent. Rather, British policy was based on the proposition that by the time the opponents' intentions were clear, it was too late to affect them.

3. *Deterrent power* is the ability to prevent certain threats or actions from being carried out by posing an equivalent or greater threat.

There is no inevitable symmetry between offensive and defensive power. Some states have had little of the first but much of the second. Switzerland, for example, has managed to combine inac-

3

cessibility of terrain with the ability to mobilize a considerable proportion of its national resources. States in this position have been able to prevent other countries from imposing their will. On the other hand, they have not played a very active role in international affairs.

Power has no absolute measurement; it is always relative. In the seventeenth century, it would have been futile to try to compare the power of Japan and that of Great Britain, since they possessed no means of bringing their strength to bear on each other. This geographical separation of power remained a fact until the middle of the nineteenth century. And, after that, one small continent, Europe, was physically far superior to the rest and could dictate international affairs.

Power also depends on psychological as well as objective factors. Until it is actually used, it is what people think it is.

All these factors have been dramatically altered in the contemporary period.

Until the industrial revolution, total war in the modern sense of fully mobilizing all national resources was impossible. Subsistence economies simply could not spare the manpower or the resources for protracted large-scale operations. Armies were, therefore, largely composed of mercenaries, and they were small because the economy could not support a substantial standing force. A mercenary army did not possess the morale of modern citizen armies; the soldiers were not personally concerned with the fate of the country for which they fought. In the crudest sense, their ability to carry on their profession depended on their survival. Typical battles of the eighteenth century involved complicated maneuvers, which determined the relative position of the two sides. They caused relatively few casualties because both commanders were eager to conserve their resources and could not rely on the staying power of their troops. Citizen armies, on the other hand, which appeared during periods when political or religious passions ran high, could not conduct uninterrupted operations; in the absence of a surplus of manpower, they frequently had to disband during the harvest season.

Of course, wars fought by countries with subsistence economies did produce great suffering. The very narrow margin of survival ensured that any disturbance of the economic balance was likely to produce cataclysmic effects on society. As a result, until the industrial revolution, the collateral effects of war (casualties caused by starvation or pestilence) were usually more severe than those of the battlefield.

The industrial revolution made possible the total mobilization of modern war. This trend was given impetus by the relatively small destructiveness of what is now called conventional technology. Until the middle of the nineteenth century, weapons were simple and easy to manufacture and their destructive power was relatively low. In order to put a premium on industrial potential, weapons must be sufficiently complex to require a substantial production effort, but not so destructive as to drain the national substance before industrial mobilization can make itself felt. As a result, industrial potential proved strategically most significant when there existed a balance between the destructiveness of weapons and the complexity of the means of their delivery. Any substantial increase either in the power of weapons or in their number could then be translated into a strategic advantage. This situation led to the total mobilization of the two World Wars.

Modern technology has changed these conditions dramatically. Modern weapons are enormously destructive; they are always in a high state of readiness. If the stockpiles of weapons available at the beginning of a war suffice to destroy the opponent's industrial potential, it is clear that industrial potential has lost a great deal of its significance, and that the side whose forces-in-being are superior will gain a decisive advantage. Above all, the nature of strategy has changed fundamentally when the decision to go to war hazards the lives of tens of millions instead of thousands, when what is risked is no longer the loss of a province but the survival of society itself.

This situation reflects the basic paradox of contemporary technology. Power has never been greater; it has also never been less useful. In the past, the major problem of strategists was to assemble superior strength; in the contemporary period, the problem more frequently is how to discipline the available power into some relationship to objectives likely to be in dispute. Yet, no matter what spectrum of power the major contenders may have at their disposal, the fear of escalation is inescapable. Though states have an unprecedented possibility to devastate their opponent, their threats to use this capability have only a limited credibility. This is because the ability to destroy is not related to the ability to disarm—so that using one's nuclear arsenal indiscriminately against a major opponent only guarantees self-destruction.

This problem is made more acute because the primary purpose of modern weapons is deterrence. But deterrence is as much a psychological as a military problem. It depends on the aggressor's assessment of risks, not the defender's. A threat meant as a bluff but taken seriously is more useful for purposes of deterrence than a "genuine" threat interpreted as a bluff.

Moreover, if deterrence is successful, aggression does *not* take place. It is impossible, however, to demonstrate why something has *not* occurred. It can never be proved, for example, whether peace has been maintained because a country pursues an optimum strategy or a marginally effective one. Finally, the more effective deterrence is, the more credible becomes the argument that perhaps the enemy never intended to attack in the first place. An effective deterrent strategy may thus have built-in pressures to strengthen the arguments of those who argue that a defense effort is unnecessary.

Even when the necessity for a military policy is not challenged, serious disputes are produced by the novelty of modern weapons. Never before in history has so much depended on weapons so new, so untested, so "abstract." Nuclear wepons have been used in wartime only against Japan, which did not possess means of retaliation. No one knows how governments or people will react to a nuclear explosion under conditions where both sides possess vast arsenals.

Then, too, modern weapons systems are relatively untested. During the debate over the Nuclear Test Ban Treaty, a great deal of attention was focused on the adequacy of nuclear warheads. In fact, the other components of modern weapons systems contain many more factors of uncertainty. The estimated "hardness" of Minuteman silos depends entirely on theoretical studies. Of the thousands of missiles in our arsenal, relatively few of each category have been tested under operational conditions. There is little experience with salvo firing. Air-defense systems are designed without any definite knowledge of the nature of the offense. A high proportion of the phenomena discovered in nuclear testing has been unexpected.

The novelty of modern weapons is compounded by the difficulty of forming a plausible conception for their use. How does one threaten an enemy with solid-fuel missiles? As these are always in an extreme state of readiness, how does one demonstrate an increase in preparedness, which has historically served as a warning? During the Cuban missile crisis of October, 1962, dispersing Strategic Air Command planes to civilian airports proved an effective warning. What will be an equivalent move when strategic forces are composed entirely of missiles?

DEFINITION OF NATIONAL SECURITY POLICY

National security policy in the nuclear age thus goes far beyond the traditional concept of assembling overwhelming power. It includes political, psychological, economic, and social factors. In its widest sense, it comprises every action by which a society seeks to assure its survival or to realize its aspirations internationally. This definition embraces all measures that have a bearing on the strength and vitality of society. A more significant definition of national security policy is the way in which the term is used within the United States Government: the policy area where power impinges on national objectives. In this sense, national security policy includes defense policy—the development of a country's military potential—but it also involves the attempt to influence the actions of other countries either by organizing them in efforts of collective defense or by creating an environment in which neutrality is possible. It involves a policy for dealing with what the West calls insurgency and the Communists define as wars of national liberation. National security policy embraces the efforts to discipline the arms race through formal or informal arrangements. Arms control and disarmament, in short, are not alternatives to national security policy but an integral part of it. Finally, any consideration of national security policy must deal with the organizational machinery by which it is devised and implemented.

Therefore, this book is subdivided into the following sections:

I. Strategic Doctrine and American Defense Policy
II. Alliances in the Nuclear Age
III. Neutrality and the Problem of Insurgency
IV. The Control of Modern Weapons
V. National Security Policy and Governmental Organization

I have introduced each section of the book with a brief explanatory note outlining the theoretical framework of the issues discussed. Each of the chapters, in addition, is prefaced by a brief note in which I summarize the main points, identify the author, and explain the significance of his argument.

HENRY A. KISSINGER

Cambridge, Massachusetts
August, 1965

PART I

Strategic Doctrine and American Defense Policy

Every advanced country has more technical choices to make than it can afford. Whether it selects missiles with large or small warheads, whether it emphasizes nuclear or conventional power, will depend more on its strategic doctrine than on the technology available to it. But strategic doctrine must not be thought of as something theoretical or dogmatic. Its role is to define the likely dangers and how to deal with them, to project feasible goals and how to attain them. It must furnish a mode of action for the circumstances it defines as "ordinary." Its adequacy will be tested according to whether these ordinary events do in fact occur and whether the forces developed in their anticipation are adequate to deal with the real challenges.

In the period between the world wars, French strategists exalted the value of the defensive and built their plans around the Maginot Line. However, the likely German attempts to overthrow the Treaty of Versailles could be prevented only by French offensive action. By the time the Maginot Line might prove useful, in other words, the Versailles settlement would already have been over-turned. Thus, French strategic doctrine contributed to the paralysis of French policy. When German armies re-occupied the Rhine-land and attacked France's allies in Eastern Europe, French power remained passive and French diplomacy stood impotent. Even when the long-awaited attack in the West finally came, it turned the flank of the French fortifications.

A wrong strategic doctrine can lead to disaster. An excessively rigid strategic doctrine can absorb great energy in the attempt to reconcile what happens with what is expected. If it is too complicated, it can break down under the stress of decision-making. The

9

Schlieffen Plan, Germany's military design for World War I, provided for every contingency except the psychological strain on the commander. It failed largely because the German leaders lost their nerve. In the face of Russian advances into eastern Germany—foreseen by the Schlieffen Plan—they rushed reinforcements from the West, weakening their offensive power at the crucial moment. It adds to the irony of the situation that these reinforcements were in transit when the decisive battles in both the East *and* the West were being fought.

But if there is no doctrine at all and a society operates pragmatically—solving problems "on the merits," as the saying goes—every event becomes a special case. More energy is spent deciding where one is than where one is going. Each event is compartmentalized and dealt with by experts in the special difficulties it involves, without an adequate understanding of its relation to other occurrences.

Considerations such as these are especially relevant to the strategic debate as it has developed in the United States since World War II. The United States emerged from the war in a position of unchallenged military superiority. The war seemed to have confirmed all traditional American strategic axioms. Despite its late mobilization, the United States had, together with its allies, crushed the aggressor. Victory had been achieved by a massive outpouring of matériel. Strategic bombing, in which the United States could engage without fear of retaliation, was seen by many as a key to victory, and victory was conceived in terms of unconditional surrender.

Inevitably, this caused American strategic thought in the postwar period to start as an adaptation of World War II maxims. Nuclear weapons were incorporated into existing practices as a more efficient explosive. In 1948, General Omar N. Bradley said:

Plans for national security must consider the possibility that the United States will be subject to air and air-borne attack on the outset. The likelihood and the practicability of this kind of attack increases daily. . . . We would [therefore] have to immediately secure bases from which an enemy might attack us by air. Next we will have to launch an immediate counterattack . . . predominantly through the air. . . . To make our counterblows we will need bases which we do not have now. The seizing and holding of [these] bases . . . will require Army combat elements. . . . Lastly comes the phase of total mobilization and maximum offensive efforts. In conjunction with the air and naval arms, the Army will engage in joint operations designed to carry the war to the enemy with ever increasing intensity. The closer we get to the enemy, the more determined will be his resistance.[1]

The theory of massive retaliation was far from new when Secretary Dulles proclaimed it.

During the 1950's, it became evident that the growth of Soviet long-range nuclear power presented new problems. For the first time, an aggressor could mount a threat to the United States not only from outlying bases but from its homeland. The subtle studies of Albert Wohlstetter (two of which are reprinted here; see below, Chapter 2, pp. 34 ff., and Chapter 10, pp. 186 ff.) demonstrated that the strategic balance was "delicate" depending on such factors as the vulnerability of the bases of the retaliatory force, the relative state of active and passive defense, and the ability to reach enemy targets.

Though the intention of these studies was to call attention to the vulnerability of U.S. strategic forces, they could also be used to emphasize that military victory remained a significant concept even in a general nuclear war. American strategic doctrine of the 1960's, strongly influenced, therefore, by these concepts, has the following major components:

1. *Flexible Response.* In the late 1950's, United States strategy emphasized a single all-out response. If general nuclear war proved inevitable, the goal was to be to destroy the opposing society essentially in one blow.

The Kennedy Administration replaced this with an approach that offered more alternatives. An attempt was made to develop the maximum number of options even for the contingency of general nuclear war—a strategy summed up in the phrase "flexible response." This strategy was described by Secretary of Defense Robert S. McNamara in 1962 as follows:

> Our forces can be used in several different ways. We may have to retaliate with a single massive attack. Or, we may be able to use our retaliatory forces to limit damage done to ourselves, and our allies, by knocking out the enemy's bases before he has had time to launch his second salvos. We may seek to terminate a war on favorable terms by using our forces as a bargaining weapon—by threatening further attack.[2]

[1] U.S. House of Representatives, *National Military Establishment Appropriation for 1949*, Hearings before the Subcommittee of the Committee on Appropriations, 80th Cong., 2d sess., pp. 3–4.

[2] Address before the Fellows of the American Bar Foundation Dinner, Chicago, Illinois, February 17, 1962, Department of Defense, Office of Public Affairs, *News Release No. 239–62* (February 17, 1962).

The purpose of the flexible-response strategy as first enunciated was victory in the traditional sense:

> To the extent feasible, basic military strategy in a possible general nuclear war should be approached in much the same way that more conventional military operations have been conducted in the past. That is to say, principal military objectives . . . should be the destruction of the enemy's military forces, not of his civilian population.[3]

Thus, flexible response, when it was first developed, was identified with counter-force strategy.

2. *Hostility to National Nuclear Forces.* Flexible response presupposes a centralized system of command and control and highly invulnerable strategic forces. Whatever possibility exists of limiting nuclear war depends on the ability of planners aware of the strategic context to use nuclear weapons according to an over-all concept. American doctrine has considered the existence of strategic nuclear forces not under United States control inconsistent with these requirements. Secretary McNamara said:

> We are convinced that a general nuclear war target system is indivisible, and if, despite all our efforts, nuclear war should occur, our best hope lies in conducting a centrally controlled campaign against all of the enemy's vital nuclear capabilities, while retaining reserve forces, all centrally controlled.[4]

President Kennedy described the French nuclear program as "inimical" to NATO. Secretary McNamara called European nuclear forces "dangerous," "expensive," "prone to obsolescence," and "lacking in credibility." Under Secretary of State George Ball criticized these nuclear forces because "the road toward nuclear proliferation has no logical ending."[5] In short, the Pentagon interprets the requirement of central control to mean the integration of strategic nuclear forces in a way that forecloses the technical possibility of independent use. If any of our allies are to have nuclear forces of their own—and the clear United States preference is that they do not—these must be an adjunct to United States strategic forces and under what amounts in practice to American control.

[3] McNamara, Address at the Commencement Exercises, University of Michigan, Ann Arbor, Michigan, June 16, 1962, *Department of State Bulletin*, XLVII, No. 1202 (July 9, 1962), 67.

[4] *Ibid.*, p. 68.

[5] "NATO and World Responsibility," *The Atlantic Community Quarterly*, II, No. 2 (Summer, 1964), 211.

3. *Tactical Nuclear Weapons.* United States strategic doctrine has shown considerable ambivalence about tactical nuclear weapons, which in the 1950's were considered a key element of the military establishment. On the one hand, the number of tactical nuclear weapons has been considerably increased—according to official Pentagon estimates, by some 60 per cent in NATO alone. On the other hand, tactical nuclear weapons do not really fit the Administration's strategic concept.

Tactical nuclear weapons in the hands of front-line units are extremely difficult to subject to the central command and control envisaged by the new doctrine. If used for local defense, they would be likely to pass rapidly beyond the control of governments or high-level commanders. The Administration has repeatedly stressed the danger of such escalation. As former Deputy Secretary of Defense Roswell Gilpatric put it, "I, for one, have never believed in a so-called limited nuclear war. I just don't know how you build a limit into it once you start using any kind of a nuclear bang."[6] And, in the spring of 1961, Secretary McNamara said that, in his concept, limited war in effect excluded the use of *any* nuclear weapons. "I think by 'limited' war we simply mean war that is carried on for the most part with non-nuclear weapons."[7] Deputy Assistant Secretary of Defense Alain C. Enthoven said on February 10, 1963:

> There has been, in recent years, the development of small nuclear weapons having yields equivalent to a few thousand tons of TNT or less. The day will come, if it has not already, when there will be nuclear weapons of smaller yield than the largest high-explosive weapons. When that day comes, will there no longer be a distinction between nuclear and conventional weapons? Some have argued to that effect. But they are mistaken. There is and will remain an important distinction, a "firebreak" if you like, between nuclear and non-nuclear war, a recognizable qualitative distinction that both combatants can recognize and agree upon one. And in the nuclear age they will have a very powerful incentive to agree upon this distinction and limitation, because if they do not there does not appear to be another easily recognizable limitation on weapons—no other obvious "firebreak"—all the way up the destructive spectrum to large-scale thermonuclear war.[8]

[6] *The New York Times*, June 7, 1961.

[7] U.S. House of Representatives, *Department of Defense, Appropriations for 1962*, Hearings before the Subcommittee of the Committee on Appropriations (87th Cong., 1st sess., 1961, Part 3), p. 136.

[8] U.S. Senate, Committee on Armed Services, *Military Procurement Authorization: Fiscal Year 1964*, Hearings on H.R. 2440 (88th Cong., 1st sess., 1963), p. 168.

4. *Conventional Defense.* In the 1960's, American strategic doctrine placed new emphasis on conventional defense. "The decision
to employ tactical nuclear weapons," testified Secretary McNamara
before the House Armed Services Committee in January, 1963,
"should not be forced upon us simply because we have no other
way to cope with a particular situation."[9] Enthoven stressed this
view in a major statement, reproduced in Part II of this book, a
little later that year:

> We will have no sensible alternative to building up our conventional
> forces to the point at which they can safely resist all forms of non-
> nuclear aggression. Our forces will be adequate if we can never be
> forced because of weakness to be the first to have to resort to nuclear
> weapons.[10]

The logical attractiveness of this theory obscured many difficulties. This was particularly true of Secretary McNamara's proposition at Ann Arbor in June, 1962, that a general nuclear war could
be conducted on the basis of purely military consideration—the so-
called counter-force strategy. It soon became apparent that the
reliability of a counter-force strategy was bound to decline as the
retaliatory forces multiplied and became more dispersed. As missile
systems become more diversified and sophisticated, some will be
hardened as underground installations; some will be mobile on
land, others at sea. This will enormously complicate the problem
of coordinating an attack.

Thus, even if the percentage of the Soviet retaliatory force the
United States is able to destroy were to remain constant for the
next decade—an unwarrantedly optimistic assumption—the absolute number remaining is bound to increase. Whatever its technical
feasibility, there are certain to be increasing political and psychological obstacles to a strategy that is based on fragmentary intelligence and that depends on large numbers of weapons for which
there is no operational experience in wartime.

Moreover, the counter-force theory implied that because the
United States was numerically superior and therefore in a position
to spare Soviet cities, the Soviet Union would have an "incentive"
to spare those of the United States. Of course, Soviet military theorists have consistently denied the possibility of this kind of war.

[9] U.S. House of Representatives, Committee on Armed Services, *Fiscal Year
1965–68, Defense Program, 1964 Defense Budget,* January 30, 1963, p. 18.
[10] Address to the Loyola University Forum for National Affairs, Los Angeles,
February 10, 1963. See below, Chapter 6, pp. 120 ff.

This would not be decisive were it not in accord with the realities of the strategic equation. For a war of attrition, even if it were technically feasible, cannot be in the interest of the weaker side. Against a numerically superior opponent, the sensible strategy would be to shock him into stopping his attack while some forces remain, by attacking objectives of great value to him—such as cities.

This is why United States doctrine has grown more modest. Within two years of the enunciation of the counter-force theory, Secretary McNamara started to set much more limited aims for the strategy of flexible response. "Fully hard ICBM sites can be destroyed but only at great cost in terms of the numbers of offensive weapons required to dig them out," he said in 1964:

> Furthermore, in a second strike situation, we would be attacking for the most part empty sites from which the missiles had already been fired. The value of trying to provide a capability to destroy a very high proportion of Soviet hard ICBM sites becomes even more questionable in view of the expected increase in the Soviet missile launching submarine force.[11]

The purpose was primarily to limit the damage to the United States in follow-up attacks:

> Thus, a "damage-limiting" strategy appears to be the most practical and effective course for us to follow. . . . While there are still some differences of judgment on just how large such a force should be, there is general agreement that it should be large enough to ensure the destruction, singly or in combination, of the Soviet Union, Communist China, and the Communist satellites as national societies, under the worst possible circumstances of war outbreak that can reasonably be postulated, and, in addition, to destroy their warmaking capability so as to limit, to the extent practicable, damage to this country and to our allies.[12]

In his testimony before the Armed Services Committees in 1965, Secretary McNamara pointed out that under the then projected programs, *fatalities* in a general nuclear war would not be lower than 122 million—or more than half of the population of the United States. In these conditions, it is no longer meaningful to

11 U.S. Senate, Armed Services Committee, *Hearings, Military Procurement Authorization Fiscal Year 1964*, 88th Cong., 1st sess., pp. 40–41.

12 U.S. House of Representatives, Subcommittee of the Committee on Appropriations, *Hearings, Department of Defense Appropriations for 1965*, 88th Cong., 2d sess., Part 4, pp. 25–28.

speak of nuclear war as involving the same principles as traditional military operations.

United States strategic doctrine has thus had to face the fact that in the nuclear age, a general war fought by purely military criteria must have catastrophic consequences. Many of the traditional tenets of national security policy have been shaken by this realization.

ONE

HERMAN KAHN

Escalation as a Strategy

[*Editor's Note: "Escalation as a Strategy" provides a comprehensive presentation of the whole range of conceivable international conflict, beginning with official expressions of disagreement and concluding with resort to all-out violence. The approach is analytical and descriptive, not narrative. National security policy is treated as a logical and reasoned extension of foreign policy. In Mr. Kahn's view, escalation is a process whereby measures which individually appear logical and reasonable generate a momentum of their own. This argument, as it appears in the essay here, represents a substantial evolution from Mr. Kahn's earlier point of view as he expressed it in* On Thermonuclear War, *published in 1960, in which he tended to treat war as a catastrophe whose effects could, to a considerable degree, be controlled and modified by rational and painstaking planning and preparation. The most serious danger lay in a widespread view that thermonuclear war was incalculable, an attitude that would guarantee a catastrophe if war did break out.*

"Escalation as a Strategy" examines thermonuclear war from another perspective: as the "next step" in a process whose previous stages have appeared to be obvious, logical, and justifiable. In On Thermonuclear War, *Mr. Kahn warned that if thermonuclear war was considered so "different" as to be incalculable, the result might invite disaster. In "Escalation as a Strategy," he shows how assimilation of thermonuclear war into the conventions of "the manipulation of violence" can cause the chief actors to slide towards the abyss because they lose the ability to make vital distinctions.*]

Escalation is a relatively new word in the English language. Though it is becoming more common in newspaper headlines, especially in connection with Vietnam, the dictionaries have yet

EDITOR'S NOTE: Condensed from *On Escalation: Metaphors and Scenarios.* Copyright © 1965 by Frederick A. Praeger, Inc. Reprinted by permission.

to define it in a military sense. To many people, escalation connotes an automatic rise in the scale of warfare from the level of an incident to the level of catastrophic nuclear exchange. But to more and more students of military strategy and tactics, it has also come to describe the kind of calculated risk taking that is an established factor of limited conflict in the nuclear age.

Strategies that emphasize the possibility of escalation are associated with the term "brinkmanship." Under modern circumstances no nation wishes to play at brinkmanship recklessly. But to the extent that any nuclear nation is serious in any incipient conflict—or to the extent that it *pretends* to be serious—it will have to face the consequences of being on the escalation ladder. However, a strategy of escalation, carefully carried out, can actually reduce the dangers of insensate, spasmodic nuclear destruction.

Events in Vietnam provide a case in point. Our opponent in Vietnam can function with great success in one dimension of warfare: guerrilla combat and subversion. The U.S., in turn, has an immense superiority in air and naval power and, beyond that, in nuclear power. Behind the North Vietnamese are the Russians, with their nuclear forces, and the Chinese, with their major but ponderous land armies. But how close the ties may be, and how willing North Vietnam and its allies might be to involve themselves against the U.S., remains uncertain. In this complex situation, the U.S. has been attempting to use its areas of advantage to counter the special strengths of the opponents, to "escalate" the war in a calculated way, all the time trying to make it clear that it intends to abide by certain limitations—unless further provoked. In Vietnam, the U.S. is clearly a nation practicing the new dimensions of escalation, reflecting its new understanding of the reasoned and restrained, yet determined, use of limited force in a world of political challenge and nuclear danger.

To make this study concrete, I have devised a ladder—a metaphorical ladder—that provides a convenient list of some of the more important options facing the strategist. This ladder indicates that there are many continuous paths between a low-level crisis and an all-out war, none of which are necessarily or inexorably to be followed. My ladder provides a useful framework for the systematic study of a crisis. There is no attempt here to recommend any courses of action. What is attempted is to describe the way stations of ascending conflict so that the elements can be recognized, and the distance from all-out war estimated. There are, of course, those who think a study of escalation is dangerous and perhaps immoral; I believe that it is dangerous and perhaps immoral *not* to understand how nations might act under the pressures of successive crises. Hence this study of the rungs and thresholds is the best contribution I know how to make to the avoidance of recklessness or panic.

RUNG 1: OSTENSIBLE CRISIS. In this stage, one or both sides asserts, more or less openly and explicitly, that unless a given dispute is resolved in the immediate future, the rungs of the escalation ladder will be climbed. These threats are made credible by various hints as to how important the government considers the issues. There may be officially inspired newspaper stories to the effect that the chief of state takes a serious view of the matter. There may be explicit announcements or speeches by other important officials—but none of them of the bridge-burning variety, none deliberately designed to make it really difficult for these same officials to back down later.

RUNG 2: POLITICAL, ECONOMIC, AND DIPLOMATIC GESTURES. Legal but unfair, unfriendly, inequitable, or threatening acts are carried out against the opponent to punish or put pressure on him.

RUNG 3: SOLEMN AND FORMAL DECLARATIONS. Such declarations go much further than Rung 2 in demonstrating resolve and commitment, but they need not be deliberately hostile. They may provide merely an executive declaration to other states of a nation's policy in a certain area, perhaps deliberately avoiding a precise statement of the policy's applicability and limitations. An example of such ambiguity is the Congressional Resolution of August, 1964, passed at President Johnson's request as a result of the escalation in the Gulf of Tonkin. Congress resolved that "the United States is, therefore, prepared, as the President determines, to take all necessary steps including the use of armed force, to assist any member or protocol state of the Southeast Asia Collective Defense Treaty requesting assistance in defense of its freedom."

Such a proclamation is usually a warning to a potential opponent not to climb farther up the escalation ladder, at least in the area covered by the announcement. The declaration may be thought of as pre-emptive or preventive escalation, which tries to forestall further escalation by the opponent. It also marks the limit to which either side can go without dangerously rocking the boat.

RUNG 4: HARDENING OF POSITIONS. As soon as negotiations take on much more of a coercive than a contractual character, I would argue that we have passed the "don't-rock-the-boat" stage and reached Rung 4. Certainly this is true if either or both of the antagonists attempt to increase the credibility of their resolve and committal by irretrievable acts. Such an act might be an announcement by the Soviet Union that it has signed a peace treaty with East Germany and no longer has any direct control over the access routes to Berlin.

In such confrontations, either side could point out vividly to the other side's population or to its allies the totally destructive character of thermonuclear war, and state that there is thus no alternative to peace—with the clear implication that, unless the madmen on the other side come to their senses, all will be lost. Alternately, one can reassure one's own side by pointing out that the other side is not mad and will therefore back down.

RUNG 5: SHOW OF FORCE. As the crisis intensifies, one side or the other may draw attention to the fact that it does have the capability to use force if need be. There are various ways of showing such force—direct or indirect, silent or noisy. In a direct show of force, one or the other nation might move naval or air units, mobilize reserves, conduct provocative military exercises or maneuvers (particularly in sensitive areas), or even order "routine" deployment of naval and military units in such areas—all with widespread publicity. In an indirect show of force, one could test missiles in a provocative way, conduct normal maneuvers but with possibly abnormal publicity, publicize the use of military equipment in "normal" but special maneuvers that simulate an element in the current crisis—e.g., the use of tanks to break roadblocks.

RUNG 6: SIGNIFICANT MOBILIZATION. A show of force can be accompanied by a modest mobilization that not only increases one's strength but also indicates a readiness to call on more force or to accelerate the arms race. An example of this was President Kennedy's call-up of reserves in the Berlin crisis of 1962. As always, private communications, either direct or indirect, through principals or intermediates, or through the use of more or less deliberately arranged leaks, can all play an important role.

RUNG 7: "LEGAL" HARASSMENT. One may harass the opponent's prestige, property, or people legally. That is to say, one may act in a very hostile and provocative manner but within the limits of international law.

RUNG 8: HARASSING ACTS OF VIOLENCE. If the crisis is still not resolved, one side or the other may move on to illegal acts, such as acts of violence, or harassments intended to confuse, exhaust, frighten, and otherwise harm, weaken, or demoralize the opponent or its allies. Bombs may be exploded by unauthorized or anonymous means. Enemy nationals within one's borders may be badly mistreated or killed. An "aroused" citizenry may stone or raid the other nation's embassy. Frontier guards may be shot. There may be the limited covert use of guerrilla warfare, piracy, sabotage, or terrorization. Both sides could step up reconnaissance probing operations or other intelligence activities. One side or the other may launch overflights or other invasions of sovereignty.

If the acts are carried out clandestinely or covertly—under the guise of being individually motivated—the escalation is relatively low. As the size, scale, and degree of organization of these acts are increased and their official character made plain, the escalation is increased, until finally we reach a level at which uniformed personnel, obviously under the orders of their government, are carrying through the actions.

RUNG 9: DRAMATIC MILITARY CONFRONTATIONS. The existing permanent alert of U.S. and Soviet strategic-bomber and missile forces is an almost continual global confrontation. Under the circumstances of prolonged cold war, this may be regarded as pre-escalation. However, the situation changes if there is a dramatic local confrontation of land or sea forces (as, for example, at the Brandenburg Gate). Such confrontations are direct tests of nerve, resolve, and recklessness. They are also dramatic enough to make everyone take note of what has happened. Because it seems obvious that these confrontations can blow up, and because in the past such incidents have often caused wars, many people think of them as being closer to the brink of all-out war than in fact they usually are. But despite contemporary conditions of a relatively firm balance of terror, they do indeed indicate that large acts of violence are possible, and that the unthinkable all-out war is becoming "thinkable."

Thus we cross the "nuclear-war-is-unthinkable" threshold. It was to this threshold that we came during the Cuban missile crisis of October, 1962, at the climax of a case of abrupt escalation. President Kennedy's dramatic television address to the nation on Octo-

ber 22 explicitly told the Soviet Union where it had been unbear-
ably provocative. Both the U.S.S.R. and the U.S., he said, had
recognized the need for tacit rules in the postwar world and accordingly had "deployed strategic nuclear weapons with great care,
never upsetting the precarious status quo which insured that these
weapons would not be used in the absence of some vital challenges." He indicated that while the Americans had always been
careful, the Russians had now broken the rules in "this secret, swift,
extraordinary build-up of Communist missiles in an area well
known to have a special and historical relation to the United States.
. . . This sudden clandestine decision to station strategic weapons
for the first time outside of Soviet soil is a deliberately provocative
and unjustified change in the status quo, which cannot be accepted
by this country if our courage and our commitments are ever to be
trusted again by either friend or foe."

He went on to describe the detailed measures that the U.S. was
taking (mobilization, blockade, air alerts) and issued the famous
warning: "It shall be the policy of this nation to regard any nuclear
missile launched from Cuba against any nation in the Western
Hemisphere as an attack by the Soviet Union on the United States,
requiring a full retaliatory response upon the Soviet Union." (Of
course, anyone familiar with current U.S. policy would note that
the phrase "full retaliatory response" does not specify the form of
the attack.)

Then, and possibly most important of all, Mr. Kennedy issued
the following warning: "Any hostile move anywhere in the world
against the safety and freedom of peoples to whom we are committed, including in particular the brave people of West Berlin,
will be met by whatever action is needed." Some students of the
subject have questioned whether the President was wise to call the
Russians' attention to the option of Berlin. In fact, it is quite important to show that one is willing to face the possibility of such
counter-escalations.

RUNG 10: PROVOCATIVE DIPLOMATIC BREAK. This act would be intended to communicate to the opponent that one's reliance on the
traditional peaceful measures of persuasion or coercion is at an end
and that acts of force may now be resorted to.

RUNG 11: SUPER-READY STATUS. Strategic forces may be dispersed,
leaves canceled, preventive and routine maintenance halted, training deferred, every possible piece of equipment and unit put in a
ready status, and limited-war forces deployed. Because of the rela-

tive invulnerability and alertness under normal peacetime conditions of the U.S. Minuteman and Polaris forces (and to some extent of the SAC bombers on alert), such actions may make a
greater difference and thus mean more to the Soviet Union than
to the U.S.

RUNG 12: LARGE CONVENTIONAL WAR. The stage has now been set
for some kind of organized military violence. It may be undeclared
war or border fighting such as occurred between the Japanese
and the Russians in 1939 (involving thousands of soldiers), a
Trieste-type occupation of disputed territory, or a major "police
action," as in Korea. If such a war is fought with any intensity, both
sides suffer casualties in large numbers but neither will use its most
"efficient" or "quality" weapons—the nuclear, bacteriological, or
chemical weapons. Paradoxically, the more "useful" these weapons
are in the narrow military sense, the less likely they are to be used.
In any case, there would be many casualties at this rung and, at
least in the initial stages of the action, a significant deepening of
the crisis.

RUNG 13: LARGE COMPOUND ESCALATION. One way to achieve a high
over-all level of escalation and still keep each separate act as an act
relatively low on the ladder is to retaliate or escalate in a completely
different theater from that in which the primary conflict is being
waged. This may be especially escalatory if the second theater is
sensitive or potentially vital: such a situation might have arisen, for
example, if the Soviet Union had moved against Berlin during the
Cuban crisis.

It is interesting to note that, except for rather small-scale excep-
tions, this obvious technique has not been used since World War
II, even though there has been much concern about the possibility.
Nearly everyone has instinctively recognized the danger of compound escalation. The sheer audacity of starting a new crisis when
another is at full force is very provocative, yet in the paradoxical
world of escalation, this might be the very reason it would be
judged in certain circumstances to be an effective measure.

RUNG 14: DECLARATION OF LIMITED CONVENTIONAL WAR. This would
be an attempt to achieve one or both of the following objectives:
(1) a clear-cut, unilateral announcement of "no nuclear first use";
(2) a setting of the limits to a conventional war, geographically or
otherwise, in a manner considered favorable or stable by the side
making the declaration. Such a declaration would have grave sym-

bolic, political, and moral effects upon one's own country and the opponent.

RUNG 15: BARELY NUCLEAR WAR. It may occur during a conventional warlike act (Rung 12) or the super-ready status (Rung 11) that a nuclear weapon is used unintentionally (accidentally or without authorization). Or one of the antagonists may make military or political use of a nuclear weapon and try to give the impression that its use was unintentional.

RUNG 16: NUCLEAR "ULTIMATUMS." One side or the other seriously considers the possibility of a central war and communicates this fact convincingly to its opponent. People begin leaving cities; in fact, one might define an intense crisis as that point when 10 per cent of the population of New York City or Moscow has left out of fear of attack.

RUNG 17: LIMITED EVACUATION (ABOUT 20 PER CENT). This would most likely be at least a quasi-official move ordered by a government either for bargaining or prudential reasons, or both. The difficulties, and possible public and political reactions, make such an evacuation a momentous decision.

RUNG 18: SPECTACULAR SHOW OF FORCE. A spectacular show or demonstration of force would involve using major weapons in a way that does no obvious damage but appears determined, menacing, or reckless. An example would be the explosion of a weapon at a high altitude over enemy territory. This would intensify the fear of war in the hope of frightening the enemy into backing down.

RUNG 19: "JUSTIFIABLE" COUNTER-FORCE ATTACK. A "justifiable" attack would be sufficiently specialized and limited to seem a reasonable response to provocation, and yet it might significantly, or even decisively, degrade the military capability, prestige, or morale of the opponent. An example would be the destruction of a submarine on the claim that it had carried out threatening maneuvers: here, a high degree of escalation could easily be involved, particularly if the casualty were a strategic-weapons submarine. A nation could invent an excuse for such an act by manufacturing an incident—perhaps by fabricating a limited nuclear attack and blaming the submarine.

RUNG 20: "PEACEFUL" WORLD-WIDE EMBARGO OR BLOCKADE. World-wide embargo would be an extreme measure of non-violent coercion brought to bear against an opponent.

Once war has started, no other line of demarcation is at once so clear, so easily defined, and so easily understood as the line between not using and using nuclear weapons. There are, of course, criticisms of this point of view. Some of them take as their point of departure a fact of physics and engineering—that it is possible to have an extremely low-yield nuclear weapon that is no more powerful than a chemical explosive. True, the distinction between very small nuclear weapons and large chemical explosives does tend to narrow under analysis. But any argument designed to refute the nuclear prohibition on purely technical energy-release grounds misses the point: even though the distinction between nuclear and non-nuclear war may have defects from some technical points of view, the distinction possesses a functional meaning or utility that transcends any purely technical question.

We should support and encourage this distinction because, for a variety of reasons that cannot be detailed in this space, it works to the advantage of both the U.S. and the world as a whole. But it is equally important to understand that once the threshold has been crossed—by an enemy, by accident, or by us—we do not stand automatically in the balance of the unthinkable war. The first use of nuclear weapons, even if against military targets, is likely to be less for the purpose of destroying the other side's military forces or to handicap its operations than for redress, bargaining, or deterrence purposes.

RUNG 21: LOCAL NUCLEAR WAR—EXEMPLARY. One side can drop a nuclear bomb or two in order to show the other side that, unless it backs down or accepts a reasonable compromise, more bombs are likely to follow. As this would be the first unmistakably deliberate use of these weapons since World War II, it would be a profoundly consequential act.

RUNG 22: DECLARATION OF LIMITED NUCLEAR WAR. A nation could use a formal declaration to set relatively exact limits to the types of nuclear action that it intends to initiate—and to indicate the type of retaliation it is prepared to countenance from the enemy without escalating further himself. In this way, eruption to all-out war might be made less likely, and the escalation itself made more explicit—which might increase the pressure to compromise. The declaration could also include a formal announcement of the conditions under which the declarer would be prepared to de-escalate.

RUNG 23: LOCAL NUCLEAR WAR. Past NATO planning has envisaged the immediate use of hundreds of nuclear weapons in reply to even a conventional attack in Europe by the U.S.S.R. As opposed to the exemplary purposes of Rung 21, NATO planned to use nuclear weapons for traditional military purposes—for defense, destruction of the opponent's local capability, etc.—and the scale of the action and the targeting were to be dictated by these military considerations. The increasing actual or potential availability of a varied inventory of small, inexpensive, nuclear weapons (including such esoteric devices as the Davy Crockett missile and the neutron bomb) is likely to renew discussion of this possibility.* It is, and will likely continue to be, an important objective of U.S. military forces to be able to wage such a war—at least in Europe, even if a "no-bomb-use policy" is explicitly adopted by all nations.

RUNG 24: UNUSUAL, PROVOCATIVE, AND SIGNIFICANT COUNTER-MEASURES. One side might carry out re-deployments or maneuvers that have the effect of increasing an opponent's vulnerability to attack or otherwise degrading its capability, morale, or will.

RUNG 25: EVACUATION OF CITIES (ABOUT 70 PER CENT). At this point, the situation may be very close to large-scale war. It might now seem advisable to evacuate a large number of people from cities. The total would probably amount to between two-thirds and three-fourths of the population—women and children and those men who are not essential to the functioning of the cities. I would judge that all important industries, communications, transportation facilities, etc., could be operated by about a quarter of the population or less.

Attacks so far have avoided the enemy's zone of interior and have thus observed a salient threshold. The line between the external world and the nation may even be stronger as a firebreak than the threshold between conventional and nuclear war, since it is an older distinction, invested with far more emotion and prestige. Under current conditions, it is reasonably clear that, in the next decade, the likelihood that a nation (including the U.S. and the Soviet Union) would invite certain annihilation for the sake of its allies is going to tend to diminish to the vanishing point, however repugnant or dishonorable this development may now seem. But the likelihood of a nation risking the kind of restrained attacks discussed below may or may not diminish so sharply, depending in

* EDITOR'S NOTE: The Davy Crockett missiles were, in late 1965, in the process of being withdrawn from Europe.

part on the decision-makers' expectations of the "rules" being observed.

RUNG 26: DEMONSTRATION ATTACK ON ZONE OF INTERIOR. An attack could be made, perhaps on an isolated mountain-top or empty desert, which does dramatic and unmistakable physical damage, if only to the topography.

RUNG 27: EXEMPLARY ATTACK ON MILITARY TARGETS. One side might begin destroying portions of the other side's weapons systems, but in a careful way, so as not to cause much collateral damage. These attacks could be launched primarily to reduce the defender's military capability significantly by finding leverage targets.

RUNG 28: EXEMPLARY ATTACKS AGAINST PROPERTY. The next step would increase the level of these limited, nuclear, strategic attacks. One possibility would be attacks on such installations as bridges, dams, or gaseous-diffusion plants. More damaging and dangerous would be limited attacks on cities, presumably after warning had been delivered and the cities evacuated. The purpose would be to destroy property, not people.

RUNG 29: EXEMPLARY ATTACKS ON POPULATION. In any crisis of the mid-1960's, this attack would probably be much higher on the ladder than I put it here. But if the balance of terror becomes sufficiently stable, and governments are believed to be under intense and graduated mutual deterrents, even this attack could occur without an eruption to spasm or other central wars.

RUNG 30: COMPLETE EVACUATION (ABOUT 95 PER CENT). At this point, large-scale warfare has begun. If at all possible, each side is likely to evacuate its cities almost completely, leaving 5 to 10 per cent of the population behind for essential activities.

RUNG 31: RECIPROCAL REPRISALS. This is a war with more or less continual exchanges. Many strategists believe that reciprocal-reprisal wars might be a standard tactic of the future when the balance of terror is judged—whether correctly or not—to be almost absolute.

Thermonuclear wars are likely to be short—lasting a few hours to a couple of months at most. In such a war it is unlikely that cities would in themselves be targets of any great military conse-

quence. But it is perfectly possible that a nation might attack cities simply without thinking it through. In Defense Secretary Robert McNamara's speech at Ann Arbor on June 16, 1962, the U.S. more or less formally enunciated a "no cities except in reprisal" strategy, but the strategy is neither clearly understood nor firmly held even here. Soviet strategists and political leaders, for their part, have declared that Soviet forces would not recognize any such "artificial" distinctions in a nuclear war. This position could be an accurate reflection of current Soviet strategic doctrine, but it is most likely that it is a very unreliable indicator of actual Soviet behavior in a "moment of truth"—or of Soviet beliefs about U.S. conduct at such a time.

Let us assume, for the moment, that a threshold between central military targets and central civilian targets (i.e., cities) can be maintained in an actual war. Thus we can consider the possibility of waging a very large, "all-out," but very closely controlled, central war, in which there is a deliberate attempt to avoid civilians and their property.

RUNG 32: DECLARATION OF "GENERAL" WAR. The formal declaration of war could indicate that the side issuing the declaration had no immediate intention of attacking (since if it had such an intention, there would be strong reasons to ignore pre-nuclear convention and simply attack). Such a declaration certainly would remove some inhibitions against the use of force and coercion, put pressures on allies and some neutrals to cooperate, and mobilize a nation's facilities for defense and tend to suppress internal opposition. It would force the other side to recognize explicitly that a formal peace treaty would have to be written before the issue is settled; delaying tactics would not settle the matter. But while tending to prevent de-escalation and to threaten future (eventual) escalation, it nonetheless might *look like* temporizing and provide an opening for bargaining.

RUNG 33: SLOW MOTION COUNTER-"PROPERTY" WAR. In this attack, each side destroys the other's property, still attempting to force the other side to back down.

RUNG 34: SLOW-MOTION COUNTER-FORCE WAR. This is a campaign in which each side attempts attrition of the other side's weapons systems over a period of time. One can conceive of a slow-motion counter-force war lasting for weeks or months during which, for example, submarines are hunted down.

RUNG 35: CONSTRAINED FORCE REDUCTION SALVO. The attacker here attempts to destroy a significant but small portion of the defender's force in a single strike while avoiding undesired collateral damage. It is especially likely to be used against weak links or high-leverage targets at the outbreak of a war.

RUNG 36: CONSTRAINED DISARMING ATTACK. The attacker tries to destroy a significant portion of the defender's first-strike nuclear forces and even some of his second-strike weapons, such as missiles in silos. But the attacks would avoid, as much as possible, civilian targets. This would make it disadvantageous for the defender to launch a counter-strike, since the defender's damaged forces might be able to do only a limited amount of damage even with a counter-strike on cities. The defender is also under pressure to negotiate since it is now probable that the attacker could threaten another attack, this one an all-out strike.

RUNG 37: "COUNTER-FORCE WITH AVOIDANCE" ATTACK. This attack differs from a constrained disarming attack by being less scrupulous about avoiding collateral damage to cities and by not deliberately sparing much if any of the enemy's second-strike weaponry. In the case of a Soviet strike against the U.S., such an attack might include hitting Tucson (a city with a population of 265,000, completely ringed with Titans) but would probably avoid the Norfolk Navy Yard and the Pentagon. If it did hit these targets or the SAC bases near very large cities, Russia might use 20-kiloton weapons rather than 20 megatons, in order to limit the collateral destruction. After such an attack, one must assume a counter-attack, but one might still try to use threats of further escalation to limit the defender's response.

RUNG 38: UNMODIFIED COUNTER-FORCE ATTACK. Although the targets would still be enemy weapons systems, the military plans would be formulated and the operation carried out with general disregard as to whether enemy civilians are killed or non-military property destroyed (though there might be disadvantages accepted, in order to avoid fallout or other dangers to allies or neutrals). No attempt would be made either to lessen or to increase collateral damage to the enemy. This attack might be described as the classical form of all-out or total war.

At this point, the warring nations are at the threshold of civilian central wars. Under current U.S. "controlled response" doctrine,

*not only does the U.S. intend to observe the city threshold, but an
enormous incentive is given to the U.S.S.R. to do so as well and to
avoid attacking U.S. cities in the first wave—whether this wave is
the first or second strike of the war. But even if population is not
the target of the first wave, it could be the target of the second
or later waves. In any case, it would always be threatened. The
residual vulnerability of the civilian hostages and cities could then
affect, to a great extent, the kind of peace treaty that the U.S.S.R.
could force on us or that we could force on the U.S.S.R. For this reason, it makes sense to try to protect people from being threatened by
second- and later-wave attacks, even though they may not have been
adequately protected on the first wave.*

*It seems to me that the U.S. should, at the minimum, undertake
a civil-defense program that is compatible with what the controlled-
response doctrine foresees in a time of war. Part of such a program
would be fallout protection for the entire population and blast protection for the 5 million to 10 million people who live within approximately ten miles of priority strategic targets. Such a program
might require $5 billion to $10 billion spread over five years or so.
In a very large range of types of wars these measures could save the
lives of 30 million to 50 million people, and in addition make it
more likely that a war, if it came, would in fact be a war of "controlled response."*

RUNG 39: SLOW-MOTION COUNTER-CITY WAR. This takes the ultimate
form—"city trading." This is, of course, the most bizarre of all the
options that are discussed in modern strategic analysis. The possibility of trading cities arises because of today's unprecedented situation, in which both sides have almost invulnerable forces while
both sides' civilians may be completely and irrevocably vulnerable
to these forces. There has never before been such a situation in
the history of mankind. This kind of war would be the extreme
and ultimate form of deliberate, selective, and controlled response
—but one not necessarily or even likely to be beyond the psychological capabilities of decision-makers, if the only alternatives were
total destruction or complete capitulation.

RUNG 40: COUNTER-VALUE SALVO. It is always possible—in fighting a
slow-motion counter-force, or slow-motion counter-*value* war—that
one side will fire a large number of missiles at civilian targets, either
in inadvertent or deliberate eruption.

RUNG 41: AUGMENTED DISARMING ATTACK. This would be an attack on military targets deliberately modified to obtain as much collateral counter-city damage as a "bonus" as feasible.

RUNG 42: CIVILIAN DEVASTATION ATTACK. This attack corresponds to the usual popular picture of nuclear war, in which there is a deliberate effort to destroy or greatly damage the enemy's society. It is distinguished from "spasm" or insensate war only by having some element of calculation and by the fact that there may be some withholding or control.

RUNG 43: SOME OTHER KIND OF CONTROLLED GENERAL WAR. It is possible to have many kinds of "all-out" but controlled as well as "all-out" but uncontrolled wars. In a "rational," "all-out," but controlled war, military action would be accompanied by threats and promises, and military operations themselves would be restricted to those that contributed to attaining victory—an acceptable or desirable peace treaty.

RUNG 44: SPASM OR INSENSATE WAR. The figurative word "spasm" is chosen because it describes the usual image of central war in which there is only a "go-ahead" order; all the buttons are pressed. A spasm war, of course, may occur, but to the extent that there is any art of war possible in the thermonuclear age, the attempt must be made to prevent it.

Down the Ladder

In the same way, the study of de-escalation and its limits and of crisis termination—how to climb down and off the ladder—is vital to the management of crises and escalation. De-escalation is even more sensitive to accurate communication and shared understandings than escalation is. The opponent may have a different conception of escalation and still understand well enough the pressures being applied to him; but, typically, in order to coordinate de-escalation moves by easing pressure, both sides must have a shared understanding of what is happening. They may not have a sufficient shared understanding if one side's paradigm of the world differs in important ways from the other's.

Because of the need for shared understanding in de-escalation, unilateral initiatives are often mentioned in connection with de-escalation. Unilateral initiatives may be quite helpful. They may relax tension to a point where it is easier to settle a dispute, or to leave it unresolved but less dangerous. Even small concessions can be significant as turning points in the escalation process. Thus, even if a move is more symbolic than meaningful in itself, its de-escalatory value may be large. A serious concern, however, may be to maintain the appearance of resolve while making conciliatory moves. For this reason, the side which is doing better may find that it should take the burden of the initial de-escalatory step.

Typical de-escalation gestures take many forms. They can include the reversal of a previous escalation move, the settling of an extraneous dispute, the freeing of prisoners, conciliatory statements, the replacement of a "hard" key official by a "softer" or more flexible individual, or simply waiting for time to have its cooling effect. Concessions need not be made explicitly. Nor need the matter under dispute be settled, as long as tension is decreased to the point where the dispute is no longer so high on the escalation ladder as it once was.

Escalation is a "competition in resolve," and resolve is often measured by a willingness to pay costs in pursuit of certain objectives. One side or the other may decide to de-escalate simply because it feels it has suffered enough. It is sometimes difficult for dedicated and resolute military leaders to accept this notion. The World War I theory of the "last fifteen minutes" (in which it was asserted that that side which could hold out fifteen minutes longer would win) is still very widespread. But this theory of conflict is often completely inappropriate for a high-level escalation and may not be the most relevant aspect of a low-level conflict. In low-level conflicts, both sides typically have virtually unlimited resources that can be deployed. Both sides thus can, and usually will, insist on a compromise solution.

Escalation is also referred to as a "competition in risk-taking." One side or the other may decide that it no longer is willing to endure these risks. In the nuclear age, this is likely to be the greatest factor in de-escalation.

Most people will accept without argument that there will always be conflict. But conflicts need not inevitably lead to the kinds of crises and escalations that lie on the rungs of the ladder I have discussed. Any crisis that reaches the upper rungs of the escalation ladder is likely to be regarded by both participants as a potential—and mutual—disaster. As both sides learn that the gains of these conflicts are small compared to the dangers and other costs, they are likely to be cautious about either starting or intensifying such conflicts. Arms control has its place in this scheme of things: it should be a major objective of arms control to prevent the kinds of crises in which the options on the escalation ladder become important, and to lessen the damage and risk if these crises arise. But our first and most important need is to escape the inertia that tends to hold us captive to obsolete notions and the desire for simplistic solutions, which can only lead to disastrous capitulation or eruption —to paraphrase President Kennedy, we need wider choices than holocaust or surrender.

TWO

ALBERT WOHLSTETTER

The Delicate Balance of Terror

[Editor's Note: This article was written in 1958, when it was generally believed that nuclear war could take only a single form: a cataclysmic final catastrophe, which was made unlikely because of its very enormity. It was also thought that the major nuclear countries would always possess overwhelming offensive strength—regardless of the scale of attack to which they might be exposed. Professor Wohlstetter was the first to call attention to the existence of a wide range of possible nuclear attacks and to the various thresholds that determine whether a country's nuclear power produces deterrence or constitutes an invitation to aggression. He showed that the balance of terror between the major powers was "delicate," depending on a subtle interplay of invulnerability and offensive power. He demonstrated that it was theoretically possible to eliminate an opposing, hostile striking force without unacceptable damage to the attacker. The existence of a powerful delivery capability, then, he argued, was not in itself an assurance of security. Its effectiveness would depend, in addition to its striking power, on its invulnerability, and the state of opposing active and passive defenses. He defined various "thresholds" to be overcome if a retaliatory force was to be effective.

Professor Wohlstetter's article has an important place in the history of the debate on national security. It demonstrated concretely how the increase in the complexity and variety of nuclear delivery systems might tend to complicate rather than simplify the problems of security and deterrence, and it underlined the need to deal not with a single all-inclusive concept of nuclear war but rather with a family of possible variants such as those on the final rungs of Kahn's escalation ladder. He emphasized the inextricable connection between strategic doctrine and the choice of weapons. More than any other individual, Professor Wohlstetter provided the intellectual impetus for the recasting of American military strategy in the 1960's.]

The first shock administered by the Soviet launching of Sputnik has almost dissipated. The flurry of statements and investigations and improvised responses has died down, leaving a small residue: a slight increase in the schedule of bomber and ballistic-missile production, with a resulting small increment in defense expenditures for the current fiscal year; a considerable enthusiasm for space travel; and some stirrings of interest in the teaching of mathematics and physics in the secondary schools. Western defense policy has almost returned to the level of activity and the emphasis suited to the basic assumptions which were controlling before sputnik.

One of the most important of these assumptions—that a general thermonuclear war is extremely unlikely—is held in common by most of the critics of our defense policy as well as by its proponents. Because of its crucial role in the Western strategy of defense, I should like to examine the stability of the thermonuclear balance which, it is generally supposed, would make aggression irrational or even insane. The balance, I believe, is in fact precarious, and this fact has critical implications for policy. Deterrence in the 1960's is neither assured nor impossible but will be the product of sustained intelligent effort and hard choices responsibly made. As a major illustration, important both for defense and foreign policy, I shall treat the particularly stringent conditions for deterrence which affect forces based close to the enemy, whether they are U.S. forces or those of our allies, under single or joint control. I shall comment also on the inadequacy as well as the necessity of deterrence, on the problem of accidental outbreak of war, and on disarmament.[1]

I. THE PRESUMED AUTOMATIC BALANCE

I emphasize that requirements for deterrence are stringent. We have heard so much about the atomic stalemate and the receding probability of war which it has produced that this may strike the reader as something of an exaggeration. Is deterrence a necessary consequence of both sides having a nuclear delivery capability, and is all-out war nearly obsolete? Is mutual extinction the only outcome of a general war? This belief, frequently expressed by refer-

EDITOR'S NOTE: Reprinted with permission from *Foreign Affairs*, XXXVII, No. 2 (January, 1959). © 1959, by the Council on Foreign Relations, Inc., New York.

[1] I want to thank Charles J. Hitch, Malcolm W. Hoag, William W. Kaufman, A. W. Marshall, H. S. Rowen, and W. W. Taylor for suggestions in preparation of this article.

ences to Oppenheimer's simile of the two scorpions in a bottle, is perhaps the prevalent one. It is held by a very eminent and diverse group of people—in England by Sir Winston Churchill, P. M. S. Blackett, Sir John Slessor, Admiral Buzzard and many others; in France by such figures as Raymond Aron, General Gallois and General Gazin; in this country by the titular heads of both parties as well as almost all writers on military and foreign affairs, by both Henry Kissinger and his critic, James E. King, Jr., and by George Kennan as well as Dean Acheson. Kennan refers to American concern about surprise attack as simply obsessive[2]; and many people have drawn the consequence of the stalemate as has Blackett, who states: "If it is in fact true, as most current opinion holds, that strategic air power has abolished global war, then an urgent problem for the West is to assess how little effort must be put into it to keep global war abolished."[3] If peace were founded firmly on mutual terror and mutual terror on symmetrical nuclear capabilities, this would be, as Churchill has said, "a melancholy paradox"; none the less, a most comforting one.

Deterrence, however, is not automatic. While feasible, it will be much harder to achieve in the 1960's than is generally believed. One of the most disturbing features of current opinion is the underestimation of this difficulty. This is due partly to a misconstruction of the technological race as a problem in matching striking forces, partly to a wishful analysis of the Soviet ability to strike first.

Since sputnik, the United States has made several moves to assure the world (that is, the enemy, and more especially our allies and ourselves) that we will match or over-match Soviet technology and, specifically, Soviet offense technology. We have, for example, accelerated the bomber and ballistic-missile programs, in particular the intermediate-range ballistic missiles. The problem has been conceived as more or better bombers—or rockets; or sputniks; or engineers. This has meant confusing deterrence with matching or exceeding the enemy's ability to strike first. Matching weapons, however, misconstrues the nature of the technological race—not, as is frequently said, because only a few bombs owned by the defender can make aggression fruitless, but because even many might not. One outmoded A-bomb dropped from an obsolete bomber

---

[2] George F. Kennan, "A Chance to Withdraw Our Troops in Europe," *Harper's Magazine*, February, 1958, p. 41.

[3] P. M. S. Blackett, *Atomic Weapons and East-West Relations* (New York: Cambridge University Press, 1956), p. 32.

might destroy a great many supersonic jets and ballistic missiles. To deter an attack means being able to strike back in spite of it. It means, in other words, a capability to strike second. In the last year or two, there has been a growing awareness of the importance of the distinction between a "strike-first" and a "strike-second" capability but little, if any, recognition of the implications of this distinction for the balance-of-terror theory.

Where the published writings have not simply underestimated Soviet capabilities and the advantages of a first strike, they have in general placed artificial constraints on the Soviet use of the capabilities attributed to them. They assume, for example, that the enemy will attack in mass over the Arctic through our Distant Early Warning line, with bombers refueled over Canada—all resulting in plenty of warning. Most hopefully, it is sometimes assumed that such attacks will be preceded by days of visible preparations for moving ground troops. Such assumptions suggest that the Soviet leaders will be rather bumbling or, better, cooperative. However attractive it may be for us to narrow Soviet alternatives to these, they would be low in the order of preference of any reasonable Russians planning war.

II. The Quantitative Nature of the Problem and the Uncertainties

In treating Soviet strategies, it is important to consider Soviet rather than Western advantage and to consider the strategy of both sides quantitatively. The effectiveness of our own choices will depend on a most complex numerical interaction of Soviet and Western plans. Unfortunately, both the privileged and unprivileged information on these matters is precarious. As a result, competent people have been led into critical error in evaluating the prospects for deterrence. Western journalists have greatly overestimated the difficulties of a Soviet surprise attack with thermonuclear weapons and vastly underestimated the complexity of the Western problem of retaliation.

One intelligent commentator, Richard Rovere, recently expressed the common view: "If the Russians had ten thousand warheads and a missile for each, and we had ten hydrogen bombs and ten obsolete bombers, . . . aggression would still be a folly that would appeal only to an insane adventurer." Rovere's example is plausible because it assumes implicitly that the defender's hydrogen bombs will with certainty be visited on the aggressor; then the damage done by the ten bombs seems terrible enough for deterrence, and any more would be simply redundant. This is the basis for the common view. The example raises questions, even assuming the delivery of the ten weapons. For instance, the targets aimed at in retaliation might be sheltered, and a quite modest civil defense could hold within tolerable limits the damage done to such city targets by ten delivered bombs. But the essential point is that the weapons would not be very likely to reach their targets. Even if the bombers were dispersed at ten different points, and protected by shelters so blast-resistant as to stand up anywhere outside the lip of the bomb crater—even inside the fireball itself—the chances of one of these bombers surviving the huge attack directed at it would be on the order of one in a million. (This calculation takes account of the unreliability and inaccuracy of the missile.) And the damage done by the small minority of these ten planes that might be in the air at the time of the attack, armed and ready to run the gauntlet of an alert air defense system, if not zero, would be very small indeed compared to damage that Russia has suffered in the past. For Mr. Rovere, like many other writers on this subject, numerical superiority is not important at all.

For Joseph Alsop, on the other hand, it is important, but the superiority is on our side. Alsop recently enunciated as one of the four rules of nuclear war: "The aggressor's problem is astronomically difficult; and the aggressor requires an overwhelming superiority of force."[4] There are, he believes, no fewer than 400 SAC bases in the NATO nations alone and many more elsewhere, all of which would have to be attacked in a very short space of time. The "thousands of coordinated air sorties and/or missile firings," he concludes, are not feasible. Alsop's argument is numerical and has the virtue of demonstrating that at least the relative numbers are important. But the numbers he uses are very wide of the mark. He overestimates the number of such bases by a factor of more than ten,[5] and in any case, missile firings on the scale of a thousand or more involve costs that are by no means out of proportion, given the strategic budgets of the great powers. Whether or not thousands are needed depends on the yield and accuracy of the enemy missiles, something about which it would be a great mistake for us to display confidence.

---

[4] Joseph Alsop, "The New Balance of Power," *Encounter*, May, 1958, p. 4. It should be added that Mr. Alsop's views have altered somewhat since he wrote these lines.

[5] *The New York Times*, September 6, 1958, p. 2.

Perhaps the first step in dispelling the nearly universal optimism about the stability of deterrence would be to recognize the difficulties in analyzing the uncertainties and interactions between our own wide range of choices and the moves open to the Soviets. On our side we must consider an enormous variety of strategic weapons which might compose our force, and for each of these several alternative methods of basing and operation. These are the choices that determine whether a weapons system will have any genuine capability in the realistic circumstances of a war. Besides the B-47E and the B-52 bombers which are in the United States strategic force now, alternatives will include the B-52G (a longer-range version of the B-52); the Mach 2 B-58A bomber and a "growth" version of it; the Mach 3 B-70 bomber; a nuclear-powered bomber possibly carrying long-range air-to-surface missiles; the Dynasoar, a manned glide-rocket; the Thor and the Jupiter, liquid-fueled intermediate-range ballistic missiles; the Snark intercontinental cruise missile; the Atlas and the Titan intercontinental ballistic missiles; the submarine-launched Polaris and Atlantis rockets; the Minuteman, one potential solid-fueled successor to the Thor and Titan; possibly unmanned bombardment satellites; and many others which are not yet gleams in anyone's eye and some that are just that.*

The difficulty of describing in a brief article the best mixture of weapons for the long-term future beginning in 1960, their base requirements, their potentiality for stabilizing or upsetting the balance among the great powers, and their implications for the alliance, is not just a matter of space or the constraint of security. The difficulty in fact stems from some rather basic insecurities. These matters are wildly uncertain; we are talking about weapons and vehicles that are some time off and, even if the precise performances currently hoped for and claimed by contractors were in the public domain, it would be a good idea to doubt them.

Recently some of my colleagues picked their way through the graveyard of early claims about various missiles and aircraft: their dates of availability, costs, and performance. These claims are seldom revisited or talked about: *de mortuis nil nisi bonum.* The errors were large and almost always in one direction. The less we knew, the more hopeful we were. Accordingly, the missiles benefited in particular. For example, the estimated cost of one missile increased by a factor of over 50—from about $35,000 in 1949 to some $2 million in 1957. This uncertainty is critical. Some but not

---

* EDITOR'S NOTE: The B-47, Thor, Jupiter, Atlas, and Snark have all been phased out. The B-70 bomber was canceled.

all of the systems listed can be chosen, and the problem of choice is essentially quantitative. The complexities of the problem, if they were more widely understood, would discourage the oracular confidence of writers on the subject of deterrence.

Some of the complexities can be suggested by referring to the successive obstacles to be hurdled by any system providing a capability to strike second, that is, to strike back. Such deterrent systems must have (*a*) a stable, "steady-state" peacetime operation within feasible budgets. (Besides the logistic and operational costs, there are, for example, problems of false alarms and accidents.) They must have also the ability (*b*) to survive enemy attacks, (*c*) to make and communicate the decision to retaliate, (*d*) to reach enemy territory with fuel enough to complete their mission, (*e*) to penetrate enemy active defenses, that is, fighters and surface-to-air missiles, and (*f*) to destroy the target in spite of any "passive" civil defense in the form of dispersal or protective construction or evacuation of the target itself.

Within limits, the enemy is free to use his offensive and defensive forces so as to exploit the weaknesses of each of our systems. He will also be free, within limits, in the 1960's to choose that composition of forces which will make life as difficult as possible for the various systems we might select. It would be quite wrong to assume that we have the same degree of flexibility or that the uncertainties I have described affect a totalitarian aggressor and the party attacked equally. A totalitarian country can preserve secrecy about the capabilities and disposition of its forces very much better than a Western democracy. And the aggressor has, among other enormous advantages of the first strike, the ability to weigh continually our performance at each of the six barriers and to choose that precise time and circumstance for attack which will reduce uncertainty. It is important not to confuse our uncertainty with his. Strangely enough, some military commentators have not made this distinction and have founded their certainty of deterrence on the fact simply that there are uncertainties.

Unwarranted optimism is displayed not only in the writings of journalists but in the more analytic writings of professionals. The recent writings of General Gallois[6] parallel rather closely Alsop's faulty numerical proof that surprise attack is astronomically difficult—except that Gallois' "simple arithmetic," to borrow his own

---

[6] Pierre Gallois, "A French General Analyzes Nuclear-Age Strategy," *Réalités*, November, 1958, p. 19; "Nuclear Aggression and National Suicide," *The Reporter*, September 18, 1958, p. 23.

phrase, turns essentially on some assumptions which are at once inexplicit and extremely optimistic with respect to the blast resistance of dispersed missile sites subjected to attack from relatively close range.[7] Blackett's recent book *Atomic Weapons and East-West Relations* illustrates the hazards confronting a most able analyst in dealing with the piecemeal information available to the general public. Mr. Blackett, a Nobel Prize–winning physicist with wartime experience in military operations research, lucidly summarized the public information available when he was writing in 1956 on weapons for all-out war. But much of his analysis was based on the assumption that H-bombs could not be made small enough to be carried in an intercontinental missile. It is now widely known that intercontinental ballistic missiles will have hydrogen warheads, and this fact, a secret at the time, invalidates Blackett's calculations and, I might say, much of his optimism on the stability of the balance of terror. In sum, one of the serious obstacles to any widespread rational judgment on these matters of high policy is that critical elements of the problem *have* to be protected by secrecy. However, some of the principal conclusions about deterrence in the early 1960's can be quite firmly based, and based on public information.

III. THE DELICACY OF THE BALANCE OF TERROR

The most important conclusion is that we must expect a vast increase in the weight of attack which the Soviets can deliver with little warning, and the growth of a significant Russian capability for an essentially warning-less attack. As a result, strategic deterrence, while feasible, will be extremely difficult to achieve, and, at critical junctures in the 1960's, we may not have the power to deter attack. Whether we have it will depend on some difficult strategic choices as to the future composition of the deterrent forces, as well as hard choices on its basing, operations, and defense.

Manned bombers will continue to make up the predominant part of our striking force in the early 1960's.* None of the popular remedies for their defense will suffice—not, for example, mere increase of alertness (which will be offset by the Soviet's increasing capability for attack without significant warning), nor simple dispersal or sheltering alone or mobility taken by itself, nor a mere

[7] See footnote 9 below.

* EDITOR'S NOTE: Actually, by 1965, missiles were the predominant part of the U.S. striking force.

piling up of interceptors and defense missiles around SAC bases. Especially extravagant expectations have been placed on the airborne alert—an extreme form of defense by mobility. The impression is rather widespread that one-third of the SAC bombers are in the air and ready for combat at all times.[8] This belief is belied by the public record. According to the Symington Committee hearings in 1956,* our bombers averaged 31 hours of flying per month, which is about 4 per cent of the average 732-hour month. An Air Force representative expressed the hope that within a couple of years, with an increase in the ratio of crews to aircraft, the bombers would reach 45 hours of flight per month—which is 6 per cent. This 4 to 6 per cent of the force includes bombers partially fueled and without bombs. It is, moreover, only an average, admitting variance down as well as up. Some increase in the number of armed bombers aloft is to be expected. However, for the current generation of bombers, which have been designed for speed and range rather than endurance, a continuous air patrol for one-third of the force would be extremely expensive.

On the other hand, it would be unwise to look for miracles in the new weapons systems, which by the mid-1960's may constitute a considerable portion of the United States force. After the Thor, Atlas, and Titan, there are a number of promising developments. The solid-fueled rockets, Minuteman and Polaris, promise in particular to be extremely significant components of the deterrent force. Today they are being touted as making the problem of deterrence easy to solve and, in fact, as guaranteeing its solution. But none of the new developments in vehicles is likely to do that. For the complex job of deterrence, they all have limitations. The unvaryingly immoderate claims for each new weapons system should make us wary of the latest "technological break-throughs." Only a very short time ago, the ballistic missile itself was supposed to be intrinsically invulnerable on the ground. It is now more generally understood that its survival is likely to depend on a variety of choices in its defense.

It is hard to talk with confidence about the mid- and late-1960's.

[8] See, for example, Gardner Patterson and Edgar E. Furniss, Jr., "NATO, A Critical Appraisal," Princeton University Conference on NATO, Princeton, June, 1957, p. 32: "Although no one pretended to know, the hypothesis that one-third of the striking force of the United States Strategic Air Command was in the air at all times was regarded by most as reasonable."

* EDITOR'S NOTE: *Study of Airpower*, Hearings before the Subcommittee on the Air Force, Committee on Armed Services, U.S. Senate, 84th Cong., 2d sess., 1956.

A systematic study of an optimal or good deterrent force which considered all the major factors affecting choice and dealt adequately with the uncertainties would be a formidable task. In lieu of this, I shall mention briefly why none of the many systems available or projected dominates the others in any obvious way. My comments will take the form of a swift run-through of the characteristic advantages and disadvantages of various strategic systems at each of the six successive hurdles mentioned earlier.

The first hurdle to be surmounted is the attainment of a stable, "steady-state" peacetime operation. Systems which depend for their survival on extreme decentralization of controls, as may be the case with large-scale dispersal and some of the mobile weapons, raise problems of accidents; over a long period of peacetime operation, this leads in turn to serious political problems. Systems relying on extensive movement by land, perhaps by truck caravan, are an obvious example; the introduction of these on European roads, as is sometimes suggested, would raise grave questions for the governments of some of our allies. Any extensive increase in the armed air alert will increase the hazard of accident and intensify the concern already expressed among our allies. Some of the proposals for bombardment satellites may involve such hazards of unintended bomb release as to make them out of the question.

The cost to buy and operate various weapons systems must be seriously considered. Some systems buy their ability to negotiate a given hurdle—say, surviving the enemy attack—only at prohibitive cost. Then the number that can be bought out of a given budget will be small, and this will affect the relative performance of competing systems at various other hurdles—for example, penetrating enemy defenses. Some of the relevant cost comparisons, then, are between competing systems; others concern the extra costs to the enemy of canceling an additional expenditure of our own. For example, some dispersal is essential, though usually it is expensive; if the dispersed bases are within a warning net, dispersal can help to provide warning against some sorts of attack, since it forces the attacker to increase the size of his raid and so makes it more liable to detection as well as somewhat harder to co-ordinate. But as the sole or principal defense of our offensive force, dispersal has only a brief useful life and can be justified financially only up to a point. For against our costs of construction, maintenance and operation of an additional base must be set the enemy's much lower costs of delivering one extra weapon. In general, any feasible degree of dispersal leaves a considerable concentration of value at a single target point. For example, a squadron of heavy bombers costing, with their associated tankers and penetration aids, perhaps $500 million over five years, might be eliminated, if it were otherwise unprotected, by an enemy intercontinental ballistic missile costing perhaps $16 million. After making allowance for the unreliability and inaccuracy of the missile, this means a ratio of some ten for one or better. To achieve safety by *brute* numbers in so unfavorable a competition is not likely to be viable economically or politically. However, a viable peacetime operation is only the first hurdle to be surmounted.

At the second hurdle—surviving the enemy offense—ground alert systems placed deep within a warning net look good against a manned bomber attack, much less good against intercontinental ballistic missiles, and not good at all against ballistic missiles launched from the sea. In the last case, systems such as the Minuteman, which may be sheltered and dispersed as well as alert, would do well. Systems involving launching platforms which are mobile and concealed, such as Polaris submarines, have particular advantage for surviving an enemy offense.

However, there is a third hurdle to be surmounted—namely that of making the decision to retaliate and communicating it. Here, Polaris, the combat air patrol of B-52's, and in fact all of the mobile platforms—under water, on the surface, in the air, and above the air—have severe problems. Long-distance communication may be jammed, and, most important, communication centers may be destroyed.

At the fourth hurdle—ability to reach enemy territory with fuel enough to complete the mission—several of our short-legged systems have operational problems such as coordination with tankers and using bases close to the enemy. For a good many years to come, up to the mid-1960's in fact, this will be a formidable hurdle for the greater part of our deterrent force. The next section of this article deals with this problem at some length.

The fifth hurdle is the aggressor's long-range interceptors and close-in missile defenses. To get past these might require large numbers of planes and missiles. (If the high cost of overcoming an earlier obstacle—using extreme dispersal or airborne alert or the like—limits the number of planes or missiles bought, our capability is likely to be penalized disproportionately here.) Or getting through may involve carrying heavy loads of radar decoys, electronic jammers and other aids to defense penetration. For example, vehicles like Minuteman and Polaris, which were made small to facilitate dispersal or mobility, may suffer here because they can carry fewer penetration aids.

At the final hurdle—destroying the target in spite of the passive defenses that may protect it—low-payload and low-accuracy systems, such as Minuteman and Polaris, may be frustrated by blast-resistant shelters. For example, five half-megaton weapons with an average inaccuracy of two miles might be expected to destroy half the population of a city of 900,000 spread over 40 square miles, provided the inhabitants were without shelters. But if they were provided with shelters, capable of resisting over-pressure of 100 pounds per square inch, approximately sixty such weapons would be required; deep rock shelters might force the total up to over a thousand.

Prizes for a retaliatory capability are not distributed for getting over one of these jumps. A system must get over all six. I hope these illustrations will suggest that assuring ourselves the power to strike back after a massive thermonuclear surprise attack is by no means as automatic as is widely believed.

In counteracting the general optimism as to the ease and, in fact, the inevitability of deterrence, I should like to avoid creating the extreme opposite impression. Deterrence demands hard, continuing, intelligent work, but it can be achieved. The job of deterring rational attack by guaranteeing great damage to an aggressor is, for example, very much less difficult than erecting a nearly airtight defense of cities in the face of full-scale thermonuclear surprise attack. Protecting manned bombers and missiles is much easier because they may be dispersed, sheltered, or kept mobile, and they can respond to warning with greater speed. Mixtures of these and other defenses with complementary strengths can preserve a powerful remainder after attack. Obviously, not all our bombers and missiles need to survive in order to fulfill their mission. To preserve the majority of our cities intact in the face of surprise attack is immensely more difficult, if not impossible. (This does not mean that the aggressor has the same problem in preserving his cities from retaliation by a poorly protected, badly damaged force. And it does not mean that *we* should not do more to limit the extent of the catastrophe to our cities in case deterrence fails. I believe we should.) Deterrence is feasible, however, provided we work at it, and, what is more, it is a crucial objective of national policy.

What can be said, then, as to whether general war is unlikely? Would not a general thermonuclear war mean "extinction" for the aggressor as well as the defender? "Extinction" is a state that badly needs analysis. Russian casualties in World War II were more than 20 million. Yet Russia recovered extremely well from this catastrophe. There are several quite plausible circumstances in the future when the Russians may be quite confident of being able to limit damage to considerably less than this number—if they make sensible strategic choices and we do not. On the other hand, the risks of not striking might at some juncture appear very great to the Soviets, involving, for example, disastrous defeat in peripheral war, loss of key satellites with danger of revolt spreading—possibly to Russia itself—or fear of an attack by ourselves. Then striking first, by surprise, would be the sensible choice for them and, from their point of view, the smaller risk.

It should be clear that it is not fruitful to talk about the likelihood of general war without specifying the range of alternatives that are pressing on the aggressor and the strategic postures of both the Soviet bloc and the West. Deterrence is a matter of comparative risks. The balance is not automatic. First, since thermonuclear weapons give an enormous advantage to the aggressor, it takes great ingenuity and realism at any given level of nuclear technology to devise a stable equilibrium. And second, this technology itself is changing with fantastic speed. Deterrence will require an urgent and continuing effort.

IV. The Uses and Risks of Bases Close to the Soviet Union

It may now be useful to focus attention on the special problems of deterrent forces close to the Soviet Union. First, overseas areas have played an important role in the past and have a continuing though less certain role today. Second, the recent acceleration of production of intermediate-range ballistic missiles and the negotiation of agreements with various NATO powers for their basing and operation have given our overseas bases a renewed importance in deterring attack on the United States—or so it would appear at first blush. Third, an analysis can throw some light on the problems faced by our allies in developing an independent ability to deter all-out attack on themselves, and, in this way, it can clarify the much agitated question of nuclear sharing. Finally, overseas bases affect in many critical ways, political and economic as well as military, the status of the alliance.

At the end of the 1940's, overseas bases appeared to be an advantageous means of achieving the radius extension needed by our short-legged bombers, of permitting them to use several axes of attack, and of increasing the number of sorties possible in the course of an extended campaign. With the growth of our own thermo-nuclear stockpile, it became apparent that a long campaign involv-ing many re-uses of a large proportion of our bombers was not likely to be necessary. With the growth of a Russian nuclear-delivery capability, it became clear that this was most unlikely to be feasible.

Our overseas bases now have the disadvantage of high vulner-ability. Because they are closer than the United States to the Soviet Union, they are subject to a vastly greater attack by a larger variety as well as number of vehicles. With given resources, the Soviet Union might deliver on nearby bases a freight of bombs with some-thing like 50 to 100 times the yield that they could muster at inter-continental range. Missile accuracy would more than double. Be-cause there is not much space for obtaining warning—in any case, there are no deep-warning radar nets—and since most of our over-seas bases are close to deep water from which submarines might launch missiles, the warning problem is very much more severe than for bases in the interior of the United States.

As a result, early in the 1950's, the U.S. Air Force decided to re-call many of our bombers to the continental United States and to use the overseas bases chiefly for refueling, particularly post-strike ground refueling. This reduced drastically the vulnerability of U.S. bombers and at the same time retained many of the advantages of overseas operation. For some years now, SAC has been reducing the number of aircraft usually deployed overseas. The purpose is to reduce vulnerability and has little to do with any increasing radius of SAC aircraft. The early B-52 radius is roughly that of the B-36; the B-47, roughly that of the B-50 or B-29. In fact, the radius limi-tation and therefore the basing requirements we have discussed will not change substantially for some time to come. We can talk with comparative confidence here, because the U.S. strategic force is itself largely determined for this period. Such a force changes more slowly than is generally realized. The vast majority of the force will consist of manned bombers, and most of these will be of medium range. *Some* U.S. bombers will be able to reach *some* targets from *some* U.S. bases within the forty-eight states without landing on the way back. On the other hand, some bomber-target combina-tions are not feasible without pre-target landing (and are therefore doubtful). The Atlas, Titan, and Polaris rockets, when available, can of course do without overseas bases (though the proportion of Polaris submarines kept at sea can be made larger by the use of submarine tenders based overseas). But even with the projected force of aerial tankers, the greater part of our force, which will be manned bombers, cannot be used at all in attacks on the Soviet Union without at least some use of overseas areas.

What of the bases for Thor and Jupiter, our first intermediate-range ballistic missiles? These have to be close to the enemy, and they must of course be operating bases, not merely refueling stations. The Thors and Jupiters will be continuously in range of an enormous Soviet potential for surprise attack. These installations therefore re-open, in a most acute form, some of the serious questions of ground vulnerability that were raised about six years ago in connection with our overseas bomber bases. The decision to station the Thor and Jupiter missiles overseas has been our principal public response to the Russian advances in rocketry, and perhaps our most plausible response. Because it involves our ballistic missiles, it appears directly to answer the Russian rockets. Because it involves using European bases, it appears to make up for the range superiority of the Russian intercontinental missile. And most important, it directly involves the NATO powers and gives them an element of control.

There is no question that it was genuinely urgent not only to meet the Russian threat but to do so visibly, in order to save the loosening NATO alliance. Our allies were fearful that the Soviet ballistic missiles might mean that we were no longer able or willing to retaliate against the Soviet Union in case of an attack on them. We hastened to make public a reaction which would restore their confidence. This move surely appears to increase our own power to strike back, and also to give our allies a deterrent of their own, independent of our decision. It has also been argued that in this respect it merely advances the inevitable date at which our allies will acquire "modern" weapons of their own, and that it widens the range of Soviet challenges which Europe can meet. But we must face seriously the question whether this move will in fact assure either the ability to retaliate or the decision to attempt it, on the part of our allies or ourselves. And we should ask at the very least whether further expansion of this policy will buy as much retaliatory power as other ways of spending the considerable sums involved. Finally, it is important to be clear whether the Thor and Jupiter actually increase the flexibility or range of response available to our allies.

One justification for this move is that it disperses retaliatory weapons and that this is the most effective sanction against the thermonuclear aggressor. The limitations of dispersal have already been discussed, but it remains to examine the argument that over-seas bases provide *widespread* dispersal, which imposes on the aggressor insoluble problems of coordination.

There is, of course, something in the notion that forcing the enemy to attack many political entities increases the seriousness of his decision, but there is very little in the notion that dispersal in several countries makes the problem of destruction more difficult in the military sense. Dispersal does not require separation by the distance of oceans—just by the lethal diameters of enemy bombs. and the task of coordinating bomber attacks on Europe and the eastern coast of the United States, say, is not appreciably more difficult than coordinating attacks on our east and west coasts. In the case of ballistic missiles, the elapsed time from firing to impact on the target can be calculated with high accuracy. Although there will be some failures and delays, times of firing can be arranged so that impact on many dispersed points is almost simultaneous—on Okinawa and the United Kingdom, for instance, as well as on California and Ohio. Moreover, it is important to keep in mind that these far-flung bases, while distant from each other and from the United States, are on the whole close to the enemy. To eliminate them, therefore, requires a smaller expenditure of resources on his part than targets at intercontinental range. For close-in targets, he can use a wider variety of weapons carrying larger payloads and with higher accuracy.

The seeming appositeness of an overseas-based Thor and Jupiter as an answer to a Russian intercontinental ballistic missile stems not so much from any careful analysis of their retaliatory power under attack as from the directness of the comparison they suggest: a rocket equals a rocket, an intercontinental missile equals an intermediate-range missile based at closer range to the target. But this again mistakes the nature of the technological race. It conceives the problem of deterrence as that of simply matching or exceeding the aggressor's capability to strike first. A surprising proportion of the debate on defense policy has betrayed this confusion. Matching technological developments are useful for prestige, and such demonstrations have a vital function in preserving the alliance and in reassuring the neutral powers. But propaganda is not enough. The only reasonably certain way of maintaining a reputation for strength is to display an actual power to our friends as well as our enemies. We should ask, then, whether further expansion of the current programs for basing Thor and Jupiter is an efficient way to increase American retaliatory power. If overseas bases are considered too vulnerable for manned bombers, will not the same be true for missiles?

The basis for the hopeful impression that they will not is rather vague, including a mixture of hypothetical properties of ballistic missiles, in which perhaps the dominant element is their supposedly much more rapid, "push-button" response. What needs to be considered here is the response time of such missiles (including decision, preparation, and launch times) and how they are to be defended.

The decision to fire a missile with a thermonuclear warhead is much harder to make than a decision simply to start a manned aircraft on its way, with orders to return to base unless instructed to continue to its assigned target. This is the "fail-safe" procedure practised by the U.S. Air Force. In contrast, once a missile is launched, there is no method of recall or deflection which is not subject to risks of electronic or mechanical failure. Therefore, such a decision must wait for much more unambiguous evidence of enemy intentions. It must and will take a longer time to make and is less likely to be made at all. Where more than one country is involved, the joint decision is harder still, since there is opportunity to disagree about the ambiguity of the evidence, as well as to reach quite different interpretations of national interest. On much less momentous matters the process of making decisions in Nato is complicated, and it should be recognized that such complexity has much to do with the genuine concern of the various Nato powers about the danger of accidentally starting World War III. Such fears will not be diminished with the advent of irbm's. In fact, widespread dispersion of nuclear armed missiles raises measurably the possibility of accidental war.

Second, it is quite erroneous to suppose that, by contrast with manned bombers, the first irbm's can be launched almost as simply as pressing a button. Count-down procedures for early missiles are liable to interruption, and the characteristics of the liquid-oxygen fuel limits the readiness of their response. Unlike JP-4, the fuel used in jet bombers, liquid oxygen cannot be held for long periods of time in these vehicles. In this respect, such missiles will be *less* ready than alert bombers. Third, the smaller warning time available overseas makes more difficult any response. This includes, in particular, any active defense, not only against ballistic missile attacks but, for example, against low-altitude or various circuitous attacks by manned aircraft.

Finally, passive defense by means of shelter is more difficult, given the larger bomb yields, greater accuracies and larger forces available to the Russians at such close range. And if the press reports are correct, the plans for IRBM installations do not call for bomb-resistant shelters. If this is so, it should be taken into account in measuring the actual contribution of these installations to the West's retaliatory power. Viewed as a contribution to deterring all-out attack on the United States, the Thor and Jupiter bases seem unlikely to compare favorably with other alternatives. If newspaper references to hard bargaining by some of our future hosts are to be believed, it would seem that such negotiations have been conducted under misapprehensions on both sides as to the benefits to the United States.

But many proponents of the distribution of Thor and Jupiter—and possibly some of our allies—have in mind not an increase in U.S. deterrence but the development of an independent capability in several of the NATO countries to deter all-out attack against themselves. This would be a useful thing if it could be managed at supportable costs and if it did not entail the sacrifice of even more critical measures of protection. But aside from the special problems of joint control, which would affect the certainty of response adversely, precisely who their legal owner is would not affect the retaliatory power of the Thors and Jupiters one way or the other. They would not be able to deter an attack which they could not survive. It is curious that many who question the utility of American overseas bases (for example, our bomber bases in the United Kingdom) simply assume that, for our allies, possession of strategic nuclear weapons is one with deterrence.

There remains the view that the provision of these weapons will broaden the range of response open to our allies. In so far as this view rests on the belief that the intermediate-range ballistic missile is adapted to limited war, it is wide of the mark. The inaccuracy of an IRBM requires high-yield warheads, and such a combination of inaccuracy and high yield, while quite appropriate and adequate against unprotected targets in a general war, would scarcely come within even the most lax, in fact reckless, definition of limited war. Such a weapon is inappropriate for even the nuclear variety of limited war, and it is totally useless for meeting the wide variety of provocation that is well below the threshold of nuclear response. In so far as these missiles will be costly for our allies to install, operate, and support, they are likely to displace a conventional capability that might be genuinely useful in limited engagements. More important, they are likely to be used as an excuse for budget-cutting. In this way, they will accelerate the general trend toward dependence on all-out response and so will have the opposite effect to the one claimed.

Nevertheless, if the Thor and Jupiter have these defects, might not some future weapon be free of them? Some of these defects, of course, will be overcome in time. Solid fuels or storable liquids will eventually replace liquid oxygen, reliabilities will increase, various forms of mobility or portability will become feasible, accuracies may even be so improved that such weapons can be used in limited wars. But these developments are all years away. In consequence, the discussion will be advanced if a little more precision is given such terms as "missiles" or "modern" or "advanced weapons." We are not distributing a generic "modern" weapon with all the virtues of flexibility in varying circumstances and of invulnerability in all-out war. But even with advances in the state of the art on our side, it will remain difficult to maintain a deterrent, especially close in under the enemy's guns.

It follows that, though a wider distribution of nuclear weapons may be inevitable or, at any rate, likely, and though some countries in addition to the Soviet Union and the United States may even develop an independent deterrent, it is by no means inevitable or even very likely that the power to deter all-out thermonuclear attack will be widespread. This is true even though a minor power would not need to guarantee as large a retaliation as we in order to deter attack on itself. Unfortunately, the minor powers have smaller resources as well as poorer strategic locations.[9] Mere mem-

---

[9] General Gallois argues that, while alliances will offer no guarantee, "a small number of bombs and a small number of carriers suffice for a threatened power to protect itself against atomic destruction." ("A French General Analyzes Nuclear-Age Strategy," p. 71.) His numerical illustrations give the defender some 400 underground launching sites and suggest that their elimination would require between 5,000 and 25,000 missiles—which is "more or less impossible"—and that in any case the aggressor would not survive the fallout from his own weapons. (*Ibid.*, p. 22, and "Nuclear Aggression and National Suicide," p. 25.) Whether these are large numbers of targets from the standpoint of the aggressor will depend on the accuracy, yield, and reliability of offense weapons, as well as the resistance of the defender's shelters and a number of other matters not specified in the argument. General Gallois is aware that the expectation of survival depends on distance, even in the ballistic-missile age, and that our allies are not so fortunate in this respect. Close-in missiles have better bomb yields and accuracies. Moreover, manned aircraft—with still better yields and accuracies—can be used by an aggressor here, since warning of their approach is very short. Suffice it to say that the numerical advantage General Gallois cites is greatly exaggerated. Furthermore, he exag-

bership in the nuclear club might carry with it prestige, as the applicants and nominees expect, but it will be rather expensive, and in time it will be clear that it does not necessarily confer any of the expected privileges enjoyed by the two charter members. The burden of deterring a general war as distinct from limited wars is still likely to be on the United States and therefore, so far as our allies are concerned, on the military alliance.

There is one final consideration. Missiles placed near the enemy, even if they could not retaliate, would have a potent capability for striking first by surprise. And it might not be easy for the enemy to discern their purpose. The existence of such a force might be a considerable provocation and in fact a dangerous one, in the sense that it would place a great burden on our deterrent force which more than ever would have to guarantee extreme risks to the attacker—worse than the risks of waiting in the face of this danger. When not coupled with the ability to strike in retaliation, such a capability might suggest—erroneously, to be sure, in the case of the democracies—an intention to strike first. If so, it would tend to provoke rather than to deter general war.

I have dealt here with only one of the functions of overseas bases: their use as a support for the strategic deterrent force. They have a variety of important military, political, and economic roles which are beyond the scope of this paper. Expenditures in connection with the construction or operation of our bases, for example, are a form of economic aid and, moreover, a form that is rather palatable to Congress. There are other functions in a central war

---

gerates the destructiveness of the retaliatory blow against the aggressor's cities by the remnants of the defender's missile force—even assuming the aggressor would take no special measures to protect his cities. But particularly for the aggressor—who does not lack warning—a civil-defense program can moderate the damage done by a poorly organized attack. Finally, the suggestion that the aggressor would not survive the fall-out from his own weapons is simply in error. The rapid-decay fission products which are the major lethal problem in the locality of a surface burst are not a serious difficulty for the aggressor. The amount of the slow-decay products, strontium-90 and cesium-137, in the atmosphere would rise considerably. If nothing were done to counter it, this might, for example, increase by many times the incidence of such relatively rare diseases as bone cancer and leukemia. However, such a calamity, implying an increase of, say, 20,000 deaths per year for a nation of 200,000,000 is of an entirely different order from the catastrophe involving tens of millions of deaths which General Gallois contemplates elsewhere. And there are measures that might reduce even this effect drastically. (See The RAND Corporation Report R-322-RC, "Report on a Study of Non-Military Defense," July 1, 1958.)

where their importance may be very considerable, and their usefulness in a limited war might be substantial.

Indeed, nothing said here should suggest that deterrence is in
itself an adequate strategy. The complementary requirements of
a sufficient military policy cannot be discussed in detail here. Certainly they include a more serious development of power to meet
limited aggression, especially with more advanced conventional
weapons than those now available. They also include more energetic provision for active and passive defenses to limit the dimensions of the catastrophe in case deterrence should fail. For example,
an economically feasible shelter program might make the difference between 50 million survivors and 120 million survivors.

But it would be a fatal mistake to suppose that because strategic
deterrence is inadequate by itself, it can be dispensed with. Deterrence is not dispensable. If the picture of the world I have drawn
is rather bleak, it could none the less be cataclysmically worse. Suppose both the United States and the Soviet Union had the power
to destroy each others' retaliatory forces and society, given the opportunity to administer the opening blow. The situation would
then be something like the old-fashioned Western gun duel. It
would be extraordinarily risky for one side *not* to attempt to destroy the other, or to delay doing so, since it not only can emerge
unscathed by striking first but this is the sole way it can reasonably
hope to emerge at all. Evidently such a situation is extremely unstable. On the other hand, if it is clear that the aggressor too will
suffer catastrophic damage in the event of his aggression, he then
has strong reason not to attack, even though he can administer
great damage. A protected retaliatory capability has a stabilizing
influence not only in deterring rational attack, but also in offering
every inducement to both powers to reduce the chance of accidental war.

The critics who feel that deterrence is "bankrupt" sometimes
say that we stress deterrence too much. I believe this is quite wrong
if it means that we are devoting too much effort to protect our
power to retaliate; but I think it is quite right if it means that we
have talked too much of a strategic threat as a substitute for many
things it cannot replace.

V. Deterrence, Accidents, and Disarmament

Up to now, I have talked mainly about the problem of deterring
general war, of making it improbable that an act of war will be
undertaken deliberately, with a clear understanding of the conse-

quences, that is, rationally. That such deterrence will not be easy to maintain in the 1960's simply expresses the proposition that a surprise thermonuclear attack might *not* be an irrational or insane act on the part of the aggressor. A deterrent strategy is aimed at a rational enemy. Without a deterrent, general war is likely. With it, however, war might still occur.

In order to reduce the risk of a rational act of aggression, we are being forced to undertake measures (increased alertness, dispersal, mobility) which, to a significant extent, increase the risk of an irrational or unintentional act of war. The accident problem is serious, and it would be a great mistake to dismiss the recent Soviet charges on this subject as simply part of the war of nerves. In a clear sense, the great multiplication and spread of nuclear arms throughout the world, the drastic increase in the degree of readiness of these weapons, and the decrease in the time available for the decision on their use must inevitably raise the risk of accident. The B-47 accidents this year at Sidi Slimane and at Florence, South Carolina, and the recent Nike explosion are just a beginning. Though incidents of this sort are not themselves likely to trigger misunderstanding, they suggest the nature of the problem.

There are many sorts of accidents that could happen. There can be electronic or mechanical failures of the sort illustrated by the B-47 and Nike mishaps; there can be aberrations of individuals, perhaps quite low in the echelon of command; there can be miscalculations on the part of governments as to enemy intent and the meaning of ambiguous signals. Not all deterrent strategies will involve the risk of accident equally. One of the principles of selecting a strategy should be to reduce the chance of accident, wherever we can, without a corresponding increase in vulnerability to a rational surprise attack. This is the purpose of the "fail-safe" procedures for launching SAC.

These problems are also relevant to the disarmament question. The Russians, exploiting an inaccurate United Press report which suggested that SAC started en masse toward Russia in response to frequent radar "ghosts," cried out against these supposed Arctic flights. The United States response, and its sequels, stated correctly that such flights had never been undertaken except in planned exercises and would not be undertaken in response to such unreliable warning. We pointed out the importance of quick response and a high degree of readiness in the protection of the deterrent force. The nature of the fail-safe precaution was also described.

We added, however, to cap the argument, that if the Russians were really worried about surprise attack, they would accept President Eisenhower's "open skies" proposal. This addition, however, conceals an absurdity. Aerial photography would have its uses in a disarmament plan—for example, to check an exchange of information on the location of ground bases. However, so far as surprise is concerned, an "open skies" plan would have direct use only to discover attacks requiring much more lengthy, visible, and unambiguous preparations than are likely today.[10] The very readiness of our own strategic force suggests a state of technology which outmodes the "open skies" plan as a counter to surprise attack. Not even the most advanced reconnaissance equipment can disclose an intention from 40,000 feet. Who can say what the men in the blockhouse of an ICBM base have in mind? Or, for that matter, what is the final destination of training flights or fail-safe flights starting over the Pacific or North Atlantic from staging areas?

The actions that need to be taken on our own to deter attack might usefully be complemented by bilateral agreements for inspection and reporting and, possibly, limitation of arms and of methods of operating strategic and naval air forces. But the protection of our retaliatory power remains essential; the better the protection, the smaller the burden placed on the agreement to limit arms and modes of operation and to make them subject to inspection. Reliance on "open skies" alone to prevent surprise would invite catastrophe and the loss of power to retaliate. Such a plan is worthless for discovering a well-prepared attack with ICBM's or submarine-launched missiles or a routine mass training flight whose destination could be kept ambiguous. A tremendous weight of weapons could be delivered in spite of it.

Although it is quite hopeless to look for an inspection scheme which would permit abandonment of the deterrent, this does not mean that some partial agreement on inspection and limitation might not help to reduce the chance of any sizable surprise attack. We should explore the possibilities of agreements involving limitation and inspection. But how we go about this will be conditioned by our appreciation of the problem of deterrence itself.

The critics of current policy who perceive the inadequacy of the strategy of deterrence are prominent among those urging disarmament negotiations, an end to the arms race, and a reduction of tension. This is a paramount interest of some of our allies. The

---

[10] Aerial reconnaissance, of course, could have an *indirect* utility here for surveying large areas to determine the number and location of observation posts needed to provide more timely warning.

balance of terror theory is the basis for some of the more light-hearted suggestions: if deterrence is automatic, strategic weapons on one side cancel those of the other, and it should be easy for both sides to give them up. So James E. King, Jr., one of the most sensible writers on the subject of limited war, suggests that weapons needed for "unlimited" war are those which both sides can most easily agree to abolish, simply because "neither side can anticipate anything but disaster" from their use. "Isn't there enough stability in the 'balance of terror,'" he asks, "to justify our believing that the Russians can be trusted—within acceptable limits—to abandon the weapons whose 'utility is confined to the threat or conduct of a war of annihilation'?"[11]

Indeed, if there were no real danger of a rational attack, then accidents and the "nth-country" problem would be the only problems. As I have indicated, they are serious problems, and some sort of limitation and inspection agreement might diminish them. But if there is to be any prospect of realistic and useful agreement, we must reject the theory of automatic deterrence. And we must bear in mind that the more extensive a disarmament agreement is, the smaller the force that a violator would have to hide in order to achieve complete domination. Most obviously, "the *abolition* of the weapons necessary in a general or 'unlimited' war" would offer the most insuperable obstacles to an inspection plan, since the violator could gain an overwhelming advantage from the concealment of even a few weapons. The need for a deterrent, in this connection too, is ineradicable.

VI. SUMMARY

Almost everyone seems concerned with the need to relax tension. However, relaxation of tension, which everyone thinks is good, is not easily distinguished from relaxing one's guard, which almost everyone thinks is bad. Relaxation, like Miltown, is not an end in itself. Not all danger comes from tension. To be tense where there is danger is only rational.

What can we say then, in sum, on the balance-of-terror theory of automatic deterrence? It is a contribution to the rhetoric rather than to the logic of war in the thermonuclear age. The notion that a carefully planned surprise attack can be checkmated almost effortlessly—that, in short, we may resume our deep pre-Sputnik

[11] James E. King, Jr., "Arms and Man in the Nuclear-Rocket Era," *The New Republic*, September 1, 1958.

sleep—is wrong, and its nearly universal acceptance is terribly dangerous. Though deterrence is not enough in itself, it is vital. There are two principal points.

First, deterring general war in both the early and late 1960's will be hard at best, and hardest both for ourselves and our allies wherever we use forces based near the enemy.

Second, even if we can deter general war by a strenuous and continuing effort, this will by no means be the whole of a military, much less a foreign policy. Such a policy would not of itself remove the danger of accidental outbreak or limit the damage in case deterrence failed; nor would it be at all adequate for crises on the periphery.

A generally useful way of concluding a grim argument of this kind would be to affirm that we have the resources, intelligence, and courage to make the correct decisions. That is, of course, the case. And there is a good chance that we will do so. But perhaps, as a small aid toward making such decisions more likely, we should contemplate the possibility that they may *not* be made. They *are* hard, *do* involve sacrifice, *are* affected by great uncertainties, and concern matters in which much is altogether unknown and much else must be hedged by secrecy; above all, they entail a new image of ourselves in a world of persistent danger. It is by no means *certain* that we shall meet the test.

THREE

ARTHUR WASKOW

The Theory and Practice of Deterrence

[Editor's Note: This article appeared in 1962 as a critique of the Wohlstetter school of thought. Accepting Professor Wohlstetter's thesis that the balance of terror is delicate (see above, Chapter 2), Mr. Waskow argues that the complexities of deterrence do not diminish the risks of war; on the contrary, they increase its likelihood. According to Mr. Waskow, each attempt to remedy the military balance has made the situation more complicated and explosive; and the attempt to make strategy scientific falsifies contemporary issues that are essentially political, economic, and social, rather than military. The world situation requires, not greater sophistication in the theory of deterrence, but abandonment of the concept. Mr. Waskow accepts most of Wohlstetter's premises, then, but draws opposite conclusions from them.

Mr. Waskow's insistence that national security policy ultimately depends on moral, political, and social factors is useful. The weakness of his position lies in his implication that strategic analysis and moral concerns are antithetical, an attitude representative of the school of thought which, in effect, considers strategic analysis in itself dangerous.]

In recent years, "deterrence" has become the fundamental concept in all official proposals for the protection of American national security. At the same time, there has developed more and more disagreement on the meaning of "deterrence." In the last several months, we[1] have attempted to clarify these various meanings, to spell out the full implications of the sometimes incoherent proposals of various defense experts, and to assess the practical worth

EDITOR'S NOTE: "The Theory and Practice of Deterrence," from *The Liberal Papers*, edited by James Roosevelt. Copyright © 1962 by James Roosevelt. Reprinted by permission of Doubleday & Company, Inc.

[1] The use of "we" and "our" in this essay is purely the result of editorial convention and connotes no one's responsibility for the opinions expressed except the author's.

of the major alternatives now presented by various spokesmen in the Department of Defense.

In addition to published materials, our chief sources for the various opinions expressed have been interviews with a number of policy-making officers and civilian officials in the various services, in the Department of Defense central organization, and in other government agencies involved in the problem, such as the Office of Civil and Defense Mobilization.

We focused on such questions as these: What kinds of wars does the Department of Defense expect to deter? What weapons systems would be involved in various methods of deterrence? What is the role of civil defense, as a component or a complement of particular weapons systems, conceived to be? What types of service reorganization are considered necessary to support any given notion of deterrence? And do particular branches of the services of particular agencies espouse particular versions of deterrence? We also tried to explore the varied theoretical explanations of how the psychology of deterrence would operate.

Finally, after examining the theories themselves, we have examined the kinds of practical action Congress can take in regard to them.

THE COUNTER-FORCE THEORY OF DETERRENCE

A number of officers and administrators, mainly in the Air Force, are convinced that thermonuclear war is possible, conceivable, acceptable, and that it will be "won" or "lost" in the classical sense. These men agree that it would be preferable to prevent such a war from taking place, but they think the only effective prevention is the establishment of a force capable of winning such a war and accepting the surrender of the enemy. Against the common belief that thermonuclear war is inconceivable, they have tried to construct a rational model of the probable course of such a war—rational in the literal sense that they expect the highest rationality to be maintained by fighters and governments on both sides. Counter-force theorists assume that the authorities who engage in thermonuclear war will, at least, attempt to restrict as far as possible the great damage that would result from thermonuclear war.

This group conceives that war might come in one of two major ways: the Sino-Soviet bloc might launch a major atomic strike at the United States; alternatively, the bloc might act against some area other than the United States in such an intensely provocative way—for example, by invading Western Europe or Japan—that the United States might decide to make a first atomic strike[2] against the Communist bloc.

In either case, this group expects the action of the United States to be "counter-force" action. They would expect American attack to be directed not against populations or industry but against the atomic capability of the enemy. They come to this conclusion through two alternative chains of reasoning. One hypothesis is that if the enemy makes a surprise attack with nuclear weapons, his first target would be American atomic forces. An American counter-attack directed against enemy cities would be suicidal, since it would invite enemy retaliation against American cities with un-scathed atomic forces. Hence, American atomic forces which survive the initial attack should be directed at enemy atomic capabilities, in the hope of destroying them. In the second chain of reasoning, the United States would respond to a major provocation by attacking enemy atomic capabilities with thermonuclear bombs. Only in this way would there be hope of preventing a Soviet atomic strike against our cities, on the theory that the Soviets would have nothing left to strike back with.

The counter-force theorists argue that both United States and Soviet atomic-striking forces are sufficiently remote from population centers; in consequence, war between *these* atomic forces would not absolutely destroy the American and Russian peoples. These theorists estimate that up to 36 million Americans might die in such a war, but they regard this as an acceptable loss. They believe that after absorbing such a blow, the United States and Soviet governments would still be able to act by rational calculation in attempts to minimize destruction. They assume that capitals would not be destroyed nor governments annihilated, simply because such annihilation would not be to the advantage of the attacking power. Both sides, they believe, would want governments left intact to minimize conflict and simplify surrender.

When mobile land missiles like the Minuteman are in operation on both sides, counter-force theorists recognize the need to pin-point the atomic forces one was trying to destroy; therefore, they suggest that an atomic war of this nature would not be a matter

[2] All segments of the Defense Department seem to assume that the United States will not be the first to make a warlike act. But some segments would want a Sino-Soviet act of low-level war (such as conventionally armed invasion or even subversion) answered by a high-level American act, even the first use of nuclear weapons.

of mere hours. Protracted air reconnaissance would be necessary to hunt down and destroy mobile missiles. During this period, civilian populations would wait (either in their home cities or in specially prepared underground "city" sites) for days and weeks while thermonuclear attacks on thermonuclear forces went on around them. This desperate war of attrition would end when the nation that had begun with the larger, more protected, and better-directed atomic force had some atomic-strike capacity left, the other having exhausted its capacity. The nation that had been ahead would demand and receive the surrender of the other.

In the event of a major Soviet provocation short of direct attack on the United States, American populations might be evacuated to previously prepared gigantic shelter areas. Such evacuation would free the United States to demand a withdrawal of the Soviet provocative act on pain of atomic attack upon the Soviet Union. Thus, whether in their cities (theoretically remote from the missile sites and air bases that would be the focus of attack) or in such mass shelters, American populations would be rescued from annihilation.

The chief weapons systems necessary to fight such a war would be the Strategic Air Command (SAC) with its B-70 bombers, the Atlas and Titan liquid-fuel ICBM's, and the mobile solid-fuel Minuteman ICBM—all of which systems are under Air Force control. In addition, to complicate the enemy's problem of discovering the American atomic striking force, such sea-based systems as Polaris would be valuable components of over-all strategy. But, because Polaris missiles are too small to destroy enemy missiles in underground, concrete silos and more difficult to aim accurately, the Polaris could be only secondary in counter-force strategy.

Two essential elements of this strategy are as yet undeveloped. First, we are several years away from an atomic-powered plane capable of the hovering reconnaissance necessary to track down mobile missile sites. Even more difficult, what is being done to create huge underground cities for evacuation, to prepare populations for evacuation and for underground life, to build in our cities effective anti-fallout shelters? These last would be necessary to keep casualties below the 30-million level while enemy thermonuclear bombs and missiles were dropping on the rockets and planes based in the United States.

Counter-force theorists feel little need for large Army and naval forces as part of their strategy. Counter-force strategy, through its threat of atomic retaliation, is considered a sufficient deterrent against limited war initiated by the enemy.

The counter-force system would not only act as a deterrent to such minor wars, according to its supporters, but would be the only way of deterring general war. In many ways, counter-force theory is an outgrowth of the classic assumption that the best deterrent to enemy attack is being strong enough both to live through the attack and to accept the enemy's surrender. Thus, in this view, "deterrence" is the building of an overwhelming force capable of winning the war if it should come and of leaving the winner in a viable position.

Objections to the Counter-force Theory

Major objections have been posed to this whole theory from a number of sources. Many of these objections have come from the two armed services that counter-force theory would downgrade—that is, the Army and the Navy. These objections have been directed, first, against the hypothetical model of thermonuclear war devised by counter-force theorists and, second, against the kind of American society that would result from acceptance of the counter-force system.

To deal first with the imaginary thermonuclear war, the possibility of actually separating atomic forces and great populations has been questioned. Several U.S. bomber bases are near cities. It seems likely that such situations as now exist in Tucson, Arizona, where Titans have been built close to the city, would become more rather than less the practice. There can be little doubt that Nike bases presently established close to American cities would have to be major targets for atomic destruction if air reconnaissance were going to be free to sniff out mobile or hardened missile sites. Thus, it seems likely that atomic attack would have to center on targets quite close to our major cities, resulting in casualties far beyond the estimated "acceptable" 30 million. A similar pattern is likely to develop in the Soviet Union, thus lessening the likelihood that the Soviets could accept nuclear attacks on nuclear-force targets and make rational and controlled responses. If even a few cities are destroyed on either side, it is unlikely that the return fire will be selectively directed against military targets only. In such a situation, the national agony would be likely to demand an all-out attack.

Indeed, such a war might easily destroy some vital link in the national chain of command, leaving small groups of atomically armed forces bewildered, fearful, and free to attack at will. Such disintegration would be a likely result of the intense pressure of continuous atomic attack lasting several weeks. If such a breakdown occurred, the war would not be fought along the lines of counter-force theory.

The feasibility of civil-defense preparations that would fit counter-force theory is open to serious question. Aside from the problems of expense, if the huge underground city shelters proposed were built, it is questionable whether they would be usable. For example, what would an enemy conclude if American evacuation to such shelters were ordered? Might he not expect our attack and therefore attack us pre-emptively? Or, once war had started, would he accept defeat so long as he might hope people in such shelters were running out of food and water and would have to emerge, becoming vulnerable to attack? Such questions point up the impossibility of basing counter-force deterrence even on the future effectiveness of such shelters, let alone the unlikelihood of their construction.

The Minuteman missile, on which much of the counter-force strategy depends, may not be a workable weapon. The special conditions necessary for the long railroad trains that support Minutemen can be found only in the West of the United States, where there are so few railroad tracks that high aerial bursts of thermonuclear weapons in a pattern above the tracks could knock all the Minutemen in the area out of operation. If the Minuteman trains were to leave the scattered tracks of the West in order to travel the complex Eastern railroad systems, they would be more likely to approach metropolitan areas and thus confuse the vital distinction between atomic forces and civilian populations.

It seems likely that as mobile, hardened, or secret missile sites proliferate on both sides, it will become more and more difficult to find and destroy atomic forces. This is particularly true of the American capability to find and destroy Soviet bases, since the U.S.S.R. exceeds the United States both in secrecy and in space. Even if counter-force strategy is conceivable in some sense today, it may not be possible ten years from now.

To summarize and clarify these objections to the feasibility of counter-force deterrence, it is useful to look closely at the concept of "rationality" in military planning. As the United States builds a counter-force system that is more subtle, more hidden, more mobile, the temptation increases for an enemy to make an overwhelming and undiscriminating attack. Rationality *to the Soviets* might dictate the use of high-burst pattern bombing to destroy the entire American society; otherwise, some of the American striking force might escape.

The history of twentieth-century war suggests that as one side uses its armed might more effectively, the other's reaction is to strike back with greater strength. We know this process well enough to have called it "total war"; there is every reason to believe that the final step in the process would result from applying counter-force theory. A serious look at what *each* side would consider "rational" thus shows that counter-force deterrence will not work out as counter-force theorists expect, and the counter-force war is not possible.

Counter-force strategy has been attacked as not only impossible of practice in war but overwhelmingly dangerous to the preservation of peace. If both sides hope to be able to destroy the atomic forces of the other, both sides are under enormous pressure to be quick on the trigger. Striking at empty missile pads is absurd; split-second calculations designed to outshoot an enemy nation may lead to madness.

With the pressure so enormous and the stake so high, there can be little doubt that each side would be forced to attempt to pre-empt the other. In any period of major international crisis, the fear of a planned attack could only lead to preparations for attack which might be strictly defensive in intent. But such acts of self-defense must appear as offensive threats to the other side, which would be forced to prepare its missiles. The sequence would lead directly to hair-trigger responses and could scarcely avoid leading to war. The chances of accidental war through some remote crisis developing into a larger threat, partial mobilization, and mutual fears of attack would be enormously increased.

Accepting counter-force strategy would also mean accepting an arms race without end. More and more mobile missiles, more and more underground missiles—the attempt to achieve ever newer counter-force weapons—would prevent the achievement of any halt in the arms race. The system is based on the goal of having the larger atomic force to begin with, so as to have more left after attack. Thus neither side can ever stop adding to its atomic-weapon stockpile. The costs of continued stockpiling and of the search for and production of more powerful weapons would be enormous both in human terms and in money and would extend indefinitely into the future. The costs simply of building huge underground evacuation centers might be expected to run into several hundred billion dollars. An American society that would become accustomed to such evacuation shelters, to recurrent evacuations, to the possibility that whole populations would cower in shelters or in cities while atomic strikes went on around them, and to the expectation of 30 million deaths, would to free men be alien and unwanted, even unworthy of protection.

In fact, counter-force theorists admit privately that the United States might, if it fell behind in the counter-force arms race, have to surrender in such a war as they imagine. Since they seem fully to expect that an atomic war of some sort is inevitable if the United States were to fall behind in such an arms race, they must regard as an important possibility that all the sacrifices they demand in money and in human feelings might not prevent our defeat.

Counter-force theory thus seems to be bankrupt. Its hypothetical war between atomic forces is so improbable that there is little possibility of convincing an enemy that preparations for such a war are a credible deterrent. Even if such a war were possible, counter-force strategy seems more likely to bring it on than to prevent it. Far from deterring, counter-force strategy might press both antagonists toward pre-emptive attack. Finally, even if counter-force strategy did not bring about the war it is intended to win, constructing the weapons systems and shelters to support such a strategy would distort the free society we are pledged to defend.

THE COMBINED-DETERRENT THEORY

Some American officers and administrators, centered in the Army and the Navy, have decided that "to win" or "to lose" a thermonuclear war is inconceivable. They believe that such a war must be prevented, and they do not believe that preparing to fight it is the way to prevent it. They prefer to make the outbreak of such a war as unlikely as possible by means of sharply increasing its terror. The result of such planning will, hopefully, be the elimination of all but the old-fashioned, conventional wars, for these members of the older military services want basically to work out a way to return to the older fashions of making war.

This theory of deterrence, not surprisingly, is based on a combination of the particular weapons systems and skills of the Army and Navy. For the theorists of this combined deterrent, the first question is how to make thermonuclear war sufficiently terrible that it cannot and will not be fought. The mission of accomplishing this ennoblement of terror belongs to the Navy, which claims to have developed an "invulnerable deterrent."

It is the Navy's theory that if both the United States and its chief enemies have great masses of the population open to atomic attack (in a sense being held as hostages) and that if, on both sides, the forces to mount such an attack are themselves invulnerable, the attack will never be mounted. The theory is that any nation which under such circumstances struck first would condemn its own population, its economy, its government, its very existence to death. For any nuclear attack would fail to destroy its enemy's invulnerable capacity, and that capacity would then be used to destroy its own cities.

The theorists of combined deterrence argue that the existence of such an invulnerable striking force would bring all the pressure of hope and fear to bear against any idea of a first atomic strike. They thus argue that the invulnerable deterrent with vulnerable populations would stabilize the international situation. Instead of pressing both sides toward a pre-emptive attack, the invulnerable deterrent would press both sides to think long and hard before attacking.

In addition, the argument runs that this situation would constitute a plateau in the arms race. It is suggested that when both sides reach the level of the invulnerable deterrent they can tacitly agree to arrest the arms build-up while understanding difficulties, they attempt to negotiate. In fact, many of the proponents of "arms control" are looking to the establishment of this state of affairs as an end in itself, rather than as a way station on the road to disarmament.

The Navy believes that the "invulnerable deterrent" is to be found in its Polaris submarine, driven by atomic motors and armed with thermonuclear missiles. The argument runs that the Polaris can cruise the oceans of the earth in secrecy, ready to strike but with every incentive not to do so unless the United States is struck first. By its very separation from the land masses and population centers of America, the Polaris would avoid attracting an attack against the continental United States. For such an attack would have no purpose if it left the Polaris still capable of striking.

The Polaris itself is not believed to be a provocative weapon, because it can be so managed as to be incapable of attacking an enemy's atomic force. This is thought to be true because the megatonnage of the Polaris missile is too small to crack through hardened missile bases or to kill a hidden base with a near miss. Nor is the Polaris missile, launched at sea with all the difficulties of precisely accurate aiming that a ship encounters, capable of direct hits on mobile missiles.[3] The only way in which the Polaris could be made capable of a counter-force strike would be to mass so many

[3] Some Navy men, however, in arguing their case to Congress, claim "pinpoint accuracy" for the Polaris. If true, this claim would gravely weaken the argument that the Polaris is not provocative.

explosions in the territory of the enemy that by sheer salvo technique atomic capability would be destroyed. Most Navy theorists
believe that the crucial point in this massing of salvos would be at
the number of forty-five Polaris submarines. To avoid turning the
Polaris into a provocative counter-force weapon, the Navy would
like to restrict the number of its Polaris submarines to no more
than forty-five.

As the Navy realizes, the form of deterrence based on the Polaris'
ability to kill whole cities can only be a deterrence of all-out thermonuclear war. If an enemy were to take any action less emphatic than
a thermonuclear attack upon the United States, the United States
would certainly hesitate long before mounting a thermonuclear
attack upon Soviet cities. For, of course, as long as our cities were
intact, they would serve as hostages against the initiation of such
an attack by the United States.

Theorists of the invulnerable deterrent therefore have to propose
some way in which lesser provocations than all-out war can be
deterred. It is in this context that the Army and Navy feel that
what is necessary is a combination of deterrents. For major provocations less than all-out war and, in fact, for minor provocations as
well, the Army and Navy look to tactical forces as the chief deterrent.

Such major provocations might be invasion of Western Europe
by the Soviet Union or of Southeast Asia or Japan by Communist
China. The question would be how to throw back such an attack
without involving the world in a thermonuclear war.

The theorists of the combined deterrent argue that the answer to
this question is modernized ability to fight on the fringes of the
Communist world. They believe that if the United States and its
allies have such ability, it will act as a deterrent and will never have
to be used; in other words, *this* kind of war can be won or lost and
the way to prevent it is to prepare to win it. War may still be "a
continuation of politics by other means" but only if the chances of
thermonuclear war are eliminated by balance-of-terror techniques.

The Army and the Navy believe that the old-fashioned foot
soldier and fleet are the keys to deterrence, provided that infantry
and naval equipment are modernized. Two important factors compel such modernization: first, compared with the Sino-Soviet bloc,
the United States and its allies are short on men but long on ma-
chines; second, the West must defend a far-flung frontier on which
tactical attack might come at any place and at any moment. In
consequence, the mobility and the firepower of Western tactical

forces should be increased; if possible, their numbers should be increased as well. On the question of mobility and numbers, there is general agreement on the need for an air-lift capability that could transport within hours sizable forces of infantrymen to any part of the world.

Sizable fleets, floating off the shores of critical areas, must also be ready to land American marines at short notice. Finally, every attempt should be made to increase the numbers of allied soldiers available to integrated Western commands; hence, emphasis on the need for a strong German army and for increased military subsidies to nations on the Communist periphery that cannot afford to build up their own armies.

Both the Army and Navy believe that increased tactical readiness not only will deter actual military invasion by Sino-Soviet forces but that it could check internal subversion and revolution. For the presence of the fleet "showing the flag" all across the globe, the availability of air-lifted infantrymen, and the existence of powerful indigenous armies—all are thought to work against the possibility of internal Communist revolutions. The three techniques of intervention to stop invasion, intervention to halt subversion, and aid to strengthen an indigenous army against either subversion or invasion were exemplified by American action in Korea, Lebanon, and Greece. In each of these cases, the Army and Navy believe that they frustrated the Communists' immediate plans and, by demonstrating American military capacity, reduced the prospects of similar Communist expansion elsewhere.

The one issue in which there is considerable disagreement among theorists of the combined deterrent concerns increased firepower for tactical forces. Some argue that because the West can never, despite mobility and military aid, match the Sino-Soviet bloc in numbers of available soldiers, the West's presumed technological superiority must fill the gap. Atomic, chemical, or bacteriological weapons must be placed in the hands of Western armies to be used against "hordes" of Sino-Soviet invaders. Unless this is done, they believe that Soviet expansion cannot be checked. On the other hand, some combined-deterrent theorists believe that atomic, chemical, and bacteriological weapons could only spread tactical war into general war. These men argue that the only observable limits are defined by the so-called conventional weapons, that once beyond this limit, there is no way of stopping one side or the other from employing still more powerful weapons up to and including the H-bomb.

But with this exception on the question of firepower, theorists of the combined deterrent are agreed on their system. They believe it can prevent the thermonuclear war that they believe is absolutely unacceptable to mankind. They also believe it can probably prevent both tactical wars and internal subversion. Even if it fails to prevent them, it can make possible American or Western victory in such situations.

Objections to the Combined-Deterrent Theory

To this whole theory, as to counter-force theory, there have been many objections on various levels. Again, some of the objections question the possibility of building a credible deterrent along these lines, and, again, some of the objections dispute the belief that a society and international order based on such a deterrent would be stable or tolerable.

The question of military possibility rests squarely on the alleged "invulnerability" of the Polaris submarine, but the invulnerability of the present Polaris even against existing methods of anti-submarine warfare has been seriously questioned. The Polaris missile has an effective range of some 1,500 miles. Most Russian cities are so far from navigable oceans that, to be capable of hitting them, the Polaris submarine must circle quite close to Communist coasts. It cannot literally "hide beneath the oceans," because only a fraction of the world's oceans are within striking distance. If this were all, the protection of the seas might be sufficient; but should the submarine launch one of its missiles, its position would immediately be revealed to enemy aircraft. It is possible that the submarine could be destroyed before firing more than one or two of its sixteen missiles.

Refinements of the Polaris may, of course, add to its range and to its ability of self-concealment, but there will undoubtedly also be refinements in the techniques of anti-submarine warfare. The Polaris system is not a technological plateau. To be a credible deterrent, it must be improved, and this improvement will undoubtedly call forth improvements in anti-Polaris systems. This "invulnerable" deterrent cannot stand still; it cannot halt the arms race. It can only give rise to a slightly different kind of arms race in which first anti-submarine warfare and later the anti-missile missile would be the chief direction of arms improvements.

By its nature, the Polaris would add to, rather than reduce, one of the major problems of effective deterrence. That problem is the so-called "*n*th-country" question. Silent underneath the ocean, the

Polaris submarine is unidentifiable. If a Polaris-type missile is fired against a city, no one can know for sure who fired it. If nuclear technology proliferates across the world with the result that many nations can build atomic submarines, no one will ever be sure what nation might deliver *or even might have delivered* a thermonuclear blow. If nuclear knowledge spreads, it might even be in the best interest of the Soviet Union and the United States to clear all atomically armed and atomically powered submarines from the sea, so as to prevent a case of mistaken identity or disguised attack. This view shows the difficulty of using the Polaris in the approaching situation when much of the world will have atomic weapons.[4]

In addition to these criticisms of the feasibility of using the Polaris as a deterrent, there have been criticisms of its moral and political implictions. Air Force theorists in particular have pointed to what they call the absolute immorality of planning the total destruction of civilian populations, compared with their own acceptance of a "limited" war bringing only 30 million deaths. There is no doubt that if the Polaris deterrent were to fail, the result would be a universal holocaust.

Finally, Polaris has been criticized because of the impossibility of continued governmental control over the acts of the submarine commander. Since the Polaris has to be free to act if governmental centers are destroyed—otherwise, in case of the assumed enemy first strike, there would be no way for it to act at all—there is no sure way to prevent independent action by Polaris crews, even in the absence of a first strike. While an American submarine crew, fearful of retaliation against their homeland, would be unlikely to take such independent action, the crews of some lesser power might seek to upset the world balance by means of provoking an all-out war. Even in ships of the major powers, the chance of an irresponsible or irrational attack should by no means be ruled out.

The other element of the combined deterrent, "tactical readiness," has also been severely criticized. The criticisms directed against the high-firepower wing of theorists have already been described. High firepower in terms of atomic, chemical, or biological weaponry is clearly capable of leading upward into a thermonuclear

---

[4] Another curious ramification of the nth-country problem could develop from the Polaris strategy. By nature, the Polaris must be ready to fire if communication with the mainland is cut off. But if communication is cut off, how can the submarine be told on whom to fire? Might it be fired on the wrong country, or even be fired because it was thought that war had begun when there was only a communications failure?

war. Certainly, few powers would want atomic or biological wars fought over their territory, and they would be likely to respond to such weapons by pressing for the use of thermonuclear weapons in their own defense.

But many who fear that such escalation would result from unconventionally armed tactical forces are also convinced that in sheer numbers the West can scarcely cope with Sino-Soviet capacities. The costs, both human and economic, of universal and lengthy military conscription would be extremely hard to bear, especially if no end to the struggle can be imagined.

The limited-war lessons that matter most are those which can be drawn from Korea and Algeria; and the lessons apply for both the domestic reactions to such wars and the results in the countries defended. Both the United States and France, during each of these prolonged and stalemated wars, experienced great difficulty in limiting the theater of the war and in preserving their civil liberties. Demands either to abandon the war or to expand it were enormous in each case. Pressures that in the United States showed up as a nightmare episode of attack on civil liberties, in France developed into an actual overthrow of the republic. Thus, the effects at home of future involvements in limited wars are not to be dismissed lightly.

In other countries, the effects of limited wars would be equally unhappy. Constant readiness to use military force against invasions or revolutions thought to be Communist-directed will not prevent such violence, for its causes are far deeper than Communist manipulation. The political, economic, and social origins of unrest in Africa, Asia, and Latin America cannot be eliminated by Western armies. Such armies can only ally themselves with privileged minorities who are interested in maintaining the *status quo* of poverty and ignorance, trying to hold down or hold back the violence born of desperation. Thus, the policy of large Western armies would not only weaken the West but tend to frustrate the necessary development of the hungry nations.

The substitution of Western-aided, native "anti-Communist" armies in the hungry nations for actual Western armies meets the same objections. Massive military aid to such nations distorts their economies and interferes with orderly economic and social growth. In fact, heavy military aid to such countries and heavy support for the military classes in such countries often intensify discontent and revolution. Such internal rebellions are frequently deflected by undiscriminating Western opposition to social change into an alliance with the Communist bloc. In some nations (such as Cuba), we have already seen the disturbing effect of such a series of events. In others, it may be possible for continued military aid to the ruling groups to suppress any upheavals; but the upheavals will not end, and instability will become a chronic factor in precisely the places where stable allies are most hoped for.

The notion of the combined deterrent thus seems to be only a temporary expedient. The "invulnerable" deterrent seems impossible to make permanently invulnerable, and hence it will not be permanently credible. Large-scale military conscription and tactical readiness would place such a strain upon the economies and the political systems both of developed and underdeveloped countries that it seems an unwise goal. The combined deterrent also seems likely to increase the chances of nth-country attack and of internal subversion and chronic instability in the poor countries. The plateau promised by the theorists of the combined deterrent is illusory. Though adopting the theory might give the great powers a few additional years to think out new solutions, the combined deterrent promises no permanent "arms control" and is in itself no goal for achieving peace.

The Theories Confounded

Although we have discussed the major arguments for and against each of the central theories of deterrence, there remain some general considerations to be raised on the nature of deterrence and the nature of the kinds of deterrence so far discussed. Among these is the difficulty of distinguishing operationally between "counterforce" and "combined-deterrent" strategies.

The blurring of the two strategies has been dignified as a theory by some elements of the Defense Department and labeled the "mix," or the "middle course." It is now almost automatic even among those who believe in the combined deterrent to say that there should be a "mix" of weapons and strategies available to the United States. In fact, the services in which the combined-deterrent theory is dominant (the Army and Navy) say specifically that they do not hope or intend to eliminate the weapons systems that fit into a counter-force strategy. In other words, the Titan, the Minuteman, and the B-70 are all to continue to exist alongside the Polaris and a limited-war capability. This position is politically inescapable for the various services, since each fears it would hurt only itself by attacking the institutionalized prerogatives, industrial allies, and political supporters of the others. But the position is rationalized on the basis that the United States must be ready for whatever kind of war the enemy initiates—must, in short, be ready to fight either a counter-force or counter-population war.

Yet there can be no doubt that a potential enemy would view the American military system as a whole. He would doubt that a combined-deterrent policy had been clearly adopted, if weapons systems alien to such a policy were continued. In such a situation, the advantages claimed for the combined deterrent—stability during a crisis—would not exist. So there is no point to choosing the combined deterrent, no chance of reaping the advantages claimed for such a system, unless the United States eliminates weapons that do not fit that concept—that is, scraps most of the Air Force. No such intention seems to exist either in the Department of Defense or in the Congress, and certainly not in the missile industry.

On the other hand, if the United States chooses counter-force theory, it must eliminate all semblance of city-busting techniques. For if, in addition to counter-force weapons, we insist on building weapons that can only be used effectively against populations rather than forces, we will make impossible the development of a war according to counter-force theories. If the enemy watches us building a force (for example, Polaris) that is obviously intended for use against cities because it would be of little use against atomic striking forces, they could only conclude that the intention was to strike against both cities and forces. Once that conclusion is fixed in the mind of a potential enemy, the rational calculations will be different from those the counter-force theorists assume. Assuming that it must forestall a general attack, the only rational action open to an enemy is to attack our capital, leadership, population, economy, and industry as well as our atomic force. Thus the war would not develop in the rational ways counter-force theorists propose. If counter-force theory is to be adopted, weapons like Polaris must be scrapped.

Furthermore, if an enemy is to believe that the United States will respond to major conventionally armed provocations (such as an attack on Europe) with an atomic strike it seems necessary to scrap our own limited-war capabilities; otherwise, the enemy will not be convinced that we really mean to use the atomic strike. Pure counter-force theory means that most of the Army and Navy would have to be scrapped, just as pure combined-deterrent theory would mean that most of the Air Force would have to be scrapped.

An exclusive commitment would have to be made to one of these theories for either of them to be believable. But the United States is such a rich country that, instead of making hard choices between costly alternatives, we try to build everything we think of. If that pattern of the past is to be continued, then attempts to argue for either the counter-force or the invulnerable-deterrent strategy are meaningless.

Confusion in an enemy's mind between counter-force and combined-deterrent strategy could be brought about in another way. Even if our choice were made in favor of a combined-deterrent strategy, there is a limit to the size of the invulnerable-weapons system that could be built if the system were not to look like a more subtle counter-force weapon. For example, Navy theorists suggest that if we build more than forty-five Polaris submarines, that force would no longer appear to the Soviet Union like a second-strike, deterrent-only weapons system; more than forty-five atomic submarines would suggest that a saturation-bombing technique was to be used. The "value" of having a not too accurate, not too powerful missile would disappear if salvos of such missiles were to be massed. Such a massing could turn the Polaris into a counter-force weapon, and, therefore, the building of a huge fleet of Polarises would seem to be an adoption of counter-force strategy. This limit is understood by the Navy men, but they do not generalize this concept to apply to the multiplication of weapons systems. If only forty-five Polarises are built, if a Minuteman intended as an "invulnerable" deterrent is also built, and if a series of similar invulnerable deterrents are built in addition, the resulting mix of weapons systems will scarcely seem to fit the combined-deterrent theory. Thus, again, the potentialities of American wealth could turn what seems to be a choice of a particular strategy into a confusion between the two strategies. But this view is little understood in the Department of Defense and seems scarcely likely of acceptance by the political forces that would determine budget and basic plans.

Finally, there is a third way in which confusion between the two strategies could arise: if the invulnerable deterrent, even in its most carefully limited form, and alongside it a major civil-defense shelter program were to be built. The theory of the invulnerable deterrent works only if populations are vulnerable and forces are invulnerable. If either the Soviet Union or the United States were to give a clear indication of an all-out program of shelter-building, the assumption on the other side could reasonably be that a city-busting attack was expected and was being guarded against. Such an attack would only be expected, according to combined-deterrent theory, in retaliation for an attack by one's own forces against cities. By these assumptions, the reason to guard against such an attack would be to free one's invulnerable deterrent to make a first strike against the cities of one's opponent.

A shelter-building program on either side would therefore contribute greatly to the instability that the invulnerable deterrent is supposed to alleviate. It would raise the specter that the deterrent was to be used for a first strike and would force the opponent into developing a counter-force strategy. Unlike the other two confusions discussed above, this one does not seem as yet built into the political structure and assumptions of the United States. No commitment has yet been made here to an all-out shelter building program. But it is noteworthy that no service, not even the combined-deterrent theorists of the Army and Navy, is willing to suggest that civil defense be abandoned, to uphold the purity of the combined-deterrent theory. As long as even the present ineffective civil defense is continued, notions of a commitment to an all-out shelter program will endure. Such a commitment would have to be prevented for the future, if the United States decided to adopt the invulnerable-deterrent strategy.

We have discussed the ways in which the United States refuses to choose between the two major strategies and thereby may bring about the worst aspects of each. Neither from this confused "mix" nor from either pure theory can we expect a halt to the arms race. Instead, we believe that present military strategies would result in a rising crescendo of destructive capacity—a crescendo in which there would be plateaus, but only plateaus like the steps of an escalator that quickly and insensibly merge into the next step up.

We suggest that there would develop, indefinitely into the future, a rising series of alternations. First there would be a period of high instability tied to a counter-force strategy. Then, as one side or the other caught up in the techniques of making its weapons invulnerable, there would be a period of moderate stability and the dominance of combined-deterrent strategies. During this period, research would continue in ways to nullify invulnerability. At our present weapons level, for example, this would mean the development of anti-submarine warfare and anti-missile missiles and reconnaissance satellites. When one side or the other had achieved a break-through in one of these techniques, a new period of extremely high instability would result, and again the counter-force theorists would dominate. But in the second period, the destructiveness of the weapons, the hostilities of the peoples, the speed of reaction would all have been heightened.

Thus it is clear that the "stability" proposed by the combined-deterrent theorists and the rationality proposed by the counter-force theorists are only true on a superficial level. Short-run stability would lead to long-run increases in the chances of war. Short-run rationality would only accomplish its own replacement by an irrational spiral.

For these reasons, it seems extremely unlikely that either form of deterrence that we have discussed, whether in its pure form or in mixture with the other, can accomplish the ends that are claimed for it. In addition, there seems to be some evidence that such theories of deterrence as those discussed do not apply when deterrence is most needed—at the height of an extreme and vital international crisis. At such times deterrence disappears—not because the weapons systems cease to exist, but because their psychological impact upon the opposing nations disappears.

Deterrence can operate only in the minds of leaders of the nations deterred. There is evidence that under conditions of extreme and growing tension, the major decision-makers in every great power become unable to pay attention to the warnings, the threats, the deterrents of their potential enemies. Such a development took place in the summer of 1914, when the Allies and Central Powers tried, by mobilizing their full strength, to deter each other from going to war. But in 1914, the only information that officials had time and energy to accept was the information about their own nation's capabilities and preparations. When attention could no longer be fixed on the threat of retaliation, deterrence failed. In neither of the views of deterrence presently held by American military experts is there any realization of the necessity to deal with this problem of the height of crisis. Still less is there any proposal for a deterrent that would work in such conditions.

From discussions with policy-makers in the Pentagon, it is clear that there has been no adequate exploration of the nature of deterrence. The inadequacy is traceable partly to the rigid quasi-scientism of strategists who have attempted to plot undeviating results from particular actions. The complexity of the hour-to-hour decisions may result in any of the myriad failures of theory that we have here detailed. *But to the theorists who have worked out these strategies, human decision-making seems a one-track operation.* The strategists have further failed to examine the nonmilitary factors—

economic, propaganda, psychological, among others—that will condition the responses to any military strategy. An adequate theory of deterrence must be far richer and more flexible—must take in many more factors and allow many more deviations from expectations.

The inadequacy of present deterrent theory may also be traced partly to a basic misconception of deterrence in the international field. Deterrence as a military, international concept claims its roots in the notion of the internal police force as deterrent against crime. But the basic assumption of the police force as deterrent does not exist in international relations. In the world at large, the situation is analogous to what has been happening in the Congo. Police forces exist in the Congo, but they do not deter violence because they do not act under agreed sanctions, under one effective national law. The police force in this context is provocative rather than stabilizing. Similarly, in the world at large, armed forces acting in the absence of internationally agreed law can only be provocative, no matter what theory of deterrence they are seeking to carry out.

For accurate and adequate notions of what deterrence can mean, we must consider the effective deterrence achieved by a police force under law. From this analogy, it would seem that only international arrangements for effective arms reductions and control leading to disarmament could be an effective deterrent. Once laws against national armaments have been promulgated and effective police forces to enforce such laws established, then deterrence as municipal policemen now practice it can come into being.

It is essential to examine the conditions under which such a result can be achieved. An international agreement effectively policed can conceivably deter any would-be aggressor. An international police force does not have to be all-powerful to be effective; it is the probability of discovery and punishment that restrains criminal action. Any national leader who attempted to breach an international disarmament agreement would have to face an international police force supported by world opinion. It seems to us that only in this way could the theory of deterrence be adequately reconciled with the facts of international military and technological life.

Often it is argued against the chances of effective disarmament that the West cannot "trust" the Soviet Union to keep its agreements, and that the risks of "cheating" would be too high. It is important to remember that counter-force and combined-deterrent theory both put enormous "trust" in the Soviets. Both theories trust the Soviets to react "rationally"—that is, as our theorists want them to act—to control their own reactions, and to abide the arms race without growing impatient, unstable, or irrational. The irony of the cold war is that we think of the Communists as irrational for having started it, and yet trust them to act in a rational manner in prosecuting it. As we have shown, the risks of such trust are enormous, for either by accident or through "cheating" on our expectations the Soviets might well help military deterrence to fail and war to come. The risks would be far less if an international police were exerting the controls and enforcing the deterrent.[5]

The idea that a disarmament agreement might be the *only* workable deterrent has not been explored by branches of the armed services, by the Department of Defense itself, or by any other branch of the government so far as we have been able to determine. This idea seems to us a hopeful avenue to pursue. We would urge upon decision makers that this view of deterrence be explored as soon as possible.

Necessary Practical Steps for Congress

The notion of an effectively policed disarmament agreement as the most likely adequate deterrent is so far distant from present international realities that it may weary those who want to take practical action. But there are practical actions available to the Congress to deal with the present inadequacy of deterrent theory.

There are four major areas in which the Congress can affect deterrent policy: through budget allocations, through setting organizational forms in the Department of Defense, through the creation of new agencies, and through the treaty power, the Congress could act to support its own views of how best to protect American security.

In budgeting for the armed forces, the Congress chooses between weapons systems, whether it intends to do so or not; and by choosing between weapons systems, Congress chooses a particular theory of deterrence, whether it intends to do so or not. If the Congress tries to support with funds all the proposed weapons systems of all the services, it gives America the confused "mix" of deterrents which, as we have pointed out, marries the worst of all possible worlds.

The Congress ought deliberately to determine what theory of deterrence it believes most adequate for the nation's security: counter-force deterrent, combined deterrent, or disarmament as

[5] Soviet disarmament proposals have, at least rhetorically, accepted the idea of careful inspection and enforcement. The rhetoric should be taken seriously long enough to find out whether the Soviets seriously mean it.

deterrent. We recommend that the relevant Congressional committees, including the House Appropriations Committee, begin at once the investigations necessary to back up such a decision. Depending on its findings, the Congress will know whether it wishes to increase funds for the B-70 and the Titan and to abolish the Polaris; or to increase funds for the Polaris and for a mobile infantry while abolishing the counter-force missile systems; or to take a more complex action that would support the theory of disarmament as deterrent.

Such support would begin by taking seriously American negotiations on disarmament with other powers. Congress should provide for budgetary changes to go into effect if disarmament agreements are reached. Provisions in the budget for reductions in particular areas of defense, according to an internationally agreed plan for disarming, could be accompanied by provisions for redirecting the money to nondefense expenditures or for reduction in taxes. Thus the machinery would be ready for the economy shift in new directions if a disarmament agreement were to be reached.

In the area of civil defense, the Congress will want to decide whether to increase enormously the amount spent and to build great underground cities, as would fit the counter-force deterrent, or to scrap all civil defense, as would be logical either to complement the combined deterrent or to move toward disarmament. The present half-hearted expenditure of funds on clearly useless plans for evacuation and partial shelter makes sense for no plan of deterrence. For protecting whole populations against counter-force attack, only entirely new shelter cities or anti-radiation shelters for every city resident would be of any use. For protection of the cities themselves against counter-city attack, no civil defense of any kind can be useful; H-bombs will kill cities, and ICBM's will allow no time for evacuation. For a policed disarmament, the shelters would be unnecessary, and building them would cause great distrust of any avowed disarmament. Our immediate recommendation to the Congress is that it abandon the present half-baked arrangement called civil defense, rather than go further into a program that would end in costing hundreds of billions of dollars, destroying liberty, and failing in its purpose anyway.

In examining the question of Defense Department organization, the Congress must take into account factors other than "efficiency." It must examine arguments for reorganization in the light of what theories of deterrence they actually support.

At present, the Air Force is by all odds the most powerful single service. Its connections with heavy industry, its long monopoly of the most "glamorous" weapons, and its willingness to plunge deep into the most advanced weapons and theories of twentieth-century war have given it the highest prestige and the largest budget in the Defense Department. As long as it retains this power, the Air Force believes that it will dominate any true unification of the armed forces, insuring for its theory—that is, counter-force deterrence—the victory in Defense Department debate. This expectation is shared by the Army and Navy, which have therefore opposed unification in the fear that their services, their weapons systems, and their theories would be submerged.

In the present practical situation, therefore, if the Congress pressed for total unification of the armed forces it would probably enthrone the counter-force deterrent. We have heard serious fears expressed that this kind of unification might result in some loss of civil and democratic control over the military. Officers in the Pentagon themselves expressed the fear that a single chief of staff over a single service might concentrate so much power, both over publicity and defense contracts, that civilian department heads, the Congress, and the public would be unable to question or to oppose his decisions. In such a unified military service, the fears expressed by President Eisenhower of the growing interdependence of an enlarged military establishment and an enlarged arms industry would be likely to become real dangers. But that is not to say that, by keeping the forces separate, the Congress is effectively choosing the theory of the combined deterrent. For, as has been shown above, as long as the American arsenal contains weapons obviously chosen for their counter-force capability, so long is the "purity" of the combined deterrent compromised and its actual goals thereby made impossible of attainment. Continuing the present system would therefore be a deliberate choice of contradictory theories.

Deep inside the present system, however, certain officials could in fact choose between counter-force and combined-deterrent theory. At present, the key to such a choice may lie with the interservice Joint Targeting Center, in which military officers are attempting to integrate the enemy targets to be selected by various branches of the American armed forces. In planning for missile and airplane strikes, such targets must be arranged ahead of time; which targets are selected—cities or atomic forces—could decide the struggle between the Air Force and Army-Navy views. For such a choice to be made without the knowledge and understanding of the Congress or the people would amount to surrender of civilian control over basic defense and foreign policy. It would be a complete Defense "reorganization" without Congressional sanction.

A similar form of "silent reorganization" so constructed as to benefit one theory of deterrence may be attempted under the cover of foreign policy and the NATO alliance. In many ways the proposal for a NATO force of Polaris submarines looks toward establishment of the combined-deterrent policy under NATO control. Building the deterrent under NATO would side-step the present Air Force dominance in the Defense Department, and for that reason the Army and Navy have supported the proposal. Quite aside from accentuating the problem of the spread of atomic weapons and probably forcing the Soviets to take similar action, the grant of Polaris to NATO, by diluting both American and civilian control over atomic weapons, would tend to deny the Congress any continued power over basic defense policy.

One kind of formal reorganization has been proposed that could conceivably fit into the combined-deterrent theory. That is the suggestion that the services should be reoriented into two functional commands: one to fight tactical and limited wars, the other to act as the great deterrent. If the Congress clearly directed and by practical provisions made sure that the great deterrent command was dominated by Navy men and ideas, the two commands would together make up the combined deterrent that the Army and Navy now support. But if the great deterrent command were to come under the control of counter-force theorists, the Navy's ideas and the weapons systems to carry them out would be abandoned. If the Congress wishes to choose this method of reorganizing the Defense Department to apply combined-deterrent theories, it must carry through by overseeing arrangements within the tactical and deterrent commands.

If the Congress decides that the view of disarmament as deterrent is indeed a correct one, a rather different view of Defense Department organization would be necessary. The goal would then clearly be the gradual dismantling of the whole defense organization and its replacement with an international police.

To move in this direction would obviously require a writing of contingent legislation by Congress, rather than a single sweeping act of reorganization. Changes in the defense structure and transfer of some personnel to an international police force would have to be made contingent upon successful negotiations with other world powers to establish such a police. The difficulties would be novel, but they would not be impossible of solution.

It is in dealing with these difficulties and attempting to work out a way toward a disarmament agreement that would act as a deterrent that Congress might effectively bring into play another of its powers—the power to create a new agency in the federal government. For the difficulties in the path of an effectively policed world disarmament agreement are so complex and possible solutions so unexplored that it would be most useful to have a new agency confronting these difficulties.

The far-reaching results of basic and applied research have in the last fifteen years become obvious in the field of weapons development. But never has the United States attempted to apply the techniques of research to the questions of how to achieve disarmament, how to reduce the international tensions that stand in the way of disarmament, and how to deal with the gaps in our society that disarmament would make.

To mobilize the techniques of social and natural science in the search for disarmament, it has been suggested that the federal government create a National Peace Agency. The proposed agency has been compared to the National Institutes of Health, in that scholars of all sorts would be encouraged to deal with the myriad questions of reducing tensions in political, economic, military, and other fields. In addition, it has been argued that the Peace Agency might include the corps of men designated by the United States for international service to police a disarmament agreement. In this fashion, the agency would make use of the manpower, the knowledge, perhaps even some of the individual men that would have been previously used by the Department of Defense.

The creation of such a Peace Agency, with its potential both for finding the steps that could bring disarmament and for dealing with the actual enforcement of disarmament, we recommend as a practical step to the Congress.

Finally, the Senate's treaty powers could be brought into play. An actual experiment could be set up in the possibilities of international inspection and enforcement, in an area not crucial to American security, if the President signs and the Senate ratifies a treaty for an atomic test ban. Atomic testing is not vital to American military security because it involves only a marginal addition to firepower and no addition at all to delivery capability. It is equally true that a ban on testing is not vital to American security as approached via disarmament, because the test ban will not stop or reverse any of the important parts of the arms race. But as an experiment in international policing the test ban would give the Congress and the nation a chance to assess what steps in true disarmament would be possible.

POSTSCRIPT

It is sometimes said that public discussion of and decision on the issues we have raised is unwise, that it is best to "keep the enemy guessing." But only by preventing all enemy guesswork can we hope to make deterrence work. If the United States intends to deter by a counter-force strategy, the Soviet Union must know this clearly in order to be deterred; if by combined deterrence, then again, there must be no doubt. And, of course, negotiations for disarmament could be successful only if we and the Soviets were each convinced the other was totally serious about deterring war through disarmament.

Not only is the policy of "keeping the enemy guessing" unwise, it is impossible to square with the democracy we are trying to preserve. For, ultimately, the policy means that we keep ourselves guessing—our people, our Congress, logically perhaps even our President. Refusing to discuss and decide the greatest question of human history means abandoning the very assumptions of the Constitution. The Congress, for the safety of the nation and the preservation of democracy, must face the issue of deterrence.

FOUR

JAMES R. SCHLESINGER

Quantitative Analysis and National Security

[Editor's Note: Professor Schlesinger's essay, published in 1963, represents another critique of the method of strategic planning that came to be dominant in the Pentagon with the advent of the Kennedy Administration in 1961. Professor Schlesinger's attack, as opposed to Arthur Waskow's (see above, Chapter 3), challenged not the concept of strategic theory, but a particular application of it known as the method of "systems analysis."

This method seeks to allocate limited resources among competing weapons systems on the basis of "cost effectiveness." The cost-effectiveness method, in brief, tries to group all relevant costs of a particular weapons system, regardless of which branch of the armed services project proposed it, project them over a five-year period, and compare them with similar costs for competing systems. This relatively simple notion presupposes an ability to define what constitutes each system's function and "mission" and what the relevant costs are. The method's utility lies in the fact that it can provide quantifiable criteria upon which to base decisions. Its drawback is that the emphasis on what is quantifiable may obscure elements of decision-making that depend essentially on value judgments.

Professor Schlesinger's article examines both the scope and the limits of the cost-effectiveness method. It shows how cost-effectiveness models are constructed and the conditions of their reliability. It explores the degree to which, by the very nature of the decision-making process, policy-makers are restricted in the range of strategic options they are able to consider. Cost effectiveness is most useful when the criteria are unambiguous; its quantitative apparatus, however, must not obscure the value choices which present the most difficult problems in the field of national security.]

The long-time neglect of the military establishment by the economics profession at large is now in the process of being rectified.[1] It hardly seems necessary to justify this awakening interest. Since resource allocation is fundamental in military problems, the economist, whose primary interest is the logic of the allocative process, is particularly well qualified to make a contribution. To be sure, this contribution is purely formal. Economics helps to select and frame the questions that should be asked, but the data necessary for the decision-maker to make a choice must be supplied from elsewhere. Though economics may be lacking in substantive content, in that it tells how to choose rather than what to choose, nevertheless such clarification of the logic of choice is not useless to the decision-maker.

The military allocation problem is normally divided into two parts: (*a*) how much resources to divert to defense, and (*b*) how to use such resources. A qualitative difference is widely believed to exist regarding what the economist can say about the two issues.[2] With respect to diverting resources to defense, the economist is admitted to have relatively little to say. Total security is unobtainable, and the real question is one of trading more or less military security for other goals. Individuals differ in their assessments, and the professional economist, who is presumably neutral, has no license to evaluate the utility patterns bearing on this exchange. It is professionally proper for economists to remind the public of the great flexibility of the economy and the consequent possibility of devoting either more or less resources to defense without provoking collapse. Such a function is not unimportant in a society in which fears are widespread either that our budgetary capacity is in danger of exhaustion or that disarmament would inevitably be followed by

EDITOR'S NOTE: Reprinted with permission from *World Politics*, XV, No. 2 (January, 1963).

[1] The writer is indebted to the Social Science Research Council for providing support for the research that this article entailed. It has been immeasurably improved by the comments of Daniel Ellsberg, George Hall, Almarin Phillips, and Rutledge Vining, but the writer alone retains final responsibility for the content.

[2] Charles J. Hitch and Roland N. McKean, for example, in *The Economics of Defense in the Nuclear Age* (Cambridge, Mass., 1960), before devoting a major section of the book to the problem of achieving what they call "efficiency" in military decisions, treat the question of how much should be diverted to defense in one page of excellent though formal principles (p. 48). Though the authors make every attempt to avoid substantive judgments, the difficulty of avoiding discussion of how much to divert to defense is illustrated by a statement that refers to the postponing of "vital actions such as the dispersing and hardening of our deterrent force" (p. 54).

deep depression. Yet such counsel is quite limited when compared with the much more relevant advice which, as we shall see, the economist is supposed to be able to offer regarding problem (b)—allocation within the defense establishment.

The sharpness of this supposed dichotomy arises from two sources. One is the exaggeration of the degree of assistance in formulating policy offered to the decision-maker by systematic quantitative analysis (systems analysis or operations research). The other is the result of unconsciously accepting the element of arbitrariness in traditional budget-making that systems analysis has now made it possible to reduce. Conventional budgeting methods prescribed a two-step process of deciding how much could be devoted to defense, *prior to* determining how such resources would be used.[3]

More will be said below about how much economics can contribute to the problem of diverting resources to defense. In one sense, this decision seems a much simpler one than allocation within. It constitutes one figure, one budget allotment, one announced decision. But it also reflects a congeries of decisions regarding internal allocation. Unless the budgeting procedure is rule-of-thumb, the decision regarding resource diversion emerges as a result of a process of evaluating the particular uses to which resources can be put in achieving national security. Conceptually, the answer to diverting resources emerges simultaneously with decisions on internal allocation, and the economic point of view is equally relevant to both.

To be sure, the weakness of guidance on internal allocation has properly been viewed as the most serious defect in defense planning. In the past, the absence of a market mechanism has meant that budgetary allotments have been based on the dominant enthusiasms of military planners. Defense can, however, no longer be planned on the assumption that one will be able to catch up with modern weaponry some years after the outbreak of war; it must now be planned five to ten years in advance. Economists have consequently been called upon to provide a substitute for the market mechanism that will offer some guide to efficient resource allo-

[3] *Ibid.*, p. 105. Though some qualifying remarks take note of interdependence, this is the procedure the authors follow. Arthur Smithies provides a brief discussion of the recent history of this procedural method, and a partial defense of it, in *The Budgetary Process in the United States* (New York, 1955), pp. 121–30, 237–40. In light of the political nature of the decisions that must be made, he seems to regard the practice as inevitable—and he expresses a certain sympathy not only for establishing ceilings, but even for the widely criticized Congressional meat-ax.

cation. By contrast, it has been easier to continue to accept the
diversion of resources to defense as "a purely political decision,"
because here the mechanism works tolerably well. However, this
pragmatic difference should not be taken to imply that there is an
intrinsic difference between the insights that economics contributes
to the two problems.

I

Can the economist really provide a precise framework for deciding allocations within the defense establishment? To the enthusiastic practitioners of systematic quantitative analysis, the answer
seems obvious. To this writer, however, such confidence is based in
part upon the failure to recognize the importance of a distinction
between the two different types of problems and the methodologi-
cal approaches to them that are the subject matter of quantitative
analysis. This distinction is so fundamental that it might well be
made the basis of a permanent division of quantitative analysis. In
certain problems, "output" can be measured. In other cases it cannot be, for the "objective" is only a general phrase that melts together a number of discrete subgoals. In the latter case, the technique of quantitative analysis is to measure inputs in alternative
employments for the light such analysis casts on decision-making—
a highly sophisticated form of cost accounting, but still only cost
accounting. It would be fruitful if the techniques employed to deal
with these different sorts of problems were recognized as distinct
entities. One way to underscore the distinction would be to redefine, as analytically separate, systems analysis and operations research, terms that continue to be employed interchangeably in
general usage. At present, the only distinction sometimes drawn
between the two is that the former deals with "higher-level" and
the latter with "lower-level" problems.[4] Such a distinction points in

---

[4] How commonplace is the usage of "operations research" and "systems
analysis" as interchangeable terms may be gathered from any one of several
standard sources; see *Operational Research in Practice*, Report of a NATO
Conference (New York, 1958). Charles J. Hitch uses the terms interchangeably in "Economic and Military Operations Research," *Review of Economics
and Statistics*, XL (August, 1958), 200, though mentioning that broader,
longer-range, operations research studies are frequently called "systems analyses." Roland McKean may be credited with developing the association between systems analysis and "higher-level criteria" (see *Efficiency in Government Through Systems Analysis* [New York, 1958], p. 9), though he also does
not distinguish between the two on the basis of the type of problem with
which each can cope.

In the present article, the position taken is that the term "operations rethe right direction but fails to bring out the full import of what should be recognized as the remarkable transition from operations research to systems analysis.

The problems with which economics deals may be classified as maximization problems, completely subject to control through mensuration, and choice-of-objects problems, which are not. In maximization problems, one is attempting to optimize a clearly definable objective function; the solution is embodied in the available data, if they are used correctly. These are the problems for which operations research was initially designed, although one should not underestimate the skill required to select the objective or achieve its maximization. In choice-of-objectives problems, on the other hand, the fundamental question is the selection of the appropriate mix of goals. The data suggest no solution in themselves. Even after the quantitative data are collected and organized, the pressing question still remains: what does one want to do? Sophisticated costing may provide considerable assistance in revealing the trade-offs among various alternatives—but the ultimate decision, the choice of the strategic approach to the problem, remains a matter of faith that will always elude rigorous quantification. The attempt has been made to apply the methods of operations research to this class of problems and—when this is done—as frequently as not the term "systems analysis" is tagged on. But the two classes are not amenable to the same type of treatment. The chief danger in the first sort of problem is that of mathematical miscalculation or mishandling of the data, whereas in the second the danger is something akin to consumer ignorance.

Unfortunately, the fact that the systems-analysis approach to the choice-of-objectives problem developed out of operations research, in addition to the fact that there is some parallelism between the techniques of the two analytical methods, has hidden the very great differences between them. The conceptual difference between the two types of problems and analytical methods should be emphasized. Failure to do so, up to the present time, helps to explain an

---

search" should be confined to *efficiency* problems and "systems analysis" to problems of *optimal choice*—thereby avoiding the confusions that have existed. Unfortunately, the conventional use of the term "operations research" both to describe a technique that some experts feel should be limited to lower-level operational problems, and also to encompass all quantitative analysis, is confusing. I have attempted to differentiate by using "operations research" when the limited meaning is intended, and by using "operational research" as an inclusive and general term incorporating systems analysis.

atmosphere of misunderstanding and mutual distrust that sur-
rounds the subject. Technology-oriented practitioners who believe
that operational research should be confined to problems where
there is a clearly defined objective function view with suspicion, if
not contempt, the systems-analysis approach because of its impre-
cision and "unscientific" nature. Those analysts who fail to see the
complexity of the criterion problem and who see no limits to operational research are likely to feel, with some justification, that no
one understands or appreciates them. Economists, by comparison,
are inclined to view both groups, the little-O.R. and the big-O.R.
people, with skepticism, owing to the frequency with which inadequate or improper criteria are chosen. Recognition that there are
really two techniques, each with its own limitations and one of
which may be usefully employed in casting light on problems in
which a multiplicity of objectives exists, would reduce such misunderstanding.

Although an attempt is made in this article to deflate some of the
claims made in behalf of systematic quantitative analysis, this
should not be taken to imply that the writer has any doubt that
both techniques have an increasing and a welcome role to play.
Systems analysis, which is of primary interest to the economist, has
become the rage in Washington. The ideas of Charles J. Hitch,
who is both a high official in the administration and one of the
seminal minds in the development of systems analysis,* are now
having upon budget-making a revolutionary effect—one which conventional economics never was able to achieve, for the terminology
and method of thought of systems analysis possess a bureaucratic
acceptability that the more abstract concepts of marginal analysis
lacked. Traditionally, government bureaus have been split (in a
sort of internal cold war) between the "planners" and the "budget
people," the former living in a fictitious world where programs were
developed on the hypothesis that resources were free, while the
latter were engaged in trimming the fondest aspirations of the
planners in light of the funds made available. Optimal decisions
could not be attained when the budget people had to choose, sometimes indiscriminately, among plans and portions of plans drawn
up as if resource limits did not exist. Not only were the planners in
a state of continual frustration, but resources were not employed as

---

* EDITOR'S NOTE: Charles J. Hitch was Chief of the Economics Division of
The RAND Corporation, 1948–61. From 1961 until 1965, he served as Assistant
Secretary of Defense (Comptroller) and is now Vice President of the University
of California.

effectively as they might have been under more suitable circumstances. Systems analysis is now helping to bridge the gap between the two groups. When planners have learned to visualize programs in terms of resource limits, they will recognize that the budget people are more than negativists to be shunned and can provide valuable assistance in achieving the most effective employment of the resources made available.

This change in budget-making technique is a remarkable accomplishment. But there is a very real danger that the nature and limits of systems analysis will go unperceived. Systems analysis provides assistance to logical thinking, but it can never "solve" problems in the same sense that operations research can. Neglect of this fact in itself will lead to less-than-optimal solutions, and undo at least some of the benefits that systems analysis can bring.

II

It was perhaps inevitable, in view of its successful employment during the war and its suitability in assisting corporate management in decision-making, that a broadly construed operational research would be seized upon as the guidepost for efficient resource use where the market provides little or no guide. Originally designed for the solution of low-level operational problems, the range of operational research has gradually been extended over the years, despite the protests of many of the older practitioners, so that it now includes higher-level problems. This transition is fraught with dangers chiefly because the habits of thought developed in dealing with operational problems may readily prevent the analyst from thinking through the complexities of higher-level problems. If operational research has become a mechanical contrivance, the danger becomes quite great that, in the press for quantification, the nonquantifiable elements will be obscured, and in higher-level problems it is the nonquantifiable elements that are of greatest importance. Most obviously is this true in the process of choosing the pattern of goals, which is quite likely to be reduced in practice to a single, quantifiable "objective function." As issues analyzed become more complicated and more "qualitative," the greater becomes the value of recalling the traditional outlook of economists embodied in the simple precepts of marginalist thinking.

The extent to which operational research falls within the purview of economics is debatable, and it is perhaps wise not to enter that tangled thicket at this point. Suffice it to say that the attempt to apply quantitative methods to choosing between competing goals clearly falls within the domain of economics. Even for low-level problems, which are fundamentally engineering in nature, it is probably the duty of economists to check whether important considerations have not been overlooked. In the name of technical efficiency, technologists have regularly committed innumerable acts of waste. Since O.R. has been designed in the main by engineers, mathematicians, and scientists, it has acquired certain characteristics of the technological outlook. A tendency exists to oversimplify problems and, especially, to think that definitive answers to social or economic problems may be readily obtained. If it is too difficult to obtain a nonlinear expression of a relationship, why, a linear one will do. Everything significant is assumed to be quantifiable, and, conversely, whatever is not quantifiable is not significant. The tendency is therefore to narrow fundamental questions down to that part of the whole which is solvable by a narrow technique.

While recognizing the inadequacies of economists in dealing with technological issues, it would seem incumbent on economists —who are doubtful whether all relationships are linear or even expressible, who are alert to the fact that returns must be measured in "values" of an abstract nature, and who are not seduced by mere physical quantities no matter how sublime the technology—to examine both what O.R. is doing to decision-making and what it should be doing.

Without attempting to discuss the more recondite techniques of the discipline, a brief examination of the method and limitations of O.R. is necessary. Special note should be taken of what Dorfman refers to as "the style of operations research,"[5] since it is here that habits of mind rather than the general theory of the discipline are reflected. The doctrine itself, though vague, is perfectly satisfactory in principle; it comes to little more than a prescription to apply orderly analysis to organizational problems. By using a *team* of specialists to look at an organization from the standpoint of over-all objectives, the benefits of the division of labor may be obtained while avoiding narrowness, and through O.R. the optimum decision from the standpoint of the whole system may be obtained.

The analytical method is something different—reflecting perhaps the scientific cast of mind of the progenitors of O.R. and the dominance of schools of technology in curricular training in O.R. After formulation of the problem under review, the second step is to con-

[5] Robert Dorfman, "Operations Research," *American Economic Review*, L (September, 1960), 577.

struct a *mathematical model* to represent the *system* under study. The assumption that an organizational system can usefully be expressed in terms of a mathematical model may be regarded as the chief postulate of O.R. in practice—for it is reconcilable with the belief that O.R. represents orderly analysis only if orderly analysis and mathematical expression invariably coincide.

The solution to a given problem is obtained by testing alternative methods of achieving the objective by the formal model that has been constructed. Estimates of the relative gains and costs from each alternative method may then be obtained. The applicability of the techniques of O.R. thus depend upon the fulfillment of the following conditions: (1) that the objective can be defined with precision; (2) that a formal model can be constructed expressing the relationship between that objective and the variables and constraints involved in its attainment; and (3) that sufficient quantitative information is available to permit an intelligent calculation of the parameters. In practice such conditions are most likely to be realized in low-level, technical, and repetitive functions—in other words, in narrow operational decisions rather than broad policy ones.

The possible impediments are many. Selecting the criterion or objective is no easy task. Even if it is obvious, it may not be subject to quantification through a formal model. In fact, the more quantifiable the objective, the greater may be the doubts that the proper one has been selected. If there are several objectives, these may be incommensurable. The problem of uncertainty is, to put it mildly, difficult to handle; in practice its treatment may be close to guesswork.[6] How does one treat problems of time—what rates of discount should be applied, and how should this be varied (if indeed it should be) as the degree of uncertainty changes?

Enough has been said to indicate that O.R. is most satisfactory for low-level decisions. This remains true in military matters, where O.R. found its beginnings in dealing with operational problems.

[6] The conventional approach is to make estimates (guesses?) of the probabilities, the ultimate decision being based on probability densities. One must remember, however, that these are not large-number cases but usually unique events. In addition, the significance of the Knightian* distinction between risk, which can be calculated far in advance, and uncertainty, which cannot be so calculated and where the decision-maker (entrepreneur) must take upon himself the burden of deciding on the incalculable, has not been fully explored.

* EDITOR'S NOTE: Frank Knight, Professor of Economics at the University of Chicago, is author of *The Economic Organization* and *Risk, Uncertainty, and Profit*.

Logistical or inventory problems, or choosing the composition of a fleet of transport planes, or deciding where to put runways and how long to make them are all problems that may be handled effectively through O.R. The trouble is that higher-level policy decisions cannot be treated so readily. How can one decide on "efficiency" grounds among allocating resources to civil defense, ICBM's, Polaris submarines, anti-submarine warfare, limited-war capabilities, and so forth?

The higher one goes in decision-making, the more difficult it is to define the objective. No single criterion is appropriate, other than a meaninglessly broad one like "national security" that obscures the complexities of choosing a strategy. The higher one goes, the less commensurable become the several goals, and the greater are the difficulties created by time and uncertainty on account of the lengthening of the time horizon. Finally, the higher one goes in the decision-making process, the less quantitative and the less systematic becomes the analysis. This happens because one is examining rare events, single events, or mere possibilities—rather than repetitive and routinized operations.

One may conclude that the clear-cut benefits to be obtained from operations research for low-level decisions begin to disappear at higher levels. Though undoubtedly the latter category includes the vital ones, one should not overlook the cumulative importance of many low-level decisions even in the over-all sense. In this respect, O.R. will be especially useful in the military establishment, not only because there is no substitute guide to efficiency, but because the savings to be obtained due to the rapidity of technological change may be greater than in private industry.

III

As decision-making moves to higher levels, it is generally recognized that it becomes, if not qualitative, at least "more qualitative." The emphasis shifts from measurement to "evaluation." The attempt is made to employ the methodology of operations research in dealing with these higher-level problems. In this case, the term "systems analysis" is as commonly used as "operations research." Systems analysis is newer[7] and has not earned such universal ac-

[7] Herman Kahn comments, "About six or seven years ago there was a 'technological breakthrough' at The RAND Corporation in the art of doing Systems Analysis." (*On Thermonuclear War* [Princeton, 1960], p. 119.) Despite a certain flamboyance in the remark, the institutional pride is justified. Much

ceptance as has operations research. The purity and force of the original discipline begin to disappear along with its precision. It is to be noted that some of the keenest practitioners of the art have warned against this attempt to push the operations-analysis type of approach to higher and higher levels. O. M. Solandt, who must be numbered among O.R.'s founders, has been especially direct in his comments. While recognizing that the new emphasis on systems analysis may be a good idea, it is a long way from the equipment problems in which the worth of O.R. was first demonstrated. He observes: "Systems research that is not based on a thorough knowledge of the elements that go into the system can become sterile. I think it is particularly dangerous for operations-research workers to deal with continually larger and larger systems until finally they study the political and social systems of the whole world."[8]

Despite a similarity in the way of looking at problems, it is essential to recognize that systems analysis is basically a different tool from traditional operations research. In O.R., the objective may be precisely expressed and readily quantified; in systems analysis, there are normally a number of different objectives, which are incommensurable. In O.R., the goal is to obtain the most efficient method for achieving a given objective; but in systems analysis one is concerned not with a simple means-end problem but with the actual selection of the mix of objectives or the choice of a strategy.

---

of the pioneering work and much of the very best work in systems analysis has been done at RAND. Many of the criticisms that follow, regarding tendencies in systems analysis, do not apply to RAND work. RAND analysts have been particularly cognizant of the multiplicity of objectives. Kahn and Irwin Mann have criticized the emphasis on mathematical models. They have lampooned the diseases they refer to as "modelism . . . analysitis . . . and technocratism." Albert Wohlstetter has dealt sharply with the use of "manipulatory techniques . . . cookbook fashion." The fact that these men have felt it necessary to emphasize these points is, however, not without significance; it is suggestive of the tendencies and tenor of much of the work in systems analysis. Nevertheless, RAND studies have rarely been guilty of ignoring either the multiplicity of, or conflicts among, objectives. On the contrary, such studies have frequently served to counteract very simple (if non-mathematical) models in the minds of policy-makers. Not infrequently, it is the policy-makers themselves who come to believe that there is a single objective to be maximized, when this is not the case. In such circumstances, systems analyses may provide a corrective.

8 O. M. Solandt, "Concluding Remarks," in "A Decade of Military Operations Research in Perspective—A Symposium," *Operations Research*, VIII (November-December, 1960), 857. See also Dorfman, *op. cit.*, pp. 613–22, and G. D. Camp as cited in Dorfman.

The quantitative information is sought not to provide data on least-cost methods of production but to provide data on the terms of exchange as among different objectives, so that the decision-maker is better able to choose among the possibilities on the basis of his utility pattern or system of preferences. It is important to recognize both this difference and the fact that this is not an efficiency problem but a choice-of-objectives problem. What systems analysis does is to provide data on costs or prices of achieving different objectives through the several alternative systems. But if the "demand" for particular objectives is inelastic, then the technical substitutability of weapons systems is low, and, consequently, prices and costs should matter relatively little in selecting the weapons-system mix. Information on costs is highly desirable in decision-making, but the rational decision-maker may be no better advised to alter his strategy on the basis of costs than the rational consumer would be to buy brewer's yeast (or candy) instead of vitamin pills because of their seeming cheapness. The rationality of the purchaser in determining his wants is in both cases a more fundamental question than accuracy in manipulating quantitative data. The great danger in systems analysis is that it may result in an attempt to transform problems of optimal choice into measurable problems of efficiency, a possibility that disappears when one moves outside the framework of a given weapons system. One ought not deceive oneself: when choosing among weapons systems, one is selecting a strategy—a decision into which, under the best of circumstances, some degree of prayer and hope must be infused.[9]

As long as the nature and limitations of the analysis are kept firmly in mind, there is little cause for concern, but several obvious dangers exist. The first is that the distinction between choosing a strategy and obtaining efficiency will be obscured—particularly through the use of nebulous terms like "qualitative."[10] Such phrase-

[9] One is reminded of the story of General Marshall, who dozed off one day during a meeting of the Policy Planning Staff. When he awoke, his aides were *still* groping with "on the one hand . . . on the other hand, etc." "Are you still wasting your time on the preliminaries?" asked the general. "Make a decision." These problems do *not* yield to analysis, simple or complex; a decision must be made for which the statesman bears the burden of responsibility: "The buck stops here."

[10] The very name "Weapons System Evaluation Group" (the operational analysis organization for the Department of Defense) implies recognition of the qualitative or evaluative nature of conclusions regarding higher-level problems, but this seems to forestall perception of the more vital ends-efficiency dichotomy. Consider, for example, the following description: "We are likely to be deeply involved in the doctrine of the total system—and in the choice of

ology leaves the impression that the only difference between systems analysis and the more traditional operations research is the difficulty in *measuring* the results,[11] whereas the really important difference is the difficulty of deciding on goals and selecting as preferable one pattern of results over another. The basic problem is that there is no obvious criterion. When it is strategy that is under consideration, this fact should be recognized, rather than assuming that measurement is the problem.

A second danger is more elementary—the failure to recognize the unsuitableness of quantitative analysis. Both the methods employed and the training of the practitioners provide a psychological pressure to quantify[12]—or, what is equally harmful, to make the quantitative element predominate even where it is inappropriate. One might even observe that a ritualistic recitation of the dangers of excessive quantification characteristically precedes the attempt to push quantitative analysis too far.

Experienced and detached practitioners argue that it is the *approach* of quantitative analysis which is most useful. It provides for a more orderly review of a problem by indicating what is known, what is unknown, and what one would have to know in order to

---

the appropriate mixture of weapons in the total system. This is a field in which quantitative parameters are particularly difficult to find. Consequently more of our work is done in qualitative terms than is the case for other operations-analysis groups." (George E. Pugh, "Operations Research for the Secretary of Defense and the Joint Chiefs of Staff," in "A Decade of Military Operations Research," p. 842.) In light of the pressure for quantification, it is interesting to note that the author later looks longingly toward the day when more of the work can be done in quantitative terms.

[11] See, *inter alia*, Hitch, "Economics and Military Operations Research," *op. cit.*, p. 200.

[12] In this regard, take note of the words of the retiring president of the Operations Research Society of America, Martin L. Ernst: "The plea for improved measures of effectiveness was sounded early in the Society's career. Unfortunately, there has been little response to this plea, and there are few indications that any progress whatsoever has been made in this most fundamental area of operations research. Basically, we still make claims to being one of the quantitative sciences, *with employment of qualitative measures being reserved as a last resort*. If we engage increasingly on major problems, we will in due course be faced with a choice of alternatives. Following one path, we may give up the emphasis on quantitative analysis, and simply employ nonquantitative logic as the basis of our effort. To follow the other path, wherein we maintain our quantitative capabilities, we will be completely dependent on improving our abilities to measure fundamental characteristics of the objects of our studies. *Quantitative science simply cannot exist without yardsticks*, and herein perhaps lies our greatest weakness." ("Operations Research and the Large Strategic Problems," *Operations Research*, IX [July-August, 1961], 443-44; italics added.)

obtain a solution to the problem. Even under such circumstances, however, it is not unlikely that the analysts will become excited about the numbers and come to think that a problem is truly quantitative. This may be another variant of Whitehead's "fallacy of misplaced concreteness." It leads to a tendency to adopt decisions that are justified because they are supported by numbers—and by an entranced researcher who fails to provide his chief with the proper (qualitative) warning. Under somewhat poorer circumstances, the drive for quantification takes the form of manufacturing dubious formulas for which little supporting evidence can be provided. Every analyst can mention numerous examples. They are particularly prevalent in the business community, where they are retailed by the thousand (this may be a form of poetic justice, since the business community in its marketing policy adheres to *caveat emptor*).

A third and more obvious danger arises from those who see no limits to the fields that operational analysis can conquer. Ellis A. Johnson, for example, has argued that in the age of the computer, the policy confusions and the administrative cross-currents in the Department of State can and should yield to the methods of operations research.[13] There are few who would insist that State has reached such a pinnacle of efficiency that there is no room for improvement, though it is clear that many of the conflicts within the Department that may strike the outsider as signs of inefficiency are

[13] "Operational research is badly needed in the United States State Department. The State Department is faced on the one hand by a population, industry, Congress, Senate, and Administration primarily engrossed with domestic affairs, and on the other by a set of world societies, many in the process of national revolution and all in a most vigorous sociological interaction. All aspects of this sociological interaction—political, economic, military, and cultural value system—are in a state of violent and revolutionary change. . . . The State Department is as yet unprepared for the modern technical aspects of diplomacy, either by education or *by prior studies by operational research*. This makes it very difficult for its traditionally trained executives to understand and always bear in mind the great twentieth-century interdependence between technology and diplomacy when political policy is being established or political decisions are being made. . . .

"I believe that it is in the State Department and in politics that *the greatest possible advances in operational research can be made in the future*, and that here there can be *a tremendous use of symbolic logic and computers* to provide for all of the interrelations in a way that is presently beyond the comprehension of any single human being or of any group of diplomats of reasonable size." (Ellis A. Johnson, "The Long-Range Future of Operational Research," *Operations Research*, VIII [January-February, 1960], 7–8; italics added.) By contrast, one might consider the words of Solandt, quoted above.

simply built-in organizational devices for recognizing the multiplicity of objectives to which attention must be paid. A naïve attempt to streamline the Department in the name of efficiency might readily lead to less optimal policies. Nevertheless, it would be unwise to assume that O.R. has no role to play—particularly for such agencies as AID, in which using the dollar most effectively may have some operational significance. But even here, it is not at all clear what the objective of foreign assistance is. If it is to maximize the contribution to the growth of the gross national product, some useful calculations can be made, but to what extent are we more interested in propaganda or in power relationships as opposed to economic progress or political stability, taken by themselves? In the quest for efficiency, the enthusiastic operations researcher may ignore the intangibles and complexities of the real world and urge violation of the rules of his discipline. This reflects the failure to recognize the vagueness and incommensurability of objectives, the immense weight of uncertainty, and the impossibility of providing a precise model.

IV

Operational research is a new field, and, in the early years, practitioners of new arts tend to regard them as panaceas. This enthusiasm for technique has characterized all of the newer branches of mathematical economics, as well as human relations, communication theory, cybernetics, etc. Unlike Columbus, explorers of the intellectual realm ordinarily assume that they are discovering new worlds. Until experience breeds a sense of proportion, such enthusiasm is contagious and may prove dangerous. Among others, Charles Hitch has warned against what he calls the "naïve" use of quantitative analysis—i.e., the tendency to extract more than warranted from the data. But he argues that, at least under present circumstances, any tendency to push systems analysis too far will be held in check by those in the operating departments who rely on the intuitive approach.

In the long run, however, as systems analysis becomes more readily accepted in the government, will the situation remain as comforting? The ordinary practitioner of a discipline must be expected to accept the formulas of a discipline uncritically and to apply its methods mechanically. In quantitative analysis, a long-run threat to optimal decision-making exists in the pressure for quantification and in the failure to recognize not merely the qualitative but the *inherently subjective* nature of the decisions that must be made. While estimates of exchange ratios can be made more or less accurately on the side of costs, they cannot be on the side of objectives. Precise utility maps exist only in the textbooks. In quantitative analysis, energy is diverted to the search for numbers, and, what is worse, a decision may be distorted because of the disproportionate weight given to those aspects of a problem that are quantifiable.

In a sense, this represents a deficiency of all high-powered mathematical techniques when applied to situations both too complex and amorphous. (Would Henry Adams exchange the computer for the dynamo as the symbol of the modern age?) A complicated reality is oversimplified and distorted. Important insights are excluded from precisely formulated models, and the results may be ludicrous. Both Marshallian and Keynesian theory, to cite examples, suffered from more rigorous formulation than the originators intended. It is unwise to use tools that are too sharp in relation to the material with which they are used. Mathematical treatment becomes inapplicable or misleading under two sets of circumstances. In the first, the formulation of the model leads the researcher, in order to reveal the parameters, to seek quantitative evidence that is really unobtainable.[14] At best this represents a misdirection of effort; at worst, it leads to a misleading model based on flimsy evidence. In the second, the formulation of the model results in the exclusion of important variables or relationships. As it happens, such is the case in a large number of strategic problems. Under these circumstances, systems analysis *should* become a synonym for the logical ordering of a problem, and refined techniques become superfluous.[15] In R. G. D. Allen's words, "Some

---

[14] Wherever sufficient data are lacking, the attempt to give quantitative significance to a model is useless, at best. This need for sufficient data to ascertain the parameters explains why O.R. is most suitable for repetitive, technical operations. To take a simple example, the problem of diabetic control in principle should be susceptible to the methods of O.R. In principle, diabetes is a relatively simple inventory problem. But O.R. offers no assistance to the practitioner, because in practice sufficient quantitative information is unobtainable without causing endless discomfort and loss of time to the patient. The result is that medical practitioners continue to operate, as they must, by "feel" and intuition.

[15] In an excellent analysis of the national security problem with the suggestive title "The National Security Dilemma: Challenge to Management Scientists" (*Management Science*, VIII [April, 1961], 195–209), Marshall Wood argues that management scientists, through an inclusive systems approach, can help solve our security problem. The orderly analysis that follows, however, would have come into being even if management science had never existed.

problems are adequately treated by relatively simple logical reasoning and the introduction of mathematical symbolism is then only destructive of clarity."[16]

At this point, one can recognize certain advantages of the traditional marginalist method of economic analysis, which by its nature readily lends itself to a sympathetic interpretation of qualitative problems. Its mathematical underpinnings, which represent the simple logic of maximization, are sufficiently rudimentary that it need not become bogged down in either unobtainable or manufactured quantitative evidence. Yet it does point clearly to the intuitive or subjective nature of the decisions that must be made in strategic matters, by its acceptance of the fact that, whenever a number of goals exist, we can do little more than consider carefully how much of one goal we are willing to trade to obtain more of another. Of course, some of the present difficulties with quantitative analysis also were experienced in the attempt to press forward with the statistical formulation of marginal concepts. Nevertheless, wherever quantitative information is absent or insufficient, marginal analysis is most convenient for dealing with subjective evaluation, partly because the tools are not sharper than the nature of the material warrants, and partly because it has traditionally been used to indicate the principles of public finance.[17]

There is no intrinsic reason why problems of subjective evaluation cannot be dealt with under the heading of systems analysis. The insights of marginal analysis might be regarded as part of or a supplement to the newer field. The barrier lies in the scientific-quantitative origins of operational research, which make it psychologically difficult for practitioners to accept such a procedure. To put it another way, the difficulty lies not with operational research, the *theory* of which is sufficiently broad to incorporate any logical procedure, but with the operational researchers. If systems analysis

[16] R. G. D. Allen, *Mathematical Analysis for Economists* (4th ed., London, 1949), p. 2. Is there any reason to believe that Lord Keynes' judgment is no longer appropriate? He wrote: "Too large a proportion of recent 'mathematical' economics are mere concoctions, as imprecise as the initial assumptions they rest on, which allow the author to lose sight of the complexities and interdependencies of the real world in a maze of pretentious and unhelpful symbols." (*The General Theory of Employment, Interest and Money* [New York, 1936], p. 298.)

[17] Hitch refers to these as "pretty empty principles" in "The Uses of Economics," *Research for Public Policy* (Washington, 1961), p. 99. This is perfectly true, in that they are devoid of quantitative guidance in expenditure decisions, but it is their "emptiness" (or formality) that makes them useful in evaluating goals.

is adapted so that it is recognized as dealing with issues wherein the clash between multiple and incommensurable goals must be settled by judgment; if it is accepted that the lack of quantitative guidance is a permanent condition and not a temporary frustration, so that "measures of merit" are no longer expected to appear spontaneously as a *deus ex machina;* then systems analysis may indeed play a large role in the guidance of resource allocation within the establishment. To be sure, it would be illusory to expect perfection, even if systems analysis were able to provide a complete substitute for the market. Markets are efficient only if one accepts the market criterion of satisfying consumers. If consumers, facing an array of products, are unwise in their choices, the results are unsatisfactory. The same is even more true in the case of strategic choice, where failure may be catastrophic. Consequently, in military resource allocation, it is essential to concentrate attention on the weighing of objectives and the choice of strategy.

If it be granted that, in coping with choice-of-objectives problems, systems analysis can do no more than provide relevant information on performance and costs that may help in making subjective decisions in problems involving incommensurabilities and uncertainties, then a few words should be added with respect to the conventional distinction, mentioned earlier, between how little the economist can say regarding resource diversion to defense and how much regarding allocation within the defense establishment. The latter part of this antithesis is based on the doctrine that operational research now makes possible scientific handling of the internal allocation problem. It has been noted that this is not the case; systems analysis does not provide a mechanism for objective decision-making. Any decision regarding internal allocation involves strategic choices based upon faith that certain objectives are of a greater order of importance than others—a position that must be taken in the face of incalculable uncertainties.

But cannot the same observation be made concerning the decision to divert resources to defense? Once it is recognized that systems analysis provides no definitive answers, the external problem becomes similar to the internal one. One attempts to compare objectives in the security field with those outside it. A certain weapons system will provide the capability for achieving a particular objective. One discovers the additional costs associated with this capability—and one decides whether it is justifiable to ask the taxpayer to make the additional sacrifices (of nonstrategic objectives) to provide the capability. Although the choice is now wider, one is still engaged in evaluating incommensurable objectives. The total amount provided for defense represents the sum of funds allotted individually to different weapons systems to achieve the objectives chosen. Systems analysis provides a means for rationally comparing different weapons systems by treating each as a unit in terms of its costs. But by permitting each potential capability to be examined on its own merits, it permits the question to be raised whether it is in the interest of the taxpayers to provide that particular capability.

Total resource diversion reflects the number of affirmative decisions in the case of individual weapons systems. No longer does resource diversion to defense have to depend upon a single decision that is based either on a rule of thumb or on the response to the global but indefinite question: how important we think defense is *in toto*. Thus systems analysis, by permitting weapons systems to be analyzed separately, has outmoded the sharp contrast of the conventional argument. Allocation decisions, both internal and external to the defense establishment, are on the same footing, because systems analysis provides exactly the same kind of data to help in the selection of objectives, security and nonsecurity alike.

Acceptance of the contention that the economist can speak with equal appropriateness about external and internal allocation would bring to an end the paradoxical situation in which economists sedulously avoid discussion of the adequacy of the amount of resources devoted to defense. The tendency to confine discussion to achieving efficient resource usage in the defense establishment may have represented a misdirection of energies. After all, it is easy to compensate for such inefficiencies by increased expenditures, and in view of the habits and attitudes of military officers in association with the vast resources of the American economy, it may be the better way. Granted that the economist has no special warrant to impose his judgments about objectives on the American public. If he were to attempt to do so he would be unsuccessful, since his preachments would reach only the ears of those already converted. But he does have the privilege—indeed, the obligation—of pointing to the need for consistency between the importance ascribed to particular objectives and the means provided to achieve those objectives. This plea for optimal resource allocation applies with as much force to comparisons between security and nonsecurity objectives as to comparisons between weapons systems themselves.

V

National security is too broad a problem to be solved by any single professional insight. In determining policy, the decision-maker draws judgments from several sources and attempts to reconcile views as diverse as those of the blind men in the case of the elephant. Inevitably clashes occur; the only thing that can be said of the ultimate decision is that it cannot and should not coincide exactly with any individual professional judgment. The conviction of the economist that "efficiency" is important will be shared by the technologist—with whom he may be associated in operational research. Differences do exist. The technologist is likely to be enamored of technological processes or hardware; he is likely to choose a single variable to be maximized. The economist will be more alert to the need to weigh intangibles and to maximize "values-in-general" rather than a single variable. But both are likely to be in a deeper conflict with the professional officer. On the surface, there would appear to be a rough parallelism between the economist's notion of his discipline and the military definition of strategy (a plan best to employ resources toward the achievement of aims). Both emphasize allocative functions, but despite the similarity of words, there is a difference in the range of considerations that reflects the conflict of professional values. Economists tend to assume that the kinds of efficiency they take into consideration are equivalent to the requirements of national security. When military officers discuss efficiency, however, they refer not only to weapons systems or organization in the broad sense, but also to organizational continuity, discipline, morale, *esprit de corps*, and tradition. The rationalist's notion of efficiency is likely to overlook the psychological elements in an organization's efficiency upon which the military is likely to lay stress. Those interested in abstract efficiency are continually generating plans for the drastic reorganization of the armed forces, which the latter resist—and properly so: it is not only a matter of vested interests, but recognition of the role of long personal associations and tradition in the building of morale. After all, organizationally speaking, what is more irrational than the Marine Corps, yet what is more useful?

Economists tend not only to calculate in terms of a particular type of efficiency, but also to assume that governments are really *interested* in efficiency, and that when information is provided it will be acted upon. Part of the conflict lies with the decision-making politician-statesman, whose training and instincts lead him toward compromise, toward reconciling different views, toward the achievement of the possible. Some of the politician's modifications are necessary and proper: externally to avoid actions alarming to allies or provocative to an enemy, internally to manage public opinion. But some of the compromises are for less respectable purposes —to maintain the image the public desires of a stable world order, or to see to it that military bases in selected Congressional districts remain undisturbed. Not only may the necessary information to provide efficiency not be acted on, but its existence may be avoided or ignored. Congress, for example, has resisted the use of performance budgets at least in part because their absence facilitates the use of the meat-ax on expensive projects that pay low political dividends, and also permits the use of resources for "uneconomic" projects that are politically productive.

The services themselves are not always delighted with the information produced in the search for efficiency. This is true in spite of the recognition by the services of their own weaknesses in selecting the most appropriate weapons-system mix and the need to turn to outsiders to provide the detachment lacking within the services. The independent operations-research groups established by the services have not always had an easy time of it when the conclusions reached were not regarded as satisfactory from the standpoint of the sponsoring service.[18]

Thus the mere uncovering of ways to increase efficiency is not sufficient. Even where a decision is clear to the disinterested observer, it is difficult to persuade committed men that their programs or activities should be reduced or abandoned. The price of

---

[18] Consider, for example, the implications of the following evaluation: "So far, the integrity and competence of the major military operational-research groups has remained high. At times, their work has been very unpopular in Washington, even within their own services, during this period of crucial decision and controversy—because integrity and honesty do not always provide the best ammunition to win Washington battles. As a result, the Services have in some cases sought with success more amenable operational-research organizations for certain studies, and in two cases have taken organizational and personnel actions to ensure better 'cooperation.'" (Johnson, "The Long-Range Future of Operational Research," p. 16.) It is noteworthy that the Army recently severed its long-time association with the Operations Research Office (ORO) because of a long-standing dispute over control of research and established the Research Analysis Corporation, whose findings would presumably be less unsatisfactory to the Army. Dr. Johnson, ORO's director, was quoted as saying that "the Army has wanted to run the research—and that we couldn't tolerate." (*Missiles and Rockets*, June 5, 1961, p. 11.)

enthusiasm is that those who have a commitment will be "sold" on their specialty and are incapable of viewing it in cold analytical terms. This may be especially true of the military establishment, where the concepts of duty, honor, and country *when particularized* lead to a certain inflexibility in adjusting to technological change and the new claims of efficiency. But it is also true in the civilian world: for conservationists, foresters, water-resource specialists, businessmen, union leaders, or agrarians, some aspects of their value systems run directly counter to claims of efficiency. The economic view strikes them all as immoral as well as misleading. (After all, is it not a value judgment on the part of economists that efficiency calculations are important?)

Even in the case of fairly low-level decisions, if they are political, systematic quantitative analysis does not necessarily solve problems. It will not convince ardent supporters that their program is submarginal. Nevertheless, quantitative analysis remains most useful. For certain operational decisions, it either provides the decision-maker with the justification he may desire for cutting off a project or forces him to come up with a non-numerical rationalization. It eliminates the *purely* subjective approach on the part of devotees of a program and forces them to change their lines of argument. They must talk about reality rather than morality. Operational research creates a bridge to budgetary problems over which planners, who previously could assume resources were free, are forced, willingly or unwillingly, to walk.

When confronted with a negative decision, to the effect that a particular program is too costly relative to its benefits to be accepted, the obvious response on the part of devotees, since they cannot argue with the cost figures, is to charge that the wrong criterion has been chosen. This contention may be correct, particularly in higher-level problems; but even if it is not, it may be advantageous because it places emphasis on the important part of the problem, the question of strategic choice. One concrete example of a current problem might be offered, and in order to reveal the striking increase in the rationality of such discussion, one might compare it with the B-36 carrier controversy of the late 1940's. Suppose one wishes to analyze the advantages of the submarine-based Polaris missile system compared with a land-based missile system (say, the Minuteman). One would note that the initial procurement costs per missile (including configuration or the pro-rated share of the submarine) are much higher for the Polaris than for the Minuteman. In addition, the maintenance and operating costs, inclusive of crew, port facilities, etc., are very high for Polaris, moderate for Minuteman. Moreover, the readiness of Polaris is much lower. Submarines will be laid up for repairs on an average of from one to two months a year; time must be allowed to provide leave for the crews; and time will be lost cruising to and from port. Polaris is also probably less reliable and possibly less accurate than Minuteman. The upshot is that to achieve equal destructive power will require a vastly larger investment of resources in Polaris than in Minuteman.

When confronted with such a presentation, supporters of Polaris are not likely to argue about the facts, but maintain instead that the criterion of destructive power on target, *ceteris paribus*, is not appropriate; the strategic problems are much broader. They are likely to emphasize that at present the Polaris system is virtually invulnerable; that it is vastly more difficult for Soviet intelligence to gather information on the whereabouts of Polaris subs than of Minutemen; and that in the event of Soviet development of a defense against missiles, it is likelier to be much more effective against the Minuteman ICBM than the Polaris IRBM. Moreover, they might point out that an additional benefit is that the Polaris system may force the Soviets to devote substantial resources to development of an anti-submarine warfare capability that they might otherwise use for other purposes. The sensible, *and highly qualitative*, conclusion likely to be reached is that the United States ought not to place all of its deterrent eggs in one basket—and that both systems should be included in the weapons mix. An example of this sort indicates how quantitative analysis is useful in concentrating attention upon realities and at the same time upon over-all strategy. It also supports the contention that a simple dedication to "efficiency" in the spirit of operations research might easily lead to the wrong decision.

FIVE

ROBERT S. McNAMARA

The Spectrum of Defense

[*Editor's Note: This speech by Secretary of Defense Robert Mc-Namara, delivered to the Economic Club of New York on November 18, 1963, four days before the death of President Kennedy, focuses on how intelligent planning and programing have placed the United States in a position to confront a wide variety of challenges through a flexible series of options. In its concern with virtuoso performance, it is notably characteristic of the intellectual atmosphere of the Kennedy Administration. It is an excellent statement of the basic objective of American national security policy as President Kennedy defined it: "Our weapons systems must be usable in a manner permitting deliberation and discrimination as to timing, scope, and targets in response to civilian authority." In succeeding pronouncements, Secretary McNamara's confidence that the decision-maker can maintain control whatever the level of violence has become somewhat tempered.*]

Before long, this Administration will be presenting, once again, the details of a proposed national defense budget for the consideration of the Congress and the public. Given the importance of these matters, their complexities and uncertainties, and the existence of real differences of opinion, a degree of controversy is inevitable and even desirable.

Some controversies, however, reveal underlying differences in perspective that scarcely suggest the participants are living in the same world. Within the past few weeks, some critics have suggested that we have literally hundreds of times more strength than we need; others have accused us of risking the whole future of the nation by engaging in unilateral disarmament. I would like to believe that criticisms bracketing our policy in that fashion prove it to be rational and sound. But a discrepancy of that order cannot be reassuring. Rather, it indicates that we have failed to convey to some part of our audience even the broadest outlines, as we see them, of the problems that our military strategy and force structure are meant to address. I believe we should be able to move from controversy on that scale toward consensus in military affairs, not always on details or components of our policies, but at least on an appreciation of the major national security problems confronting us, on the broad alternative paths to their solution and on the dominant goals, obstacles, costs and risks affecting choice.

As a prelude, then, to the coming season of debate, I should like to identify and discuss some basic matters on which a considerable degree of consensus seems to me both possible and desirable, although by no means assured.

These include those over-all comparative strengths and weaknesses of the opposing military alliances that form the bold relief in the strategic environment. In short, they are the considerations that seem to have relatively long-term significance compared to the annual budget cycle.

Matters of that degree of permanence tend to be stamped on our minds as being unchanging and unchangeable, the unquestioned framework of daily and yearly policy-making. Yet these factors of which I shall speak do change—more swiftly and more profoundly than our picture of them tends to change. Indeed, I believe it is just the fact that over the last decade this topography has changed—while many maps have not—that accounts for some apparently irreconcilable controversies.

Let me recall the earlier period briefly, for comparison. The strategic landscape at the outset of the 1950's was dominated by two outstanding features: one was the practical U.S. monopoly of deliverable, strategic nuclear weapons; the other was the Soviet Union and Communist China's virtual monopoly of ground force on the continents of Europe and Asia.

Both of these determinants of Western military policy had changed considerably by the end of the Korean War. The Soviets had produced atomic explosions and had created a sizeable nuclear delivery capability against Europe, while NATO ground forces had expanded rapidly and military operations in Korea had greatly tarnished the significance of Chinese Communist superiority in numbers. But the old notions of monopoly persisted as short-cut aids to thinking on policy matters. And they were not so misleading as they came later to be. Soviet armed forces approaching 5 million men still heavily outweighed the NATO forces in Europe; and Soviet delivery capability against the U.S. was dwarfed by that of

SAC. Moreover, tactical nuclear weapons were being heralded as a new nuclear monopoly for the West.

Even as these earlier notions of monopolies grew obsolete, ideas about the feasibility of alternative policies continued to reflect them. So did ideas about how wars might be fought. Nuclear operations, both strategic and tactical, by the U.S. in response to Soviet aggression against our allies were considered to be virtually unilateral. Hence, it was supposed that the problem of credibility of the U.S. response would scarcely arise, even in the case of relatively limited Soviet aggressions. Western reliance upon nuclear weapons, in particular strategic systems, both to deter and to oppose non-nuclear attack of any size seemed not only adequate but also unique in its adequacy.

That sort of situation is convenient for policy-makers. It makes policy easy to choose and easy to explain. Perhaps that is why throughout most of the 1950's, while the Soviets under various pressures decreased their ground forces and the NATO allies built theirs up, and while the Soviets acquired a massive nuclear threat against Europe and laid the groundwork for a sizeable threat against the U.S., the picture underlying most policy debate remained that appropriate to 1949. It was a picture of a Communist Goliath in conventional strength facing a Western David, almost naked of conventional arms but alone possessed of a nuclear sling.

Toward the end of that decade, the prospect that the Soviet Union would acquire intercontinental ballistic missiles at a time when our strategic forces consisted almost entirely of bombers focused our attention and our budget even more sharply than before upon our strategic forces. The urgency of the problem of deterring the most massive of attacks was a new reason for thinking that the West could spare neither resources nor thought to deal more specifically with lesser threats. The most urgent task was to provide for deterrence of massive aggression by assuring the survival under any attack of forces at least adequate, in the calculations of a potential attacker, to destroy his society in retaliation. It was now not the assurance of continued nuclear superiority that pre-empted the attention of policy-makers but, on the contrary, the struggle to maintain it.

But it is time for the maps to change by which policy is charted and justified. The old ones, which assumed a U.S. nuclear monopoly, both strategic and tactical, and a Communist monopoly of ground combat strength are too far removed from reality to serve as even rough guides. Neither we nor our allies can afford the crudities of maps that tell us that old policies are still forced upon us, when a true picture would show important new avenues of necessity and choice.

What most needs changing is a picture of ourselves and of the Western alliance as essentially at bay, outmanned and outgunned except for nuclear arms no longer exclusively ours. We should not think of ourselves as forced by limitations of resources to rely upon strategies of desperation and threats of vast mutual destruction, compelled to deal only with the most massive and immediate challenges, letting lesser ones go by default. It would be a striking historical phenomenon if that self-image should be justified. We are the largest member of an Alliance with a population of almost 450 million people, an aggregate annual product which is fast approaching a trillion dollars, and a modern and diverse technological base without parallel, facing the Soviet Union and its European satellites with their 100 million fewer people and an aggregate output no more than half that of the West.

And quite apart from ignoring the underlying strengths of the West, the outdated picture I have described takes no account of the military capabilities that our investment over the last decade, and specifically in the last few years, has bought for us. If new problems put strong claims on our attention and our resources today, it is very largely because we have come a large part of the way that is feasible toward solving some old ones.

Let me summarize the current status of the balance of strategic nuclear forces, that part of the military environment that has preoccupied our attention for so long. In strictly relative numerical terms, the situation is the familiar one. The U.S. force now contains more than 500 operational long-range ballistic missiles—Atlas, Titan, Minuteman, Polaris—and is planned to increase to more than 1,700 by 1966. There is no doubt in our minds and none in the minds of the Soviets that these missiles can penetrate to their targets. In addition, the U.S. has Strategic Air Command bombers on air alert and more than 500 bombers on quick-reaction ground alert. By comparison, the consensus is that, today, the Soviets could place about half as many bombers over North America on a first strike. The Soviets are estimated to have today only a fraction as many intercontinental missiles as we do. Furthermore, their submarine-launched ballistic missiles are short-range and generally are not comparable to our Polaris force. The Soviets pose a very large threat against Europe, including hundreds of intermediate and medium-range ballistic missiles. This threat is today and will continue to be covered by the clear superiority of our strategic forces.

The most wishful of Soviet planners would have to calculate as a certainty that the most effective surprise attack they could launch would still leave us with the capability to destroy the attacker's society. What is equally pertinent is that the relative numbers and survivability of U.S. strategic forces would permit us to retaliate against all the urgent Soviet military targets that are subject to attack, thus contributing to the limitation of damage to ourselves and our allies.

Deterrence of deliberate, calculated attack seems as well assured as it can be, and the damage-limiting capability of our numerically superior forces is, I believe, well worth its incremental cost. It is a capability to which the smaller forces of the Soviet Union could not realistically aspire. That is one reason, among others, why I would not trade our strategic posture for that of the Soviets at any point during the coming decade.

But given the kind of force that the Soviets are building, including submarine-launched missiles beyond the reach of our offensive forces, the damage which the Soviets could inflict on us and our allies, no matter what we do to limit it, remains extremely high.

That has been true for our allies ever since the middle and late 1950's. Soviet acquisition of a sizeable delivery capability against the U.S., and more significantly their acquisition of relatively protected forces, submarine-launched or hardened, has been long and often prematurely heralded. Its arrival at last merely dramatizes the need to recognize that strategic nuclear war would under all foreseeable circumstances be bilateral—and highly destructive to both sides.

Larger budgets for U.S. strategic forces would not change that fact. They could have only a decreasing incremental effect in limiting somewhat the damage that the U.S. and its allies could suffer in a general nuclear war. In short, we cannot buy the capability to make a strategic bombing campaign once again a unilateral prospect.

That must, I suggest, be accepted as one of the determinants affecting policy. Another is that the same situation confronts the Soviet leaders in a way that is even more intensely confining. In fact, enormous increases in Soviet budgets would be required for them to achieve any significant degree of damage-limiting capability. The present Soviet leaders show no tendency to challenge the basis of the U.S. strategic deterrent posture by such expenditures.

In the last two years alone, we have increased the number of nu-

clear warheads in the strategic alert forces by 100 per cent. During
that period, we have more than doubled the mega-tonnage of the
strategic alert forces. The fact that further increases in strategic
force size will at last encounter rapidly diminishing returns—
which is largely an effect of the very large investments the U.S.
has made in this area—should be reflected in future budgets. The
funding for the initial introduction of missiles into our forces is
nearing completion. We can anticipate that the annual expenditure on strategic forces will drop substantially and level off well
below the present rate of spending. This is not to rule out the possibility that research now in progress on possible new technological
developments, including the possibility of useful ballistic missile
defenses, will require major new expenditures. In any event, there
will be recurring costs of modernization.

In the field of tactical nuclear weapons, the picture is in important respects similar. The U.S. at present has in stockpile or
planned for stockpile tens of thousands of nuclear explosives for
tactical use on the battlefield, in anti-submarine warfare, and
against aircraft. They include warheads for artillery, battlefield
missiles, demolition munitions, bombs, depth charges, air-to-air
missiles, and surface-to-air missiles. The consensus is that the U.S.
is presently substantially superior in design, diversity, and numbers
in this class of weapons.

This is an indispensable superiority, as we can readily understand if we consider how our problems of strategic choice would
be altered if the tables were reversed and it were the Soviet Union
which held a commanding lead in this field. Nevertheless, what we
have is superiority, not monopoly, and even if tactical nuclear warfare can be limited, below some ill-defined threshold of strategic
exchange, the key fact is that if the West initiates such warfare in
the future it must be expected to be bilateral, in any theater which
engaged the Soviet Union. Again, we cannot buy back a monopoly or the assurance of unilateral use.

Finally, there is the area of what we call our general-purpose
forces. Within the last two years, we have increased the number of
our combat-ready Army divisions by about 45 per cent, from eleven
to sixteen. There has been a 30 per cent increase in the number of
tactical air squadrons; a 75 per cent increase in airlift capabilities;
and a 100 per cent increase in ship construction and conversion to
modernize the fleet.

But it is not only force size that matters. The key to the effective
utilization of these forces is combat readiness and mobility.

The most recent demonstration of our ability to reinforce our troops presently stationed in Europe occurred last month on Operation Big Lift, the first of a series of planned large-scale, worldwide exercises. For the first time in military history, an entire division was airlifted from one continent to another. That movement could never have been accomplished without a massive increase in our airlift capability, which is still being expanded. (It will have risen 400 per cent between 1961 and 1967.) It required the development of new techniques to pre-position combat equipment, of which we have two extra division sets now in Europe. It called for new techniques in military training and administration to make sure that units are really ready to move out on a moment's notice. This exercise, in which some 16,000 airmen and soldiers and more than 350 planes took part, is directly relevant to the needs of Europe, where it brought a seventh division to join the six that are to remain in place. It is also relevant to the ability of the U.S. to fulfill its policy commitments world-wide, swiftly, and in effective strength.

But, it might be asked, what is the significance of all this for the realistic security problems of the United States and its allies? To what contingencies are these forces expected to contribute and how effective might they be, measured against the strength of opposing forces? How meaningful is it to talk of sixteen or twenty or thirty divisions in opposing the ground armies of the Soviet Union and Communist China?

Such questions are often meant to be merely rhetorical, in view of the supposed masses of Communist troops. The fact is that they are serious, difficult questions, to which I shall suggest some tentative answers. But it is difficult to encourage realistic discussions of specific contingencies so long as the shadow of the Communist horde hangs unchallenged over the debate. The actual contingencies that seem to me to be most likely and most significant are not those which would involve all, or even a major part, of the Soviet Bloc or Chinese Communist armed forces, nor do they all involve Europe. Hence, aggregate figures of armed strength of NATO and the Warsaw Pact nations are not immediately relevant to them. But it is useful to make these over-all comparisons precisely because misleading or obsolete notions of these very aggregates often produce an attitude of hopelessness toward any attempt to prepare to meet Communist forces in ground combat, however limited in scope.

The announced total of Soviet armed forces for 1955 was, indeed, a formidable 5.75 million men. Today, that figure has been cut to about 3.3 million; the Warsaw Pact total including the Soviets is only about 4.5 million. Against that, it is today the members of NATO whose active armed forces number over 5 million. The ground forces of NATO nations total 3.2 million, of which 2.2 million men are in Europe, as against the Soviet ground combat forces total of about 2 million men and a Warsaw Pact total of about 3 million. Both the Soviet Union and the U.S. forces of course include units stationed in the Far East. In Central Europe, NATO has more men, and more combat troops, on the ground than has the Bloc. It has more men on the ground in West Germany than the Bloc does in East Germany. It has more and better tactical aircraft, and these planes on the average can carry twice the payload twice as far as the Soviet counterparts.

These facts are hard to reconcile with the familiar picture of the Russian Army as incomparably massive. The usual index cited to support that picture is numbers of total active divisions, and the specific number familiar from the past is 175 divisions in the Soviet Army.

This total, if true, would indeed present a paradox. The Soviet ground forces are reliably estimated to be very close to 2 million men, compared to about 1 million for the U.S. How is it that the Soviets can muster ten times the number of active, combat-ready, fully-manned divisions that the United States has manned, with only twice as many men on active duty? The answer is simply that they do not. Recent intensive investigation has shown that the number of active Soviet divisions that are maintained at manning levels anywhere close to combat readiness is less than half of the 160–175 figure.

What remains is a large number, but even that is misleading. For one thing, U.S. divisions have about twice as many men in the division unit and its immediate combat supporting units as comparable Soviet divisions. A U.S. mechanized division has far more personnel in maneuvering units, far more in armored cavalry, far more engineers, far more signals, far more light armored personnel carriers, and far more aircraft available in support than Soviet divisions. In addition to longer staying power, much of the U.S. manpower and equipment margin is muscle that would make itself felt on D-Day. If, on the other hand, we were to reorganize along Soviet lines, we could display far greater numbers of divisions comparable to those of the Soviets.

The Soviet combat-ready force remains a formidable one. Moreover, the Russians do have a power mobilization capability; in particular, they have a large number of lightly manned or cadre divisions to be filled out on mobilization. Still, this reality remains strikingly different from our accustomed maps of it.

I do not wish to suggest that such aggregate comparisons are by themselves a valid index to military capabilities. But they are enough to suggest the absurdity, as a picture of the prevailing military strengths on which new efforts might build, of David and Goliath notions borrowed from 1949.

None of this is to say that NATO strength on the ground in Europe is adequate to turn back without nuclear weapons an all-out surprise non-nuclear attack.

But that is not in any case the contingency toward which the recent and future improvements in the mobility and capabilities of U.S. general-purpose forces are primarily oriented. Aggression on that scale would mean a war about the future of Europe and, as a consequence, the future of the U.S. and the U.S.S.R. In the face of threats of that magnitude, our nuclear superiority remains highly relevant to deterrence. The Soviets know that even non-nuclear aggression at that high end of the spectrum of conflict so threatens our most vital interests that we and our allies are prepared to make whatever response may be required to defeat it, no matter how terrible the consequences for our own society.

The probability that the Soviet leaders would choose to invoke that exchange seems to me very low indeed. They know well what even the Chinese Communist leaders must recognize upon further reflection, that a nuclear war would mean destruction of everything they have built up for themselves during the last fifty years.

If we were to consider a spectrum of the possible cases of Communist aggression, then, ranging from harassment, covert aggression, and indirect challenge at one end of the scale to the massive invasion of Western Europe or a full-scale nuclear strike against the West at the other end, it is clear that our nuclear superiority has been and should continue to be an effective deterrent to aggression at the high end of the spectrum. It is equally clear, on the other hand, that at the very low end of the spectrum, a nuclear response may not be fully credible and that nuclear power alone cannot be an effective deterrent at this level in the future any more than it has been in the past.

The fact is that at every level of force, the Alliance in general and the U.S. Armed Forces in particular have greater and more effective strength than we are in the habit of thinking we have—and with reasonable continued effort we can have whatever strength we need. I have spoken already of strategic weapons, where the great superiority of the United States is the superiority also of the Alliance. In tactical nuclear weapons, a parallel superiority exists—and while many of our Allies share with us in manning the systems which would use these tactical warheads in the hour of need, it is not unfair to point out that, even more than in the strategic field, the tactical nuclear strength of the Alliance is a contribution of the United States. That strength has been increased, on the ground in Europe, by more than 60 per cent in the last two years. Today, the thousands of U.S. warheads deployed on the continent for the immediate defense of Europe have a combined explosive strength more than 10,000 times the force of the nuclear weapons used to end World War II. Tactical nuclear strength the Alliance has today, and we have provided it.

But neither we nor our Allies can find the detonation of such weapons—and their inevitable bilateral exchange—an easy first choice. At the lower end of the spectrum, therefore, we also need strong and ready conventional forces. We have done our part here, and we continue to believe it just—and practicable—for our partners to do theirs.

The most difficult questions arise over the best means for meeting a variety of dangerous intermediate challenges in many parts of the world: those which threaten the possibility of sizeable conflict while still not raising the immediate issue of the national survival of ourselves or of any member of our alliances. Conflicts might arise out of Soviet subversion and political aggression backed up by military measures in non-NATO areas in Europe, Latin America, the Middle East and Africa. There is a range of challenges that could arise from Communist China and its satellites in the Far East and in Southeast Asia. Most dangerously, approaching the upper end of the spectrum, there is the possibility of limited Soviet pressures on NATO territory itself, along the vast front running from Norway to Greece and Turkey. Both the flanks and the center contain potential targets. And always, of course, there are the contingencies that could arise in relation to Berlin.

It is difficult to say just how probable any of these circumstances might be, although they must be regarded as more likely than still larger aggressions. What one can say is that if any of these more likely contingencies should arise, they would be highly dangerous. Inaction or weak action could result in a serious setback, missed opportunity, or even disaster. In fact, if either a nuclear exchange or a major Soviet attack should occur, it would most likely arise from a conflict on a lesser scale, which Western capabilities had failed to deter and which an inadequate Western response had failed to curb in time.

Since World War II, the expansionist impulse of the Communist Bloc is clear, but equally clear is its desire to avoid direct confrontation with the military forces of the free world. In Greece, in Berlin, and in Cuba, Communists have probed for military and political weakness, but when they have encountered resistance, they have held back. Communist doctrine has counselled not only this caution, but respect for the danger that any sizeable, overt conflict might lead to nuclear war. It would follow that no deterrent would be more effective against these lesser and intermediate levels of challenge than the assurance that such moves would certainly meet prompt, effective military response by the West. That response could confront the Soviets with frustration of their purposes unless they themselves chose to escalate the conflict to a nuclear exchange, or to levels that made nuclear war highly probable—a choice they are unlikely to make in the face of our destructive power.

The basis for that particular assurance cannot be systems in development, or weapons in storage depots, or reserves that must be mobilized, trained and equipped, or troops without transport. We need the right combination of forward deployment and highly mobile combat-ready ground, sea, and air units, capable of prompt and effective commitment to actual combat—in short, the sort of capability we are increasingly building in our forces.

This capability requires of us, as of our Allies, a military establishment that is, in the President's words, lean and fit. We must stop and ask ourselves, before deciding whether to add a new and complex weapons system to our inventory, whether it is really the most effective way to do the job under the rigorous conditions of combat. We must examine constantly the possibilities for combining functions, particularly in weapons that could be used by two or more services. Given this toughminded sense of reality about the requirements of combat readiness, it should be possible for the United States not only to maintain but to expand this increased strength without over-all increases in our defense budget. As our national productivity and our gross national product expand, the defense budget therefore need not keep pace. Indeed, it appears likely that measured in relative—and perhaps even absolute —terms, the defense budget will level off and perhaps decline a little. At the same time, we are continuing the essential effort to reduce the impact of defense spending on our balance of payments.

We have already brought this figure down from $2.7 billion in fiscal-year 1961 to $1.7 billion for fiscal-year 1963, and we shall continue to reduce it, without reducing the combat ground forces deployed in Europe, and while strengthening our over-all combat effectiveness.

And it must be our policy to continue to strengthen our combat effectiveness. I do not regard the present Communist leaders as wholly reckless in action. But recent experience, in Cuba and, on a lesser scale, in Berlin, has not persuaded me that I can predict with confidence the sort of challenge that Communist leaders will come to think prudent and profitable. If they were again to miscalculate as dangerously as they did a year ago, it would be essential to confront them, wherever that might be, with the full consequences of their action: the certainty of meeting immediate, appropriate, and fully effective military action.

All of our strengths, including our strategic and tactical nuclear forces, contributed last year, and they would contribute in similar future situations, to the effectiveness of our response by providing a basis for assurance that the Soviets would not dangerously escalate or shift the locale of the conflict. But, above all, in order to fashion that response, and to promise the Soviets local defeat in case of actual ground conflict, we had to use every element of the improvements in combat readiness and mobility that had been building over the preceding year and a half, including combat divisions, air transport, and tactical air. And the last ingredient was also there: the will to use those forces against Soviet troops and equipment.

Let us not delude ourselves with obsolete images into believing that our nuclear strength, great as it is, solves all of our problems of national security or that we lack the strengths to meet those problems that it does not solve. In the contingencies that really threaten —the sorts that have occurred and will occur again—we and our allies need no longer choose to live with the sense or the reality of inferiority to the Soviet Bloc in relevant, effective force. Let us be fully aware of the wide range of our military resources, and the freedom they can give us to pursue the peaceful objectives of the free world without fear of military aggression.

SIX

ALAIN C. ENTHOVEN

American Deterrent Policy

[Editor's Note: This speech is by the Deputy Assistant Secretary of Defense (Systems Analysis) who has been largely responsible for implementing the cost-effectiveness method described in earlier chapters. Mr. Enthoven's speech represents an elaboration of a particular set of options in Secretary McNamara's list (see above, Chapter 5). His basic argument is that the most reliable "fire break" is between conventional and nuclear weapons and that once that threshold is crossed, rapid escalation is probable. He argues, therefore, that the United States should never be in a position to have to resort to nuclear weapons because of the inadequacy of its conventional arsenal—in other words, he would prefer the United States to be in a position where it is able to resist any conventional challenge with conventional arms.]

Military force is but one instrument in the hands of the President to be used in the struggle to keep us alive and free. It takes its place alongside diplomacy, economic policy, foreign economic and military assistance, alliances, and many other activities that contribute to our national security. Its ultimate purpose, like that of these other activities, is to enable the President, in cooperation with the leaders of other free nations, to establish and maintain a peaceful world order based on a belief in the worth and dignity of the individual, and on freedom for each person to develop his own capacities in the way he chooses. The role of military force, in the pursuit of this objective, is to prevent would-be aggressors who do not believe in freedom and human dignity from forcing free men to live under a system based on tyranny and coercion. The problem of formulation of defense policy is to select those forces which will contribute most effectively to these multiple objectives.

There are three related themes underlying and uniting our defense policies today. They are, first, deterrence of aggression; second, freedom for the President to select and apply the amount and kind of force appropriate to the threat at hand; and third, the controlled use of force. In the nuclear age, military force will be too dangerous to use if our objectives are not carefully chosen and limited at each step of a conflict, and if the force cannot be used in a controlled and deliberate way to achieve precisely the objectives being sought. To fight for unlimited objectives, or to fight in an uncontrolled way would almost surely bring on almost unlimited destruction.

In order to give the President the freedom of action required to be able to limit appropriately the use of force, current defense policy emphasizes flexibility, options, and choice. One of its main objectives is to make available to the President a range of military responses appropriate for each threat to our security, so that he can apply force adequate to accomplish the objectives at hand without causing any unnecessary damage or loss of life, and while holding to a minimum the risk of escalation to a more destructive level of conflict.

A few years ago, there was a great deal of public debate as to whether limited war was possible. The theory and practice of strategic bombing in World War II, the use of the atomic bombs, and the unconditional-surrender policy left in their aftermath a widespread belief that war could only be total. This belief persisted long after the armed resistance to Communist aggression in Greece and Korea. Of course, total war remains possible. But, as time goes by and the size and destructive power of nuclear arsenals increase, total war between nuclear powers will, more and more, mean total destruction. It is my own opinion that with the widespread realization of this fact will come the general belief that all wars should be limited. At no time should we deliberately choose to fight an unlimited uncontrolled war. The "limited war–general war" dichotomy that has crept into our language may be harmful if it suggests that there is a kind of war that it makes sense to fight without limits, though, of course, the limits that we adopt will have to depend on the threat and on our objectives.

What this means, in practice, is that we are working to acquire a flexible, balanced defense posture giving us capabilities for the selective use of force for all kinds of conflict, from counter-insurgency and anti-guerrilla warfare through large-scale conventional (non-nuclear) warfare, through major thermonuclear war. Although the choice of the amount and kind of force to be applied in any circumstance is bound to be a difficult one, we would like to make it possible in all cases, if I may borrow a phrase from *The Mikado*, "to make the punishment fit the crime."

Keeping the use of force appropriately limited requires control. The range, speed, and destructiveness of modern weapons makes this problem both more urgent and more difficult than it has ever been before. More than ever before, this means that the President must have communication and control facilities to provide him with timely and accurate information on the course of events and to permit him to communicate his decisions in a similar manner. It also means that the military forces must be responsive to his direction, even in considerable detail. To use President Kennedy's words, "Our weapons systems must be usable in a manner permitting deliberation and discrimination as to timing, scope, and targets in response to civilian authority."

Moreover, when force is being applied, the military action must not be allowed to control events and compel the President's decisions; rather, it should be the other way around. To borrow a term from missilery, our use of military force in the cold war must be command guided, not inertially guided.

This belief may be contrasted to the view that "peace is peace and war is war," and that in war military necessity is the only valid criterion for decision. Certainly, the requirements of the military commander must be considered very seriously, both because our security requires success in whatever armed conflicts are thrust upon us and because the lives of our soldiers are involved. But still, the President must be free to weigh them against other requirements and decide what is best for the security of the United States. This principle was important before nuclear weapons; it has taken on added importance in the nuclear age.

This was one of the hard lessons of the Korean War. The United States had to re-learn to fight for limited objectives. There were reasons which the original military commander found very compelling for expanding the scope of the conflict. But in the President's judgment, to expand the conflict would have risked touching off another world war which would have left both the South Koreans and ourselves far worse off than the final outcome that actually was achieved. The President must be in a position to make and enforce such judgments.

The same principle of control was applied in a thoroughgoing way in the recent Cuban crisis. Each military move was, in effect, a carefully formulated message from the President to Khrushchev, intended to convince him that the United States would use military force to the extent necessary to achieve removal of the offensive weapons. But each move was also intended to convince him that he could withdraw without armed conflict, if he would withdraw. Because each move was a carefully formulated message, all moves had to be carefully controlled from the White House.

All this was summarized by President Kennedy in these words:

> Our arms must be subject to ultimate civilian control and command at all times, in war as well as peace. The basic decisions on our participation in any conflict and our response to any threat—including all decisions relating to the use of nuclear weapons, or the escalation of a small war into a large one—will be made by the regularly constituted civilian authorities.

Because of the importance of such control, a great deal has been done in the Defense Department in the past two years to strengthen and make more secure the means of high-level command and control of forces.

How have these themes worked themselves out in the development of our defense program? One of the most important ways has been in the recent and large build-up in our conventional or non-nuclear forces.

To understand properly the importance of the build-up of non-nuclear forces, it is necessary first to understand that there is a very great difference between nuclear weapons and non-nuclear weapons. Nuclear weapons are not simply high explosives writ large. Their destructive power makes them a completely new kind of military force which must be understood and related to our national security objectives in new ways. Hiroshima was destroyed by a 20-kiloton bomb. We now have weapons a thousand times that size. Roughly 2.5 million tons of TNT were dropped on Germany in World War II. One B-52 can now deliver many times that amount of destructive power, and we have the ability to deliver the equivalent of thousands of millions of tons intercontinentally. As well as the familiar effects of blast and heat, these weapons can cover many thousands of square miles with deadly radioactive fallout. All this is familiar.

There has been in recent years the development of small nuclear weapons having yields equivalent to a few thousand tons of TNT or less. The day will come, if it has not come already, when there will be nuclear weapons of smaller yield than the largest high explosive weapons. When that day comes, will there no longer be a distinction between nuclear and conventional weapons? Some have argued to that effect. But they are mistaken. There is and will remain an important distinction, a "firebreak" if you like, between nuclear and non-nuclear war, a recognizable qualitative distinction that both combatants can recognize and agree upon, if they want to agree upon one. And, in the nuclear age, they will have a very powerful incentive to agree upon this distinction and limitation, because if they do not, there does not appear to be another easily recognizable limitation on weapons—no other obvious "firebreak" —all the way up the destructive spectrum to large scale thermonuclear war.

Adequate conventional forces are important. It is for this reason that, in the past two years, we have increased the number of active combat-ready Army divisions from eleven to sixteen, and our active tactical air wings from sixteen to twenty-one. It is for this reason that we have more than doubled the annual rate of procurement of army equipment, that we have speeded up the tempo of modernization of our tactical air forces, and that we have increased our outlays on naval shipbuilding. Moreover, it is for this reason that we are now urging our NATO allies to increase the size and effectiveness of their conventional forces. Why?

The reason strong conventional forces are required is that there are many situations in which the use of nuclear weapons would be inappropriate. For the same reasons that a sledge hammer does not make a good substitute for a fly swatter, nuclear weapons are not a good substitute for non-nuclear forces against a wide range of military threats. Even if they could be used to apply the minimum force required to achieve our objectives, their use would risk triggering escalation to a more and unnecessarily destructive level of conflict.

A nation or an alliance which maintains a strong nuclear posture combined with weak conventional forces thereby puts itself at a great disadvantage in the confrontation with another power that has both strong nuclear and strong conventional forces. This will be true no matter how strong and effective are its nuclear forces, provided that the other power maintains a secure second-strike nuclear retaliatory capability. Because nuclear war is so destructive, the use of nuclear weapons must be reserved only for the most desperate circumstances. But if the nuclears have to be reserved for vital issues, the side with the strong conventional forces is likely to be able to have its way on all issues less than vital. The side without adequate conventional forces will have no means for effective resistance in such confrontations. The side with conventional forces can use "salami-slice" tactics, or make its aggression piecemeal, in the confidence that it will be able to have its way on all but life-and-death matters. This is the kind of threat we have been facing in Berlin. The danger in piecemeal aggression is that erosion in the position of the free world over the years can end in world domination by the Communists.

Put alternatively, the President will be in a weak bargaining position indeed if he is confronted by the Communist bloc with a choice between suicide or surrender, holocaust or humiliation. In order to resist aggression and defend our freedom, the President must have more attractive alternatives. Without conventional forces, our choice when faced with aggression may be "red or dead"; conventional forces help to deter aggression, and if deterrence fails, they can give us the opportunity to fight to stay alive and free.

Nevertheless, the build-up in our conventional forces has been costly and controversial. Two main lines of argument have been advanced against it. The first is that it weakens our nuclear resolve. In effect, it is a message to Khrushchev telling him that we are afraid or unwilling to use nuclear weapons, and that he can commit aggression against us with the expectation that we will not use them. Of course, pushed to an extreme, such an argument would say that we ought to abolish the United States Marine Corps. But the argument is defective. The important thing is not to convince an aggressor that we will use nuclear weapons. The important thing is to convince him that we will use whatever force is necessary to preserve our freedom. In many cases, that will be non-nuclear force. Sole or excessive reliance on nuclear weapons may tempt him to believe that we will not fight for less than vital issues. The danger is that each issue can be made less than vital. Aggression can be made piecemeal and in small enough pieces so that succumbing always looks attractive by comparison with thermonuclear war. Is not Berlin Khrushchev's "last territorial demand in Europe"?

In fact, reflection on the problem should convince most reasonable men that the threat of the ultimate use of nuclear weapons, if required, is much more credible to an aggressor who sees that to accomplish his objective he must first defeat a large and effective conventional force. If he succeeds in doing that, the issue at stake is likely by then to be vital for the defender.

Still, some argue that we should try to convince our adversaries that we would use nuclear weapons even in situations in which it is irrational to do so. Interestingly enough, Khrushchev himself has recently attacked this principle as a policy for the Communist Bloc, and in attacking him, the Chinese Communists have nonetheless acknowledged the enormous destructiveness of nuclear war. When it is clear that the Communists know the facts of nuclear destructiveness, it would seem foolish for us to base our strategy on the pretense that we do not. The trouble with trying to exploit "the rationality of irrationality," as theorists of bargaining and conflict call this, is that it simply is not a viable policy in the long run for a democracy, especially a democracy with allies. We must have defense policies that make sense to the American people and to our allies. Moreover, threats to blow ourselves up along with the aggressor are not likely to be credible. Rather, the most credible kind of threat is the threat that we will do what in the event will be most in our interest to do. In the case of piecemeal non-nuclear aggression, that will be to apply conventional forces.

The other main line of argument against the build-up of our conventional forces is that it will be fruitless, extremely costly, and unable to achieve the objective of adequacy because we are so badly outnumbered by the Communist hordes. These arguments, though widely believed, are not supported by the facts. Conventional military strength requires fighting men; it also requires that the men be fed, clothed, and equipped with effective weapons and other material. Equipping and supporting armies requires wealth and industrial production. The NATO allies outnumber the members of the Warsaw Pact in population, men under arms, and even foot soldiers in active army forces. In the dire straits into which mismanagement has plunged their economy, the Chinese Communists appear to be far from being able to provide modern and effective equipment for an army the size of our own. Moreover, the gross national products of the United States and its allies are more than twice the same total for the Soviet Union and its allies; in terms of industrial production, the ratio is more than two-and-one-half to one. What all of these facts suggest is that although substantial sacrifice may be involved for us and our NATO allies in equipping ourselves with adequate conventional forces, proportionally the sacrifice is much smaller for us than it is for our adversaries. Although we do need to strengthen our conventional forces somewhat, the extra costs are not large. We have already paid the entry fee into the "non-nuclear club." It is now largely a matter of making fully effective the force levels we have already agreed to provide.

A related argument has it that limiting conflicts to non-nuclear weapons puts us at a disadvantage because of our numerical inferiority, and that we need to use nuclear weapons as an equalizer in all but the smallest of armed conflicts. Leaving aside the undesirable character of the equalization they accomplish, and the unresolved question of whether the use of nuclear weapons is to our military advantage if the other side replies in kind, let me point out that our wealth and technology confer on us some important advantages in non-nuclear combat. Indeed, the effectiveness of modern non-nuclear arms is so great that they can offset substantial numerical inferiority in isolated situations in which we might be numerically inferior. The ability to produce such armaments in large quantities is a key determinant of the effectiveness of a nation's non-nuclear forces.

In summary, conventional military force is usable force. In Korea and in the Cuban crisis, we found that the non-nuclear forces were the cutting edge of our military power. We can use conventional force with a minimal risk of self-destruction. Therefore, it provides a more credible deterrent to non-nuclear aggression. As the destructiveness of nuclear war increases, and as nuclear-weapon systems become less vulnerable to sudden attack, the effectiveness of the threatened use of nuclear weapons as a substitute for conventional forces will diminish, and we will have no sensible alternative to building up our conventional forces to the point at which they can safely resist all forms of non-nuclear aggression. Our forces will be adequate if we can never be forced because of weakness to be the first to have to resort to nuclear weapons.

But if nuclear forces are not an effective substitute for adequate conventional forces, neither are conventional forces an effective substitute for adequate nuclear forces. Rather, the relationship between the two is one of complementarism. Now that the Communist Bloc is armed with nuclear weapons, we cannot successfully fight conventional wars except under the umbrella of nuclear strength. This nuclear strength is required to deter the Communists from escalating a non-nuclear conflict which is not going well for them into nuclear war, and to convince them that an act of nuclear aggression would lead to their defeat and possibly to the destruction of their society.

This, then, is the most important objective of our nuclear posture: to make thermonuclear war unlikely by deterring deliberate calculated nuclear aggression. We also seek other objectives. We want to make accidental, unpremeditated, irrational nuclear war unlikely also. And if war does occur, we want to be able to bring it to a speedy termination on military terms favorable to ourselves, and we want to do what we can to limit the damage caused to ourselves and our allies. How do we go about pursuing those objectives?

First, we attempt to deter deliberate premeditated attack by maintaining secure second-strike retaliatory capabilities—that is, force that cannot be knocked out in a surprise first blow. This means relatively invulnerable weapons systems like Minuteman, Titan, and Polaris, and secure, protected, survivable command and control facilities that will enable our national leadership to survive an attack and direct the use of retaliatory forces against any aggressor.

There is a great deal of literature and there are many approaches to the subject of deterrence. Some argue that, in the event of a nuclear attack on the alliance, we should plan to retaliate strictly against Soviet cities. Others argue that we should plan to strike back only against Soviet military forces. Still others argue for both. Some believe that we should design our posture for an irrevocable commitment to a spasm of massive retaliation. Our approach is based on options, deliberation, flexibility, and control. Rather than decide ahead of time which targets must be hit by which weapons, and then commit ourselves to it, our approach is to give the President a range of choices so that he can select the plan whose targets and timing of attacks are most appropriate to the circumstances at hand. I won't speculate here as to which nuclear response might be used in which circumstances. Nothing useful would be accomplished by doing so. But let me make three observations about this policy.

First, it is a policy of strength, not weakness. It takes superior nuclear forces to be able to ride out any kind of attack and then retain the option to destroy most of the enemies' remaining military forces, should that be appropriate. It would be a policy of weakness to commit ourselves irrevocably to a spasm of nuclear retaliation against Soviet cities.

Second, this policy requires secure forces and secure command and control. It requires weapon systems like Minuteman and Polaris that are hard and dispersed, or mobile and concealed, and that can ride out a thermonuclear attack and be held in reserve in the environment of nuclear war. This is one of the reasons why the Defense Department's procurement of strategic weapon systems in the last two years has emphasized Minuteman and Polaris.

Third, this approach to nuclear deterrence illustrates the principle that across the spectrum of conflict, military force is to be used with deliberation and control. There is, to be sure, a danger of breakdown of control in the environment of thermonuclear war. But, short of complete destruction of Western society, there is no point at which it makes sense to choose to abandon control. Even when it comes to thermonuclear weapons, if our weapons are to be used to keep us alive and free, their use must be controlled.

This emphasis on control had led us, in the past two years, to emphasize the procurement of survivable, secure, redundant, and internetted command, control, and communications facilities. For example, we now have a SAC command post with a general officer on board constantly airborne, twenty-four hours a day. For the top civilian authorities, we have a National Emergency Airborne Command Post, command posts on ships at sea, and various hardened underground command posts, all tied together by protected communications. As well as making a major contribution to our ability to deter deliberate attack, this strengthened command structure has made an important contribution to reducing the likelihood of such unlikely eventualities as unauthorized, accidental, or other unpremeditated attacks blowing up into large-scale thermonuclear war. And, along with many other safety precautions that we have taken, it is making much less likely the possibility of accidental or unauthorized use of nuclear weapons on our side.

I would like to emphasize this point because some recent literature has suggested that there is a lack of concern among the military and civilian leaders of the Department of Defense for the safety and stability of our nuclear weapons posture. This suggestion could not be farther from the truth. In fact, both our military and civilian leaders take this problem very seriously, and they have been willing to accept considerable costs to assure the compatibility of military readiness with the highest possible degree of safety.

But, despite our best efforts, a war may still occur. In these dangerous and unpredictable times, it would be foolish to base our planning on the assumption that a thermonuclear war could never happen. Despite our best efforts, almost any kind of nuclear war would be an unprecedented disaster. But if such a war were thrust upon us, there are worthwhile things that could be done to mitigate its consequences. We are making preparations whose purpose is, in the event of war, to enable us to maintain a favorable military position, to bring the war to an end quickly, and to hold to a minimum the damage to ourselves and our allies. To limit the damage, we are making a combination of plans and preparations, including civil defense, active air and anti-missile defense, and an ability to destroy what we can of the enemy's offensive weapons. Let me explain each one.

The largest part of our civil-defense program is fallout shelters for our population. One of the most destructive effects of nuclear weapons is radioactive fallout. In a thermonuclear attack on the United States, many millions of people would die, even though they were far from the blast and thermal effects, simply from radioactive fallout. Although there are substantial uncertainties here, and the numbers vary widely depending upon the assumptions made, most studies suggest that whereas several tens of millions might die from the blast and thermal effects of a nuclear attack on the United States, because of fallout the total deaths could well be over 100 million in the United States alone. In order to prevent this, the President has directed the Department of Defense to undertake an expanded civil-defense program, which has as its first objective the provision of fallout shelters for all of our population.

Civil defense is very important for many reasons. Without it, our active defenses and other preparations for survival in a thermonuclear war would be rendered meaningless. For example, if we defended our cities with impenetrable anti-missile defenses but had no fallout protection for the inhabitants, an attacker could still destroy all the people in those cities simply by surface bursting thermonuclear weapons upwind and killing the people with fallout. If we do have a civil-defense program, then active air and anti-missile defenses can also make a very important contribution to our survival. Civil defense is also necessary if we are to have any hope of limiting the effects of a major thermonuclear war and making possible a meaningful strategy of controlled use of nuclear weapons.

As well as these measures, we are also buying strategic retaliatory forces capable of knocking out those vulnerable elements of enemy nuclear striking power remaining after an attack has been launched against us. Of course, we are up against the limitation here that, after such an attack, our counter-attacking forces are likely to be spent destroying many empty bases and launching sites. However, our studies to date suggest that, in such circumstances, it would still be likely that there would remain vulnerable forces that could be used against us in follow-up attacks, and that their timely destruction could help to limit the damage to the United States and our allies.

Beyond these physical measures, we are also opening up the option of maintaining some effective deterrence after a nuclear war begins. This was described last Spring by Secretary of Defense Mc-Namara in an address at Ann Arbor, at the University of Michigan. In his words:

> The U.S. has come to the conclusion that to the extent feasible, basic military strategy in a possible general nuclear war should be approached in much the same way that more conventional military operations have been regarded in the past. That is to say, principal military objectives, in the event of a nuclear war stemming from a major attack on the Alliance, should be the destruction of the enemy's military forces, not of his civilian population.
>
> The very strength and nature of the Alliance forces make it possible for us to retain, even in the face of a massive surprise attack, sufficient reserve striking power to destroy an enemy society if driven to it. In other words, we are giving a possible opponent the strongest imaginable incentive to refrain from striking our own cities.

Doubtless, questions will arise in your minds as to whether nuclear war can and should be limited and controlled. First, can it? The answer depends on our will to make it so. With the protected weapon systems, command posts, and communications we are now acquiring, there is no technical reason why the use of nuclear weapons cannot be controlled in a nuclear war. The destructive power of their uncontrolled use should give all participants a strong incentive to find ways of avoiding it. Moreover, as both sides acquire protected forces like Minuteman and Polaris, the prospects are that neither side will be able to improve its military position by a sudden attack on the forces of the other. Then, if massive thermonuclear attack ever did make sense, it will do so no longer.

The other question is, "Should we try?" The argument against trying, one that has been used against civil defense, is that it weakens the "firebreak" between nuclear and non-nuclear war. But any thermonuclear war would be such an unprecedented disaster that it is difficult to see how anything we could do to mitigate its consequences would effectively weaken the "firebreak." And the disaster of an unlimited nuclear war would be too great to permit us not to take whatever measures we can to minimize its likelihood. Moreover, the principle of controlled and limited use of military force is indivisible. If we believe in control in some circumstances and not in others, it will become more difficult to maintain it in those circumstances in which we should. An emphasis on control and limitations in the use of force is desirable across the spectrum of conflict.

I am sure that you are all concerned, as I am, about the moral problems raised by our military preparations. Is is right or wrong for us to be buying hundreds of intercontinental ballistic missiles, fighter-bomber aircraft, and equipment for many army divisions? Can we justify weapon systems and war plans that would enable us, if a nuclear war were thrust upon us, to fight back even though doing so might lead to the deaths of many millions of people?

These are extremely complex and difficult problems that we can neither escape nor hope to understand fully. Their moral solution cannot come from artificial simplification. What I would like to do is offer you some questions and some reflections that may illuminate some of the issues. A proper appreciation of the moral aspects of defense policy requires an understanding of theology as well as the alternative strategies and their implications. A dialogue is required, and I offer the following remarks in that spirit.

According to traditional Christian doctrine, the use of force to repress evil can be justifiable under certain conditions including the following: first, the use of force must have a reasonable chance of success. Second, if successful, it must offer a better situation than the one that would prevail in the absence of the use of force. Third, the force that is used must be proportional to the objectives being sought (or the evil being repressed). For this to be satisfied, peaceful means of redress must have failed. Fourth, the force must be used with the intention of sparing noncombatants and with a reasonable prospect of actually doing so.

It is interesting to observe that the potentially catastrophic character of thermonuclear war has forced practical decision-makers, reasoning in a secular context, to adopt a set of criteria very much like those of the traditional Christian doctrine and to apply them to the design of the military posture of the United States. Now, much more than in the recent past, our use of force is being carefully proportioned to the objectives being sought, and the objectives are being carefully limited to those which at the same time are necessary for our security and which do not pose the kind of unlimited threat to our opponents in the cold war that would drive them to unleash nuclear war. In the past, before nuclear weapons, deliberate limitations in the use of force did not present much of a practical problem because of the limited destructive power of nonnuclear weapons. Nuclear weapons have now given such constraints great practical importance.

Within the broad policy of armed resistance to aggression, which is one of the alternatives open to us, and in terms of the moral criteria of the traditional Christian doctrine, I think it is fair to say that we have made considerable progress. This is not to say that we have gone as far as we can go. But it does suggest that all the moral questions are not concerned with whether or not armed resistance can be justifiable.

During the past fifteen years, a number of commentators, theologians and others, have taken the position that although in former times the traditional doctrine was valid and, under appropriate conditions, the use of armed force could be justified, now, in the atomic age, there can be no justifiable war. The argument has been made that nuclear war does not and cannot offer a reasonable chance of bringing about a better situation than that which would have prevailed in the absence of the use of force; that thermonuclear force, being essentially unlimited in its destructive effects, cannot be proportioned to reasonable objectives; and that with it, the noncombatants cannot be spared. Therefore, many argue, the traditional doctrine is obsolete and a new doctrine must be found. Some argue that the only morally acceptable course is to renounce nuclear weapons; others believe that we must renounce the use of force altogether.

I would not want to suggest that this line of thought is not based on good and compelling reasons, even though I have not found it convincing myself. It may prove to be the case that the danger of escalation is so great that future limited non-nuclear wars will bring with them an intolerable risk of massive thermonuclear destruction. However, experience in the past fifteen years has shown that nonnuclear wars can be kept limited and that freedom can be defended from Communist aggression without massive destruction.

A question to consider in one's critical thought on this problem is whether the view that the traditional doctrine is obsolete is based on an overemphasis on unlimited nuclear war, perhaps an identification of all armed conflict with it. An unlimited nuclear war is an extreme on a broad spectrum of possible armed conflicts. Of course, it is a very important extreme because of its disastrous consequences, but it is not the whole spectrum. In fact, it is only one among many possible kinds of thermonuclear war. It can be a mistake to apply reasoning based on this extreme to all kinds of armed resistance to aggression and injustice. I think it is important to recognize this, for if our thinking is unclear on this point, and if we identify any use of armed force with unlimited destruction, we are likely unnecessarily to disarm ourselves and leave ourselves victims of Communist aggression.

It is clear that we have elected to retain the threat of use of nuclear weapons in our own defense and that of our allies. We thereby consciously accept the risk that we will have to use them. Some people believe that we should reject the use of nuclear weapons. Before accepting such a judgment, one should consider carefully the full implications of such a decision. We do have worldwide responsibilities. Many millions of people depend for their lives and freedom on our military strength. In this respect, the United States is in a very different position from any other country in the free world.

The question I would like to leave with you is whether current U.S. defense policy, which emphasizes deterrence, control, and the use of the appropriately limited amount of force, represents a good reconciliation of the traditional doctrine with the facts of life in the nuclear age? We have achieved some success with the controlled use of force. We are still alive and free today, and the missiles are out of Cuba. We are running great risks, to be sure, but would the risks be ameliorated by laying down our arms? It is tragic that nations must at times resort to armed force to resolve their differences. War is destructive and it has evil consequences. But our defense posture is being designed to make war less likely and less destructive. I am not suggesting that we can make war and violence desirable. The question is whether we have a better alternative.

I have defended our policies on the grounds that they make sense. Can they also be defended on the grounds that they are moral? Viewed with perspective, the two should be the same.

SEVEN

ROSWELL L. GILPATRIC

Our Defense Needs: The Long View

[Editor's Note: This article by the then Deputy Secretary of Defense was written toward the end of Mr. Gilpatric's tenure in office, in April, 1964. While Secretary McNamara's and Mr. Enthoven's speeches deal with America's options during the conduct of military operations (see above, Chapters 5 and 6), Mr. Gilpatric's article describes the United States military posture during a period of peace. He emphasizes that security cannot be found in the accumulation of armaments, but rather requires that the arms race be brought under control. He outlines reductions in military budgets and changes in overseas deployment that a prolonged period of relaxation of tensions could bring. Mr. Gilpatric's article thus shows that elements of Mr. Wohlstetter's concepts (see above, Chapter 2) and some of Mr. Waskow's considerations (Chapter 3) were incorporated into United States security policy.]

I

The United States may face a dilemma over the extent and use of its military power in the event the cold war with the Soviet Union eases before major steps are taken toward general disarmament.

This dilemma was foreshadowed in President Johnson's first major policy statements. In his November, 1963, message to the Joint Session of the Congress, he rededicated the government to "the maintenance of military strength second to none," and in his December address to the United Nations, he stated a new national objective: "We know what we want: the United States wants the cold war ended, we want to see it end once and for all."

Another indicator of this forthcoming dilemma was in two votes by the United States Senate on September 24, 1963. In the morning of that day, the Senate voted 80 to 19 to ratify the partial test

EDITOR's NOTE: Reprinted with permission from Foreign Affairs, XLII, No. 3 (April, 1964). © 1964, by the Council on Foreign Relations, Inc., New York.

ban treaty, and in the afternoon it voted 77 to 0 for the largest defense budget in peacetime history.

In June, 1963 President Kennedy's speech to the American University had also reflected the same two lines of U.S. policy—namely, to keep our defenses strong while seeking to improve East-West relations and stop the arms race. These were his words:

> Today the expenditure of billions of dollars every year on weapons, acquired for the purpose of making sure we never need to use them, is essential to keeping the peace. . . .
>
> Both the United States and its allies, and the Soviet Union and its allies, have a mutually deep interest in a just and genuine peace and in halting the arms race.
>
> Let us re-examine our attitude toward the Cold War.
>
> We must, therefore, persevere in the search for peace in the hope that constructive changes within the Communist bloc might bring within reach solutions which now seem beyond us.

In January, 1964, President Johnson's State of the Union message re-emphasized the same points. On the one hand, he pledged that there would be maintained the "margin of military safety and superiority" now possessed by the United States. At the same time, he promised new steps toward the control and eventual abolition of arms and undertook that, even without agreement, the United States would "not stockpile arms beyond our needs or seek an excess of military power that could be provocative as well as wasteful."

There is no fundamental inconsistency between these two policies. Indeed, the lesson to be learned alike from those modern nations which have most successfully avoided wars—the Swiss and the Swedes—or from Roman policies in the long period of the *Pax Romana*, is the truth of that harsh guidance: "If you wish for peace, prepare for war."

Today, it is not too difficult to explain any apparent inconsistency between these two approaches: that one complements and supports the other; and that unless we are willing to credit our rivals with superhuman qualities of goodness of nature and self-restraint, we had best not risk tempting them from a prudent path. Thus, at present, there is broad support for a policy which insists both on maintaining adequate military power and on simultaneously seeking out opportunities—of which the test ban, the ban on bombs in orbit, the wheat sale, and the "hot line" to Moscow are examples—to move toward a lessening of tensions and the growth of increasingly normal relations between the two major blocs.

But what about tomorrow? Will we be successful in holding to both lines of policy? Will we be able to decrease our defense effort, supposing a reduction is consistent with our national commitments and national interests, without relaxing our resolve to deter aggression and international lawlessness? Or, on the other hand, will we be able to move as freely as we should toward alleviating cold-war tensions, while still maintaining adequate defenses?

Unfortunately, there can be no confident answer to such questions. History does not provide much assurance regarding the ability of nations, especially democratic nations, to keep equally alert to both the possibilities for peace and the dangers of aggression. Too often, the tendency has been toward an all-or-nothing approach; an approach which cannot reconcile the simultaneous existence of both danger and opportunity; an approach which leads nations to view wars as either unthinkable (and so discouraging serious attention to defenses) or inevitable (and so requiring a rigid stand against the enemy)—or even as both unthinkable and inevitable, with a consequent breakdown of any semblance of rational policy.

Indeed, even today we sense a fear that the Western democracies will not be able to follow both policy lines, causing some to argue for suppression of one or the other policy goal—not on the grounds that it is unsound, but rather that if it is pursued, it will draw support away from the other. Many of those who opposed the nuclear test ban did so not on grounds that there lay in the treaty a significant military risk to the West, but rather because they feared that any easing of tensions would soon find the Western democracies inviting disaster by letting down their guard long before a real resolution of differences between the two blocs was in sight. Similarly, there are those on the other side who argue for massive cuts in defense spending not on the basis of any serious analysis of the military threat which we must be prepared to neutralize, but simply on the grounds that only by greatly reducing defense spending, and so (in their view) removing the basis of a "cold-war mentality," can the Western governments be free to move forward toward reasonable settlements with the Soviet bloc.

There are further variations of these attitudes, but in all of them the central assumption is the same: that we cannot pursue simultaneously more than one of the two goals—reducing tensions and keeping our defenses strong—not because the goals are inherently incompatible but because there are flaws in our societies which make it impossible for governments to pursue both effectively. As noted earlier, there is, unfortunately, a good deal of historical example to support this bleak view. As Walter Lippmann has pointed out (in describing the "malady of democratic states"): "The unhappy truth is that the prevailing public opinion has been destructively wrong at the critical junctures. The people have imposed a veto upon the judgments of informed and responsible officials. They have compelled the governments, which usually knew what would have been wiser, or was necessary, or was more expedient, to be too late with too little, or too long with too much, too pacifist in peace, and too bellicose in war, too neutralist or too appeasing, or too intransigent."

As a result, the best answer we can give to those who counsel that it is dangerous even to attempt a balanced policy is not that they are clearly wrong—for there is too much history which says they may be right—but that to fail to try a balanced policy is even more dangerous. We cannot afford a policy which, in effect, deliberately avoids seeking a reduction of tensions in order to keep the public alert to dangers. Nor can we afford a policy which deliberately seeks to lull the public, and ignore dangers where they exist, in order to make it easier to build support for a policy of peaceful accommodations.

II

I stress all this partly because it is so important that it bears frequent repeating, partly to avoid any misunderstanding about what I have in mind when I discuss, as I now propose to do, the kind of military establishment which might be appropriate for the United States should there develop a continued easing of the level of East-West tension such as we have seen during the past year. I am not talking about an inevitable major decline in U.S. defense spending, but about one that might be feasible should the present amelioration of East-West relations prove more permanent than the "Spirit of Geneva" or the "Spirit of Camp David."

I do not know how permanent the present relaxation may be and would not attempt to predict. I do know that there is evidence that responsible leaders of both blocs are increasingly aware of the consequences of nuclear war, and of the dangers of limited wars or even of intense crises getting out of control. Consequently, it is clearly in the national interests of nations in both blocs to exercise restraint in the conduct of their foreign and military policies. For no one can foresee what might happen should any nation, through miscalculation or folly, infringe on the vital interests of another or invoke a morally binding commitment given by another nation. Recognizing, as I believe both sides do, the dangers of our situation, the need for restraint and the need to search for greater international stability, I think it at least possible, though not assured, that we shall at last find a more than temporary easing of East-West tensions.

Should that possibility develop into reality, we would not want either to see armaments continue at unnecessarily high levels, with the various dangers and instabilities that they could bring, or to see a prematurely drastic cut in military preparedness, with the dangers and instabilities that it could bring. And since military planning has so often been out of phase with the realities of the moment, we had better start thinking now about "after-the-cold-war" defense policies, if we are to be prepared to respond sensibly to the opportunities we hope will arise. It is in that spirit—and in the hope of stimulating attention to these issues—that I propose to discuss a possible military posture for the United States which, it seems to me, might be a reasonable one for a midway point between cold war and a genuinely peaceful world with effective international law and minimal national defense establishments.

Already there has been, in fact, a modest turndown in the arms race. In December, 1963, Premier Khrushchev announced a cut of 600 million rubles in the Soviet military budget for the calendar year 1964. Of course, we cannot be sure this is a genuine cut rather than an exercise of statistical legerdemain. But it did follow announcements by senior U.S. officials in the fall of 1963 that our defense budget would probably decline modestly in the years immediately ahead. The budget for fiscal-year 1965 (which begins July 1, 1964), presented to Congress in January, provided approximately $2 billion less for defense than would have been called for by continued spending at the previous year's rate, after taking into account uncontrollable increases such as military, civilian and retirement pay. By coincidence, both the Soviet and the U.S. cuts in military spending for the next budget year come out at the same percentage: 4 per cent of the base figure.

The principal U.S. budget decreases were not, however, based upon reduction in tension but were essentially a consequence of the energetic efforts during the previous three years to close certain gaps in our defense posture. There was the fact that we were putting behind us the accumulated deficiencies in conventional force equipment inherited from the 1950's. The correction of those deficiencies had required an increase in the Army procurement budget from $1.5 billion in fiscal-year 1961 to $3.2 billion in fiscal-year 1964. Once this was substantially accomplished, normal programming of conventional equipment procurement could be safely resumed. More important, we are past the peak of the very large expenses involved in building up our Polaris and Minuteman missile forces. A figure of $5.5 billion was included for Polaris submarines in the fiscal-year 1962, 1963, and 1964 budgets, and $2 billion for additional Minutemen in the fiscal-year 1964 budget alone; and we have increased our alert-force mega-tonnage by more than 100 per cent in the past three years. As a consequence of these large increments, we were approaching the point at which further increases in strategic delivery vehicles promised little meaningful military advantage. Consequently, we had a substantial decline in the expenses of this part of the strategic force. Finally, the intensive Cost Reduction Program instituted by Defense Secretary McNamara in 1962 allowed for further significant reductions of cost.

Thus, the cut in defense expenses for 1965 does not imply a cut in the level of U.S. military preparedness. Nevertheless, this was the first real reduction in our defense spending in a decade. It reflected the conviction of senior defense officials that the level of defense expenditures in one year does not have to be regarded as the floor for expenditures in the following year.

As to the Soviet cut, we can only speculate. Indeed, because of the character of the public Soviet budget, we have no firm data on which to estimate how great a cut is really involved. It might be either more or less than the 4 per cent announced, or conceivably no cut at all, although this is not likely. If the cut is roughly equivalent to that announced in the Soviet public budget, we can attribute it in part to factors similar to those which allowed a decrease in our own military spending: that is, in part to pressures arising from the desire to allocate a larger share of resources to other sectors of the economy and in part to a desire to take a small symbolic step to indicate that arms budgets need not inevitably spiral upward from year to year.

The question then arises how far the U.S. and Soviet military efforts can decline, in the absence of formal arms limitation agreements, through this kind of complementary action—what Khrushchev has called a "policy of mutual example." To the extent that the Soviet cut reflects a genuine reduction in military forces, it reduces the level of the military threat which the West must be prepared to negate, and so allows for some reduction in that countervailing effort. Similarly, to the extent that the U.S. budget decline reflects, as it does, a tapering off in the growth of our strategic nuclear forces, it presumably makes possible a decision by prudent Soviet planners to slow their own effort. The prospect of diminishing marginal returns from further force increments affects the utility of Soviet force increases at least as much as it does those of the United States, although for somewhat different reasons.

Let us assume that this process of "mutual example" continues —perhaps not in an unbroken decline in tensions, but at least with a definite trend toward less troubled relations in the military sphere and a clear, if not uninterrupted, trend downward in the intensity of military preparations on both sides, while we continue to compete vigorously in the economic and political spheres. Under such circumstances, what kind of U.S. force structure might be envisaged by the end of this decade? Our security requirements would remain, in principle, substantially as they are today. But they could lessen quantitatively in face of parallel declines in the balance of forces on both sides.

Several elements must enter into the resulting power equation:

1. The forces, including those for strategic deterrence, which the United States must possess to counter the threat represented by the Soviet forces as they then exist;

2. The forces needed to contain whatever level of aggression the Chinese Communists and their allies are capable of mounting, bearing in mind that at some time they will have nuclear weapons; and

3. The forces which may be required for the United States to project its power presence to deter or arrest conflict in areas where there is no confrontation of the super-powers but where subversive insurgency, aided directly or indirectly by the Soviets or the Chinese Communists, constitutes a threat to the stability of nations aligned with the United States or looking to it for assistance. A *détente* with the U.S.S.R. would not necessarily cause the Soviets to relinquish their objective of supporting what Khrushchev calls "wars of liberation."

In recent years, there have been a number of instances where a U.S. military presence has served to avoid or damp down conflict in parts of the world where the United States and the Soviet Union have not been directly involved. Such has been the case in South Korea since 1953, in Thailand in 1962, in Saudi Arabia in 1963 during the dispute with the United Arab Republic over Yemen, and in the recent joint U.S.-U.K. air exercises in India. The same motivation lies behind the current proposal for the Seventh Fleet to put a task force in the Indian Ocean. The British Commonwealth similarly projected its military power during the crisis over Aden in 1962 and is in the process of doing so again to counter the current Indonesian threat against Malaysia. In order to preserve peace and prevent the spread of externally supported subversion throughout Latin America, it may also be necessary in the years ahead for the United States to maintain a larger military presence in the Caribbean area. The difficulties in Panama may be only symptomatic of more serious troubles to come, particularly if Castro retains, or enlarges, his capacity to foment such troubles.

III

A combination of U.S. military forces tailored to the strategic situation which would prevail in the absence of major confrontations between the Soviet Union and the West could, by 1970, look something like this:

Strategic retaliatory forces. A deterrent force, consisting only of hardened and dispersed land-based and mobile sea-based missiles, with all of the vulnerable, earlier-generation missiles deactivated, and all manned bombers retired from active deployment. Such a force, comprised of weapons systems invulnerable to surprise attack, would be capable of destroying the centers of Soviet and Chinese Communist society.

Continental air and missile defense forces. Only warning systems, such as the big ballistic-missile detection and tracking radars in Alaska, Greenland, and Scotland, and the current generation of surface-to-air missile systems for tactical deployment would be maintained. Manned interceptors with their ground-control counterparts and all other bomber defense and warning systems would be phased out, unless the Soviets changed their presently indicated intention of concentrating their strategic power in missiles. There would be no production or deployment of anti-ballistic-missile systems in the absence of Soviet moves to proceed beyond experimental installations of such systems.

Reconnaissance forces. Both aircraft and satellite-based reconnaissance systems would be retained and improved to take full advantage of state-of-the-art developments, so as to provide the United States at all times with a world-wide capability for the collection of both strategic and tactical intelligence.

General-purpose forces. No significant changes would take place in this category except for a reduction of Army divisions that might be withdrawn at some stage from Korea or from Europe (if a decline in the Soviet threat there allowed). The remaining Army ground forces and the existing Marine divisions, with presently planned air support and airlift (consisting of all the Tactical Air and Military Air Transport units, plus the Marine Air wings), would be needed to deter or counter threats of aggression not directly inspired or supported by the U.S.S.R. The bulk of the U.S. forces now assigned to the Pacific Command are there primarily to meet the threat from Communist China and her satellites, plus Indonesia. Hence, in the event of a *détente* with the Soviet Union alone, it would not be safe to reduce U.S. force levels in the Pacific.

It should also be possible to reduce the National Guard and Reserve forces, retaining—in the case of the Army—only the high-priority divisions plus round-out units capable of quick call-up.

Such a cutback force, if made possible by a true *détente* between the United States and the Soviet Union, should require an annual level of defense expenditure about 25 per cent under the current (fiscal-year 1964) rate, and 10 per cent or so below that at the end of the Eisenhower Administration. At the new reduced levels, force strengths would be little below those prior to the 1961 build-up. The main difference between the two sets of forces would be in their mix, those postulated for 1970 being better balanced with far less emphasis on nuclear-weapon components.

The force sketched above leaves many questions unanswered. There probably would be little argument within our national security establishment about retiring the older, unprotected missiles. These weapons do not constitute, in any case, a major element of our force numerically and are the most vulnerable and least reliable of our missiles. There would be, again, little argument about keeping intact the later-generation missile systems, such as the Minuteman and Polaris. These are the most effective elements of our strategic force, both as deterrents and as fighting weapons in time of war. It is difficult to conceive of circumstances under which it would be sound to cut back these forces in the absence of explicit, effectively policed, arms-control arrangements.

Deactivation of the bombers would raise more of an issue. Modified B-52's and the newer B-58's could probably be kept operable into the 1970's. On the other hand, particularly if the Soviet Union were undertaking similar steps, there seems to be no compelling reason why the bombers need be kept in the active force. We would have to consider the effectiveness of a bomber reserve force, including the time required for a call-up, should that ever be necessary, and the storage arrangements (presumably reflecting a maximum practical dispersal), and the degree of assurance we could have, lacking formal inspection, of the retirement from active service of the Soviet bomber fleet. We should also take into account the effects on the military balance and on over-all stability of various alternatives, ranging from development of a next-generation strategic bomber or keeping a large part of the bomber force on active duty to a complete phase-out of a substantial share of the force. All of these questions, and many more affecting our strategic forces, will have to be looked at carefully in the years immediately ahead if we are to be ready to proceed intelligently should the opportunity for a major slowdown in the arms race develop during the latter half of this decade.

Similarly, in air defense, we would have to consider what degree of confidence we could expect to place in our estimates of Soviet retained bomber strength, if any; the significance of an interceptor force in a period when both sides are heavily armed with long-range missiles; the effect of deployment of ballistic missile defenses, given the limitations on the effectiveness of any system that could be developed in the foreseeable future; and many other questions. We might, as I have suggested, find it consistent with our interests to retain only warning systems and short-range surface-to-air missiles. As with offensive forces, we will be able to proceed with reasonable confidence only if these questions have been carefully considered prior to the time a decision must be made. It was the earlier period of study and debate which made it possible for the new Administration to move forward on its defense programs with speed and confidence in 1961. Issues such as survivability, non-nuclear options, and controlled response had been extensively examined for several years prior to 1961. Since then, we have been living on that intellectual capital, and we have an urgent need to replenish it.

The most difficult problems arise in trying to establish proper levels for our general-purpose forces. These do not lend themselves to the relatively precise analysis of alternatives and mixes that can be applied to strategic offensive and defensive forces. On the other hand, because they are intended primarily for non-nuclear engagements, their effect on problems of military stability in the world is less dramatic than the effect of nuclear forces. Probably it would be prudent to retain substantially the forces we now have, decreased only to the extent that Soviet reductions in Eastern Europe permitted an offsetting decline in NATO in Western Europe. Similarly, it may be possible to make reductions if, through changes in the world situation and through the improvement in mobility which is playing such a marked role in modernizing our forces, the United States can reduce its garrison forces in Korea.

Strong efforts, meanwhile, would presumably continue in research and development, to assure that we were not left behind in major technological developments that could upset the balance of power between the blocs. Consequently, military research-and-development expenditures would remain high, such declines as did develop being the result mainly of savings on the large expenses of final engineering and testing of full-scale new strategic systems, rather than from a reduction in the breadth of our research programs or in pushing new frontiers of technology.

We would continue to put major effort into improvements in the command and control, reliability and flexibility of our strategic forces and would proceed with exploratory development of some new systems. But, assuming similar restraint on the other side, we could probably, without injury to our national security, exercise a good deal of restraint over the deployment of any major weapon systems beyond those already programmed.

All of this, I emphasize again, is not to lay out a plan for a military program at the end of the decade. It merely suggests the kind of program that might be adequate to meet our commitments and defend our interests, while at the same time contributing to general military stability, provided the present movement toward *détente* with the U.S.S.R. continues to progress in the years ahead. Under these conditions, the kind of restraint outlined here (although not necessarily the details suggested) would be in our interest, provided similar restraint were exercised by the Soviets. Greater reductions probably could not be achieved in the absence of explicit arms-control arrangements, including a substantial degree of international inspection.

IV

What is clearest in all this is that the United States, in order to safeguard its best long-term interests in the decade ahead, must remain alert to the changing requirements—and opportunities—that will develop over the remainder of this period. The world changes fast these days, and the state of the military arts fastest of all. We can be quite sure that among the important factors in the military situation at the end of the 1960's will be some which few people are seriously concerned with today. Yet our ability to safeguard the peace is going to depend in large measure on our ability to keep pace with the realities of military defense as they change over the years.

This essay selects one possible situation and outlines one possible set of military forces that might be appropriate to it. There are other situations we should be thinking about: a hopeful world in which substantial measures toward disarmament and international inspection have begun; a more dangerous world in which the cold war is renewed in bitter form; and a world in which tensions last at about the level where they are today but complicated by various kinds of technological developments. We should be thinking about appropriate military postures in each situation, and thinking through the long-term implications of possible new ventures in armaments—such as, for example, major antiballistic-missile deployments—so that we may try to shape the military environment that will exist at the end of the 1960's and not merely stumble into it.

The power of the United States in the years ahead might take on entirely different forms and proportions than the mix of armed forces which comprises our military establishment today. New characteristics may be desirable to meet power requirements in the changed conditions that have been assumed. The most important requirement must always be "usability," but the qualities which make a military force usable may vary as conditions vary.

Our military power must be such that the President can apply the measure and kind of force appropriate to any provocation, so that he may use force, when justified, with some confidence that history will judge his actions as serving the best interests of the nation and of the world, and not merely as the trigger for massive mutual destruction. Thus, one constant will be that our military power must always provide a variety of capabilities suitable for dealing with a broad range of contingencies. Our military power must not only serve to deter but also, if deterrence fails, to defend. It may also be important that it assume a more unobtrusive character than it has in the past. Sea-based power, for example, offers political advantages not possessed by the stationing of ground troops and air units on foreign soil.

We can discern some things which will probably remain good guide-lines even amid these uncertainties. Readiness will always be an essential requirement for our future military forces. A highly advanced state of technology and a broad industrial base are no longer a sufficient foundation for the projection of armed force to back up foreign policy. Never again can this nation expect to be allowed the time to start mobilization after a crisis has already developed. Today our contingency plans call for immediate deployment of forces in being or capable of being called up within sixty to ninety days at most. This condition assumes a really ready reserve force and existing stocks of equipment. Mobilization plans for civilian training and conversion of commercial production will not suffice.

Further, there must always be a balance in the U.S. power base. We should never again have troops without modern equipment, or units immobilized by lack of airlift, or ground forces unprotected by air cover. At all times, the complexion and shape of the U.S. forces must reflect the forward thrust of military technology and be sensitive to quick shifts in the power equation. In the past, our military doctrines have too often been out of focus with the political realities at the moment. This lack of balance has existed even under relatively static conditions such as we cannot hope for in the future.

In view of the prospect that such a major reshaping of the military and political situation faces the United States in the years immediately ahead, the wisdom and appropriateness of our defense policies may be tested more severely than ever before. Indeed, as suggested earlier, the need for restraint and firmness, for the pursuit of both political stability and military security, for both resistance to aggression and an unfailing search for an honorable *détente*— all this complexity merely reflects the complexity of the world we must live in and reminds us that the ability of democratic governments to act rationally and effectively to preserve themselves is itself in question.

EIGHT

FREEMAN J. DYSON

Defense Against Ballistic Missiles

[Editor's Note: As James Schlesinger's article indicates (see above, Chapter 4), one of the major problems in national security policy is to define the boundary-line between the technical expert and the policy-maker. The process of technological change can produce dilemmas in which technical feasibility turns out to be the least significant aspect. When scientific change brings in its train major strategic and political upheavals, the scientific expert can, by default or by a transfer of expertise from one field to another, shape national policy in a major way. Much of the strategic debate has been conducted by scientists whose entry into the field came through a consideration of the technical aspects of particular weapons systems.

This article by Professor Dyson, a British physicist who has lived and worked in the United States since the late 1940's, illustrates this point. Starting from a demonstration of the technical feasibility of an anti-ballistic missile system, Professor Dyson goes on to argue the political and strategic undesirability of such a program. It is Professor Dyson's view that an anti-ballistic missile program will upset the strategic and political balance in a way that will outweigh any military benefits. Nevertheless, Professor Dyson is somewhat fatalistic about the future. He feels that the technical feasibility of an anti-ballistic missile program and the likelihood of Soviet progress in that area will eventually force us to enter this aspect of the arms race.]

Wise men have been saying consistently since 1945 that there is no defense against nuclear weapons. This statement does not mean that it is impossible to shoot down an airplane that may happen to be carrying an atomic bomb. The statement means that no defense

EDITOR'S NOTE: Reprinted with permission from the *Bulletin of the Atomic Scientists*, June, 1964. Copyright 1964 by the Educational Foundation for Nuclear Science, Inc., 935 East 60th Street, Chicago, Illinois 60637.

would be lasting, or proof against countermeasures, or reliable enough to offer a country any real security from nuclear destruction. Interpreted in this sense, the statement is still true and is likely to remain true in the future.

Although the prospect of any absolute defense is remote, the race to develop means for shooting down nuclear-weapon carriers continues vigorously. The United States and the Soviet Union have deployed enormous systems of surface-to-air missiles to protect cities and military bases against bombing airplanes. Now that the main offensive threat is shifting from airplanes to ballistic missiles, the engineers on both sides have designed and built prototype anti-missile missiles which can intercept and destroy offensive missiles.

Although missiles are immensely more difficult to hit than airplanes, the defensive systems have had some substantial successes. Problems that ten years ago seemed unapproachably difficult are now either solved or close to being solved. The builders of anti-missile systems do not claim to provide absolute defense, but they can now justifiably claim to be able to provide a partial defense, a defense which would make some significant difference to the strategic balance. In some special circumstances (for example, in case of an accidental attack by a small number of missiles), a defense system might well be able to save the attacked cities and thus prevent a general holocaust.

The development of defensive systems has now reached the point at which serious decisions have to be made. It is not enough to repeat the slogan "there is no defense" and leave it at that. Engineers now offer us systems which have a definite, although limited, military effectiveness. Until now, all the work on anti-missile missiles has been developmental—that is, design and construction of prototype models only. The question which now faces us is whether to deploy—that is, whether to build an operational system for the actual defense of our cities. The existing development program is costing us about half a billion dollars a year; a deployment program would be at least ten times as expensive. Almost everybody agrees that the development program should be continued. The controversy centers around the question of deployment.

A most important factor in the situation is the attitude of the Soviet Government. We know that there has been a massive and sophisticated Soviet program for the development of anti-missile missiles. Khrushchev and other Soviet leaders have frequently boasted of the successes of this program, and have implied that it would lead to the deployment of an operational defense. The nature and time-scale of such a deployment have never been clearly stated. There have been several newspaper reports to the effect that an operational anti-missile system already exists around Leningrad. Whether or not these reports are true, the Soviet Government is probably still hesitating to deploy a massive system all over the U.S.S.R. Any decision by either side to deploy defenses will undoubtedly react strongly on the other.

In addition to the anti-missile missile systems which have been designed and tested, other more exotic forms of defense against ballistic missiles are conceivable. Some exotic systems aim to destroy the missiles on their way up, soon after take-off, and others are supposed to destroy missiles without using defensive nuclear warheads. It is characteristic of exotic systems that they probably do not work at all, but if by any chance they do work they may be spectacularly better than conventional systems. In considering the future of ballistic missiles beyond the next five years, it is most important to keep the possibility of exotic defenses in mind. In this paper, the phrase "anti-missile missile," or ABM, will mean a conventional defense system, while the phrase "ballistic missile defense," or BMD, will include both conventional and exotic methods. The central problem which will be discussed is whether in any foreseeable circumstances the deployment of BMD by the United States would be necessary or advantageous to our security. So far as the immediate future is concerned, the only kind of BMD deployment which is under consideration is an ABM deployment.

The decision to deploy BMD must be considered as an indivisible one. The technical, military, and political factors involved in the decision cannot be clearly separated. Nevertheless, it is convenient in this discussion to make such a separation. Thus, the next three sections will be concerned with technical, military, and political questions, respectively. In the final section, an attempt will be made to summarize the argument and arrive at some balanced conclusion.

TECHNICAL FACTORS

The most important factor for the layman to understand about the technology of BMD is that the race between offensive and defensive systems is a never-ending one. If at any time the defense stood still and committed itself to a fixed Maginot Line system, the offensive could quickly find means to penetrate the defense. If at any time the offense stood still and committed itself to a fixed "finite deterrence" system, the defense could, though more slowly and with much greater difficulty, find means to nullify the offense. As long as research and development in the field of BMD continue, whether or not any BMD systems are actually deployed, there can be no final stabilization of strategic weapons.

Neither side need hope or fear that a "solution" of the BMD problem may be found, if a "solution" means a scientific invention which could reliably destroy all incoming missiles. The only kind of "solution" which is in prospect is a defensive deployment whose capability will be limited but increasing with time. At any particular time, a sufficiently massive attack will be able to overwhelm the defense and reliably destroy the defended targets.

The last five years have been a historically exceptional period in which the technology of offensive weapons (missiles) so far outstripped the technology of defense that many people fell into the habit of thinking of the supremacy of the offensive as permanent and automatic. Defensive technology is now beginning to catch up. In the future, the supremacy of the offensive will not be automatic. In the future, we shall have a strategic choice, either to devote such efforts to the improvement of our offensive weapons as will maintain their effectiveness in spite of Soviet defenses, or to attempt to upset the supremacy of the offensive by building defenses ourselves. This is the essential content of the decision which is confronting us. Until we can establish an international control over military research and development, the choice of stopping the technological arms race does not seem to be open to us. We have only a choice between two different ways of conducting the arms race.

Another important technical fact about BMD is that it is monstrously expensive. Exotic BMD appears to be just as bad as ordinary ABM in this respect. Prices quoted for a complete system intended to protect a big country range from $10 billion to $100 billion, the high figure being the more realistic.

More crucial than the absolute cost of a BMD system is the relative cost of the system when compared with the cost of an offensive system which would nullify its effect. Many studies have been made of the economic balance in a hypothetical arms race between defense on one side and offense on the other. In almost all such studies, the offense has a clear advantage. Unfortunately, the "rules of the game" must be chosen arbitrarily. One possible rule, which gives to the defense the benefit of many doubts, is to assume that the defense will destroy any target which it can detect and engage.

In this case, the offense cannot defeat the defense by cleverness but must rely on sheer force of numbers. The offensive response to a given defense system is to build more offensive missiles than the defense has ammunition to engage. Under these unfavorable conditions, the offense is still substantially cheaper than the defense, so long as the numbers of weapons are comparable with their present levels. If the numbers of weapons on both sides were enormously increased, the economic advantage would tend to swing over to the defense, but just in this case of very large numbers the rule of 100 per cent effective "kill" of engaged targets seems particularly unrealistic. Economic prognostications in the technological sphere are notoriously unreliable, but the result of all the economic studies has been to make the deployment of BMD look unattractive in two distinct ways. First, BMD itself appears wastefully expensive. Second, deployment of BMD would be likely to stimulate a large increase of offensive forces on both sides, with no gain to the security of either.

A further technical fact concerning BMD is its close connection with civil defense. The immediate decision which must be soon taken in the U.S. is whether or not to deploy a specific ABM system which is called Nike-X. For various technical reasons, the Nike-X system does not do well, even on paper, unless it is supplemented by a massive civil-defense program.

On this subject, McNamara spoke very explicitly in testimony before the House Armed Services Committee on January 27, 1964:

> In the absence of adequate fallout shelters, an active defense might not significantly increase the proportion of the population surviving an "all-out" nuclear attack. Offensive missiles could easily be targeted at points outside the defended area and thereby achieve by fallout what otherwise would have to be achieved by blast and heat effects. . . . Moreover, before we make the huge investment required for the deployment of an ABM defense system, we must carefully consider what additional civil defense measures might be required for the population. The effectiveness of the Nike-X system against attacks employing decoys would vary with the altitude at which the incoming warheads must be engaged. The lower the altitude, the better the chances of discrimination, but the greater the chance that the weapon might be detonated before it is intercepted. But the lower the altitude at which the weapon is detonated, the higher the blast and thermal effects on the ground for any given yield. Thus, to the extent that we can protect the population against the blast and heat of a nuclear explosion, we can wait longer before

engaging an enemy missile and can thus be surer that we engage the warhead, not a decoy.

The Nike-X system thus requires both fallout shelters and blast shelters for the defended population. The same weakness will exist in any BMD system which defends local areas rather than an entire country. The high yield of probable Soviet warheads makes this problem particularly acute for American BMD systems.

There are many reasons for considering massive civil defense programs to be unwise and dangerous. It would require too long a digression to discuss the problems of civil defense adequately here. Suffice it to say two things: first, the cost of blast shelters for the U.S. urban population is comparable with the cost of a major BMD system. Second, the combination of BMD with massive civil defense would require very extensive participation of the civilian population in quasi-military activities. In the U.S., the preparation of the population for disciplined use of a massive shelter program could possibly have profound effects on the internal political balance of the country, tending to convert us into what the strategists call a "hard society." The meaning of the phrase "hard society" is that a whole population may be trained and hardened in a spirit of unquestioning obedience in order to withstand a nuclear attack, just as a missile silo is hardened by encasing it in a certain thickness of concrete. In the U.S.S.R., the social effects of a massive civil defense and BMD program would probably be less serious, since Soviet society is already highly disciplined on a local level and is in a certain sense already "hard."

MILITARY FACTORS

In making any military assessment of BMD, it is first of all necessary to have some idea of the kind of military situations with which BMD is supposed to deal. On the U.S. side, we know fairly well what these situations are. We are concerned primarily with a possible thermonuclear war in which the U.S. and the U.S.S.R. attack each other in full fury during a brief period of a few days or weeks. It is generally assumed that the war is over after this brief exchange of fire, either because the U.S.S.R. has been so completely destroyed that no further organized military operations are possible, or because the threat of such complete destruction has persuaded the surviving Soviet leaders to accept American terms of peace. This

American picture of thermonuclear war we shall call the "short-war" doctrine. It has the important consequence of making war appear to be more accurately predictable now than it has been in the historical past. The outcome of the war is essentially determined by the outcome of the initial attacks, and the outcome of the initial attacks is calculable if the numbers and performance of the weapons on both sides are known.

The short-war doctrine has a wide acceptance among American civilian strategists. It makes possible the elaborate and quantitative military analyses which are their stock in trade. American military men are often more skeptical, and incline to a more old-fashioned view of war. The professional soldier is less impressed by electronic computations and more impressed by the historical accidents which caused German short-war strategies to fail disastrously in 1914 and again in 1941.

Whether the American short-war doctrine is true or false we shall not attempt to decide. The vital point, upon which no doubt can exist, is that this doctrine cannot give a correct basis for understanding Soviet policy. Any Soviet strategist who is not an out-and-out defeatist must repudiate the short-war doctrine. And indeed we find, for example, in the recently translated volume *Military Strategy*, edited by Marshal Sokolovsky,* that the Soviet picture of war is quite different.

The Soviet doctrine is almost exclusively long-war in its emphasis. Future war is envisioned as differing only in severity but not in essence from past wars. Soviet military leaders are still dominated in their thinking by the experiences of World War II in which they rose to prominence. They think of a future war as beginning with a devastating nuclear exchange launched by the crazy and power-mad imperialists, but this first exchange will not destroy the Soviet people or end the war. After absorbing the terrible losses of the first attack, the two sides will continue to fight to the best of their ability with whatever they have left. The war will then pass into a long and messy phase in which the traditional Russian strategy of attrition and endurance will be employed. In the long run, the superior will power and discipline of the Russian people, aided by the geography of their country, will prevail as they prevailed in 1812 and in 1945.

The difference between short-war and long-war doctrines has a decisive effect on any assessment of the military usefulness of

* EDITOR'S NOTE: Marshal V. D. Sokolovsky, ed., *Military Strategy: Soviet Doctrine and Concepts* (New York, 1963).

BMD. For advocates of short-war doctrine, the aim of analysis is to make war into something calculable, and the unpredictability of BMD is a grave disadvantage. Short-war analysts also take seriously the results of calculations which indicate that BMD would be militarily less useful than offensive forces of equal cost. For both these reasons, the consensus among American civilian strategists is against the deployment of BMD.

For Soviet military men, who live by the long-war doctrine, the situation is quite different. These men do not believe that war is calculable in the first place. After all, if they had stopped to calculate the chances of a successful Soviet defense in 1941, they would probably have found it hopeless. Their picture of war is of a desperate chaos, where the only way out is to fight as hard as possible with whatever weapons happen to be available. It makes no sense to them to try to calculate whether a BMD system would be useful under such conditions. Against sporadic and uncoordinated attacks in the later phases of a long war, a BMD system might prove to be extremely effective, especially after the defending crews have had time to learn by experience and to improvise tactics accordingly. For believers in long-war doctrine, defensive weapons gain in value as the quality of the offense is degraded, and therefore the deployment of BMD may seem to be a sound military investment. This is the point of view which probably prevails in the Soviet military establishment. It is not surprising to find similar views held by senior officers of the U.S. Army, the men who would in fact have operational responsibility for Nike-X if it were deployed.

The last military factor to be considered here is the effect of BMD deployment on strategic stability. By stability is meant a situation in which neither side is tempted to an unprovoked attack on the other by hopes of a cheap victory. Among American civilian strategists and, in particular, among experts on arms control, the notion of stability has come to be identified with the notion of the supremacy of the offensive. It has become a dogma that the maintenance of stability demands the existence of invulnerable and irresistible retaliatory offensive forces. Each side must be deterred from a first strike by the threat of an immediate and irresistible second strike. This dogma, equating stability with mutual vulnerability, has the consequence that deterrence and defense are regarded as incompatible. A country which deploys BMD is expressing a serious intention to make itself invulnerable, and is thus automatically threatening to upset stability. This reasoning has led the majority of American civilian experts to oppose violently the deployment of BMD by either side. The debate on the ratification of the atmospheric test-ban treaty showed very strikingly the intensity of the fear aroused in Americans by Soviet BMD deployment.

The incompatibility of deterrence and defense is, however, only valid if short-war doctrines are accepted. In a short war, the only possible deterrence is the threat of immediate retaliation, but the Russians have never considered that deterrence rests primarily on the results of a single strategic exchange. In the Russian view, deterrence of war rests ultimately on the capacity and determination of the U.S.S.R. to drag a war out into a long struggle of attrition, in which the traditional Russian defensive strategies can operate successfully. Nobody is likely to begin a war which he knows he cannot finish. Soviet experts who accept the long-war doctrine find no incompatibility between this kind of deterrence and a reliance on the most modern defensive weapon systems, including BMD.

It is particularly unfortunate that the divergence between American and Soviet doctrines of deterrence is increased by purely linguistic misunderstandings. The Russians translate the English word "deterrence" by "ustrashenie," which in its emotional connotations is much closer to our word "blackmail" than to "deterrence." It is thus totally naïve to suppose that any Soviet leader could be persuaded to forego "defense" for the sake of preserving "deterrence." Attempts from our side to pressure the Soviet government into abandoning deployment of BMD would almost certainly backfire.

POLITICAL FACTORS

The political factors involved in deployment of BMD are mostly internal to the countries concerned. Let us look first at the political aspects of BMD in the U.S.

It is generally agreed among the experts that a limited or token deployment of BMD in the U.S. would be politically impossible. It is difficult to imagine the Congress voting large sums of money for the defense of New York and Washington while leaving Detroit and San Diego out in the cold. For internal political reasons, the minimum deployment that is judged to be feasible would cover 50 or 100 cities and would cost at least several tens of billions of dollars. It is this all-or-nothing quality that makes the decision to deploy BMD so crucial. The usual practice when a new military weapon is introduced is to build first a few, to see how well they work, and then decide whether to build a lot more. Only in the case of BMD is this gradual approach excluded. A decision to deploy

BMD will commit the U.S. immediately to a vast and probably permanent addition to our military establishment.

A decision not to deploy will of course not have the same irrevocable character. For example, a negative decision made in 1905 could be reversed in 1970. However, there are reasons why a negative decision is unlikely to be reversed rapidly. The main reason is that any particular BMD system becomes technically ripe for deployment at a certain date and is then superseded by a newer one. For example, the Nike-Zeus ABM system became ripe for deployment in 1961, but the decision was then made not to deploy it; nobody would think now of reviving Nike-Zeus, since the much better Nike-X system will soon be available. The next two years will be crucial for deciding whether to deploy Nike-X. If the decision is again negative, it will be several years before the designs for the next generation of ABM systems are ready.

Another political factor influencing BMD in the U.S. is interservice rivalry. The Nike ABM program has been the pride of the U.S. Army. The U.S. Air Force takes an equal pride in the ability of its offensive missiles to penetrate Soviet ABM defenses. The political struggle for and against U.S. deployment of BMD occasionally degenerates into a squabble between Army and Air Force vested interests. However, there is no evidence that these interests have played any improper part in the decisions which have been made heretofore. Since in the U.S., the Air Force is the most influential of the three services, the effect of inter-service rivalry tends to be favorable to offensive missile systems and adverse to BMD.

We now turn to consider internal political aspects of BMD in the U.S.S.R. We find here, even more than in the technical and military aspects, profound differences between Soviet and American preoccupations. First of all, the Soviet leaders do not need to worry about treating all their cities fairly. They may decide to defend Leningrad only, or Leningrad and Moscow only, or any other selection of cities. So they are able to deploy BMD gradually, as any rational military man would wish to do, without committing themselves at once to a countrywide program.

The effects of inter-service rivalry are probably greater in the U.S.S.R. than here, and certainly work in the opposite direction so far as BMD is concerned. In the U.S.S.R., the defensive commands, particularly the Army and Air Defense commands, have acquired the big budgets and the political pull which in the U.S. have gone to the offensive Strategic Air Command. The men in the Soviet establishment who correspond to our General LeMay are mostly graduates of army artillery. All through the 1950's, the U.S.S.R. spent a major part of its military budget in building up an enormous system of defenses against manned bombers, starting with anti-aircraft guns and ending with sophisticated ground-to-air missiles. During this period, the Soviet offensive forces remained unexpectedly small and were comparatively starved of funds. It was inevitable that, when the external threat began to change from manned bombers to missiles, the huge and prestigious defense command should turn its attention to BMD. It was likewise inevitable that Khrushchev should support large investments in BMD, unless he was prepared to overturn the balance of power within his own military establishment. Thus, the status of BMD is quite different in the two countries. In the U.S., a decision to deploy BMD would be a major disturbance of the internal *status quo*; in the U.S.S.R., a decision not to deploy would probably be an equally great disturbance. In both cases, the disturbance may be made to occur, but the forces of inertia work against it.

The last political aspect of BMD which shall be considered here is its use as a weapon of bluff. Any BMD system is admirably suited for bluffing purposes, since nobody will ever know, short of a major war, how good or bad the system really is. It is possible to imagine a successful bluff based on plywood dummies of BMD installations.

The problem of bluff introduces yet another divergence between American and Soviet attitudes to BMD. Serious bluff is impossible for the U. S. Government to maintain. Congress and the press compel the U.S. Government to play its cards openly. As usual, the American public has converted this necessity into a virtue and has come to regard American openness as morally right and Soviet secrecy as morally wrong. Thus, most Americans become highly offended and antagonistic when they find that they have been the victims of a Soviet bluff.

The Soviet regime, on the other hand, has a long tradition of the successful use of bluff. Indeed, the original seizure of power by the Bolsheviks in 1917 was defended by nothing else. In more recent times, the U.S.S.R. has consistently exploited its advanced weapons for psychological purposes. There were public displays of massed parachutist landings in the 1930's and public displays of advanced jet bombers in the 1950's. The most spectacular example of the political use of weapons was the demonstration of the Soviet ICBM capability by means of the first Sputnik in 1957. In each case, the U.S.S.R. took the opportunity provided by a new weapon to make an impressive show of strength. The weapons displayed were in fact prototypes, but the general public naturally assumed that they were in mass production and would soon be available in large numbers. In this way, the Soviet leaders have been able to exaggerate their military strength and to distract attention from their weaknesses. The existence of rigid internal secrecy has made such tactics possible and effective.

The Soviet emphasis on BMD is entirely consistent with the tradition of defense by bluff. In this connection, it is significant that Khrushchev has said he wanted to make public a film showing a test of his ABM but that his advisors persuaded him not to do it. Presumably this indicates a difference between Khrushchev thinking of the weapon mainly in political terms and the advisors being more seriously concerned with its military function.

The danger of the Soviet habit of defense by bluff is that it usually succeeds too well. The ICBM bluff of 1957–60 succeeded so well that the U.S. was frightened into building an ICBM force far larger than the actual Soviet force. There is a corresponding danger that the Soviet ABM bluff will frighten us into another exaggerated response. The response this time might be either the counter-deployment of a massive ABM system on our side, or a further large expansion of our offensive forces. In either case, our response would no doubt force the U.S.S.R. to make a correspondingly large counter-response. Force levels on both sides would increase rapidly, and their growing destructive capabilities would soon outweigh any possible saving of lives that might be expected from the ABM systems. An intensified arms race of this character could never bring us security but would lead only to increased fear, frustration, and danger.

It would, of course, be a splendid thing for everybody if the U.S.S.R. would give up the habit of bluff and the secrecy that goes with it. But the chance of this happening is remote. It is therefore up to us in the West to learn to live with Soviet bluffing, to avoid exaggerated reactions, and to understand that bluffing usually conceals weakness rather than strength.

CONCLUSION

A consistent pattern emerges from this discussion of technical, military, and political factors. For many and diverse reasons, Soviet military and political leaders find the deployment of an ABM system convenient and reassuring to their feelings of security. For equally diverse reasons, deployment of ABM in the U.S. would be neither convenient nor reassuring to us. It is therefore logical to expect that, as time goes on, a Soviet ABM system will be deployed whereas an American ABM system will not. Such a course of events would answer to the objective needs of both countries. American security would be assured by an invulnerable retaliatory missile force equipped with the most modern penetration aids, and Soviet security would be assured by the possession of the most modern defensive weapons combined with modest offensive forces.

It may seem paradoxical that the U.S.S.R. should derive security from a defense system, at the same time as we derive security from being able to penetrate their defense. The paradox is not real, because the meaning of security on the two sides is different. On our side, security is adequately protected if the analytical computations of thermonuclear exchanges indicate that enough of our second-strike force will certainly penetrate the Soviet defenses. On their side, security is adequately protected if the Soviet armed forces have the finest weapons that anybody knows how to build, irrespective of paper calculations.

Unfortunately, there is one obstacle to the achievement of this objectively tolerable situation. The obstacle is the intense political pressure that exists in both countries to duplicate whatever the other side does. It will require unprecedented self-restraint for the American people to accept a Soviet ABM deployment and not embark on a much bigger deployment in response.

Supporters and opponents of American BMD deployment all agree that a vigorous program of BMD research and development must be maintained. Our own BMD development program is of vital importance in learning how to build offensive missiles that will penetrate Soviet defenses. Therefore, the more we resist BMD deployment and put our trust in our offensive weapons, the more we should continue BMD development. Another good reason for continuing with BMD development is, of course, the uncertainty of all technical predictions. Although the technical outlook for BMD at present looks dim, it is always possible that in the 1970's or later a really satisfactory and effective defense system will emerge. If this should happen, we would then be free to deploy such a system. The essential point is that any American decision to deploy a BMD system should be made only when a careful review of military, economic, and political circumstances clearly indicates that a defensive deployment would be of greater value to the security of the United States than other programs of equal cost. We should not deploy merely because the Russians have done so, or because we believe that the Russians may be about to do so. Our decision to deploy, if we ever take it, should be based upon our own analysis of our own interests, not upon a panicky reaction to Russian moves or boasts.

Heretofore, the American people has always viewed the Soviet ABM program as intensely threatening to its security. The fear of Soviet ABM, as shown for example in the recent test-ban debate, seems to be more deeply felt than the fear of Soviet offensive forces. The fear of Soviet ABM is rationalized by the following syllogism: we decided not to deploy Nike-Zeus because we calculated that it could not defend us from a full-scale Soviet attack; the U.S.S.R. decided to deploy an ABM system; therefore, the Soviet ABM system must be technically far ahead of Nike-Zeus and must be capable of nullifying the American second-strike forces. This logic has led many people in the Senate and elsewhere to consider the Soviet ABM program as primarily intended to allow the Soviet Union to attack the U.S. without fear of retaliation.

The Soviet ABM program cannot, in fact, be technically capable of fulfilling such a purpose. There is no black magic in ABM technology, and we know enough about the Soviet system to set reliable upper limits to its possible performance. Also, from everything we have seen of Soviet military and political motivations, it is easy to find many reasons for a Soviet ABM deployment other than an intention to commit aggression on the grand scale. The syllogism is false because the decision of the U.S.S.R. to deploy an ABM system would not be based upon theoretical calculations of effectiveness of the kind which we used in evaluating Nike-Zeus.

The present policy of the U.S. is to keep a careful watch on Soviet ABM activities and to equip our offensive missile forces with such penetration aids as may be necessary to ensure their effectiveness. This policy can and should be maintained in the future. So long as it is maintained, there is no reason why we should consider the Soviet ABM deployment to be threatening to us. Indeed, we ought to feel glad if the U.S.S.R. devotes its resources to an ABM system instead of enlarging offensive missile forces which threaten us directly.

The crucial problem that remains is to convince the American Congress and public that Soviet ABM systems are not necessarily a deadly threat. The American people must become accustomed to the idea that they may be better off without an ABM system, even if the Soviet people believe they are better off with one. Perhaps this re-education of the American people cannot be achieved without some help from the Soviet Government. For example, some unmistakable evidence of restraint in Soviet ABM procurement would help a great deal. With or without such help, we must do the best we can.

PART II

Alliances in the Nuclear Age

In the past, alliances have been created for three basic reasons: (1) To provide an accretion of power. With conventional weapons, overwhelming power could generally be assembled only by way of coalition. The wider the alliance, the greater its power to resist aggression. (2) To leave no doubt about the alignment of forces. It has often been argued that, had Germany known at the beginning of both world wars that the United States—or even England— would join the war, aggression would have been averted. (3) To express as a formal obligation what may otherwise be an inchoate interest in mutual assistance.

To be sure, even before the advent of nuclear weapons, there was some inconsistency among these requirements. The attempt to combine the maximum number of states for joint action occasionally conflicted with the desire to leave no doubt about the collective motivation; the wider the system of collective security, the more various were the motives animating it and the more difficult the task of obtaining common action. The more embracing the alliance, the more intense and direct the threat had to be that would produce a united response.

This traditional difficulty has been compounded in the nuclear age. Nuclear war requires tight command and control of all weapons. This is to some degree inconsistent with a coalition of sovereign states. Moreover, the enormous risks of nuclear warfare affect the credibility of traditional pledges of mutual assistance. Traditionally, alliances have been operative because it was believed that the *immediate* risk of conflict was less than the *ultimate* danger of facing a preponderant enemy alone. But when nuclear war risks the lives of tens of millions, some allies may consider the outbreak of a war the worst contingency and, in time of crisis, act accordingly.

As a result, many theories of nuclear control have a tendency either to turn alliances into a unilateral U.S. guarantee or to call into question their utility altogether. American strategic thought verges on the first extreme; some French theorists have hinted at the second.

As for the United States, official spokesmen have consistently emphasized that the European contribution to the over-all nuclear strength of the NATO alliance is negligible. The United States has made various proposals for nuclear sharing; the common feature of these has been the retention of the United States veto over the nuclear weapons of the alliance—a tendency well exemplified in writings by Albert Wohlstetter, Malcolm Hoag, and Robert Bowie. (See below, Chapters 10, 11, and 12, pp. 186 ff., 213 ff., and 237 ff.)

However sensible such schemes may appear from the point of view of division of labor, they would perpetuate American hegemony in nuclear matters. Allies are considered necessary not so much to add to over-all strength as to provide the ability for applying power discriminately. Allies are useful because they permit resistance to aggression by means less cataclysmic than all-out war. In such a structure, American decisions must continue to be paramount. The nuclear weapons have to remain under central control, which in effect means American control.

According to the opposing view, alliances have lost their significance altogether. The French theorist General Pierre M. Gallois argues, for example, that nuclear weapons have made alliances obsolete. (See below, Chapter 13, pp. 264 ff.) Faced with the risk of total destruction, no nation will jeopardize its survival for another. Hence, he maintains, each country must have its own nuclear arsenal to defend itself against direct attack, while leaving all other countries to their fate.

This formula would mark the end of collective security and would be likely to lead to international chaos. In the face of the growing nuclear arsenals of the major protagonists, it would be idle to deny that the threat of nuclear retaliation has lost some of its credibility. The Gallois theory would transform a degree of uncertainty, however, into a guarantee that the United States would *not* come to the assistance of its allies, thus greatly simplifying an aggressor's calculation.

The preponderance of nuclear power in the hands of the United States poses one set of problems; the range of modern weapons raises another. In the past, a threatened country had the choice of either resisting or surrendering. If it resisted, it had to be prepared to accept the consequences in terms of physical damage and loss of life. A distant ally could generally be helpful only if it was able to bring its strength to bear in the area of conflict.

Modern weapons have changed this. What each member country wants from the alliance is the assurance that an attack on it will be considered a *casus belli*. It strives for deterrence by adding a distant ally's strength to its own. But, equally, each state has an incentive to reduce damage to itself to a minimum, should deterrence fail. For the first time, the range of modern weapons provides the technical possibility of combining these objectives. In 1914, Belgium could not base its defense on a strategy that transferred to Great Britain the primary risks of devastation. In the age of intercontinental rockets, this is technically feasible.

Part of the strategic dispute within the Western alliance, therefore, involves jockeying to determine which geographic area will be the theater of war if deterrence fails (though this obviously cannot be made explicit). A conventional war confined to Europe inevitably will appear in a different light to Americans than to Europeans who remember the casualty lists of two world wars and on whose territory such a war would be fought. (On this point, see the essay below by Bernard Brodie "What Price Conventional Capabilities in Europe?" Chapter 15, pp. 313 ff.) A nuclear exchange that spares their territory may seem to them a more attractive strategy and the threat of nuclear retaliation a more effective deterrent. Although the interests of the alliance may be indivisible in an ultimate sense, this does not guarantee that there will not be sharply clashing perceptions about methods to reach common objectives.

Thus, the pressures of the new technology run counter to traditional notions of national sovereignty. The risks of nuclear warfare may be too great to be combined reliably with what has heretofore been considered a key attribute of sovereignty: the unilateral right of a sovereign state to alter its strategic or political views.

The nature of alliances has changed in yet another way. In the past, one reason for joining an alliance was to impose an additional obligation for assistance in time of need. Were each country's national interests completely unambiguous, it would know precisely on whose assistance it could count; a formal commitment would be unnecessary. Both the aggressor and the defender would understand what they would confront and could act accordingly. Wars could not be caused by a misunderstanding of intentions. They would occur only if the protagonists calculated the existing power relationships differently.

Traditionally, however, the national interest has not been unambiguous. Often, the aggressor did not know which countries would ultimately be lined up against it; in 1914, Germany was genuinely surprised by Great Britain's reaction to the invasion of Belgium. Occasionally, the defenders could not be certain of the extent of their potential support—as was the case with the allies in both wars regarding U.S. participation. Historically, the existence of a tacit or explicit understanding on this point has often been the determining factor in the decision to go to war. In the decade prior to World War I, the staff talks between Great Britain and France that led to the transfer of the French fleet to the Mediterranean were one of the key factors in Britain's decision to enter the conflict in August, 1914. (Thus, the talks achieved one objective of traditional alliances: to commit Great Britain to the defense of France. They failed in another: to make the alignment clear to the potential aggressor.)

One of the distinguishing features of the present period is that ideology and technology have combined to produce a global confrontation. This, in turn, has rendered the national interest of the major antagonists less ambiguous. Neither the United States nor the Soviet Union can permit a major advance by its opponent, regardless of whether the area in which it occurs is formally protected by an alliance or not. Neutral India was no less assured of American assistance when Communist China attacked it than Pakistan, allied with the United States, would have been in similar circumstances. In these conditions, the distinctions between allies and neutrals is likely to diminish. A country gains little from being allied and risks little by being neutral.

Inevitably, this results in the weakening of allied cohesion, producing what some have described as polycentrism. But polycentrism does not reflect so much the emergence of new centers of physical power as the attempt by allies to establish new centers of decision.

The gap in military strength between the United States and its European allies has in fact widened, not narrowed, in the past decade. What *has* changed is the use to which the power can be put. On the one hand, the enormous risks of nuclear warfare call into question traditional pledges of formal assistance. On the other hand, the issues with respect to which nuclear threats *are* credible are so clear-cut as not to seem to require reinforcement by formal undertakings. Polycentrism is on the rise not because the world has ceased to be bipolar, but because with respect to nuclear weapons it essentially remains so. When allies became convinced that their actions cannot fundamentally affect the circumstances in which the

United States might be prepared to resort to use of its nuclear weapons, the American commitment need not be purchased by conciliation and cannot be jeopardized by intransigence—within very wide limits, at least.

Thus, more and more allies see little risk and considerable potential gain in political independence. In a curious way, it is possible that they can add the senior partner's power to their own, even for measures contradictory to those of the senior partner. Although, traditionally, a state's diplomatic influence corresponded roughly to its military strength, this is no longer inevitably the case. Influence can now be achieved by using another country's protection even for policies not in accord with its preferences.

NINE

THOMAS C. SCHELLING

Nuclears, NATO and the "New Strategy"

[Editor's Note: Professor Schelling's essay deals with one of the major areas of national security policy: the debate within the Atlantic Alliance about nuclear weapons and strategy. It examines the relationship of nuclear delivery systems to various prevalent concepts of national interest and international relations. These systems are treated as counters in a bargaining process involving not only potential enemies but also traditional allies. Professor Schelling's dominant thesis is that the members of the Atlantic Alliance are subject to two contradictory pressures: as individual nations, they are tempted to try to achieve maximum freedom of action; yet, the Alliance can be effective only if there is a measure of mutual responsibility.

Because, in the early 1950's, Western Europe was too weak to pursue independence, the illusion was created that the Atlantic Alliance had escaped tensions inherent in other coalitions. But the political and economic recovery of Western Europe has made the coordination of autonomous military policies one of the key problems of the Atlantic Alliance. Because each member of the Alliance pursues simultaneously somewhat contradictory purposes, an effective strategy depends on the ability to achieve some consensus on strategic doctrine. Professor Schelling deals with the background and strategic components of American policy, emphasizing that just as the European members of NATO have individual as well as collective interests, the United States has strategic responsibilities and capabilities that overlap, but do not coincide with, those of its NATO partners. (See also below, Chapter 18.)]

I

Many Europeans appear puzzled about present American military policy. And most Americans appear willing to straighten them out. What I want to try is to sort out the main lines of thought that lie *behind* American policies. Some of these can be discerned in public statements directed toward Europeans; some can be heard when Americans talk among themselves; and some can be perceived in what the American Government does with its military force. It is particularly easy to be confused by the several strands of American policy if it is not recognized that they *are* separate strands.

One reason for confusion is that Americans—commentators as well as officials—often fail to distinguish between a valid argument and a strong one. In making a good point, we often argue as though it were a decisive one. Many Europeans are understandably wary of accepting some fundamental idea that has been used as an argument, for fear it commits them to the conclusions that were associated with it. And there is probably some tendency for Europeans to suppose that all the components of American policy that *apply* to Europe reflect American policy *toward* Europe.

It is helpful to remember that there is an important alliance other than NATO involved in American decisions. It is the "alliance" known as the American Government. As in NATO itself, there is probably no single mind in the government that contains a blueprint of "present American policy." It is often evident that in the American Government—probably in any government—busy officials can agree on a policy (or on language to describe policy) without agreeing on the reasons for it or the premises that underlie it.

Whole strategies, furthermore, get described by a single word— often some descriptive catchword that magnifies some part of the strategy. Strategies change, names often stick. "Counter-force," "no-cities," "controlled response," and "conventional strategy" are among the current names. It is unlikely that these terms can be anything more than a popular shorthand. It is equally unlikely that, within a government, responsible officials share a common interpretation of these terms. Communication is not perfect even within

EDITOR'S NOTE: Slightly different versions of this paper appeared as "Les armements nucléaires, l'OTAN et la nouvelle strategie,'" *Politique Étrangère*, No. 2, 1963, pp. 114–40; and "Wie neu ist die 'neue Strategie' der Vereinigten Staaten?", *Europa-Archiv*, No. 15, August, 1963, pp. 551–64. Reprinted with permission of the author and publishers.

a government, if only because there are but twenty-four hours in a day.

Finally, many disputes over nuclear arrangements in Europe are not mainly concerned with military strategy vis-à-vis the Soviet Union. There is a tendency, though, on both sides of the Atlantic, to argue nuclear arrangements in the traditional terminology of deterrence and defense—whether the American deterrent has lost credibility, whether an independent French force will patch a hole in the deterrent posture. These issues of current military strategy—of military posture vis-à-vis the Soviet Union in the 1960's—are often, however, of secondary importance in the motivation of European governments. Neither American nor European arguments about nuclear arrangements will penetrate to the real problems so long as we act as though the main issues involve military relations with the Soviet Union in the 1960's, rather than political relations within the alliance in the 1970's.

Let me put this bluntly. French commentators have argued that, because the American deterrent is not (or may not be) fully credible, a modest French retaliatory force can make a difference. American commentators respond either that the American deterrent is fully effective or that the French force would be so ineffective as to add nothing and that the cost of the French program is not warranted. But even if French proponents of an independent nuclear program did become so persuaded or so pressured by the military arguments against the program that they had to concede the point about deterrence, I doubt that their interest in a French nuclear program would be much diminished. It is important to get the military arguments straight; but I doubt they are decisive in the present controversies. (And we may get the military arguments straighter if we can stop using them as proxies in a political argument.[1])

II

Let me speak first about the development of American ideas on local and regional warfare with the Soviet bloc. Their origins go

[1] I suspect that the interest in additional "deterrent" forces, which is often alleged to reflect diminishing confidence in American deterrence as Soviet nuclear power grows, is in fact a reflection of increased confidence. With growing confidence that the Soviets are deterred from a major onslaught against Europe, governments and commentators can turn to longer-term problems within the alliance. As countries become more assured that they *can* rely on U.S. strategic forces, they can more safely consider whether they wish to.

back at least to controversies in the early 1950's about massive retaliation, limited war, graduated deterrence, and the special problems of controlling the use of nuclear weapons. American thinking
on this subject, even by many who are now officials in government,
is probably well represented in the published literature. Many
senior American officials—Assistant Secretary Paul Nitze, General
Maxwell Taylor, and President Kennedy himself—were outside the
executive branch of government for part or all of the past decade.
Some of them spoke and wrote at length. There is also no doubt
that commentators outside government were read or listened to
with interest over the last decade both by people who were then in
government and by people who are now in government. So, although the published literature is by no means the whole story,
it is surely an important part of the background.

One impression an American gets is that the thinking on local or
regional conflicts has developed as much with Formosa, Vietnam,
the Middle East, or even, recently, India and Cuba in mind, as
with Europe. One difficulty with dialogue on military policy is that
it is not easy to distinguish, at least in America, between policies
primarily oriented toward Europe and policies primarily oriented
toward other countries, especially if the policies are still in dispute.

There has been for a long time a widespread belief that the
United States should not be wholly dependent on nuclear weapons
in peripheral areas. At the landing of American troops in Lebanon,
the United States must have had to think seriously about whether
nuclear arms were appropriate, either to engage an enemy or to
threaten engagement in the Middle East, especially when it was
not clear who the enemy might be or what his relations with the
Soviet bloc were. It is probably in a crisis, when action is required,
that what everyone knew all along becomes so unmistakably pertinent that it can no longer be ignored or postponed. Policies always
relate to anticipated contingencies; if unanticipated contingencies
arise, policies have to be enriched to deal with them. The Cuban
crisis was a dramatic reminder that not everything one might like
to do with military force can be done more effectively with nuclear
weapons.

For a long time, the argument about nuclear weapons in local
war seemed mainly concerned with the psychological impact on
third areas. There was concern with what Asians would think if
Americans used nuclear weapons on Asians. That is important, but
while it may be the most easily expressed consideration, I doubt
whether it has been the most important. More important for most
Americans was probably another consideration: that engagements

with the Soviet bloc—even with Soviet-bloc troops, but particularly with forces receiving support from the Soviet bloc—might be much more in the nature of strategic-political maneuvers than local military contests. Call it a "competition in risk-taking." In contests of this sort, getting in first with a "pre-emptive maneuver," confronting the other side with a *fait accompli* rather than being confronted with one, starting an engagement that faces the enemy with a choice of withdrawing or enlarging his own risk, and demonstrating an American (or allied) commitment and involvement that would not permit our backing down, will often be at least as important as the local capability for tactical victory in a particular area. (It is sometimes said that the Cuban crisis of October, 1962, went in favor of the United States because the United States had an overwhelming local naval and air superiority in the Caribbean. That explains half; the other half is that the Soviet Union went along with *our* definition of where and what the conflict was. They did not, for example, choose to make it a contest in the harassment and blockade of each other's island allies.)

Such tactics were frequently thought about for areas where the most obvious encroachments could be of a more political and less directly military sort, or where Soviet objectives might be more exploratory and less determined than in the area of Western Europe. But even for Western Europe, it has long been recognized in the United States that Soviet probes or minor military ventures, not only in flank areas but even on the central front, ought to be anticipated with something other than a massive nuclear response. Former Secretary of State Dean Acheson's interest in a sizeable conventional capability for Europe was articulated a good many years ago (for example, in his book *Power and Diplomacy*, published in 1958). It is sometimes forgotten that Secretary of State Dulles was expressing similar views at the same time.[2] This Ameri-

[2] Secretary Dulles was more interested in small nuclear weapons than in conventional capabilities at the time, but his language was strikingly similar to Secretary Acheson's: "In the future it may thus be feasible to place less reliance upon deterrence of vast retaliatory power. . . . Thus, in contrast to the 1950 decade, it may be that by the 1960 decade, the nations which are around the Sino-Soviet perimeter can possess an effective defense against full-scale conventional attack and thus confront any aggressor with the choice between failing or himself initiating nuclear war against the defending country. Thus, the tables may be turned, in the sense that instead of those who are nonaggressive having to rely upon all-out nuclear retaliatory power for their protection, would-be aggressors would be unable to count on a successful conventional aggression, but must themselves weigh the consequences of invoking nuclear war." (J. F. Dulles, "Challenge and Response in U.S. Policy," *Foreign Affairs*, xxxv [October, 1957].)

can interest in a graduated capacity for military action in Europe, and the recognition that below some threshold of provocation the threat even of *local* nuclear response would not be sensible, is no sudden innovation of the New Frontier.

Parenthetically, I should stress that these ideas about the use or non-use of nuclear weapons in local engagements appear to have a different parentage from thoughts about the controlled use of strategic forces in case of general war. Both ideas can be described in terms of the controlled, flexible, restrained, or political use of military force and of nuclear weapons in particular. But the concept of controlling nuclear weapons in general war—of continuing "deterrence" into war itself—and the concept of limiting or controlling the use of nuclear or other weapons in regional engagements reflect quite separate lines of thought, even if they reflect somewhat similar philosophies.

Within the area of conventional strategy (or conventional forces), I perceive several different strands of thought. First, we should distinguish between an American interest in developing strategies for contingencies in which conventional weapons would be most appropriate, and an American interest in increased European force levels based on a conventional strategy. American policymakers have been exhorting their NATO allies to contribute more troops and larger budgets to NATO defense during most of the period since the Korean War. Arguments pointing toward European manpower and economic potential as indicative of a greater European military potential are not new. Even in the years of the greatest apparent American reliance on nuclear weapons for NATO's defense, European governments were still urged to greater efforts. It should not be surprising that the American Government continues to advocate greater efforts, particularly when European economies have shown such strength. At a time when the American Government is urging on the Europeans a greater interest in the role of conventional force, while maintaining its usual insistence on a greater NATO effort, it is probably natural that the two be combined into an argument for "larger conventional forces."

But an interest in conventional strategies can exist independent of an interest in enlarged troop commitments. I doubt whether the American interest in a wider range of strategies would disappear if the Americans became convinced that European troop commitments had hit their ceiling. To anticipate contingencies in which conventional forces would be most appropriate, to engage in planning for such contingencies, and to think about troop locations and the deployment of weapons in the light of those contingencies should not stand or fall with the wisdom of an "all-out" conventional defense of Europe or of any particular increase in troop levels.

In other words, the argument for higher troop levels and the argument for flexible strategic planning with greater emphasis on the anticipation of conventional engagement are two quite different arguments. They combine so readily that there is a temptation to think of them as two sides of the same coin. And certainly some of the published American expositions of a "conventional strategy" have failed to make the distinction.

There are a number of different views about possible conventional engagements in Europe. They do not all lead to the same conclusions, though most of them tend toward a heightened interest in the number of troops. The extreme view was recently restated by Secretary Acheson.[3] This view insists on the value and feasibility of troop levels capable of defending successfully against almost any Soviet conventional frontal attack on the central front. According to this view, European and North American manpower can provide enough troops (something like thirty divisions deployed plus thirty mobilizable within thirty days) to resist such an ambitious Soviet onslaught. There is, in this view, strong reason to believe that the Soviets would not initiate the use of nuclears in those circumstances. It is also argued that this strategy has a strong deterrent implication: if the Soviets are in any doubt about Western willingness to use nuclears, or Western willingness to commit a full-scale defense if that implies large-scale use of nuclears, and if the Soviets might be willing to try their luck if they thought they could succeed conventionally, *that* particular temptation would be removed.

My personal view is that this extreme form of conventional strategy, providing for the "all-out" defense of Europe conventionally, is interesting but only moderately so. I doubt very much whether a war that directly engaged twenty divisions—NATO divisions about to be overrun, with half a dozen American divisions among them—could last long without the introduction of nuclear weapons by somebody. This is something of a hunch, but I am doubtful whether anything on the scale of World War I or II in Europe, or even the Korean War if it had persisted, could be fought to successful conclusion with the kind of restraint on the NATO and the Soviet side that the Acheson theory presupposes. (My

[3] Dean Acheson, "The Practice of Partnership," *Foreign Affairs*, XLI (January, 1963), 247–60.

doubts would be even stronger if, in the interim, nuclears had been used in anger anywhere in the world, breaking an eighteen years' tradition of non-use and signalling an intention to use them again. The whole strategy would have to be re-examined if nuclear weapons were used in the Caribbean, the Far East, or anywhere else.)

If present troop strength in Europe is insufficient to get an impressive engagement going (which I doubt), so that there might be a shred of a doubt in the Soviet mind whether the West could accept an easy defeat rather than introduce nuclears, then surely more troop strength *is* necessary. But the criterion for this increase would be different from the standard of all-out successful conventional defense. "Trip-wire" is an insulting term for describing NATO ground forces, but there must be *at least* a trip-wire at some level significantly short of the level at which full-scale conventional attack could be reliably stopped. Still, because all-out conventional defense looks as though it may be within reach, and because a capability for it would be of some positive value, this goal can be disputed only on grounds of costs or of some offsetting reduction in deterrence that the strategy overlooks.

I do not see any offsetting reduction in deterrence. I am fully persuaded that a vigorous Western response is the more likely, and would be the more prompt, and would have behind it the greater political unity, the more available is conventional force to meet conventional attack. I am also fully persuaded that the timely introduction of nuclears is the more likely, the more promptly and vigorously *some* Western engagement occurs. And *I* am quite persuaded that the *Soviets* are so persuaded. I see no sign that the current emphasis given to conventional strategy in Washington is in any way related to notions of "nuclear disengagement" or anything of the sort, though I am aware that some American commentators claim to see it that way.

As to the economic problem of force goals on the scale advocated by Acheson, I have nothing new to say. I prefer to emphasize another cost that may be incurred in exhorting Europeans to accept that goal. That is the tendency to focus excessive attention on the need to measure our strategies and troop strengths primarily—almost exclusively—by the standard of a massive Soviet deliberate effort to conquer Western Europe or a large part of it. This is the problem that motivated NATO in 1949 and for many years thereafter. If there is any military adventure in the world that the Soviets could embark on only if they were out of their minds, it would be that one. To do it without launching—not simultaneously, but beforehand, in the interest of surprise—a major attack on American strategic forces would be an extraordinary long-shot gamble.

If there is any place where deterrence works, it is there. Even if some people doubt whether the American Government would—coolly in its own interests, or warmly for its NATO commitments—deliberately launch general war in retaliation, it is hard to believe that a large nuclear war could be averted when the Soviets were smashing through central Europe defeating the bulk of NATO forces on the way. War on that scale is noisy, brutal, and inflammatory; and if anything is "incredible," it is that American strategic nuclear forces could stay patiently grounded while NATO was methodically smashed to bits and its territory overrun.

But there are more likely military contingencies, most of them of a subtler sort, in which conventional or other non-massive action is not only pertinent but even essential, if the alternative is not to be inaction. Such contingencies ought to receive attention. They get little attention as long as the classic problem of 1949 on the Central Front dominates discussion. Not all of these call for Western action that can be characterized as "defensive," at least not in the tactical military sense. I totally agree with Secretary Acheson's reference to the Hungarian uprising of 1956 as suggestive of the kind of thing that could really challenge the ability of the Atlantic nations to use their military assets in support of their foreign policy. Recent Berlin crises have suggested a number of ways that the gauntlet might be thrown to Western forces to take some initiative.

There are countries outside the NATO area, even in Europe, where the influence of NATO military force may need to make itself felt. It does not require a talent for fiction to imagine events over the next decade in Finland or Yugoslavia, even Spain or Portugal, Sweden as well as Norway or Greece, where the effectiveness of Western military force will not be measured by its purely military capability for tactical victory. Pre-emptive maneuvers, the quick involvement of a Western presence, the erection of some new trip-wires, a persuasive threat of intervention unless the Soviet Union stays out, and an ability to keep Soviet troops preoccupied and to deny them flexibility of action may be as important as the exercise of a local firepower advantage.

Not all of these contingencies may be covered by the NATO treaty. There may be national constraints on what forces can be used, particularly if they must be used quickly, as well as numerical restraints on what can be subtracted from a particular front for use elsewhere.

One does not have to be aggressively oriented toward "roll-back" to foresee that contingencies can arise in which Western inaction can involve a serious net loss, particularly if this inaction were assured in advance to the Soviets. "Flexibility" may be precisely what NATO military forces will need, as a successful NATO begins to think about its over-all foreign policy and not just the traditional contingency of a major Soviet attack.

For many of these purposes, some advance planning may be more important than troop strength. The location and mobility of troops may be at least as important as their aggregate number. Alliances find it particularly difficult to respond quickly to unforeseen contingencies. Foreseeing some, at least in general outline, has value in itself, whether or not concrete preparations result from it.

It would be unfortunate if the enthusiasm for enlarged conventional *forces* should overshadow the need for a flexible political-military *strategy*. It would also be unfortunate if the argument for increased conventional strength became—or became interpreted as —an argument for almost exclusive reliance on conventional strength, even in some of the smaller contingencies. Any strategy is bound to be conventional *and* nuclear in the weapons implicitly available. The nuclears in the background will be decisive in determining the shape and scope of any conventional engagement, even one in which no shots are fired.

III

We come now to another strand of American thinking, sufficiently wide-spread among commentators to suggest that it may have influenced official thinking. It relates to the possibility of "controlled use of nuclears" in a local or regional engagement—to the fact that there *is* such a thing as potential escalation and that the Soviets may have to be confronted with it. Two things may be implied.

First, nuclears, if they need to be used, might not suddenly be declared "released" from their "unconventional" status and declared generally available for tactical use. They might instead be used selectively and with restraint. Second, they might be consciously used not only to destroy targets and to defeat an enemy locally, but to make the Soviets unwilling to proceed with further escalation or even to prosecute their local war vigorously. Nuclears would *signal* something, as well as *destroy* targets. Getting the right signal across would be an important part of the policy. This could imply, for example, deliberate and restrained use earlier than might otherwise seem tactically warranted, in order to leave the Soviets under no illusion whether or not the engagement might go nuclear. The only question then would be, how nuclear.

In its extreme form this restrained, signalling, intimidating use of nuclears for brinksmanship has sometimes been called the "shot across the bow." There is always a danger—Churchill and others have warned against it—of making a bold demonstration on so small a scale that the contrary of boldness is demonstrated. There is no cheap, safe way of using nuclears that scares the wits out of the Russians without scaring ourselves too. Nevertheless, *any* use of nuclears is going to change the pattern of expectations about the future use of nuclears. Even those who have argued that nuclears ought to be considered just a more efficient use of artillery will surely catch their breath when the first one goes off in anger. Something is destroyed, even if not enemy targets, if ever-so-few nuclears are used. Whatever a few nuclears prove, or fail to prove, about their user, they will change the environment of expectations. And it is expectations, more than anything else, that will determine the outcome of a limited East-West military engagement.

We have been talking about something that can be called the "controlled" use of nuclear weapons or a "flexible strategy of response," and it involves important questions of command and control in war time. But it relates less to *who* controls the nuclear weapons than to *how* they are controlled in their use. And it is distinct from the notion that general nuclear war itself might involve, or ought to involve, a high degree of control and restraint.

IV

Lastly, we come to strategy for what has usually been called "general nuclear war." Secretary McNamara, in his commencement address at the University of Michigan a year ago, is widely regarded to have unveiled a "new strategy" with respect to the conduct of general war. He suggested that population centers would not necessarily be primary targets in a general war, that general war might have some of the characteristics of "limited war" with reciprocated restraint on both sides, and that the primary targets ought to be the enemy's nuclear forces. He also strongly implied that, in consequence, coordination among nuclear forces would be of extreme importance during general war; such coordination would be difficult without single-nation control of weapons and target selection; and it would be particularly difficult if some members of an alliance were busy retaliating on population centers while other members were carefully avoiding such targets.

In America, this "new strategy" has been publicly criticized both for its restraint and for its bellicosity. Some commentators have seen it as a new infatuation with pre-emptive or preventive war as the solution for most of our problems and an alternative to locally limited war. Others have deplored it as a weakening of our deterrent threat by the introduction of restraint. Still others have just considered it unrealistic, assuming that general war means cataclysm and that any attention given to a possibility of limitation is wasteful and deceptive. In Europe, there have been at least some commentators who have seen this new strategy as a grand and contrived excuse for keeping a national monopoly of nuclear decisions. The Soviet verbal reaction is an alleged skepticism about the possibility of limited nuclear war, coupled with the accusation of thinly disguised effort to make war acceptable. So there are about four groups of opponents and two brands of skeptics, all of whom seem agreed on only one thing: that the strategy is new.

As an idea, it surely is not. In the published literature, a number of commentators have been talking about it for several years. President Kennedy's first defense budget message contained language strongly suggestive of this "new strategy." Ideas of this sort do not get invented, developed, accepted, and articulated within a period as short as a couple of months. We can conclude that the "new strategy" was at least a few years old and not invented under the incentive of a commencement address. More seriously, it was not invented in 1962 as a debating point against General de Gaulle.

My personal opinion is that it was a mistake in diplomacy to use this conception of general war as an argument against independent nuclear deterrents in Europe. I say this with hindsight. The new strategy was new enough, at least in public discussion, to need a sympathetic audience. Because it was used as an argument against French (or British) independent strategic forces, it has had the effect of making some proponents of independent nuclear forces attack the premise rather than the conclusion. It has thus incurred the opposition or cynicism of many Europeans. This is a high price to pay for winning the argument. If the argument is not won, it will be a serious misfortune if European governments are predisposed against the kind of strategy that the American government seems to be adopting.

I am not going at length into the merits of this strategy, which

Secretary McNamara described as one of keeping available the "option" of possibly sparing cities in a general war if the enemy reciprocates. In honesty, I shall say that I am sympathetic toward it, that it is a complex of ideas still in process of development, and that public discussion has been more obstructed than helped by nicknames like "counter-force" and "no-cities."

I do want to put this so-called "new strategy" into perspective, though, and especially to see whether and how it relates to European defense. It may be helpful to trace the development of these ideas, insofar as traces can be found in the public record. A good starting place is 1957, when the first Soviet announcement of a successful ICBM test, together with the first Sputnik, dramatized the problem of vulnerability. The vulnerability that was dramatized was not that of population centers but of strategic retaliatory forces.

There was every evidence that the Eisenhower Administration became increasingly concerned with the problem of how to deter enemy surprise attack with a force of fragile bombers located on a limited number of bomber bases. Proposals for a suddenly augmented "airborne alert" reached the point of active Congressional discussion; Air Force officials discussed the emergency dispersal of B-47 bombers to civilian airfields to reduce their vulnerability to Soviet attack. Proponents of the Polaris submarine emphasized its expected invulnerability to enemy pre-emptive attack. Albert Wohlstetter's article on "The Delicate Balance of Terror"* set off a lively public discussion of this issue and helped to draw public attention back to the problem of deterring general war after a period of several years during which commentators had often taken for granted that general war had been ruled out as a serious possibility. President Kennedy, then a Senator, and Assistant Secretary of Defense Paul Nitze, then a private citizen, both expressed concern for American development of a genuinely invulnerable strategic force.[4]

This increased concern had effect. Not only in the new Administration but under President Eisenhower, and not only with respect to missile forces but in the alert status of the bomber force, important steps were taken. Once efforts were made to avert the sudden

---

* EDITOR'S NOTE: See above, Chapter 2.

[4] See, for example, Senator Kennedy's speech on "The Missile Gap" in the United States Senate, August 14, 1958 (reprinted in John F. Kennedy, *The Strategy of Peace*, Allan Nevins, ed. [New York, 1960]). See also *Developments in Military Technology and Their Impact on United States Strategy and Foreign Policy*, prepared by the Washington Center of Foreign Policy Research for the Committee on Foreign Relations, United States Senate (Washington, December 6, 1959); Paul H. Nitze was a co-author.

destruction of a strategic force, there was bound to arise a technical interest in providing similarly for the security of communications, reconnaissance, and all the other elements of "command and control" of the surviving force. Furthermore, once general war came to be taken with renewed seriousness, thought had to be given to how it might be conducted as well as how it might be deterred. For the purpose of pure deterrence, one may be content to occupy himself solely with how war might start. But if one has to take seriously the possibility that it *might* start, he has to consider also how it might be finished. A renewed interest in the "control" of military forces and in their relation to national policy is probably, therefore, a natural consequence of the renewed concern with general war that was manifest in the late 1950's.

Another idea, related and coincident, can also be traced back to about 1958. This is the idea that "invulnerable" or well-protected strategic forces not only may promise better deterrence but can avert the need for hair-trigger decisions about their use. Vulnerable forces, if not launched instantly upon warning, may not be available to launch at all. In the event of ambiguous warning, a government possessing a force that might cease to exist within a fraction of an hour would be in an acute dilemma—to wait and risk the destruction of its strategic forces, or to launch them and make certainty of a war that might yet have been averted. A less hasty response—a more "controlled" response or a more flexible or graduated response—is not only important but all the more feasible as the forces themselves become less vulnerable. This idea was being clearly expressed even before the Kennedy Administration came into power: for example, in public discussion of the advantages of mobile Polaris and hardened Minuteman.

Still another related idea can be discerned. Strategic forces are bound to play a sensitive role in any heightened military crisis short of general war. It is important that strategic forces not be fatigued and disrupted by alarms and excursions; it is equally important that they not react to emergencies in a way that makes the enemy believe an American attack is on the way. Concern for this problem had already been expressed during the Eisenhower Administration; it is one more aspect of the "control" of strategic forces—their responsiveness to national policy in an aggravated crisis.

Finally, one element of the "new strategy" is comparatively new in its official expression. This is the suggestion that even general war, depending on the circumstances of its outbreak, might have some of the characteristics of "limited" war. According to this idea, population centers would not be the most urgent targets in the event of general war; even some deliberate avoidance might make sense. In public discussion, this notion has often been coupled with the idea of a vigorous disarming attack on enemy strategic forces, a "counter-force" campaign, sometimes with the implication that the strategy particularly suits a nation with such superior strength that it can do the job decisively (and perhaps only if it is willing to initiate the war).

Questions have been raised whether such a strategy, if it could appeal to the United States, would not for similar reasons be rejected by the Soviet Union, or whether such a strategy can only appeal to the United States as long as it enjoys a strategic superiority over the Soviet bloc. Authoritative answers are yet hard to find in the public record.

One ought, nevertheless, to distinguish two quite different dimensions of this so-called "counter-force" strategy that can exist somewhat independently of each other. One is the notion that "deterrence" might be extended into the war itself, maintaining for coercive purposes the continued *threat* of city destruction, in place of the instant destruction of "hostage" population centers. In other words, general war might be subject to some reciprocated restraints, might be terminated short of "unconditional destruction" and the sheer exhaustion of weapons on both sides, and might involve the continuation of conscious military *policy* rather than indiscriminate military action. The second aspect, which is especially pertinent if one does envisage the possibility of some city avoidance, is the question of what targets *are* attacked.

"Counter-force" action designed to reduce the enemy's capacity for destruction is undoubtedly affected by, but by no means wholly dependent on, deliberate restraint with regard to population centers. Preservation of a city-destroying potential—by withholding weapons from city destruction in a manner that preserves the continued threat, rather than the instant expenditure of the weapons in city destruction—is affected by the kind of campaign that might be waged against military targets but is by no means dependent on a particular "counter-force" campaign. Whatever the merits of a vigorous "counter-force" campaign, they are only partly affected by one's interest in avoiding cities, and whatever the merits of attempting to restrain the war against populations, they are only partly affected by the kind of campaign that is waged against military targets.

For this reason, the name "counter-force" that is often used to describe the whole idea may be a serious misrepresentation, as is the alternative name, "no-cities," which may equally describe only one of the several conceptions that might make up such a strategy.

I would emphasize that, while this conception appeared to be "new" in its public recognition about a year ago, it should not have been unexpected. What I have tried to indicate is that over the past half dozen years there has been a serious concern, both in and out of government and under both administrations, with a conscious development of policy about general war and its deterrence. As the problem has come to be viewed more seriously and realistically, especially by civilian authorities and not just the military services, there has been a natural tendency to try to relate available military force to over-all national policy and to design future military capabilities so that they could be more closely related to national policy. Whether or not general war was "unthinkable," it was apparently not much "thought about" except by those who knew they would have to fight if it occurred. The spirits of the 1955 Geneva Summit and Camp David seemed to prevail for several years. But as new attention was given to the possibility that general war might actually occur, thought was bound to be given to how it might responsibly be conducted. The conception that a nuclear showdown would be so "all-out" that once it started there would be nothing to do but wait until it was over—no decisions to make, and no "policy" involved—it was bound at some stage to begin to look like resignation rather than wisdom.

I doubt, therefore, whether we should be surprised to find the American Government considering general war a somewhat more complicated notion than the word "all-out" can convey. I also doubt whether any of us, including the present Administration, have reached a final understanding on the subject.[5]

[5] General Pierre Gallois has credited Khrushchev with a shrewd understanding of the politics of deterrence, evidenced by his "irrational outburst" in the presence of Secretary Harriman. In case the West tried to use military force over Berlin, "Our missiles will go off automatically"; and the men surrounding Khrushchev echoed "automatically." By his behavior, according to Gallois, Khrushchev "added to the risk which, for its part, Washington must run in holding out in Berlin." Yet Gallois "hardly sees Moscow launching its atomic missiles at Washington because of Berlin." ("Mr. McNamara's Sophisms and the Departure of General Norstad," *Revue de Défense Nationale,* October, 1962.) Granted, however, that somebody important may be somewhat intimidated by this responsive chorus on automaticity, must the American Government rely for the credibility of its deterrent on a corresponding ritual? Can we not get something a little less idiosyncratic for $50 billion a year? A government that is obliged to appear responsible can hardly cultivate

Let me sum up the three points I have tried to make on the topic of general-war strategy and deterrence. First, whatever the "new strategy" is, like any strategic concept it is a complex of ideas, not a single idea, some parts of which may be transient while others may endure, some parts of which may relate to today's technology but not tomorrow's, some parts of which are still in process of development. Second, while Europe is bound to be so central to American strategy that no over-all strategic policy could be developed without regard to it, many of the ideas about strategic warfare that we can see developing over the last several years have a momentum of their own and are not to be explained mainly by reference to NATO. They impinge on NATO defense in extraordinarily important ways, but can probably not be best explained or interpreted by reference to a parallel development in NATO policy. Third, whatever the strategy implies about the wisdom of single-nation control of strategic forces, it has equal implications for the control and coordination of strategic forces owned by an alliance or by individual members of the alliance. Even if these ideas are rejected as a sufficient argument for tight national or multilateral control, they should be taken seriously by any nation that finds itself a partner in strategic deterrence or warfare. What has come to be known as the careful control of strategic forces in warfare should be *at least* as interesting to France or any other nation as to the United States. That ought to be so, whether the independent strategic force is expected to be used by itself or in the context of a larger war.

---

forever the appearance of impetuosity on the most important decisions in its care. Khrushchev may need a short cut to deterrence, but the American Government ought to be mature enough and rich enough to arrange a persuasive sequence of threatened responses that are not wholly a matter of guessing a President's temper.

TEN

ALBERT WOHLSTETTER

Nuclear Sharing: NATO and the
N + 1 Country

[Editor's Note: The possession of nuclear weapons is regarded by some of America's allies—especially Great Britain and France—as the key factor in the attainment of strategic independence. However, complete independence is unattainable in the nuclear age, and the quest for it runs counter to Alliance policy. One of the chief problems in NATO has been to determine how allies can achieve access to nuclear control without proliferating nuclear weapons and ultimately undermining the Alliance. In one of his seminal articles, Professor Wohlstetter discusses the various methods of nuclear sharing and the strategic and political problems arising from them. He evaluates four logical possibilities: (1) the rejection of nuclear weapons, of the American guarantee to defend Europe, and of all association with nuclear powers; (2) the development of autonomous national forces; (3) a jointly controlled nuclear force, specifically, a NATO multilateral force; and (4) reliance on the United States guarantee.

Professor Wohlstetter firmly advocates the last option. He believes that any drastic modification of the existing nuclear structure and, more important, any attempt by America's allies to develop autonomous nuclear forces would undermine the United States nuclear guarantee and thus the political and military stability of the North Atlantic Alliance. A proven and credible arrangement would be replaced by something unfamiliar that would invite constant probing. Professor Wohlstetter's views on nuclear control in NATO have been dominant in the Pentagon through the 1960's.]

Is the spread of nuclear strike forces good or bad? When we regard the diffusion of nuclear weapons as bad or at least worrisome, we refer to it as the nth power problem. In this guise, it appears as the principal menace lending a sense of urgency to our negotiations on arms control and as a trend to be fought. In particular, it is the chief justification offered for a test ban. During most of the time since the summer of 1958, we have been in negotiation with the Russians to conclude a treaty prohibiting the explosion of nuclear weapons. We do this largely because we hope that other countries will join us in abstaining from tests, and so find it harder to get a nuclear capability. Meanwhile, we ourselves have stopped testing and hope that the Soviet Union has too. Quite apart from the test ban, of course, we have for a long time so regulated our study, manufacture, and operation of weapons as to reduce the chance of information of weapons design spreading to other countries, including our allies. These self-constraints have been embodied in our Atomic Energy Law. In both our atomic-energy legislation and our arms-control negotiation we act on the assumption that it is bad to increase the number of nuclear powers.

On the other hand, at least some of our military policies seem to proceed from the notion that it is good. Some contemplated NATO policies suppose in particular that we want to disperse the power to decide to use nuclear weapons, to have more than one center for such decision in the West. We have, of course, deployed nuclear weapons under our own control in many parts of the world. In several countries we have put weapons under the dual control of ourselves and our host. While we have not transferred warheads to the independent control of other countries, we have, in the case of several allies, sold or given them significant parts of a total system—delivery vehicles, personnel training, and the like. We contemplate assisting the Dutch and the French to construct atomic submarines, or—in order to avoid a formal clash with the Atomic Energy Law—we might at least help them build the submarine hull and the non-nuclear parts of the propulsion machinery. In the case of the United Kingdom, we have actually given not only atomic-submarine plans but also designs and special materials for nuclear warheads. We modified the MacMahon Act in 1958 so as to justify this special treatment of the United Kingdom, but we did it in such a way as to seem to offer incentives to our other allies to demon-

EDITOR'S NOTE: Reprinted with permission from *Foreign Affairs*, XXXIX, No. 3 (April, 1961). © 1961, by the Council on Foreign Relations, Inc., New York.

strate a nuclear capability of their own, and so become eligible for help.[1] We are now contemplating the transfer to NATO of the major components of an entire weapons system—submarines, Polaris missiles and warheads—possibly for use without our veto. In many of these actions, we appear to have been the initiators of moves toward diffusion. In most of them, we have tended at least to view the spread of nuclear capabilities benignly. We use an appropriately benign word, "sharing," which has overtones of fairness, Christian charity and right behavior.

It is conceivable that these two sets of policies are consistent—that we are *for* sharing nuclear weapons with some of our allies, and just against spreading them to enemies or neutral powers or certain of our allies. But, in fact, it has always been clear that the two sorts of diffusion are not so easily separated, that the acquisition of nuclear military power by some of our allies can impel its acquisition by enemies and that it is particularly hard and divisive to select among our allies. The spread occurs in chain. It seems more likely that this division in our policies expresses a divided purpose.[2] The arms-control moves that we have made to limit diffusion are largely formal or declaratory, tied to complicated and uncertain negotiations with the Russians, and, in fact, likely to depend on the cooperation of potential nth powers. On the other hand, the moves we have made in alliance policy which favor diffusion are strong. If our military and foreign policies are to be consistent and effective, we ought to decide whether the nth power problem really worries us, or whether we favor sharing and the state of the world it may bring about.

But perhaps there is no point in deciding how we feel about the diffusion of nuclear capabilities. It is frequently claimed that the trend toward diffusion is inevitable. There are cheerful as well as pessimistic views of the trend. The pessimists, who are (correctly,

---

[1] It would be hard to imagine a deeper goad for the French than the statement by the Secretary of Defense on April 22, 1960. According to *The New York Times*, Mr. Gates indicated that "the United States did not regard two nuclear explosions as qualification for French admission to the 'nuclear club.'" "I am not sure there is a demonstrated ability," he is quoted as saying. "France would have to show a high level of technical competence." It appears that even our restraints offer a considerable incitement.

[2] The Russians appear to be not entirely clear about how *they* regard the diffusion of nuclear power. They have not hurried to give bombs to the Chinese or the Warsaw powers; yet they have repeatedly opposed safeguarding reactor programs against diversion of nuclear materials to military purposes in the underdeveloped countries.

I believe) concerned with the enormous instabilities and dangers of a world with many nuclear powers, call somewhat wanly for an immediate and comprehensive program of international controls. Some of the optimists, on the other hand, suppose that if bombs are spread much more widely, they will be less likely to be used, that stability will increase. Others, not quite so cheerful, hold that, since diffusion is inevitable, we should go along with it or try to direct it into less harmful channels, but in any case that we should help our friends in NATO by reducing the costs.

However, both the gloomy and lighthearted prophets of inevitable diffusion have been rather unclear as to precisely what sorts of nuclear capability will be diffused and how fast. A more analytic understanding might make the optimists less cheery and lead the pessimists to a less fatalistic view. It seems very likely that *some* new countries will acquire *some* sorts of nuclear capability in the next decade, but it is by no means certain just how many countries and which ones will acquire what sorts of nuclear capability. Though even a little diffusion has important implications for strategy, it makes a great deal of difference whether twenty-odd countries develop or are given bombs and delivery capabilities in the next six or seven years, or whether it is two or three of the more industrialized powers.

A mechanical view of the inevitability of the trend toward nuclear diffusion places the entire burden of stopping or slowing the spread on effective international agreements—which are hard to come by. It tends to ignore decisions that the United States can make on its own and so fails to exploit some possible brakes on nuclear dispersion stemming from the immediate self-interest of prospective nth powers. Their decisions will affect the trend, too. It is worth pointing out to the responsible prospective nth powers in the NATO community that the undertaking is not merely arduous; it is unlikely to pay off. A failure to pay in terms of immediate national self-interest is likely to affect the intentions of nth countries more strongly than arguments about the stability of the world system.

So far as long-run world stability is concerned, the nth country tends to think of the problem as beginning with n plus 1. The original irony intended by the label "nth-power problem" was seated precisely in the fact that the United States and the Soviet Union thought of the trouble as the third-power problem, Great Britain thought of it as the fourth-power problem, France as the fifth-power problem, and so on. Each new or prospective nuclear power thinks of the problem as that of stopping the next country after itself. This is the $n + 1$ country problem.

As for world stability through arms control, France and England, for example, have tended to think of their own acquisition of nuclear weapons as entirely beneficial. Macmillan has justified British weapons and V-bombers on the grounds that they permit the English to exercise influence on arms-control arrangements between the two major nuclear powers. General de Gaulle speaks of the increased effect on nuclear disarmament which France would have by becoming a nuclear power. In the limit, one might suppose that unanimity for nuclear disarmament may be achieved by distributing bombs to everybody.

The choices among alternative nuclear policies confronting members of NATO are likely to play a key role in the diffusion of nuclear capabilities—especially in Europe—and in the problem of avoiding small or large nuclear wars. For this reason I would like to consider, from the standpoint of the national interest of the individual members, some of the major alternatives open to them. What sorts of nuclear capability are the lesser industrial powers in the West likely to achieve? What are the motivations for achieving independent capabilities? What is the role of the American nuclear guarantee? Is it, as it is currently fashionable to say, "incredible"?

The four main alternatives open to the European powers are these: (1) the rejection of nuclear weapons, of the American guarantee, and of all association with nuclear powers; (2) the development of national strike forces; (3) a jointly controlled force, and especially the NATO-wide force; (4) reliance on the United States guarantee. Let us examine the relevance of each for avoiding large-scale nuclear war and for meeting lower levels of aggression in Europe.[3]

1. THE REPUDIATION OF NUCLEAR WEAPONS

The rejection of any reliance on nuclear weapons, even an ally's, to deter Russian nuclear attack has been prominently advocated in England in the last few years, and very recently it has gained some adherents in the United States. It deserves more extended comment than can be included here.

[3] I am indebted for comments or stimulation to Michael Arnsten, F. C. Iklé, Malcolm Hoag, F. S. Hoffman, Herman Kahn, Ciro Zoppo, and especially to Daniel Ellsberg and William Kaufman. The views expressed are those of the author.

According to this view, nobody in his senses believes that either the Russian or American government would deliberately initiate a nuclear war, since this would amount to self-annihilation. None the less, it is thought, there is almost a "statistical certainty" that a continuing policy of mutual deterrence will result eventually in accidental war and the devastation of most of mankind. The diverse representatives of this view range from those who, like A. J. P. Taylor and Frank Cousins, call for exclusive reliance on conventional weapons, through those like Stephen King-Hall and the traditional pacifists who recommend passive resistance to Russian occupation, and finally to Philip Toynbee who contemplates surrender. A common thread in their arguments has it that the danger of war with the Soviet Union and the Soviet military threat itself are a consequence rather than a cause of the arms race, and that East-West differences are susceptible of settlement now, since the Soviet Union is a satisfied, *status-quo* power. Near one extreme of this view, Bertrand Russell takes Soviet desires for Communist transformation of the world as analogous to, and hardly more menacing than, Christian desires to convert the world to Christianity. The other end of the scale approaches those who, like some heads of Western states, are merely optimistic about early diplomatic settlements with Russia, including extensive disarmament. The United States is seen not as a defender of areas menaced by Soviet aggression, but as one half of a power conflict which threatens to crush third countries. In fact, it is held that the United States will not fulfill its commitment to defend its allies but is quite likely to implicate them in a war.

This view wishfully understates the conflict of interest between the East and the West, and, by repeating the familiar clichés about an automatic balance of terror, it shows no understanding of the difference between defensive military postures which would ensure damage to the aggressor and those which would make it highly probable that the aggressor would come off unscathed. It exhibits the weakest and most inconsistent form of the dogma about the automatic balance by failing to recognize that unilateral nuclear disarmament would insure the aggressor against retaliation. It is sometimes said that total disarmament and submission to Soviet demands would remove any motive for attack, but it is hard to take seriously the belief that the West at the height of its industrial and political power would follow a policy of *total* submission. Lord Russell himself regards this possibility as academic. The more likely result of "unilateralism" would be a partial disarming and resistance that would actually increase the danger of the nuclear war which advocates of nuclear repudiation want to avoid. Specifically, it would increase the danger of deliberate war. . . .

II. NATIONAL STRIKE FORCES

The justification for the spread of national nuclear forces—as elaborated, for example, by Pierre Gallois—is based on the belief that no nation can be counted on to defend another from atomic aggression, since in doing so it would chance annihilation. Thermonuclear weapons, however, favor the prospective victim of aggression, it is said, by making it comparatively easy to retaliate effectively. So a lesser power can deter even a major nuclear power such as the Soviet Union. Thermonuclear wars, therefore, will be unlikely when nuclear forces are widespread. And because limited wars risk escalation to thermonuclear war with its attendant destructiveness, they too are improbable. It would seem hard to find a more lighthearted contrast to the unilateral disarmers' grim estimate of the consequences of the diffusion of nuclear capabilities. But there may be more persuasive ones.

Let us begin with the rather paradoxical claim that it is not very difficult for a small power to deter a Soviet nuclear attack. This claim has had a long history, dating almost from the time of Hiroshima. A number of distinguished analysts then held that nuclear bombs would be the poor countries' weapon, a kind of equalizer in international politics, giving their smallest possessor the power of retaliation over the largest. However, such judgments were not based on any sophisticated analysis of the requirements for deterring the Soviet Union. Even at the time that Britain and later France decided to become nuclear powers, there was little evidence that the distinction between a first- and a second-strike capability was understood. Later justifications were excessively optimistic: the British exaggerated the time that would be available in the event of surprise attack; French military theorists overestimated the number of Russian missiles required to destroy sheltered missiles, miscalculating their accuracy by factors no lower than 5 and sometimes as high as 25. Now, methods of keeping bombs and delivery vehicles on the move are being looked to in the hope that mobility will permit them to survive.

But the job of retaliation is more complicated than simply assuring the survival of a few bombs and delivery vehicles in the face of an initial strategic assault. Its analysis involves much more complex and uncertain quantitative interactions than the simple duels, now abounding in the literature of nuclear strategy, in which the aggressor's strategic missiles hit the victim's, and the remainder of these in turn automatically destroy the aggressor's cities. In the last year or two, it has become somewhat better understood that, even for the United States, getting a responsible deterrent to Russian attack is far from easy. It is vital and feasible, but hard. Yet the United States has incomparable advantages of distance, size and industrial strength. While there are many barriers to retaliation besides surviving strategic missile attack, in what follows I shall focus on one which plays an especially crucial role in an examination of theories of multiple national strike forces and joint deterrents. This is the critically important problem of maintaining a protected and responsible command and control.

This obstacle to assuring retaliation against a major power would be less formidable if we were willing to be sufficiently irresponsible, if in fact we were to institute the sort of automatic and decentralized decision system by subordinate commanders which Lord Russell infers to be the present arrangement. If our response system were sufficiently hair-trigger, we might make it unlikely that our missiles would be caught before launching; even very ambiguous indications would trip our nuclear response. However, the chance of starting a nuclear war by mistake or without authorization would then be very much larger than it is. If one takes a sufficiently responsible view and requires positive orders from high authority to launch a retaliatory blow, there is the problem of protecting that authority, and the flow of information to and from it.

The United States has not set up a response system which involves starting World War III automatically on the basis of radar or infra-red signals, or as the result of a failure in communication, or even on the detection of an unidentified nuclear explosion. On the contrary, it has set up "fail-safe" procedures and positive controls. Frequently, those who are most concerned about the nth country problem and the dangers of accidental war believe that "the maintenance of deterrent stability is relatively easy to achieve," but they base this belief in part on the notion that we should or will inevitably erect a completely automatic system for deciding to go to war.[4] It is not surprising, then, that these theorists take the accident problem as something which will have to be solved by the

[4] National Planning Association, "1970 Without Arms Control," Special Committee Report, pp. 32–33, 44. Quotation from p. 48.

deus ex machina of international agreement. However, to adopt an automatic procedure, which these theorists themselves regard as extraordinarily dangerous, is not inevitable but a matter of choice. Such considerations suggest that the problem of forestalling deliberate attack is inseparable from that of preventing war by miscalculation. The solution of one can be made comparatively easy only at the expense of the other. The task of both national defense and arms control is to solve them simultaneously.

With the multiplication of national strike forces, the control problem becomes especially acute. If many nations have the power of decision, and if, in addition, each nation decentralizes its control to a multiplicity of subordinates, or—worse—to some electronic automata, it is evident that the situation could get out of hand very easily. The difficulty of distinguishing accidents from attacks or, if the attack is actual, of identifying its source would be enormously increased. Diffusion therefore places increased burdens on control. Yet precisely because it is hard to get a responsibly controlled deterrent with a small national force, some advocates of diffusion have proposed such desperate expedients as huge "dirty" weapons with only the most primitive guidance and possibly no control.

There are other barriers to retaliation and analysis of them would reinforce the point: the task of getting and keeping a force able to survive Russian attack and hurdle all the barriers to retaliation, including the preservation of control and the flow of information necessary for intelligent decision, is much more difficult than proponents of independent strike forces have been willing to recognize. Not many nations will solve the problems involved. England's cancellation of its costly program for the Blue Streak missile marked the conscious transition from a hopefully "independent deterrent" to the much less ambitious "independent contribution to the deterrent." And it is not without reason—as François Mauriac has pointed out—that France's first "deterrent" vehicles will be called "Mirage."

The problem of deterring a major power requires a continuing effort because the requirements for deterrence will change with the counter-measures taken by the major power. Therefore, the costs can never be computed with certainty; one can be sure only that the initiation fee is merely a down payment on the expense of membership in the nuclear club. For the same reason, the alternative idea that a lesser power ought to be given a deterrent which it cannot get by itself should be regarded with caution by both the donor and the recipient. The gift is not only expensive; it is obsolescent as soon as given. It is not a grant of independence but of continuing dependency.

It follows, therefore, that both the pessimistic and cheerful prophets of the wide diffusion of "cheap" retaliatory systems forget that this is not a simple matter of improving technology to cut the cost of a standardized product. Unfortunately, the job of building barriers to retaliation is subject to improvement too. Published studies of the diffusion problem consider only the requirements for making bombs, not those for securing retaliatory systems. An effective system of retaliation must meet changing demands placed upon it by the aggressor. Retaliatory systems in the last decade have become no cheaper. They *may* in the future, but it is dubious, and the simple affirmation that they will is not very persuasive. The cost of the first 100 B-58's, Atlases, or submarine-launched Polarises —including development and all other fixed and variable expenses needed for five years of peacetime operation—will be from three to five times greater than the costs of the first 100 B-47's.

Growing awareness of the complexities of retaliation has brought into prominence the argument that a smaller power, just because it is a less important prize, need not have a capability to do much damage in order to deter, and that a capability of sufficient size is not hard to acquire. This theory of "proportional deterrence" relies on several unfounded assumptions. Nothing quite so simple as a proportionality works here. There are huge "entrance fees" for getting even one's first strategic missile and the communications and other elements to go with it. The costs of a small force are disproportionately high. The research and development costs of American missiles have been extremely heavy. It might appear that such expenses will be substantially less for nth countries, since they will benefit by the results of our work. This belief rests in part on ignoring the dynamic aspects of the problem and the possibility of counter-measures: the missiles which the nth countries learn about after a time lag, and develop after a further time lag, are likely not to be relevant for their original purpose. Surely the history of development programs among the lesser powers for both missiles and aircraft is not very encouraging.

But there are two additional factors, which weigh heavily against secondary powers. First, the United States and Russia benefit in any specific development program from parallel programs in progress or completed. Navigation systems or systems of propulsion, for example, may be transferable. So the Atlas was able to use a booster developed for the Navajo, and the Navy Ship Inertial Navigation System has several uses. Perhaps most important, the research, managerial, and production skills, and the physical plant developed for earlier weapons are useful for the next. The major countries, in short, benefit in any particular missile development by the fact that they have created a huge space technology and rocket industry. This will be much less the case for a small country. Second, the United States and the Soviet Union spread their fixed or initial costs, including research and development, over a great many units—the lesser powers over only a few. The per-unit cost tends therefore to be much higher for *n*th countries.

Although this discussion has focused on *system* problems (specifically, command, control, co-ordination), rather than simply the vehicles, this does not mean that vehicles or their numbers are unimportant. It will not be easy for lesser powers to obtain their first missiles, much less an adequate number. Moreover, it should not be assumed that a force of ten missiles—even assuming they are safely launched—will do one-tenth the damage of 100 missiles. Here again, the proponents of the small deterrent have vastly oversimplified their problem. By means of active defense—to take just one example—a major power can reduce the effectiveness of a small force perhaps to the vanishing point. The development of decoys to aid the offense in penetrating defenses requires particularly costly and sophisticated study of re-entry into the atmosphere. While active defense against another major power is extremely difficult, it should not be very hard for a major power to erect an active defense capable of handling the retaliation, say, of Guatemala, supposing Guatemala had a few ballistic missiles. In fact, one of the consequences of nuclear diffusion would be to impose the necessity for such defenses on the major powers. A small strike force, then, could inflict, not proportionately small damage, but possibly no damage at all.

It is sometimes argued that the small power need not be able to offer much of a probability that damage will occur at all. Even a very small probability of retaliation—a mere "shadow of incertitude," it is suggested—will be enough to deter, especially because a nuclear war might escalate and lead to almost "boundless" harm. As Raymond Aron has put it, any finite probability of a boundless injury is too much to make attack worth while. This line of reasoning parallels Pascal's famous argument that, even if there were only a small probability of eternal damnation, the risk would be excessive. Yet, some have risked hellfire. It is important to observe that this argument for the adequacy of national strike forces also removes their principal reason for being—at least as it is currently avowed. The proponents of national strike forces claim they are necessary because of the lessened credibility of the American guarantee. But even the strongest enthusiast for an independent deterrent would concede there is some finite probability that the United States would fulfill its commitments, and the harm done to the enemy by an undamaged American strike force, if not boundless, is at least as great as that to be inflicted by a damaged national strike force. The advocates of national strike forces, in short, seem to place incompatible requirements on the credibility of American retaliation as compared to what they ask for themselves.

Even if the lesser power can assure only "a shadow of incertitude" of retaliation, the aggressor, in order to eliminate the possibility of retaliation, might have to effect enormous destruction. This might make aggression less attractive. But the victim's ability to force his own destruction is quite a different thing from a promise to do direct and extensive damage to the aggressor. It is rather more like the method of lying down on the railroad tracks or fasting until death used (sometimes successfully) by non-violent resisters. It is doubtful that it could be counted upon against a totalitarian opponent. And it is likely to wear heavily on the nerves of any but a nation of saints and heroes.

Of course, the advocates of nuclear diffusion are only unintentionally non-violent. Yet in effect their tactic resembles the methods consciously chosen by some of those who repudiate the bomb altogether. And, in spite of the obvious contrast, there are several strong points of resemblance between those who would distribute bombs to everybody and those who reject them altogether. It may be that the reaction of the unilateralists to the reckless nuclear policy characteristic of the diffusion advocates is made easier by the assumptions they hold in common. When General Gallois develops his view that no nation can be counted on to defend another in the atomic age, he sounds a little like Mr. Nehru and other members of the neutralist camp who talk of alliances as things of the past. It is not only the unilateral disarmers who call for the end of overseas bases and the withdrawal of American forces; the possibility of withdrawal is offered as bait by those Europeans and Americans who want us to give our allies bombs and, hopefully, the ability to shift for themselves. Both views share an underestimation of the problem of deterring deliberate attack, and specifically a deliberate Soviet attack.

Theorists of nuclear diffusion, in order to reassure us on the unstabilizing effects of the proliferation of weapons, sometimes say that no nation would use them except when confronted with annihilation or slavery. But anyone who believes this must, like the unilateralists, discount Russian nuclear attack, since the West does not confront the Soviet Union with these alternatives. It is significant that the moves toward nuclear independence in the last half dozen years have accompanied a lessening rather than a growing fear of Russian attack.

Whatever the motives for the national strike forces, they have a dubious utility for deterring Russian nuclear attack. There are, however, other functions which have been contemplated for them, and two are worth mentioning: (*a*) the deterrence of Russian non-nuclear attack; and (*b*) the defense of national interests in conflicts with lesser powers—possibly, for example, the defense of overseas interests in underdeveloped areas. Both of these have the familiar defects of the doctrine of massive retaliation which flourished in this country until recently; both lead directly to diminishing efforts in the field of conventional defense. As to the first, it is not hard for an enemy to devise a plan of aggression or a set of demands which are less than would seem to justify a nuclear response and, if conventional defenses are allowed to lapse, a small nuclear power will be extremely vulnerable. . . .

The use of nuclear status as a bargaining weapon to attain a special position within NATO is of course an acknowledgement of interdependence. The English have talked of the position of leadership conferred by their nuclear power. And the French, quite willing to believe in the existence of an Anglo-Saxon duumvirate, hope by attaining nuclear status themselves to restore the triumvirate. But it is not likely to stop there. Such an objective for a weapons program is by its very nature divisive. Not all members of the alliance can be "more equal" than the others. The allies who are slighted are bound to resent the superior position of the others, especially if, as is quite probable, it is obtained by diverting national resources from alliance obligations, and by getting the help of the United States. The British nuclear force was a direct spur to the French, and every real or fancied discrimination made in favor of England has added more incentive for the French to follow suit. It is hard to believe that the Germans will not be moved to follow the French, if we reward the French for their efforts to develop an independent nuclear power. Influence in the alliance might better be determined by contributions to NATO's defense. National nuclear forces have not added significantly to either the sword or the shield by comparison with equal amounts spent for conventional defense.

Up to this point, we have been examining the worth of a nuclear capability largely from the national standpoint of a prospective nth power. I have deferred speaking of the implications for "world stability" or, more concretely, the probability of small or large nuclear wars. It is easier to do this now when we can make a little more precise the sorts of nuclear capability that might be widely diffused. To begin with, we should distinguish the capabilities of the lesser powers against the major powers, and the sorts of capability a lesser power might have against various other lesser powers. This last in particular has been neglected.

First, to deter a major power such as the Soviet Union is hard, and this ability is not likely to be widespread. Second, the ability to disarm a major country and so to preclude extensive damage to oneself is likely to be still harder, if the major country exercises care, and particularly if it is a totalitarian country exploiting the characteristic advantages of secrecy. Against totalitarian Russia, I know of no *reliable* way even for the United States to achieve and maintain such a "preclusive first-strike capability." There remains a third capability—to strike first and do damage without precluding retaliation. Against a major power only this third sort is likely to be at all general. But this is a good deal less useful to its possessor than either a deterrent or a preclusive first-strike capability.

Against lesser countries, a secondary nuclear power might have any one of the three capabilities described. It might be able to do a little or a lot of self-destructive mischief. It might be able to attack and prevent all damage to itself. This obviously would be the case if the victim were not a nuclear power, but it could also be the case if both the aggressor and the victim were nuclear powers. Each might have the ability to preclude the other from striking, depending on who struck first. The only live question then would be which one would be dead. Finally, between some pairs of lesser powers there might be a relation of mutual deterrence.

What does this mean for the likelihood of nuclear war? The view that widespread diffusion will be stabilizing assumes that the prototype relation among the many powers will be mutual deterrence. But it would in fact be a miracle if *every* pair of countries out of a large number of nuclear powers stood in this relationship. These countries are at different stages of development and in different relative strategic positions. It would be remarkable if there were not strong asymmetries and sometimes symmetrical "preclusive" capabilities. Relations, moreover, would shift constantly with changes in the military technology of the various powers and with the shifting coalitions among them.

If one starts with the assumption that all prospective *n*th countries are interested in deterrence rather than aggression, one might suppose that an addition of nuclear weapons to their arsenal might merely add to the deterrent. However, in the real world, if there are many nuclear powers, some are likely to be interested in aggression and some able to get away with it without response from the victim. While the more responsible powers would be hard put to it to find a use for their nuclear capability, diffusion is likely to bring some less responsible recruits into the club. Then, with the major powers eager to avoid involvement, a lesser nuclear power might feel that he could attack one of his brethren with impunity. On the other hand, if, as may happen, a potential conflict looks as though it will be hard to isolate, it may be less likely to occur, but much more serious.

The probability of war by "mistake" as well as by deliberation is likely to increase. Vulnerability to attack and the incidence of "mistakes" can, it is important to observe again, be affected by the way we shape our posture, including our decision-making processes. However, the proliferation of nuclear forces has an essential connection with the difficulty of solving these two problems simultaneously. It places an increased burden on a system of positive control, and therefore increases also the problem of its protection. A dispersion of nuclear weapons complicates the problem of responsible deterrence by increasing the ambiguity as to sources of attack. One must decide not only whether one is under attack, but who has attacked; or one may feel obliged to attack all possible culprits including powers so far not involved; or the powers not yet attacked might pre-empt in order to diminish the consequences to themselves of a probable spread of the conflict. The instability would be a world-wide problem. Even if, with large-scale proliferation, each new nuclear power adopted a positive control system with a high standard of responsibility, there would be an increase in the possibility of mistakes, simply because there would be *more* control centers. It is apparent that this problem is not widely understood. When it is, this should reduce any temptation to cut the costs of a national force by "volume" sales to other powers.

To sum up the case against national nuclear forces: from the national standpoint of a responsible power, they are costly and of dubious military value. Their political value has been exaggerated, for, as the English have learned, it encourages emulation and is therefore transient. From the standpoint of world stability, wide nuclear diffusion would be gravely disruptive. It would increase the likelihood of the use of nuclear weapons both by accident and by deliberation.

III. JOINTLY CONTROLLED STRIKE FORCES

Joint forces, such as the proposed NATO strike force, have been suggested as a means of strengthening the alliance and of heading off the diffusion of nuclear control—in particular, to offer the French some substitute for a national force and thereby to remove a stimulus to the Germans. Some very thoughtful analysts and policy-makers have supported these proposals, and, given the disturbing implications of nuclear diffusion, they deserve the most sympathetic consideration. None the less, I believe the proposals for joint nuclear forces are mistaken. They are likely to propagate the diffusion they are intended to control. They are expedients, and their precise content is unclear. I believe, therefore, that they will weaken rather than "save" the alliance.

Proposals for a NATO strike force usually take at face value the claim that Europeans are genuinely fearful of a massive nuclear attack to which the United States would not respond and that it is this fear which motivates diffusion. To begin with, let us also take this claim at its face value. Would a NATO strike force in fact satisfy the problem? Would it be more credible as a deterrent to nuclear attack on Europe than the U.S. guarantee? There are several reasons for believing that it would be considerably *less* credible. I shall focus once more on the command and control problem.

What is it that members of NATO want—the power to launch a nuclear strike or the power to say "No"? There is much evidence to suggest that Europeans have been worried most about the possibility that the United States may be trigger-happy; they are mainly interested, therefore, in the power to say "No." Even General de Gaulle, who has said that it is intolerable for France to depend on other countries for its defense, has indicated that he would like the ability to veto the use of nuclear weapons by the West anywhere in the world. But if those who jointly control the NATO force are principally interested in the power to say "No," then the response of the joint force is less credible than the U.S. guarantee. For one thing, as a member of NATO, the United States has a vote, and if a strike is not in our interest, we would presumably exercise our veto. But even if we did not have a vote or did not exercise it, the chance that at least one of the European powers would vote "No" seems extremely high—higher than the chance of an American veto, simply because there are many powers voting. But ironically, the power to veto the use of a NATO strike force would not offer much satisfaction to those who are worried about the control of their fates, and specifically control over supposedly trigger-happy Americans. Giving the members of NATO a smaller strategic force to veto during a crisis would not by sympathetic magic prevent Americans from invoking the tremendous power of SAC. Plans for joint controls, then, provide no assurance that the NATO strike force will itself respond, and none that SAC will not.

On the other hand, if the purpose of joint control is to say "Yes," then what is its meaning? No one to my knowledge has suggested that the NATO strike force be at the disposal of any member of NATO who desires to use it, regardless of what the others think. This of course would be the extreme short cut to the nuclear decentralization which the NATO strike force is supposed to avoid. Is the decision, then, to be taken by majority vote? By all or a majority of a subcommittee? Suggestions that have been made for committees of five or three powers to launch the NATO strike force raise in the most acute form questions of national sovereignty. They are not likely to be more practicable than the modest proposals for a division of labor in NATO, which have so far presented insurmountable obstacles. For the fifteen countries to define "rules of engagement" for the use of a strategic force means that each must state in advance the precise circumstances under which it is willing to be committed to a general thermonuclear war and to whom it would give this power of commitment. Agreement here would offer the greatest political difficulties. The hope that the problem can be solved by the formation of a United Europe, in which there would be no separate considerations of national interest, seems at the present date rather forlorn.

Another alternative, and the one most frequently discussed, is to delegate the decision to the Supreme Allied Commander for Europe (SACEUR). But SACEUR is at present a highly responsible American general, and it seems doubtful that any other than an American could be agreed on. (There is at any rate little enthusiasm for an English SACEUR in France, for a German SACEUR in England, for a Turkish SACEUR . . . and so on.) But is it really easier to place confidence in a decision by a responsible American SACEUR than by the American President? If retaliation were not in the American interest, SACEUR would order it only if he were not responsible to that interest and to the President: that is to say, only if he were not a responsible American general.

This point will stand out with greater clarity if it is understood that the launching of the NATO strike force is intended—quite explicitly in the minds of most of its proponents—as a trigger for central war and the use of SAC. The firing of Polaris missiles from NATO-controlled submarines would be indistinguishable from the firing of missiles under U.S. control. Russian retaliation is then likely to be directed at the United States and, since the United States would expect this, it would have little choice but to launch its weapons in anticipation. The power to launch the NATO strike force is therefore the power to decide on World War III. The President of the United States has not delegated the authority to make war to the Commander of SAC. It is unlikely that he would give to SACEUR an irrevocable power to commit the United States to war, especially for a contingency in which the United States is not attacked and the President is alive and able to make the decision. In fact, it is hard to see just how much power could be made irrevocable. But if it is revocable, how has it helped the supposed problem of "credibility"?

I have suggested that protecting command and control and making them responsible are crucial for avoiding accidental war and at the same time deterring deliberate attack. If, as we have seen, it is difficult for the European countries individually to solve this problem, it is still harder for a *joint* command and control close to the enemy. The joint decision is more complex, involves more parties, and will be extremely hard to protect. It seems dubious that the NATO strike force will be a convincing substitute for the American guarantee in the event of massive nuclear attack on Europe.

On the other hand, the NATO strike force has sometimes been suggested as a substitute for the American guarantee, not in the event of a massive nuclear attack on Europe, but in case of a nuclear attack on a single NATO nation. However, it is hard to see in this case why the unattacked NATO countries would be more likely than the United States to exchange their cities for a few Russian cities in retaliation for their fallen ally. We would have to presume that, say, Turkey is more closely identified with Norway, or Iceland with Greece, than is the United States.

In sum, it seems unlikely that a NATO strike force would provide a deterrent to the Soviets more credible than that of the dubious national strike forces. It is still more doubtful that it would improve the American guarantee.

Let us now examine critically the assumption that the Europeans are moved to seek nuclear independence or a Nato strike force by a deep concern about a Soviet thermonuclear attack on Europe to which the United States would not respond. In good part, the American estimates of European fears project some American emotions. We have initiated much of the movement toward reliance on nuclear weapons in Europe, and our advocacy of nuclear sharing and of European union has been reinforced by an implicit isolationism: a hope that somehow a Europe capable of self-defense would enable the United States to reduce its overseas burdens and commitments. Such American views in turn unsettle the Europeans.

We greatly oversimplify the diverse fears and motives of the Nato powers. The only Nato countries that have attempted nuclear independence are England and France, and their programs started long before anyone was raising grave doubts about the American response—the English in the 1940's, the French in 1954. While these programs have been rationalized variously at different times, there is little evidence that the dominating incentive has been an urgent fear of Russian nuclear attack. On the contrary, diminishing efforts in national defense, hopeful statements about the prospect of resolving East-West antagonisms, and many explicit avowals suggest that the Europeans are little worried about a deliberate massive nuclear attack. If they are not worried, then their doubt about an American response to such an attack becomes an academic question. In discussing national strike forces, I have already listed motives for nuclear military programs which have nothing to do with fear of Russian nuclear attack, and may even be incompatible with such a fear. The Europeans, of course, do have legitimate worries, but these center on the adequacy and appropriateness of Nato response to lower levels of aggression.

The Nato strike force is no more relevant for other objectives of national nuclear forces. For deterrence of Russian non-nuclear attack, it has roughly the same defects as national forces. Like them, it may favor the illusion of providing a suitable response to conventional attack, though many of its principal proponents have the opposite intent. As in the case of those who advocate multiplying national nuclear forces on condition that conventional forces be expanded, the condition seems hard to impose. The joint force obviously could not be used for defense of purely national interests or in conflicts with other lesser powers; especially in the case of overseas interests, it is hardly likely to receive the consent of other members of the alliance. It is no use at all as a bargaining weapon for special position in the alliance, and it opposes completely the affirmation of national sovereignty. In short, it satisfies neither the surface nor the underlying motives for national nuclear military programs, and it is not likely therefore to head them off. In fact, many of the French have been explicit on this point. Like President de Gaulle, some members of the National Assembly oppose the NATO force. Others openly favor it as a boost to the French national force, because, for one thing, they believe it will further weaken the MacMahon Act. But with or without the NATO force, the French Government intends to get its own *force de frappe*. In the words of General Billotte, the NATO strike force "does not respond even partially to the exigencies imposed for the security of France. . . . It could in no manner be substituted for the French project."

Another hazard of a NATO force is that one of the members might withdraw some part of the force in time of crisis or, perhaps, to realize some purpose of its own. As a safeguard against this withdrawal, it has been suggested that installations be manned by mixed teams from all the member nations. Operational commanders, however, question whether such an arrangement is workable. In any case, the questions of sovereignty are here raised in a particularly acute form; General de Gaulle has resisted much less thorough integration. (The recent compromise on integrating French air defense in Europe applies only to the very small fraction of French fighters on German soil.) This safeguard of multi-national teams seems destined to be compromised out of existence also.

One omen of such compromises is that the NATO strike force has among its supporters not only those who want to restrain nuclear diffusion, but some who are simply unclear and many who are actively in favor of the spread.[5] These gentlemen are like the stout lady who drinks her Metrecal as an appetizer before a full-course dinner.

Some proponents of the NATO strike force concede that its military worth would be low, but feel that its political value is high. Its

---

[5] For example, *The New York Times* of July 23, 1960, reported that the Secretary General of NATO explored with General de Gaulle the possibility of France's accepting a gift of nuclear missiles under its own control, provided they would also accept some others to be placed under joint control.

political worth, however, may be negative. First of all, its political effects cannot be divorced from its military content. If, as I have suggested, the alleged merits of a NATO strike force will not bear analysis, this will be evident in time and is bound to trouble our allies. Second, the automatic-decision features in some versions of the proposal have disturbing political implications and would be likely to feed the fires of unilateralism both here and in Europe. Third, the probable refusal of some of our principal NATO partners to join in the project would tend to break the alliance into blocs. Fourth, it may be interpreted as a move toward withdrawal of the American umbrella. Some of the French are quick to catch suggestions to this effect in the American press. During the November debate in the French senate, Philippe Dargenlieu used these suggestions to justify doubts about the American guarantee, and as evidence of the need for a national nuclear force. Fifth, it lends a little substance to the fashionable statements about the incredibility of the American guarantee.

In many indirect as well as direct ways, then, the NATO strike force seems more likely to be a step along the way to diffusion than a means to inhibit it. Both its military and its political worth are more than doubtful.

IV. THE AMERICAN GUARANTEE AGAINST NUCLEAR ATTACK

It is fashionable to say that an American response to a Soviet nuclear attack in Europe is incredible. Is the statement true? What precisely does it mean?

Perhaps the first thing to observe is that it means nothing very precise. To talk in terms of credibility or incredibility suggests that the alternatives are simply Yes or No. But, in fact, neither our response nor our failure to respond is certain. The real questions center on how likely we would be to respond in circumstances that are worth considering. What risks would the Russians undertake if they attacked Europe on the assumption that we would not reply? How safe would the Russians feel? These questions are connected with others: How large is the American stake in defending Europe from annihilation or take-over by the Communists? From the American point of view, how would the risks of failing to react—if bombs were dropping on Europe—compare with the risks of retaliation? What are the chances of irrational decision? What would be a rational decision in terms of American self-interest?

Sober thought would suggest that the American response is by no means "incredible." The fashionable notion, I believe, is wrong, even if we interpret "incredible" as meaning simply "very unlikely." In any plausible circumstance of thermonuclear attack on Europe, we would be likely to reply today, and, if we and our allies choose our policies carefully, this will remain true. It seems clear that the Russians do not find an American response hard to believe, since they have been deterred from taking over Europe by fear of this response, and not by moral scruples or an inability to overwhelm purely European defenses.

There are many reasons why the Russians should doubt their ability to isolate Europe and attack it alone, without attacking the United States. For one thing, a considerable portion of American nuclear power is dotted over Europe in a great many places from the United Kingdom to Turkey. It would be difficult to distinguish between a massive nuclear attack on Europe alone and the first wave of a wider attack which would almost immediately engulf the United States. There are profound questions as to whether we could stand by while our allies were being taken over and destroyed piecemeal, without expecting a basic shift in power which would threaten eventual annihilation or takeover of the United States it-self. But quite apart from such relevant long-term questions, there would be a large risk of imminent destruction of much of the con-tinental United States.

To understand this a little better, we might contemplate how such an attack might look in the awful moments of the crisis itself. Is it likely that the Russians would stage a massive nuclear attack on Europe and leave untouched the several dozen points where American nuclear forces are stationed? It would be extremely dan-gerous; most would agree, very improbable. On our control boards in the basement of the Pentagon, in Colorado Springs, and else-where, we would see that a considerable portion of our nuclear capability had been eliminated, that a large portion of our forces had not yet been hit. Could we be counted on not to use these forces while they were still alive?

To fill out the picture a little, we should recall that around and about the United States at any particular moment there are un-known aircraft not definitely identified as friendly. From time to time, the number gets quite large—large enough to be "critical," that is, to be explicable only as an extremely out-of-the-ordinary configuration of air traffic or as errors in identification or possibly as an enemy raid headed toward or already infiltrating the United States. Experience shows that crises tend to generate false reports of over-flights or incursions. These and several other types of false alarm are ordinarily taken in stride. They are evaluated along with other indications of hostile action. But the coincidence of such an alarm with unmistakable confirmation of a Russian attack on Europe, if not certain to get us going, would surely add appreciably to the Soviet risk.

If we add to this picture of great menace to the country the knowledge that hundreds of thousands of Americans as well as millions of our close allies would already have been killed, it should not be hard to believe that we would make the decision to send our forces off. It is quite absurd, in fact, to think that the Russians have nothing to worry about. They would have to calculate our reactions under enormous stress, and they would have to risk a good deal more than a "shadow of incertitude." To destroy part of our strike force and leave a larger part of it untouched would involve the utmost risk.

There are other ways in which we have identified our own defense with that of Europe. The most obvious one deserves considerable weight: we have signed a treaty saying that we do. For the United States it is not merely a figure of speech to say that we will treat an attack on Europe as an attack on ourselves. A failure to fulfill a commitment on a much less momentous matter would mean a tremendous loss in political power. While our promise alone may not be enough, it would be a mistake to underestimate the seriousness of our undertaking. We have predisposed ourselves to act.

Even if a cold calculation were to suggest that the balance lay in favor of *not* responding to Russian aggression, there is obviously a very considerable chance that in the circumstances we would not calculate coldly. In any event, there are immediate and long-run risks in failing to respond. The analysis presented so far should make clear that our response would not simply depend on the possibility of our acting irrationally. If Europe had suffered a massive nuclear attack, it would be *reasonable* for us to expect the same at any instant. An aggressor who did not take this into account would himself be extremely irrational, for he would have put himself in an extraordinarily dangerous position, inviting by his delay an attempt by us to blunt his strategic force. The situation would be terribly unstable and would not recover quickly. If an attack on the United States did not immediately follow an attack on Europe, we would be justified in assuming either that the act was unauthorized or that some tremendous miscalculation had been made. And whether or

not this were true, the aggressor would have to be concerned about
the possibilities of pre-emption. The temptations on each side to
forestall the other would be enormous.

Even if the aggressor were to take pains to make clear that he
was attacking "only" Europe, and leaving America intact, this
would be so unreasonable that it is unlikely we could be convinced.
It is hard even to imagine a sensible motivation for an attack of this
sort. A somewhat more plausible scenario might be trumped up for
an attack against a single ally that had become a menacing, independent nuclear power. This, it should be observed, would be the
result of diffusion, rather than a justification for it. But no plausible
motive suggests itself for a massive attack on Europe in isolation.
Such an attack seems to be a creation of some overly simple models
of the world, rather than anything likely to occur in it. For Europeans, it would seem that the last contingency to worry about is a
deliberate massive nuclear attack on Europe which ignored the
United States.

One final point should be recalled. To deter such an attack our
response need not be certain. It must be probable enough to make
the aggression excessively dangerous to the aggressor. The probability of our response is clearly large.

In examining the probability of our response, I have concentrated on the risks to us of failing to respond. We can and should
also reduce the damage we could expect if we did respond. It is
important, however, not to exaggerate what can be accomplished
in this area. We should attempt to control the violence and diminish the frightfulness of a thermonuclear war. We should do this
primarily because, in spite of our best efforts to avoid it, thermonuclear war may come, for example, as the result of an "accident" or
an irrational or unauthorized act. But no active or civil-defense or
other program for limiting the damage done to us in a thermonuclear war is likely to be so reliable that it would seem reasonable for
the United States to go to war unless the alternatives were enormously risky. For this reason, a program to limit damage is not
likely to make the United States be or seem aggressive. For the
same reason, it would not reassure the Europeans that we would
respond if there were not substantial risks in failing to respond.[6]

[6] The military editor of the London *Times*, for example, finds it as hard "to
imagine an American President willing to risk death of 5 million Americans
as of 50 million." His comments were prompted by some widely discussed
American doubts about the credibility of American response to nuclear attack
on Europe. However, these American doubts envisage quite incredible hypo-

The most important purpose of our commitment to Europe and the deployment of our forces there is to make explicit to the Russians, to the Europeans, and to ourselves that we are aware of the enormous risks to the United States in not defending Europe against massive nuclear attack.

What sort of risks would the Russians take? When we are not thinking wishfully about the Russians, we tend to think of them as if they represented the complete negative of our desires. But a move which would damage us would not necessarily be useful to them. It is important to consider a Russian threat from the standpoint of Russian self-interest. From their standpoint, the problem of successful aggression in Europe is to find a level and kind of attack large enough to be useful but small enough to be well below the threshold risking American nuclear response.

NATO's problem is to try to make sure the Russians cannot manage a useful attack without making it so large that it would be hard to distinguish from the start of a central war. Europe's principal strategic disadvantage is that it is susceptible to attack with conventional weapons, whereas the United States is not. It is becoming more and more widely accepted among critics of NATO that the most important task for the alliance today is to raise by conventional means the threshold of attack that the Russians would have to launch in order to be successful. The main defect of NATO strategy in the 1950's was a refusal to face this problem. Since 1954,

---

thetical circumstances in which our decision would be made. Herman Kahn (*On Thermonuclear War* [Princeton, N.J., 1960], pp. 27 f.) constructs his hypothesis as follows: (1) The Russians "simply to demonstrate their strength and resolve" wipe out London, Berlin, Rome, Paris, and Bonn. (2) Following this event, which must be the classic case of all time for simply flexing muscles, the American decision-maker is prevented from making any decision for twenty-four hours. (3) During these twenty-four hours, he is assumed to contemplate first the fact that 180 million Americans would be killed if he should say "Yes" and, second, the fact that no attack on the United States would be made if he said "No." Kahn varies the numbers of Americans assumed killed in the raid to let the reader determine the "price" he would be willing to pay to fulfill American commitments to Europe. But he does not vary the probabilities of either the number of Americans dead, given that we strike, or the number of Americans dead, given that we do not strike. In effect, he suggests one alternative with a very large price and another one that carries essentially no penalty.

In the real world, the alternatives are not likely to be tens of millions or 180 million dead with certainty versus the certainty of total survival. Kahn leaves out all of the factors favoring a rational decision to respond, the large risks likely to be incurred by not responding.

NATO policy has been based on the assumption that the Alliance would respond with nuclear weapons to any kind of aggression other than a local or temporary incursion. NATO military theorists took the view that the West had no choice but to adopt a policy of nuclear response to Soviet attack. The Russian hordes, we were told, could not be matched by NATO manpower but only by the increased firepower derived from nuclear weapons. This argument was doubtful both in its estimate of NATO capabilities for non-nuclear defense and in its notion that nuclear weapons would redress the balance in favor of the West. . . .

To sum up the four alternatives for avoiding nuclear attack on Europe: for the Europeans, the first alternative, to repudiate all reliance on nuclear weapons including the American guarantee, would increase the likelihood of Soviet attack. Such an attack would still be dangerous for the Soviet Union, since the long-run interests of the United States would be critically injured by it. Yet, it is apparent that, in so far as the attempt to disentangle the immediate fate of Europe from that of the United States was successful, it would lessen the probability of American response and the consequent risks of aggression. But the second and third alternatives are hardly better than the first. A European effort to achieve nuclear independence, either in the guise of national forces or of any of various joint enterprises, would have much the same effect. It would weaken the American guarantee against Soviet attack without putting anything of substance in its place. The fourth alternative, the American guarantee of Europe, is a necessity for both the United States and Europe.

To keep the American guarantee valid, it is important not to diminish American nuclear power in Europe until conventional forces have expanded to close any gap; but, in any case, it is essential for us to stay in Europe. To remove any doubts about the responsible use of nuclear power, it is vital to keep that power under centralized control. For deterrence and responsibility we must do what we can to inhibit the diffusion of nuclear weapons.

Such a policy is best from the standpoint of both American and European security. It happens also to be sound from the standpoint of the stability of the world system and—in so far as the Soviet Union has a common interest with us in avoiding the chance of nuclear miscalculations—it may be in their interest too. This last is not necessarily a demerit. Our interests are not the negative of Russian desires, any more than the reverse is true. We should not assume that the acquisition of nuclear weapons by China or the Warsaw powers is good for us because it is bad for the Russians.

A good many people today favor unilateral steps toward disarmament, even at great risk, in the hope that this will lead the Russians to take similar actions. My point is quite different. The policies advocated here would *improve* alliance defense. We should take these measures, so to speak, "even though" they are in the interests of both East and West—for example, in reducing the chance of war by miscalculation or "accident."

It may be felt that such a national policy to abate, delay, or control nuclear diffusion is too uncertain or slow, that only an extensive arms-control agreement and perhaps even the imposition of a world authority are worth trying. However, we should not think of the achievement of arms control as if it were going to take place in one millennial, transfiguring instant. The serious control proposals on the agenda for negotiation today would themselves be at best very small steps, very indirect and uncertain. A verifiable test-ban agreement could have a modest utility, but it would be a long way from stopping the diffusion of nuclear capability and would fail to offset the strides toward diffusion taken by several of our alliance policies. By the same token, a reversal of such alliance policies is likely to be a more effective brake on nuclear diffusion. Both in our national security policies and in our arms-control agreements, we can only hope to work on the problems of stability piecemeal. The probability of nuclear war, however, can be affected year by year.

ELEVEN

MALCOLM W. HOAG

Nuclear Strategic Options and European Force Participation

[Editor's Note: In this article, Mr. Hoag offers a detailed examination of the practical requirements for achieving the third of the nuclear options set out by Professor Wohlstetter in the preceding chapter: a jointly controlled nuclear force. His position combines aspects of Schelling's and Wohlstetter's theses: he shares Schelling's concern with relating the strategic preferences of the various members of the Alliance to each other, and supports Wohlstetter's insistence on central control of all the nuclear weapons of the Atlantic Alliance. He argues that it is impossible to prevent nations which possess advanced technology from becoming nuclear powers if their strategic assessment demands it. If central control over nuclear weapons is to be achieved in an alliance of technologically advanced countries, the problem becomes how to prevent allies from developing a desire for an autonomous nuclear capability.

Mr. Hoag recommends the creation of a multi-national nuclear striking force, including the existing national forces together with NATO-manned elements. Such a force, in Mr. Hoag's view, would reinforce the concept of a greater Atlantic Community and eliminate any doubt about the credibility of the American commitment to the defense of Western Europe. He argues that any joint solution, whatever its difficulties and risks, is far preferable to a strategy that emphasizes national nuclear forces.]

Whether or not the United States should assist European members of NATO toward nuclear forces under their control, a greater share in policy governing strategic forces, or participation in particular strategic forces of the alliance, are open questions. Further, if there

EDITOR'S NOTE: Reprinted with permission from *The Dispersion of Nuclear Weapons*, edited by R. N. Rosecrance (New York and London: Columbia University Press, 1964) pp. 222, 226–51.

is to be greater European participation, should it be collective; and, if so, should it take the form of a European force or a NATO-wide force?

Many answers have been given, with different opinions about how a particular policy should be implemented. Political discussion has been plentiful but frequently naïve. It has often suffered, understandably, from insufficient technical and strategic comprehension of the new American policy for possibly controlled nuclear response; but also, inexplicably, from insufficient attention to conflicting elements in European preferences. Before turning to more difficult problems about collective nuclear-force possibilities, an analysis of the usual arguments for American aid to the projected French strategic force can illustrate both deficiencies in the discussion. . . .

IMPLICATIONS OF CONTROLLED NUCLEAR RESPONSE

NATO unity demands a better answer for nuclear defense against the threat of overwhelming attack against Europe, and American policy and prospective capabilities already supply one. There is, first and foremost, our pledge. That we view and express ourselves as part of NATO, and not apart from NATO, is mandatory, as are the deeds that back the words. Our military presence in Europe is not a mere token. An effective Soviet surprise attack upon West Germany could hardly avoid some of our nuclear capabilities. It would probably kill more American than German soldiers, and certainly many more Americans than Frenchmen. To further enhance the credibility of American nuclear response after so direct an attack upon us and our allies, if that response be needed, our strike capabilities greatly exceed those required to cover only Soviet cities. We can employ the strategy of a rich nuclear power, not a poor one; contrary to popular belief, there remains a vast difference between the two.

The difference lies not so much in greater numbers of retaliatory instruments available to us (although these are important) as in their greater protection and more sophisticated capabilities for planning and continuing control. We obviously could and might launch the all-out strike that fits the usual image. This strike would be designed to minimize Soviet capabilities to counter-retaliate, which implies that Russian civilians in large numbers would be killed as a by-product of smashing Soviet retaliatory capabilities. But in cold self-interest, as well as moral revulsion, we might well choose to do otherwise. What our strategic plenty gives us is the ability to choose among alternative tactics, each of which poses so formidable a threat to Soviet interests that it is a compelling deterrent even where we impose severe restraints upon ourselves. Smaller and less sophisticated nuclear systems in order to pose a serious deterrent, must promise to be used in as blunt and bloody a manner as possible. Since "city-killing" is commonly assumed to be relatively easy, the small independent national deterrent force tends to be directed to that purpose. The idea of "city-sparing" in otherwise full-scale general nuclear war is a heresy that, consistent with formidable deterrence, can be entertained only by a big nuclear power.

Here lies the novelty of an American policy that NATO, above all, needs to understand. At the University of Michigan on June 16, 1962, Secretary McNamara stated plainly that, "principal military objectives, in the event of a nuclear war stemming from a major attack on the alliance, should be the destruction of the enemy's military forces, not of his civilian population."

Why spare enemy cities in a nuclear attack prompted by an extreme Soviet attack upon Europe? The answer is as simple as it is upsetting to established patterns of strategic thought. Our ultimate deterrent power is that we hold enemy cities as hostages, and the enemy knows it. The bargaining power over him that these hostages give us is an asset we should be loath to throw away. We surely want to compel restraint in whatever retaliation he is capable of after our attack, and the way to compel restraint is to bring home to the enemy that most of his civilization remains hostage to us and that its survival is contingent upon his own restraint. With great and secure strategic power, we can withhold enough from an initial counter-military attack to keep his cities always under an overriding threat.

For us to leave his war industry alive another day or two is, contrary to yesterday's dogma, a trivial price. To leave untouched those military control facilities that are situated in cities may, in contrast, be costly because it permits him to retaliate; or it may yield enormous benefit, because only then can enemy political leaders stop or restrain retaliation. The measure of this last gain or cost must be left open, and we need not commit ourselves to only one retaliatory plan. But we can preserve the option to choose, by city-sparing, to carry the power to deter powerfully through nuclear war, rather than deem deterrence wholly to have failed if nuclear war occurred. And for this element of American policy and capabilities, as for emphasis upon conventional forces, our seriousness is demonstrated in the most tangible way. We are spending billions of dollars to purchase the necessary capabilities.

In describing this novel possibility in our nuclear policy, the term "counter-force" is best avoided. Traditionally, this term has implied the all-out strike, with city destruction regarded as a bonus rather than a disadvantage. The opponents of traditional counter-force strategy find it attractive only when it can confidently be expected to be nearly 100 per cent effective, and, because they forecast dimmer and dimmer hopes for such effectiveness, they dismiss the strategy. But city-sparing becomes more, not less, important as enemy retaliatory capability becomes less vulnerable to the classic counter-force strategy. If a nation is sure that hitting the enemy all-out will lead to intolerable counter-retaliation, then it must gamble on inducing restraint in the enemy rather than on reducing his capability. It may well choose to do so by restrained counter-military attack, even when most enemy forces are thought to be invulnerable, as the best of bad gambles in a situation desperate by assumption.

The novel aspect of possible American nuclear strategies rests firmly upon a lasting concept of what *not* to hit. What specifically it *is* feasible to hit may change, although common sense suggests that no collection of military targets is likely to be composed entirely of targets that are either very easy or very difficult to destroy. At any moment of time, there will be a mix. Consider the strategic retaliatory program that we know most about—the American. Now and in the foreseeable future, it contains some soft, fixed elements which are expected to be vulnerable as well as some that are hard or mobile; no doubt it contains some elements that are not expected to be vulnerable but will unfortunately turn out to be so. Unless the enemy is in magically better shape, a city-sparing attack against him will not lack for important targets.

These ideas are simple, but not their execution. The strategic forces must be able to go on one strike option or another, and some of them must be able to ride out enemy attack and still be available for use in a later wave of retaliation. The vulnerability problems of these withheld forces are accordingly more acute. Because they are of reduced usefulness unless they can be redirected, the worst survivability problems are faced by commanders who must be able to receive and absorb information, replan quickly, and send new orders. Command, Control, and Communications are now the key labels. Beyond "Which option?" on a first wave, there now lies "What reassignment of available vehicles to what remaining targets?"

The world will have changed drastically in minutes before this question is answered. The planners will not know as much as they would like to know, and they will not be able to handle all that they do know. But a capability to get and process much relevant information in so adverse an environment can, at great trouble and expense, be attained. It is very useful to know which of your missiles survived, which survivors launched and which did not, and still more useful to have some ideas about which arrived. Even crude information may permit major re-allocations of remaining forces to remaining targets that might double or treble the effectiveness of remaining threat power, provided that withheld forces are so well controlled and integrated that fast adjustments are possible. More important, to know what further threats to make, you have to know roughly what the enemy did to you; and, both you and he have to know what you have not yet done to him but can. What message would go over a "hot line" to Moscow if this knowledge were critically lacking?

The designer of any new nuclear force in NATO—national, European, NATO multilateral, or whatever—should appreciate these operational matters and decide whether and how the new force is to fit. The decisions he makes now will determine, among other things, what capabilities his force will and will not have years from now, because the lead-time from concept to specific forces is long for everybody. One implication is that operational coordination of some nuclear forces in the alliance—those that aspire to pose withheld threats against enemy cities—has become far more complex and demanding than before.

A broader political implication is that American nuclear protection for NATO, given its ability to hit both enemy capability and intent, continues to have great comparative political appeal. Note where the hypothetical situation now ends that begins, implausibly, with extreme Soviet attack confined to Europe and proceeds to an American retaliatory attack upon Russia. If this be a damaging but city-sparing attack, it is Khrushchev, not President Johnson, who then faces the decision whether to exercise restraint or "commit suicide." The possibility that the Soviets might face such a paralyzing choice is the strongest deterrent to any such extreme attack upon Europe in the first place. Barring always that the Soviet leaders are blind or mad, this makes such an attack exceedingly unlikely. Yet, even if it happened, an American response that spared cities would offer the best remaining chance that some measure of deterrence and meaningful defense will be preserved for Europe. The restraining power upon the Soviets, to keep the Red Army and medium-range missiles in check, will be tremendous.

If America supplies the best ultimate deterrent, plus the last best hope in war for stopping short of a holocaust, Europeans more than anyone should wish to make sure that this deterrent is able to perform. But could our strategic forces fulfill their promise if concurrently the French strategic force were doing what it will presumably be designed to do—namely, to destroy Soviet cities—while American forces are taking pains to spare them? Would Soviet political leaders then have reason to be restrained? In their rage and dismay, would they, supposing they were still alive, have time to reason? The success of a city-sparing strategy depends crucially upon tight operational control of all striking forces, designed and coordinated to supply maximum leverage to one concurrent offer of terms. Both politically and militarily, NATO nuclear policy requires what General de Gaulle so publicly despises—integration. A world with such terrible weapons is too small for anything else.

Granted, general war is improbable; even if it comes, a *force de frappe* might cooperate in operations, might even have become formally integrated to insure coordination, or might be simply inactive or ineffective. The worst situation is unlikely to arise. Where the fate of all NATO may hang in the balance, however, even very small probabilities need to be taken seriously. Independent nuclear operations have become anachronisms; they should be consistently opposed, not subsidized. This proposition applies as much to Bomber Command, of course, as to a *force de frappe*. But with Bomber Command, we have operational coordination through the same unified target planning that coordinates our services; even in 1962, Britain's White Paper on Defense spoke no longer of a British deterrent but of a British "contribution to the Western strategic deterrent."

General de Gaulle speaks otherwise, and surely we should accord him the honor of believing that he means exactly what he says, especially when he takes such pains to be clear and eloquent. And we should respectfully disagree. About our nuclear aid to Britain, which is so galling to France, we can try not to exacerbate matters in the future while we reasonably explain the past. Born of shared wartime nuclear and bomber programs and nurtured by the earliest postwar governments, the origins of Anglo-American cooperation are not hard to explain. It is far easier not to create a Bomber Command than to kill one that flourished in victorious war. Also, co-operation took place in the context of strategic thought that started from consideration of cities as the natural targets, then slowly moved to cities as bonus targets, and then, possibly, to cities as exempt targets. Consequently, integration in operations used to appear easy and desirable rather than hard and imperative. Finally, aid has been continuously reciprocal, without the distressing spectacle of an ally conspicuously withholding needed facilities until America has been bludgeoned into assistance. Hard bargaining there undoubtedly has been, but bases in Britain have been continuously available to our airplanes, complete with nuclear storage; and recently we have the Polaris base in Scotland and use of Christmas Island. For all these reasons, past aid to Bomber Command can be rationalized as a special case. Yet, continuance of special status for Britain now is undesirable. Our policy toward the United Kingdom should likewise be made compatible with our global arms policy, which is why the Nassau Agreements of December, 1962, are so much to be deplored.

SHARED POLICY DIRECTION IN NATO

If American opposition to independent national deterrent forces elsewhere is well based on global arms imperatives, these should also constrain American independence. We cannot simultaneously preach Atlantic community and practice unimpaired sovereignty on life-and-death matters. To try to satisfy vulnerable and proud allies with vague and secretive reassurances will increase anxiety and resentment rather than produce cooperation. We must somehow reconcile the operational need for unitary nuclear control with allied political participation and partnership.

To repeat, the most important step is the one we took a long time ago to pledge ourselves to common defense, so that, for example, a nuclear bomb on West Germany would provoke an appropriate American counter no less than would a bomb on Maine. We are now taking other steps to reassure and inform our NATO allies about our defense policies and capabilties, and these could be very important. For instance, if we fail to provide data sufficient for our allies thoroughly to criticize and review our strategic capabilities relative to the Soviets, they may doubt Western superiority. If one globally integrated force is to be the ultimate custodian of their interests, our allies are surely entitled to know that this force is ample and securely protected.

Yet, even this minimum of reassurance involves information about what the Soviets have, estimates about how it might be used in the manner worst for the West, and about liable outcomes—given the ability of our forces to survive and respond. Such information is not lightly held or given, but, with appropriate security safeguards, its sharing fulfills a deep political obligation. Our allies are also entitled to be convinced that we are not skimping in our strategic budget at their expense—for example, by failing to cover a known Soviet medium-range missile site in our target planning while covering a known intercontinental missile site. Such information is still more delicate, but the worst for a security officer is yet to come. Our allies ought to know and influence the general outlines of plans for various contingencies, so that the intellectual core of our policies is as reassuring to them as our capabilities.

How much is being done about sharing such information cannot be publicly known, although the communiqués after the NATO ministerial meetings in 1962 and May, 1963, made clear that some progress has been made. Secretary McNamara's policy statement at Ann Arbor is explicit: "We want and need a greater degree of alliance participation in formulating nuclear weapons policy to the greatest extent possible." The United States has shared more knowledge with its partners about the "what" and "how" of our nuclear power and is open to counsel about the "when."

At this point arises a dilemma: perhaps each ally desires to possess both a trigger and a safety catch, while denying them to other allies for fear that strategic power will be either too loosely controlled or paralyzed by multiple vetoes. Perhaps this dilemma is best resolved by measures that involve no diffusion of physical control but that attempt instead to achieve a consensus about the general circumstances for nuclear employment. A foreign critic may find the United States cast here in the role of the secretary of a committee who guards jealously his prerogative to write what the "sense of the meeting" is. Nonetheless, NATO consultations about what should govern nuclear employment matter deeply to all, and, incidentally, should serve to bring home to others that it is not America alone that blocks some aspirants from uniquely influential positions. Even where consensus in NATO cannot be achieved, participation in moving toward partial agreement should satisfy some national desires and clarify matters for all.

An "Atlantic deterrent" requires no less than this, but does it require more? If more is needed beyond shared understanding and as full political consultation as possible, allied physical participation is possible, even in the most sensitive area of all—command and control. A component of the Atlantic deterrent could be Europe-oriented and could be organized as a symbol of unity in the West. Any one of many technological alternatives is possible for this component in terms of various basing and delivery-vehicle combinations, but technical discussion can be minimized here. The political image should be the dominant one, provided only that suitable protection and secure control be supplied in any one of several ways. One possible combination was suggested by President Kennedy as early as May, 1961, when he spoke at Ottawa about "the possibility of eventually establishing a NATO seaborne missile force which would be truly multilateral in ownership and control, if this should be desired and found feasible by our allies once NATO's non-nuclear goals have been achieved."

Clearly this suggestion is conditional, as it should be. The United States does not need such a force for any overriding military reason, and the test of its need should be European enthusiasm. If European NATO members are satisfied with new assurances and a greater political voice in nuclear matters, splendid. Or even if they are dissatisfied, even if they disagree more than they agree about further steps, it is only prudent that we not push for measures that breed more discord than harmony. But if there are deep-seated pressures in Europe for a nuclear force that is not wholly American, President Kennedy has suggested a way to meet them. The American offer is unprecedented for all its necessary caution, and Europeans need only agree in order to achieve such a force.

Unlike the French force, such a force would symbolize interdependence rather than national dependence, especially if the meaning of "truly multilateral" were made clear. A seaborne force could be made international in ownership and operation, down to and including mixed ship crews of different nationalities, so that not even one ship with its missiles could revert as an operable force to any nation in time of crisis or internal unrest. People worry little today about "Ultras" coming into power over SAC or Bomber Command, but if the number of national nuclear powers grows large, the specter of bellicose control, like those of heightened risks of accidental and catalytic war, cannot be ignored. If there is to be any growth in the number of nuclear powers, better a safeguarded collective addition than many national ones.

Nor should the possibility be dismissed that a multilateral force could eventually lessen the number of nuclear powers rather than increase it. Great Britain now has operational V-bombers, and

France is acquiring a force of Mirage IV light bombers. What then follows? Both propose to have operational missile forces before the decade is out, but this is years away. Perhaps the British and French governments will persevere in seeking missiles of their own, perhaps not. Surely their future choices will not be made wholly without regard for costs and available alternatives. Is it beyond the ingenuity of such experienced powers as France and Great Britain to devise a political compromise in terms of a NATO deterrent acceptable to all, while they gracefully phase out outmoded airplane forces?

If they try, the awkward question will be, of course, that of control, and we are back to the multi-trigger and safety-catch dilemma. The symbols of European uniforms on ships that carry part of the ultimate deterrent are important, as is the assignment of American Polaris submarines to a NATO commander. Control over firing missiles from a multilateral force is more important still, but so hard an issue that many find it impossible. Yet it can be solved, if necessary, along familiar lines.

What most worries some Europeans is that there would be no guaranteed nuclear response by America after a Soviet attack on Europe that overwhelmed other defense possibilities. If we let a multilateral NATO force be designed to insure European control over some nuclear response in this worst case for them, we give them a trigger for the case where we already expect to respond. Consequently, we give nothing away *if* the nature of the response fits our global operations. This vital proviso can be simply met— for example, by keeping the missiles of the European force aimed at key vulnerable Soviet military installations. These installations are almost certain to be included as targets within any strike we launch, unlike less vulnerable military targets that we may not be able to hit and very vulnerable people that we may not want to hit. So the requirements for integrated operations can be met.

The political essentials are more troublesome. Assured response implies that the North Atlantic Council will pre-authorize the commander of a multilateral force to retaliate against overwhelming Soviet attack, for time will not permit consultation then, and the enemy must not be allowed to expect that the most reluctant among fifteen nations would stop retaliation. Do Europeans really want control made so grimly explicit, with its feared automaticity in any nuclear response? Perhaps they do not, in which case their public admissions will be clarifying to them in their own parliamentary debates. If they shrink from assured response in the worst cases of Soviet attack, what are national deterrents credible against?

Debates on these matters in NATO should also be illuminating, for the more restrictions our allies want to place on any nuclear response, the more they must admit the utility of non-nuclear alternatives in credibly facing Soviet challenges. Facing the issue will be unpleasant but educational. Probably, restraints upon any automatic element in response that NATO will authorize will be severe, which is good. There must be an irreducible element, for no sudden removal of the White House and related top political echelons can be allowed to promise immunity to the Soviet Union. A little more is dangerous, but not unthinkable. What could safely be allowed, although left to European initiatives for advocacy, would be a firing pre-authorization that falls short of response based either upon fallible radar warning systems or sweeping military autonomy. Yet such authorization can still insure against paralysis of the NATO multilateral force by any one of fifteen nations in the worst of military contingencies for Europe.

Thus, constructive alternatives to a proliferation of national nuclear forces are possible for NATO; they include a militarily meaningful NATO deterrent, if it be necessary to go this far. The United States has made these alternatives possible, perhaps not fully, clearly, or consistently, but nonetheless publicly, and at the cost of renouncing any narrow interpretation of purely national interests. We have a policy, and it is a good one that should not be abandoned to please France, but improved and solidified as we move toward a greater Atlantic Community.

Post-Nassau Multilateral Purpose

The Anglo-American Nassau Agreements of December, 1962, and General de Gaulle's shattering press conference of January 14, 1963,* compelled a reappraisal of American nuclear policies in NATO. The immediate results of Nassau can be quickly summarized: the British bought both an option upon Polaris missiles and American slogans for NATO; General de Gaulle bought neither; and the United States is left with worries that its policies were compromised.

The pertinent policy slogans are a "multilateral" nuclear force,

---

* EDITOR'S NOTE: It was at this press conference that de Gaulle announced that France would continue to develop a wholly independent nuclear force and that it would, for the time being, insist on the exclusion of Great Britain from the European Common Market.

"indivisible" nuclear defense of the Western alliance, and more effective conventional forces. A compromise of the first two of these is implied by the famed escape clause in the Nassau Statement: "Except where Her Majesty's Government may decide that supreme national interests are at stake, these British forces will be used for the purposes of international defense of the Western alliance in all circumstances." How seriously does this clause qualify "multilateral" and "indivisible"? Opinions differ, but British strategic systems committed to NATO command by the Nassau Agreement can revert to Great Britain as operable forces in crises, which is what matters. For, as President Kennedy so clearly recognized in his off-, then on-the-record press conference of December 31, 1962, "The British will have their deterrent. It will be independent in moments of great national peril, which is really the only time you consider using nuclear weapons anyway."[1] A provision that covers all relevant contingencies is an escape clause indeed.

There is no need to impugn British dependability or standards of responsibility. An attack upon any NATO country so overwhelming that it might require strategic nuclear retaliation would convince every NATO country that its supreme national interests were at stake. Still, agreements matter that establish vital precedents about what a country can do. How is another NATO member now to view participation in a future multilateral force that yields it no comparable privileges for national reversion? Alternatively, to give NATO members fully comparable status would be to create a multinational force that could splinter that "indivisible" nuclear defense into many national forces. To do so would be to foster rather than deter a proliferation of nuclear powers, and national rather than collective defense, and so contradict other basic goals of American nuclear policy.

More effective conventional strength is also impeded as doubts are cast upon nuclear "indivisibility." A multilateral force need not be very costly to loom large in NATO European defense budgets, which, in the aggregate, are about one-third the American defense budget. If, as noted for the French force, a multilateral force can be depended upon to operate integrally with American strategic forces but not without them, another missile abroad may permit one fewer at home. Yet even then, the other half of the implied bargain—more GI's in Europe than would be needed if more of the increased European effort were directed toward conventional

[1] *The New York Times* (Western edition), January 11, 1963.

strength instead of European missiles—would supply the world's most vivid example of uneconomic trade pursued for overriding political reasons. The worst case, of course, would combine this division of conventional labor with a multilateral force so liable to fragmentation that no specific part of it could be counted upon for global strategic operations. Then no fewer American missiles will be made possible, and there will be no budgetary offsets. Where we shall fall between the worst and best cases remains to be seen.

A more immediate possibility for competition with strengthened conventional forces also deserves mention. Before any NATO multilateral missile force is established to implement Paragraph 8 of the Nassau Statement, existing forces, including "tactical nuclear forces now held in Europe," will presumably have been allocated to a multinational force under the terms of Paragraph 6. How this is done may be militarily harmless but symbolically beneficial, or it may not. For example, some tactical strike fighters may now be reserved at all times for predetermined priority nuclear missions, for the eminently sensible reasons that there are not enough securely based missiles that could hit targets quicker, while the bulk of strategic bombers could only hit them hours later because they are an ocean away. This situation is changing rapidly as Minuteman and Polaris missiles phase into operation. It may become desirable to let these or other missiles take over the priority nuclear assignments, and so free the tactical aircraft to exploit their flexibility in a variety of lesser nuclear or non-nuclear contingencies as these may develop. Thus, NATO's limited-war air capabilities may grow, while the fixed general-war assignments are better covered by more securely based missiles whose ability to penetrate enemy air defenses is greater.

To block this possibility by freezing tactical aircraft to priority nuclear missions via multinational-force "strategic" assignment could be militarily costly. More generally, to implement Paragraph 6 by widespread commitment of existing forces would be to impose additional political constraints upon military planning. As weapons change, so should the way in which some particular tasks are to be done, but Paragraph 6 constraints could inhibit efficient adaptation.

Such are the gloomy possibilities after Nassau, which suggest cautions in implementing the Agreements. Specifically, allocations of existing nuclear units to multinational strike forces should be confined to those that are almost certain to remain efficient com-

ponents of strategic general war forces; the cost of new European
contributions to a multilateral force should be held to moderate
levels; and the nuclear defense of the alliance should not be made
all too readily divisible because multilateral degenerates further
into multinational. Continental contributions should not lead to
revertible national forces, nor should the possibility be foreclosed
that future British contributions will take a less national form.

What, then, should be done, especially about the multilateral
NATO deterrent that was reaffirmed as a future goal at Nassau and,
for a few months, was pressed harder by the American administration? Above all, we need to articulate our purpose more clearly, face
the control problem, and suggest more concretely a force design
and use. Given these, our allies can shape their own views more
readily. Diplomacy will be facilitated, although perhaps not the
creation of a force. But surely the aim is not speedy creation of a
force that can fit the label—so that what the force is to do for whom
is a question to be put off for later consideration. To proceed this
way would be to start building a house before calling in the archi-
tect. Or, more pertinently for NATO discussion, it would be to emu-
late France in its zeal for a force first, complex strategic considerations second, and so to embarrass the inquiries that allied and
domestic critics alike should put to France.

The long discussions about multilateral-force purpose can be conveniently condensed under three headings: participation, voice,
and control. The first involves European physical sharing in strategic weapon systems; the second, political sharing in strategic decisions; and the third, perhaps, specialized command and control
arrangements.

Participation is costly but easy and would be designed to blur
the invidious line between "American nuclear knights and European foot-sloggers" in the alliance. European status and prestige
would be served. There might also be technological by-products
for European economies, although other avenues are open for
peaceful uses of atomic energy; the civilian by-products from missile guidance systems, solid-fuel propellants, and nose cones are
not liable to be great. Still, a world where the less developed countries prematurely seek steel mills, research reactors, and national
airlines while the United States races to be first on the moon is a
world grown accustomed to the expensive pursuit of prestige, and
it would be surprising if NATO countries were an exception. A reasonable burden of participation can be borne.

Control, in contrast, raises both hard issues and frightful risks, while a voice in nuclear strategy raises only the former. This distinction needs to be sharpened, for some speak of a multilateral force as the principal means for Europeans to participate in strategic discussion. Surely that should not be. Why exclude a nonparticipant from the deliberations that influence NATO nuclear plans, force posture, and declaratory policy? More pertinent still, why exclude such an ally from crisis consultations about whether to use nuclear weapons, when, and how? Its survival is at stake too, and it deserves to be informed and to be heard no less than those who participate directly in a multilateral force. To give all members a greater voice in these fundamental questions, as has been done, is to move toward Atlantic partnership. To give some a lesser voice would be a divisive step back from the achievements already noted at Athens in May, 1962:

> The Council noted the progress which has been made in the direction of closer cooperation between member countries in the development of the Alliance's defense policy. . . . So that all member states may play their full part in consultation on nuclear defense policy, it has been decided to set up special procedures which will enable all members of the alliance to exchange information concerning the role of nuclear weapons in NATO defense.[2]

Participants in a multilateral force would naturally determine its size, composition, and day-to-day management and support. But its strategic control could be left to them only if its use threatened to bring retaliation against them alone, which is unlikely. The logic of "no annihilation without representation" applies as much to such a force as it does to existing American and British strategic power, and for the same reason. It would not apply to a particular Western strategic force if that force were known to be based in one particular area by itself, and if the Soviet Union were certain to have reliable quick means for determining when firings against it came only from that area. Then the Soviets would know when that one Western force had fired at them and might confine retaliation to the one country; allied disengagement from the firings would be possible. But these stringent conditions are exceedingly unrealistic.

Consider the North Atlantic a few years from now with American, British, and possibly French submarines plus, say, several

[2] *NATO Letter*, June, 1962, p. 13. See *NATO Letter*, June, 1963, p. 16, for the Ottawa Communiqué.

NATO-manned ships with Polaris or comparable missiles. If the Soviets are ever hit hard by missiles from the Atlantic, with what NATO country can they afford to assume they are not at nuclear war? One thing can certainly be said: the atmosphere would not be conducive to calm, trustful, and reflective Kremlin consideration of any messages about Western bombers in the air and other readiness measures being undertaken solely for defensive purposes, especially when a deceptive disavowal of special national rather than alliance responsibility may be as much in the interest of the powers that fired or intend to fire as a sincere disavowal is for others. Under the enormous shock of thermonuclear attack, with crucial decisions to be made while enemy vulnerabilities decline by the minute and one's forces are in jeopardy, the urge to use remaining retaliatory power widely will be tremendous. The least that a NATO nation could reasonably fear would be an attack upon any vulnerable nuclear-strike elements that might be in its territory such as aircraft; the most, the kind of attack upon its very existence that Soviet propaganda and published doctrine stress.

The "indivisible" nuclear defense of the alliance rests upon a strong idealistic foundation. It is also based, however, upon realities even less open to question: the awesome power of anybody's deliverable megaton, linked to time (measured in minutes) for mass intercontinental exchanges. One frequently hears the comment that if one NATO nation proposes to join the nuclear club in order to be able to start a war she cannot finish, the others should feel equally free not to join the war—which may be fair but is irrelevant. There may be no way to decline in the event, so allied interests must be safeguarded in advance. Thus, any political guidelines for the employment of a multilateral force should be as much subject to full alliance debate and influence as those for the employment of American strategic power. Equally, no nonparticipant should be excluded from crisis consultations when nuclear war looms, whenever circumstances permit consultation. A voice in these fundamentals must be preserved for each, but not necessarily, of course, a veto.

These are considerations to bear in mind when some speak of assisting European nations, nationally or collectively, toward independent nuclear status. Independence in possibly starting a war but not in prosecuting it is the likely result. And if interdependence in consequences is expected, should its fuller recognition not be the avowed purpose of NATO nuclear policy, including the multilateral force? A European component of an Atlantic nuclear force, not an insulated European force, can be created, and its operations should be viewed accordingly.

Such a multilateral force component would make the permanence of the American strategic guarantee less subject to question, especially in political terms. A force that would be more than a coordinated group of national strike elements is constitutionally novel in NATO and requires a supplementary treaty. A missile-carrying ship that is financed and operated jointly, controlled at all times by NATO or a sub-group within NATO, flies what flag and belongs to whom? The Jupiter squadrons in Italy and Turkey were under the peacetime command of SACEUR, but they were nationally owned. Many important NATO installations have been jointly financed under the infrastructure program, but they revert to host countries once common use ceases. A multilateral force would be more NATO-committed than anything that has preceded it. NATO is a marriage whose bonds are strong, and a multilateral component will make divorce still more difficult. Deeper nuclear commitments that clearly apply to the 1970's are now especially pertinent evidences of intent, because Article 13 of the North Atlantic Treaty stipulates that any party may denounce membership after notice in 1969.

FORCE CONTROL

Control Requirements

What, then, of control? Suppose that a multilateral sea-based force is created and that, as earlier suggested, its missiles are ordinarily assigned to some of whatever military targets remain vulnerable. Then the first operational requirement for global coordination could be met as other strategic forces (American) were able to shift partially to other targets. A second requirement for compatibility with all possible strike options would be met because these particular targets would be chosen to fit within any of them. A global strategy could incorporate this inflexible component and yet remain flexible as a whole because other components had options. The multilateral force then could and presumably would fire with the first wave of any American general-war strike, rather than as a part of forces withheld to threaten the enemy with subsequent attack. As part of the first wave, the multilateral force would have to be well protected, but not as elaborately as forces designed for possible withholding throughout a period of nuclear attack. Thus, for example, missiles might be held back in more secure, if more expensive, American submarines, while missiles were fired from the surface ships of a multilateral fleet.[3]

Before turning to the crucial trigger issue, one implication for operational coordination with a *force de frappe* should be noted. General de Gaulle's references on January 14 to the "possibility of the action of that force being combined with that of similar forces of its allies," and to "strategic cooperation" were auspicious, despite the over-all context, which rejected integration. Yet if France orients her force toward city attacks, as all the justifications of its strategic significance despite small size indicate, it would not fit within all global strike options. Accordingly, it could not be a rigid part of a first wave without threatening the very purpose of a possible restrained strike. But will it be designed to meet the very taxing criteria for survivability throughout nuclear attack and subsequent reprogramming that must be met by a withholdable and flexible strategic system, as distinct from a system that needs to be secure only until unambiguous warning of attack is received, after which missiles can be fired in a predetermined plan? If so, will French striking power be withheld in situations where cities have not yet been subject to nuclear attack, but other targets have been? Answers are needed before the meaning of cooperation can be established, and—given the extent to which blueprints today bind strategic possibilities many years from now—answers now are none too early.

A Control Illustration

If the multilateral force is targeted to be part of any first general wave, it can be made more quickly responsive to attack. Then the "trigger" issue can be made less intractable, because the technical features will have been designed to ease the political problems by making the firing less "suicidal." There are two related problems: first, how to assure that an order is given to release warheads that may be in American custody, and possibly curtail the unique American veto that warhead control involves; second, how to determine that a firing order is given to the force, and possibly limit the veto power of European countries as well. Although they might be combined in practice, two command channels are in question. A partial prescription for the first can also serve to raise pertinent issues about the second.

[3] For a contrasting advocacy of more complex withholdable strategic systems, see Timothy W. Stanley, "Decentralizing Nuclear Control in NATO," *Orbis* (Spring, 1963).

Suppose the missiles are put in a European line of command that goes at the top, say, to the Secretary General of NATO, while the warheads are in the custody of an American line of command that goes to the President. Such a custodial arrangement would fit existing American law and practice. But for illustrative purposes and with no official sanction whatsoever, let us add an element: the presidential signal, without which no missile warhead can be armed, will be automatically transmitted if more than a pre-established number of nuclear-bomb alarm indicators at key places in Europe are triggered by Soviet nuclear attack.

Objections leap to mind. Would such a scheme risk nuclear war by electronic accident? Would it make nuclear response too easy, or, conversely, to Europeans would it offer no additional assurance of response? For these and other reasons, why do it? But it could be done, and therefore such a scheme serves at least to sharpen the policy questions. Technically, many arrangements are feasible, and a choice among them would make political issues explicit. Thus, would a Soviet nuclear attack on 90 per cent of the key strategic places in one European country, unaccompanied by attacks elsewhere, be enough to trigger the signal, as well as, say, a more general attack that hit 30 per cent or more of such places through Europe?

Legally, such a scheme probably is within the Constitutional powers of the American President as Commander in Chief, for warhead release would be pre-authorized only against massive nuclear attacks that would be certain to include strategic American elements and demand fast response. Custodial detachments at European strike bases and elsewhere would be hit as a minimum. More generally, the point of the system would be to confirm that the probability is zero, for all practical purposes, that a rational Soviet Union would ever strike massively at Europe but not America at the same time. In extreme circumstances, electronics would thus substitute partly for federation in making NATO an inseparable target entity in terms of the retaliation that Soviet attack would generate. Nuclear attack upon West Europe alone, or the American Pacific Northwest alone, would be equally absurd for the Soviets and equally dangerous to them.

A command to fire missiles—as distinct, possibly, from release of one signal required for their arming—need not and should not be automated. For safety against accidental or unauthorized firings, independently required human checks would be inserted in the missile and possibly the warhead release sequences. For assured weapon responsiveness, on the other hand, extra sources and communications can be provided at each check level to make the system less vulnerable. A system could be created comparable in principle to a two-combination safe, with a warhead release sequence to operate one combination, and a command sequence to operate the other. The "numbers" for each combination could be held at separate levels. The first number of the first release combination could be the President's, releasable by him, by highest surviving American political authorities, or possibly, as sketched above, by the impact of extreme Soviet attack. The first number for the first launch combination might be similarly releasable by NATO's Secretary-General or his highest surviving political associates, while a second number must be released by top military commanders. The NATO military commanders would not possess the first number but would be assured that it existed in enough secure places, each with access to many protected communication links, so that Soviet action could not in all probability block its transmittal. After attack, such a number might even be broadcast in uncoded form over all surviving radio stations. If all this appears complex, mechanistic, and horrible, so it is; controlled retaliatory nuclear systems can be like that, and uncontrolled ones are much worse.

Operational Implications

If safety against irresponsible firing can be provided, what assurance of responsible firing does such a scheme offer Europe that it does not already have? In American and many European eyes, nothing. But to the Soviets and to European governments that doubt the American guarantee, or more precisely to their parliamentary opponents, it would strengthen the NATO remedy for the Suez syndrome. This feared sequence involves a European country in forceful actions somewhere, followed by Soviet threats to launch missiles at the European country unless it desists. Sometimes, it is claimed that the involved country would have no alternative between compliance and holocaust unless it had a nuclear deterrent of its own, which is certainly too simple a view. A third alternative is always open: continue, and test whether the threat is a bluff, as the scores of Soviet missile threats have so far been. If one's nerve to test the bluff is bolstered by a secure national deterrent, rather than undermined by fears that a possibly insecure national deterrent might act as a lightning rod to draw Soviet fire, how much more would it be bolstered by tangible assurances that the strategic power of the entire West was geared to retaliate against Soviet execution of any such threat? Better yet, would not the assurances make the Soviets less inclined to utter such threats?

This partial remedy is important, because the Suez syndrome is prominent and because European national remedies for it, upon close examination, promise less. But to go farther is difficult. The difficult-to-dissolve feature of a multilateral force and its joint operation—the need for dependability in its part of possible global strategic strikes—and, above all, the interdependence of consequences through NATO should all or part of it be fired, combine to form one restrictive premise for control procedures: however the decision is made to fire all missiles in accord with Plan A or some missiles in Plan N, the force should operate as an integral unit. No sizeable part should be withdrawable as a national force either to fire or to try to disassociate from firing.

To premise in contrast a right and ability to disengage in a crisis changes the entire course of argument, and naturally leads to different prescriptions for control.[4] To write a new treaty for a multilateral force that explicitly contains procedures for crisis withdrawal is not to reaffirm the "attack on one or more . . . shall be considered an attack against them all" Article in the original treaty, but to subvert it. If such procedures were suggested by the United States in particular, decision-making for future contingencies might be anticipated by precipitating an immediate crisis of confidence. Those who already misread American policies as implying withdrawal from Europe would seize upon any such suggestions as confirming their suspicions. Therefore, the United States should not propose withdrawal rights even if isolation from strategic nuclear actions were feasible and all the more should not when isolation is unfeasible. The "indivisibility" theme is doubly right.

As a lesser but related operational consideration, the ability to rely upon a multilateral force to strike as a coordinated unit and the confidence that it will strike with American strategic forces are prerequisites for real military utility. Otherwise, the unfortunate military planner can only estimate highly uncertain but sizeable discounts for political unreliability for different contingents of the multilateral force, with these added to similar discounts for missiles out of commission, losses before use, unreliability in use, attrition,

---

[4] See Klaus Knorr, A NATO Nuclear Force: The Problem of Management, Princeton Center of International Studies, Policy Memorandum No. 26 (February 5, 1963), for a structure for decision-making which is ingenious and clear but which is incompatible with those suggested in this paper because derived from this contrasting premise.

and so on. He would end up with expected contributions so low and variable that they must be treated only as unpredictable "bonuses" in target coverage, with high-confidence coverage required fully from other sources. A multilateral force will be expensive enough, and pride in its real military utility important enough, to merit procedures that breed confidence.

Given these reasons for integral operations within Western strategic forces as a whole, no control procedures can be tolerated that disrupt global coordination as to what is hit, when, and by whom. That reduces the remaining big issues to influence upon decisions to strike, and what kind of a strike it shall be—the famed "Go–No Go?" and "Which Option?" questions. These questions are linked, and control procedures about the first must take full account of the second. Thus, automatic release of warheads to the force possibly becomes acceptable, not merely because enemy attack would be extreme, but because the targets for reflex retaliation would fit all options. If the targets do not fit all options, reflex operation would be unacceptable. Imagine a sweeping Soviet nuclear strike against military targets in Western Europe, but one that sought to paralyze retaliation by sparing cities and keeping them under threat. A resultant paralysis of NATO would be intolerable, but so would a reflex retaliation against Soviet cities that would generate mutual holocaust. An appropriate retaliation to any such bizarre Soviet attack might likewise be city-sparing, but drawing from the strategic resources of the entire West and covering military targets in the Soviet Union as well as the satellites. The prospect of such retaliatory damage should be a formidable enough deterrent for anybody, even though, by the standards of the nuclear age, it would be "restrained," while its nonsuicidal character would enhance its credibility as a deterrent.

Criteria for Release

To provide even the limited degree of automatic release in our illustration, given acceptable targeting and operating coordination, does two things: it qualifies the American veto, and it raises complexities about weighted voting in the control of a multilateral force. Different weights for different European countries would be implicit in defining what strategic targets in Europe are "key" ones and in valuing one of them relative to others. In a sense, each such target must be assigned a basic number of points plus possible extra points for a country if almost all key targets there are hit; and the total points required to release the warheads, as registered by a bomb alarm system, must be established. Worse yet, what constitutes a "hit" must be defined—what combination of blast overpressures, thermal effects, radioactive contamination, and so on. Should an utterly devastating hit register more points than one that just measured over the mark? How many more? The complexity is evident, and because the definition would be needed in peacetime, there would be plenty of time to debate about alternative combinations. Problems that had been conveniently buried would have to be faced.

Before dismissing any such scheme for its dispute-producing complexity alone, the standard caution applies. The difficulty about criteria arises inescapably from the problem, not from a particular proposal for its solution. How would NATO go to what kind of war, especially nuclear war? Sweeping this and other troublesome questions under the rug is a time-honored procedure and one that is sometimes of great political value. Yet fuller nuclear partnership in the alliance implies, at the least, intellectual engagement. Are proud allies to busy themselves about nuclear weapon effects first, strategic issues second: to learn to walk before they run? Ideally, yes; practically, no. One must even quarrel a bit with Acheson's magnificent speech: "But it does seem to me a waste of time to chase its [multilateral force's] distant implications of control and command to drily logical extremes before there is anything to control or command. Our allies can hardly have very solid ideas about how they want to participate in nuclear defense until they know something about it."[5] They already know something, and nothing is more clarifying about what is known and agreed, and what is not, than debating explicit proposals that do not permit the essentials to remain vague. To answer "What's the system?" before answering "What's the job?" is the way to get a bad system.

The difficulties about explicit release criteria, or "points" in the illustrative scheme, would in any case be greatly eased in practice by two considerations. First, for deterrent purposes, the Soviet Union need be informed only in very general terms and would not be able to calculate attacks that fell just below the critical threshold. Second, any rational Soviet attack would tend anyway to avoid the half-way tactics that risk the worst of all results: so limited in scope that they hardly affect the strategic balance, but so provocative as to invite retaliation that is unlimited in geographic scope. Much of NATO Europe for years to come will contain nuclear strike

[5] Dean Acheson, "De Gaulle and the West," The New Leader (April 1, 1963), p. 22.

components that are simultaneously dangerous to the Soviets and vulnerable. For the Soviets to attack such components in one country but not others may be tempting but incredibly dangerous, as would be Europe-only attacks. Over a broad range within which the threshold for release might be set, the deterrent to geographically limited Soviet nuclear attack would be strong.

Establishing the criteria for retaliatory release in any such schemes would undoubtedly involve heavy weights, for example, for Great Britain and the Federal Republic of Germany. Each contains a big population and many NATO nuclear installations. Lesser weights would naturally apply to others, but they should be significant for all. Specially, there should be weights also for nonparticipants in the multilateral force. No new force should in any way appear to remove the American strategic guarantee from a cooperative ally, especially in the eyes of the Soviet Union. Nor should any ally be excluded from strategic discussions that affect the fate of all unless full consultation is impossible—which effectively means when the enemy permits too little time. The political guidelines for the employment of nuclear weapons, and the more precise criteria that possibly may specify release procedures or rules of engagement, should be discussed by all in peacetime. At the other extreme, the sudden, overwhelming attack that precludes consultations will have to be met. In the one case, all discuss; in the other, no one. In between lie the ambiguous contingencies for which special voting procedures are often proposed, with these to apply in crises where only partial consultation is possible and action cannot be hamstrung by multiple vetoes.

TWELVE

ROBERT R. BOWIE

Strategy and the Atlantic Alliance

[Editor's Note: Professor Bowie's article takes Mr. Hoag's arguments (see above, Chapter 11) one step further. While Mr. Hoag is willing to tolerate existing national nuclear forces provided they are part of an integrated command system, Professor Bowie regards the existence of national nuclear forces (other than those of the United States) as an insurmountable obstacle to the unity of the Alliance. Independent nuclear forces, however coordinated, would generate independent strategies according to Professor Bowie; these, in turn, would have political repercussions that would greatly weaken the Alliance. Not the least important of these results is the impetus given to the nuclear appetites of other countries.

Professor Bowie's proposed solution is the creation of a multilateral NATO force (the MLF) jointly manned by crews drawn from the countries participating in it. This, in his opinion, would prevent autonomous action; it would symbolize Atlantic unity; it would provide the twin options of an evolution toward a purely European force or else toward a completely integrated NATO force in which the United States, without a veto, would be one member.]

The debate over strategy, forces, and nuclear control that now divides the North Atlantic Treaty Organization is framed largely in military terms: what is the best way to protect the NATO area and its members from aggression? The military aspects are complex in themselves, but the import of these issues extends far beyond defense. Their handling will greatly affect prospects for a partnership between the United States and a strong, united Europe.

A viable NATO strategy must therefore meet two criteria. Militarily, it must assure the security of the NATO members and give them confidence to withstand Soviet nuclear blackmail or threats.

EDITOR'S NOTE: Reprinted with permission from *International Organization*, XVII, No. 3 (Summer, 1963).

Politically, it must pull the members together rather than split them apart.

In this perspective, we shall consider first the sources of the present differences and the nature of the Soviet threat, especially for Europe. Then we shall analyze the implications for: (1) NATO strategy and forces; (2) the control of nuclear weapons; and, briefly, (3) the machinery for strategy within the alliance.

SOURCES OF NATO TENSION

The current stresses and strains within NATO arise mainly from two causes which have roots well back in time.

The first factor is the changing strategic environment for the United States and the Soviet Union. This shift has been steadily taking place over the last five or six years, as the Soviet Union has developed a larger stockpile of improved weapons and advanced means of delivery.

The strategy which NATO developed in the 1950's rested almost entirely on the vast United States superiority in nuclear weapons and delivery systems. Against the whole range of Soviet threats to Western Europe, NATO depended on taking the initiative in using nuclear weapons and in carrying retaliation to the Soviet Union itself. The shield forces, it is true, were to counter border forays or minor incursions, if they occurred. In all other cases, however, any Soviet intrusion was to be met with nuclear weapons from the outset, whether or not the attacker used them. If strictly applied, this strategic concept would have reduced the ground forces and supporting services to little more than a trip-wire. In practice, NATO plans continued to call for sizeable ground forces, which NATO members were in no hurry to furnish.

In the 1950's, this strategy posed unacceptable risks for the Soviet Union and acceptable risks for NATO for all levels of Soviet aggression. The Soviets could not disarm the NATO nuclear strength even by a first strike; NATO could threaten the first use of nuclear weapons and mean it. In case of war, Europe would have been badly damaged but would not have been destroyed.

The growth of Soviet nuclear-missile capability has been eroding the credibility of this strategy. The United States and its NATO partners still have much larger nuclear forces than the Soviet Union. But even if NATO remains "superior," the Soviet Union has, or soon will have, the means severely to damage the United States with intercontinental ballistic missiles and Europe with medium-range ballistic missiles, even on a second strike. And Soviet nuclear plenty offsets the NATO advantage in tactical nuclear weapons. Nuclear strategy is still credible to deter general war against Europe or the United States, or attempts to overrun Europe.

In view of its costs, however, can the threat to unleash nuclear weapons from the outset assure that the Soviets may not undertake more limited probes or threats in order to reap political gain? Is it prudent to continue to rely so exclusively on this threat? If the Soviets should impede access to Berlin, for example, would NATO have to choose between large-scale nuclear war and doing nothing?

If the NATO threat proved a bluff, the damage to the whole structure of collective defense would be catastrophic, regardless of the extent of any Soviet probe. The alliance might then be subjected to severe strains merely by the skillful use of threats or blackmail by the Soviet Union. The risks of undue reliance on nuclear weapons have therefore become excessive. Of course, strategic and tactical nuclear weapons still have a major role to play in the deterrent. That is not at issue.

The question is a narrower one. Should the alliance expand and improve its conventional capability to provide more flexibility? Or will such a build-up erode the deterrent and tempt Soviet probes and limited actions?

The second source of cleavage in NATO has been the changing political balance between the United States and Europe and within Europe. At the time of NATO's inception, Europe was stagnant, weak, and fragmented. Despite the mutual interest in the defense of Europe, its members were wholly unequal in size, power, or influence. Now economic revival and the European Community have restored the strength and self-confidence of Europe and nourished the sense of a common European destiny.

This emerging Europe deeply wants a more self-respecting role in the world. This desire is already genuine and strong and will gradually become more of a force. Europeans do not like the feeling of being wards of the United States. One consequence has been questions about Europe's share in NATO and, especially, in the control of the nuclear deterrent. Among some, this interest has been reinforced by concern lest the shifting strategic balance impair the reliability of United States protection.

Despite its progress and potential, Europe cannot act yet as a great power in most fields, including defense and foreign policy. Even if the European Community develops rapidly, some years will elapse before it can act as a single entity. In the meantime, the gap between aspirations and capabilities for effective action will cause serious tensions.

Moreover, the positions of Britain and France add a further complication. Britain has seen herself as a focal point within three circles of power: the Commonwealth, the Atlantic grouping with the "special relation" to the United States, and Europe. Under de Gaulle, France, a leader for an integrated Europe in the 1950's, now aspires to greater independence, based on a sort of French predominance in a loose European grouping of sovereign states. For both, national nuclear forces appear to be a symbol and basis for status and influence beyond their actual power.

These two factors—the changing strategic and political balance—substantially affect the kind of strategy and forces which NATO requires for its defense, and the respective roles for the United States and Europe in the alliance. In assessing their effects, the allies have had different time lags: Europe, in recognizing the real meaning of the changing strategic balance; the United States, in responding to the shifting political balance. The succeeding sections will deal with these issues in turn, with particular attention given to their political, as well as their military, aspects.

NATO STRATEGY—CONVENTIONAL FORCES

In the debate over NATO strategy, the main issue has been how far NATO should seek to widen the scope of alternatives for responding to threat or aggression. To extend NATO's options, the United States has urged its allies to build up conventional forces to about thirty divisions, with adequate equipment and reserves, and has developed the concept of controlled response, especially for strategic nuclear weapons.

Many in Europe have opposed any major change from the 1954 strategy, with its heavy reliance on immediate use of strategic and tactical nuclear weapons. They shy away from the greater costs of more and better ground forces and reserves. They fear that stress on such forces may impair the deterrent or tend toward inciting, instead of deterring, war. Some critics charge the United States with seeking its own protection at the expense of European security. Hence the debate raises serious issues of confidence among allies.

Does the emerging nuclear balance create real conflicts of interest between the United States and Europe? Would the proposed revisions sacrifice European security for the benefit of the United States? In my opinion, there is no basic conflict of interest. The necessity for change stems from the strategic situation and would exist even if NATO were a single national entity. The purpose and effect of the shift are to enhance the safety of the NATO area as a whole, taking account of changing conditions.

The Nature of the Soviet Threat

Any serious analysis of NATO strategy should surely begin with the actual nature of the Soviet threat today. How do the Soviets view force in the nuclear age? They have tremendous nuclear capability and large ground forces within reach of Europe, which they will doubtless use in pursuit of their foreign policy. But whatever their desire to expand their sway, the Soviets seem fully conscious of the strategic environment and of the restraints it imposes on their freedom of action.

Party and official documents, speeches of leaders, and other writings and statements reveal a definite pattern of Soviet thought regarding force under modern conditions. It embraces several elements:

1. Soviet leaders are convinced that all-out nuclear war would be a disaster for the Soviet Union as well as for its enemies. They realize that their country could not be defended in the usual sense and would suffer enormous damage in case of nuclear war. The Party statement of 1960 and Soviet comments on it underscore the nuclear danger:

> Monstrous means of mass annihilation and destruction have been developed which, if used in a new war, can cause unheard-of destruction to entire countries and reduce key centers of world industry and culture to ruins. Such a war would bring death and suffering to hundreds of millions of people, among them people in countries not involved in it.[1]

Since the Twentieth Congress of the CPSU, the Soviets have revised their dogma that wars are inevitable as long as capitalism survives, on the ground that the Communist states are now powerful enough to deter wars by the "imperialists." There is no reason to doubt that Soviet leaders want above all else to avoid large-scale nuclear war. And it is safe to assume that they will persist in this attitude as long as the United States and NATO retain a secure strategic force.

2. The Soviet leaders are also keenly alive to the dangers of es-

[1] *The Current Digest of the Soviet Press*, XII, No. 48 (December 28, 1960), p. 7:1.

calation of limited wars. In his report on the Moscow Conference in January, 1961, Khrushchev stressed this concern. After discussing the necessity for preventing all-out war, he went on:

> There is much talk now in the imperialist camp about local wars, and small-caliber atomic weapons are even being made for use in such wars. A special theory of local wars has been devised. Is this mere chance? Of course not. . . .
>
> There have been local wars in the past and they may occur again in the future, but the imperialists' possibilities of unleashing such wars are becoming increasingly limited. A small imperialist war, regardless of which of the imperialists starts it, might develop into a world thermonuclear, rocket war. Therefore we must wage a struggle both against world wars and against local wars.[2]

In general, Soviet military and other official writings emphasize the danger that any limited war, especially in the NATO area, would mushroom into general nuclear war.

3. The Soviet leaders have not, however, forsworn all use of force or threats of force. They undoubtedly view their military forces as mainly a political instrument. That is made clear in their attitude toward wars of "national liberation" or "popular uprisings" (such as Communist subversion or takeover):

> What attitude do Marxists have toward such uprisings? The most favorable [says Khrushchev]. These uprisings must not be identified with wars among states, with local wars, because in these uprisings the people are fighting to exercise their right to self-determination, and for their social and independent national development; . . . Communists fully and unreservedly support such just wars and march in the van of the peoples fighting wars of liberation.[3]

4. The Soviet approach to force and the threat of force under present conditions is essentially one of "controlled" risk. This does not mean that they are not ready to take risks. What it does mean is that they do not wish to create or provoke situations which are likely to get out of their control. They are quite prepared to exploit fear of nuclear war or other forms of force as long as they feel able to manage the situation should it threaten to get out of hand or to entail serious risks of large-scale nuclear war.

[2] *The Current Digest of the Soviet Press*, XIII, No. 4 (February 22, 1961), p. 8:2.

[3] *Ibid.*, p. 9:2.

In short, the Soviets appear to consider force and threats as a useful instrument of their policy under two types of conditions. In the unstable, less developed world, they will assist Communist-dominated regimes in their struggle to come to power and will extend the mantle of their military force to prevent the overthrow of such regimes by the Western powers. In other areas, Soviet use of force or threats will be mainly directed to the purpose of dividing the West and weakening NATO.

The crises in Berlin and Cuba are examples of the Soviet approach to force. In Berlin, they sought to exploit fear of nuclear war in order to change the political status of the city and to create friction and division among the NATO allies. From time to time they built up crises and tensions, but they took care to assure that the situation never got out of their control. For example, when the Berlin Wall was built, the initial steps were tentative and were taken by the East Berlin authorities. Thus, the Soviet Union could readily have called off the effort if it had appeared that Western reaction would have unduly raised the risks.

Cuba shows the same tendencies. Some have construed the effort to place missiles in Cuba as a rash act indicating the readiness of the Soviet Union to take great risks. Actually, their later response to the American embargo leads to quite a different conclusion. They recognized, of course, that the placing of missiles in Cuba would arouse American opposition. But apparently on the basis of Laos, the Berlin Wall, the Bay of Pigs, and the various comments about "defensive" weapons, they had concluded that the United States would not respond precipitately but would protest and allow time for maneuver. Thus, whatever the ultimate outcome, they expected to be able to manage the situation so as to keep it under control and avoid undue risks. The embargo posed the danger of direct clash with United States forces, which might escalate out of their control, even if it began at the level of conventional forces. Hence, they backed away.

Both Berlin and Cuba show that the Soviet Union is quite willing to use its force or the threat of force to jeopardize major interests of the West when it can do so without undue risks of losing control. Both cases also demonstrate that the Soviets are alert to find vulnerable spots which they can exploit under these conditions. Their primary aim is not military conquest, but weakening the NATO alliance by creating tensions, doubts, and conflicts over the handling of such challenges.

Implications for NATO *Strategy*

If this appraisal is valid, it has great importance for the devising of an effective NATO strategy.

Obviously, adequate NATO strategic forces remain essential. They are the backbone of the deterrent and the foundation for the present Soviet attitude toward force. Such strategic forces must be sufficient to cover all the targets related to deterring Soviet resort to large-scale war, whether threatening Europe or the United States. But these essential weapons need not be located on the continent of Europe. On the contrary, there are strong reasons for preferring more remote locations, such as the high seas or the continent of the United States. With greater invulnerability, they will provide better guarantees of the security of the members of the alliance, allow more time for decision in case of attack, and reduce the dangers of accidental war.

If NATO has adequate and secure strategic nuclear forces, there seems virtually no risk that the Soviets would actually contemplate a massive military assault on NATO. The specter of a Soviet effort to seize Europe while holding the United States at bay with the threat of nuclear holocaust seems fanciful. Such a Soviet move could not fail to bring on general nuclear war and to be suicidal. The United States would have no choice whatever. It is bound by its most solemn commitments to the defense of NATO. It has more than 400,000 soldiers in Europe, more than the French and British together. If Europe came under Soviet control, the United States would face an overwhelming complex of industrial and scientific power. Its very survival would at once be in jeopardy. Can anyone seriously think that the Soviets would gamble that the United States would abandon its vital interests in this fashion? Nothing in the record of the Soviet leaders gives any ground for supposing that they would play in any such reckless way with the very existence of Soviet society.

The real danger lies elsewhere. If NATO depends almost wholly on the prompt use of nuclear weapons, then the Soviets might be tempted to exploit this dependence as a gap in the NATO armor. As in Cuba, they might seek to create a limited *fait accompli* so as to confront the NATO nations with the choice of doing nothing or of doing too much. If NATO lacks an adequate conventional response, then the NATO nations might end up by doing nothing. As we have said, the political consequences would go far beyond the immediate stake. In seeking to divide the Western nations and to create frictions and cleavages among them, Berlin is still an excellent lever for Soviet purposes. In this case, the NATO nations might have to initiate the use of force to restore access to Berlin. Similarly, the Soviet Union might try to make or threaten minor grabs of small areas, in the belief that many in Western Europe would urge some compromise to avoid large-scale nuclear response. Finally, there might be risk of actions against the periphery of the alliance. Here again, the primary aim would not be the taking of territory for its own sake, but the fatal blow to the confidence in collective defense and the solidity of the alliance.

Suitable conventional capability is essential to escape this danger. If NATO has adequate ground forces, its members can respond promptly to any such probe or thrust without being torn between two fears: that an excessive response will destroy them for seemingly small stakes; or that no response will leave them fully exposed to Soviet power.

Tactical nuclear weapons will not fill this need. NATO forces must certainly have such weapons as long as the Soviets have them and might possibly use them. They could deter Soviet use of tactical nuclear weapons and inhibit the Soviets from concentrating ground forces in preparing an attack. But tactical nuclear weapons are no substitute for the option of using conventional forces. To be sure, such weapons were a special benefit to NATO until the Soviets also enjoyed nuclear plenty. Now tactical nuclear weapons offer no unique advantage to NATO defense. In Europe, their use could well mushroom rapidly into a conflict which would be indistinguishable from all-out war for the Europeans. NATO should seek, of course, to develop more selective means to utilize such weapons, but there are serious obstacles in an area as densely populated as western Europe. To destroy opposing missiles which were concealed, mobile, or hard, both sides would have to resort to much higher yield weapons, to saturation bombing of mobile targets, or to heavy ground-burst weapons for fixed hard targets. Thus, tactical nuclear weapons, if used on a large scale by both sides, would be disastrous in terms of destruction and civilian casualties. Indeed, the fear of such mushrooming could inhibit any response which depends primarily on tactical nuclear weapons from the outset. Of course, NATO should not reassure the Soviets that some tactical nuclear weapons would not be used early; their uncertainty on this point adds to the deterrent, if the conventional option makes NATO response more certain. But tactical nuclear weapons in Europe are credible mainly as a part of the deterrent against all-out Soviet attack, just because their use would be so likely to escalate rapidly. But for deterring and, if necessary, resisting such an attack, strategic forces, which can threaten vital targets in the Soviet Union, must be the primary component.

This analysis seems to me to make an overwhelming case for an adequate conventional component of the NATO deterrent. But the critics raise several questions: (1) Will not greater stress on conventional capability seriously weaken the deterrent? Will the Soviet Union conclude that the NATO nations will seek to forgo the use of nuclear weapons? Will it then feel free to launch major attacks to conquer Europe in the belief that it could do so without the risk of nuclear war? (2) What scale of forces is required, and can the NATO members provide them? Does this strategy imply that the West would have to build up conventional forces sufficient to conduct all-out defense of Europe by ground forces? These are, of course, legitimate questions.

Effects on the NATO Deterrent

There are good reasons to conclude, however, that strong ground forces would not impair the total deterrent but enhance it. The wider NATO option should discourage the Soviet Union from initiating any use of force or threat of force in Europe.

Stronger conventional forces would reduce the heavy dependence on initiating the use of nuclear weapons for defense, especially against limited non-nuclear attacks. In this way, NATO would avoid the ghastly dilemma which current strategy would invite: the choice of accepting local defeat or of promptly using nuclear weapons. Instead, NATO would be able to combat such non-nuclear threats in kind at substantial levels. Then the Soviets would face the risks of nuclear expansion or spiraling, knowing that NATO could not be paralyzed by nuclear blackmail.

The central point is that adequate conventional forces increase the certainty that NATO will respond to any probe or limited threat and reduce the likelihood of splits among NATO members about responding. With the conventional option, its members will be far less likely to hesitate to react to any such threat than they might be if NATO were virtually limited to nuclear response. The added certainty of response does not mean that the Soviets could count on hostilities remaining at the conventional level. On the contrary, they would recognize that, if the conventional fighting should develop to substantial levels, the risk of the situation getting out of control would be tremendous. Certainly, in the NATO area no one could expect that fighting which might involve up to thirty divisions on each side, plus reserves, could be turned on and off according to Soviet pleasure. Violence under these conditions would not at all fit the pattern of their preference.

Thus, the revised strategy should reduce the risks of any fighting in Europe. Against all-out war to conquer Europe, it would offer just as strong a deterrent as before: the threat of strategic retaliation. An all-out attack against Europe alone, whether non-nuclear or nuclear, would allow—indeed, force—the United States to launch the first strategic strike, which would be even more devastating than if they struck first at both the United States and Europe. But the Soviet Union seems fully aware that any such move against either Europe or the United States would be suicidal and would serve no rational Soviet purpose. This kind of deliberate attack does not seem a real possibility as long as the strategic deterrent on our side remains strong and secure.

At the lower end of the military spectrum, better NATO ground forces could hardly mislead the Soviets into risking limited actions which would not otherwise tempt them. The prospect seems exactly the opposite. As long as NATO had no real choice except nuclear response, the Soviets might consider that lesser actions would impose very severe strains on the alliance. But with adequate conventional forces and reserves, NATO could deal with any such threats by actions more in keeping with their extent and would, therefore, be less likely to hesitate to act. The effect would be to deprive the Soviets of leverage by blackmail. And the certainty of at least ground response would not mean that the Soviets could count on controlling the situation in view of the nuclear context in which they were acting. Once fighting began, it might spiral into large-scale nuclear war and might trigger serious disorder or revolt in eastern Europe. Both risks would make the Soviets more uncertain about the ultimate costs. Their cautious approach to crises which might get out of hand and their firm determination to avoid all-out general war would, therefore, reinforce their hesitancy about starting any such actions.

Amount of Conventional Force

How much conventional capability would NATO require on the central front for these benefits?

No one could claim to know exactly how many divisions and reserves would be necessary. And certainly a layman should be the last to do so. Even so, the preceding analysis of the Soviet attitude toward force and the inherent uncertainty of the nuclear environment suggest certain criteria relevant in fixing the amount and kind of forces required.

Critics who talk of an effort to re-enact World War II are wide of the mark. For an adequate deterrent, NATO does not need forces to deal with all-out conventional conflict resulting from deliberate massive Soviet attack. The necessary Soviet reinforcements for such an attack would surely give advance notice to NATO that they were planning a major aggression, and forfeit the benefit of surprise which they would otherwise enjoy. Any such Soviet action would not make sense for them, for the reasons already discussed. For the Soviets to count on NATO not to use its strategic and tactical nuclear weapons against such an attack would constitute an incredible gamble, wholly out of character.

What NATO needs for an adequate conventional component of its deterrent is the means to cope with more limited types of Soviet threats or thrusts of the sort discussed above. On the central front, such actions might involve the existing Soviet forces in East Germany and Poland, which might be substantially reinforced from the Soviet Union, and possibly supported by some of the thirty-five satellite divisions. NATO might have to resist a concentrated action at some vulnerable point or take the initiative to reopen access to Berlin. In either case, it would need to be able to handle this action without denuding or exposing other sections of the border. Adequate conventional capability for such purposes would assure that fighting could reach levels of violence which could readily get out of control. The Soviet attitude toward force should make clear why they are not likely to take the risks involved. With adequate NATO conventional defenses, therefore, there is little prospect that the Soviets would start limited hostilities which could spiral into all-out conflict. They would realize that an expanding conflict would greatly heighten the risks of general war by decision, accident, or mistake.

The NATO target of some thirty divisions appears suitable for these purposes in terms of numbers. But the required capability depends on much more than numbers. Existing and future forces need to be trained, equipped, and deployed more explicitly to perform such missions. Besides bringing divisions up to strength, it is essential to improve greatly the mobility of a major part of them and to unify logistics systems to allow this. And their training, artillery, air support, etc., must be adequate for conventional combat and not dependent primarily or entirely on nuclear weapons.

Sufficient reserves would also be essential, but they could be provided if the NATO nations were determined to do so. A major cost would be re-equipping the forces and providing adequate equipment for reserves. The real problem, however, is not resources. What is essential is that the NATO nations understand how the proposed ground forces relate to the maintenance of an effective deterrent.

CONTROL OF NUCLEAR WEAPONS

Nature of the Problem

With NATO strategy depending so heavily upon nuclear weapons, their control has been central to the alliance from the start and especially after 1954. The question of control has become a matter for serious debate, however, only in the last four or five years. The issue has come to the fore as growing Soviet strength made the United States itself vulnerable, as Britain created her V-bomber force and France sought to develop her own nuclear force, and as Europe revived its self-confidence and strength.

While cast in military terms, the issues are at bottom political and deeply enmeshed with the broader problems of adapting to new conditions the relations between the United States and Europe and within Europe. The handling of these issues will in turn profoundly affect the future Atlantic bonds and the shape of Europe as well.

Any serious discussion of nuclear control within NATO must recognize that no solution will fully satisfy all the desirable criteria. As in most foreign policy questions, each course has its advantages and weaknesses. The problem is to compare the merits and defects of the alternatives in order to make the best choice.

What should be the criteria for such a comparison? Any solution for nuclear control, it seems to me, should be judged mainly by how far it fulfills three requirements:

1. It should reinforce Western unity. The growth of the European community and the steady move toward Atlantic partnership have been the most significant developments since the end of World War II. In the last year, they have suffered serious setbacks. Whatever is done in the nuclear field should foster the progress and vitality of European integration and Atlantic partnership and should not undermine or weaken these constructive trends.

2. The solution should also assure responsible political control over the weapons and unify the deterrent. It should be designed to

take full account of the integral character of the defense of the NATO area. It would be foolhardy to suppose that a separate defense of either the United States or Europe is feasible. But this need not mean a monopoly of control in a single hand.

3. Finally, any solution should take account of the fact that the situation is still evolving and evolving rapidly. The shape of Europe is not yet finally determined. Obviously, various tendencies are contending for the ultimate outcome. And the relation between the emerging Europe and the United States also continues to develop. Hence, one should not assume that it will be feasible to strike off a definitive answer now. What is needed is to lay the basis for a constructive solution which can be worked toward over a period of time.

Broadly, three approaches have been proposed for sharing nuclear control in NATO:

1. The United States could share with its allies the planning, targetting, and guidelines for nuclear forces, while retaining the ultimate decision on use.

2. National French and British nuclear forces could be supported, with a view to grouping them and some or all United States strategic forces under some form of NATO force.

3. An integrated multilateral nuclear force could be created, composed either of Atlantic or European membership.

How do these several solutions compare in terms of the suggested criteria? We shall examine them in turn.

Appraisal of Sharing of Planning

Greater sharing of data and cooperation in targetting and planning for nuclear forces and in developing guidelines for their use seem highly desirable. Over the last year or so, such guidelines have been agreed on within NATO. The steps are already under way to introduce NATO officers into the headquarters of the United States Strategic Air Command and to expand the allied role in the nuclear planning in the Supreme Headquarters of Allied Powers in Europe (SHAPE). These measures should be pursued vigorously and extended. The fuller NATO awareness of the United States nuclear capability and greater NATO participation in the plans for its use should reassure the NATO partners and enable them to discuss nuclear issues more realistically.

But will a larger share in planning, guidelines, and targetting satisfy the other allies? Will it reconcile them to a virtual monopoly on the ultimate decision of use by the United States?

In strictly military terms, it is probably true that the alliance would be best served by such a unified control in the United States' hands. The evolving nuclear stalemate has made the defense of the NATO area more than ever a single problem. A separate nuclear war in Europe or in the United States would be out of the question. Moreover, with the approaching nuclear balance and the growing stockpiles, the need for controlled response is more and more apparent. If nuclear weapons should ever be employed, it would be in the interest of all to make certain that they were used to the minimum extent necessary and under conditions which would create the least possible damage and destruction. That presupposes highly centralized control.

Moreover, the idea that the United States would not be prepared to use its nuclear weapons to defend Europe under appropriate conditions is hardly tenable. The interests of the United States are so deeply involved in Europe and its integrity that it must treat any effort to conquer the NATO area in Europe as an attack on itself. If Europe were under Soviet control, the United States would clearly be at the mercy of the Soviet Union. Hence, it would have to treat any Soviet move to destroy or control Europe as a direct threat to its own survival. It is true, of course, that all-out nuclear war is not a suitable response for every kind of threat or danger. But this limitation on massive retaliation does not arise from United States control of nuclear weapons or from diverging interests between the United States and Europe. It would apply regardless of who might have control. If the European nations, or any one of them, had the full United States strategic capability, they would still find themselves under the same constraints against using it against lesser contingencies.

But continuing monopoly by the United States does not seem feasible any longer. For one thing, Britain and France have launched their own programs. They might be prepared in the future to merge these into some larger integrated force in which they had a significant part; there seems little prospect that either or both will simply abandon the nuclear field without any participation in some other way. But the problem really goes deeper.

The debate over strategy and nuclear control partly reflects discontent over the position of Europe in the NATO alliance. With their enhanced confidence and revived strength, many European members inevitably desire a larger part in the planning of NATO strategy and in the control over the forces for its defense, especially nuclear forces. Thus, many Europeans now feel that a virtual monopoly in United States hands is no longer appropriate or acceptable for the long term. This feeling is mainly political, but it must be recognized and treated as genuine and real.

If this analysis is correct, the desire of other allies for a role in nuclear control is not likely to be satisfied solely by measures for sharing knowledge and planning. As has been said, such steps are overdue and should be valuable in solidifying the alliance and mitigating some types of doubts or concern. But they fall short of offering the Europeans a position as real partners, even for the future. They are likely, in the long run, to feel that they remain wards of the United States, if the real power of decision rests indefinitely with the President of the United States.

Appraisal of National Nuclear Forces

How well do national nuclear forces fit our criteria? Britain and France are, of course, engaged in developing such national forces. By the Nassau Agreement, the United States, which has been assisting Britain since 1958, undertook to help her create a Polaris submarine force with American missiles and guidance systems, and the British agreed to devote their nuclear force to the defense of NATO, except in extreme national emergency. For some years, France has likewise been building a national force, which will mainly consist of Mirage bombers with atomic weapons in the 1960's and which will be converted to submarines with missiles in the early 1970's, according to present plans. After Nassau, de Gaulle rejected the United States' offer of missiles.

As Secretary McNamara and others have said, national nuclear forces in Europe (1) are expensive; (2) are seriously divisive; and (3) fragment the NATO strategic force.

There is no need to argue the question of expense. The British experience with the development of warheads, missiles, and, now, submarines has shown the tremendous expense of trying to create even a small national force. The United States spends $15 billion a year for its nuclear capability. While the British Government claims that its nuclear strategic force absorbs only 10 per cent of its defense budget, this figure excludes the cost of the V-bombers. The best evidence of the burden is that Britain has had to abandon various missile programs and contributes less than 55,000 men to the ground forces in Europe. French expenditures for developing nuclear material, weapons, and delivery systems are also heavy and will grow. Naturally, the costs of producing national forces would be materially reduced by United States assistance in technology, materials, and equipment. The question then is whether the interests of the alliance justify the United States in helping such national forces. If not, the allies should not be assisted to pursue a course which does not benefit collective defense.

The political effects of such national forces are bound to be divisive within NATO. The United Kingdom and France have justified their forces on the basis of the changing strategic balance. In his January 14, 1963, press conference, General de Gaulle said, "No one in the world—particularly no one in America—can say if, where, when, how, and to what extent the American nuclear weapons would be employed to defend Europe." Thus, the French force, though minuscule, is supposed to protect France and Europe from Soviet threats and attack: it is to deter the Soviets when United States forces alone would not. In May, 1963, Pierre Messmer, Minister of the Armed Forces, wrote:

> Only [those which possess atomic weapons] . . . are capable of defending their freedom and their life; the others are doomed to subservience or satellite status. . . . That is why the Americans and the Russians are hostile to the appearance of national nuclear forces which make their policy of hegemony more difficult and risk compromising its results.[4]

In defending their national force, the British, with more suavity, have made essentially similar points. According to British leaders, a national nuclear force enhances Britain's influence on American policy and in the world; indeed, it enables Britain to have an independent foreign policy. The V-bomber and later the Polaris force, it is explained, are necessary in order to maintain an effective deterrent under the conditions of nuclear balance. In insisting on the Nassau Agreement, the British Government showed that it still hankered after an independent role; as in the 1950's, its nuclear force is the means to independence and influence in world affairs. In his main speech in the House of Commons debate on the Nassau Agreement, Prime Minister Macmillan, in supporting the independent British deterrent, said:

> I do not believe that our Western Alliance could really stand permanently if in this vital [nuclear] field the United States were given for all time the sole authority. We are allies. We must remain allies, but we must not become satellites. I can understand why the French

---

[4] Pierre Messmer, "Notre politique militaire," *Revue de Défense Nationale*, May, 1963, pp. 760–61; reprinted in English in Release No. 155 (French Affairs) of Press Service of French Embassy, p. 12.

government, who are a world power as well as a continental power, wish to develop their own nuclear force.[5]

Peter Thorneycroft, the Defense Minister, was even more explicit:

> Assuming that we did not [have a British deterrent], then any nuclear threat to this country would have to be met by a counter-threat from outside. . . . Could we always count, in the world as it is today, upon an ally at our side? Does our history really bear out such an assumption?[6]

In concluding the debate, the Prime Minister reiterated this and other arguments.[7]

But by this logic, each NATO nation would have to develop its own nuclear striking force. According to this theory, since no nation will risk suicide to defend another, the French or British forces could hardly be expected to protect other European nations. Thus the Germans and others are bound to be faced sooner or later with the question of whether they should have such forces. Against this, it has been argued, first, that Germany is forbidden by the Western European Union (WEU) treaties to make nuclear weapons; second, that domestic pressures do not yet exist in Germany for a national nuclear program; and third, that any program would be hampered by lack of test areas.

Yet these limits on German action hardly seem likely to last if the United States assists France and Britain to develop and maintain national forces. Such United States assistance would inevitably underwrite the premises used to justify such forces: they run counter to collective defense; they certainly do not reinforce it. The German leaders have repeatedly stated that the Federal Republic cannot indefinitely accept a second-class status or discrimination. Now that it is back in the family of Europe, it is entitled to be treated once more as a full partner. Indeed, this principle has been the basis of the European Community since 1950, and it was reasserted by de Gaulle on his visit to Germany. Hence, over the long pull, the 1954 WEU limitation can hardly keep Germany from demanding equal nuclear status with the United Kingdom and France. If Germany is not treated as an equal, this discrimination will produce friction and discord. Aversion to a German national nuclear force would create tensions and cleavages within the alliance which the Soviet Union would certainly seek to exploit. In

[5] Hansard, January 30, 1963 (Vol. 670, No. 46), Col. 961.
[6] Hansard, January 31, 1963 (Vol. 670, No. 47), Col. 1154.
[7] *Ibid.*, Col. 1251–1253.

either case, the unity of the alliance will be seriously jeopardized.

The damage from assistance to French and British national forces would go even deeper. The French force is mainly a means for political primacy: a symbol to distinguish her from Germany and Italy. It reflects de Gaulle's concept of a Europe based on nation-states cooperating under French hegemony. In essence, this concept is the opposite of European integration through the European Community. Hence, assistance to the French effort would endorse de Gaulle's concept of Europe and would jeopardize support for the genuine integration of the European Community. Moreover, assistance to the British force has much the same effect. The campaign of Macmillan to show that the British force is the keystone of an independent British foreign policy reveals the ambiguity of the Conservative Party's approach to Europe. In helping the British force, the United States appears to underwrite this ambiguous attitude.

Despite these objections, it has been suggested that helping the French and British forces would offer the best route to a European or joint force. Given the reasons advanced for such national forces, any such British-French force, even if agreed to, would certainly leave intact the national forces under some façade, as has been done in the so-called inter-allied nuclear force recently set up by Nato, to which the British have "assigned" their V-bombers while retaining the national command structure and the right to withdraw for national purposes. This would be a far cry from an integrated European or Nato force. Any such truly integrated force would have to be set up so that the Germans and others could take part in it as equals; to be reliable, it would need to be so organized that it could not be pulled apart into national components. Otherwise, it could be a source of jockeying and bargaining rather than unity. Half measures will hardly satisfy a German aspiration for equality. Germany and other European nations would certainly not be content with merely taking part in a "control group" for French and British national forces. Inevitably they would expect such national forces to be finally controlled by the decision of Britain or France, and not the control group. In the quest for equality, the Germans would be led to press for their own national force, whether by removal of the United States joint control of nuclear warheads, by French assistance, or in some other way.

Far from fostering an integrated force, this course could actually obstruct it. The experience of the United Kingdom suggests that the burden of a national force might ultimately generate support for an integrated NATO or European force, even in France. But United States assistance to British and French national forces, which would assure their success and reduce their burden, would tend to remove this pressure on them to move toward a genuine integrated force.

In short, support for national nuclear forces would seriously compromise or undermine basic United States and NATO interests. It would sharpen cleavages within the alliance and create new tensions between its members. Such national forces are bound to waste resources, to be ineffective deterrents, and to be divisive within the alliance. Aiding the French and British forces can only underscore and justify their asserted rationale. De Gaulle would clearly use such help to advance his own aims for a "Europe of nations" which could undermine the alliance and the European Community. If the Germans and others are driven to seek such forces, the political strains on the alliance will be severe.

The creation of a NATO or European umbrella for such forces, or even a control group including other nations, has none of the advantages of an integrated multilateral force. The national components can always be pulled out of the NATO commitment. And such a control group appears to legitimize the national forces without solving the problems of discrimination or duplication. For these and other reasons, aid for national forces, far from leading to a joint integrated European force, would tend to damage seriously both European unity and collective defense.

Appraisal of a Multilateral Integrated Force

Thus far, our analysis of nuclear control within NATO has concluded that indefinite United States monopoly is not feasible, even with shared planning and that national forces in Europe, even under some form of group control, will not meet the criteria essential for a solution reinforcing the alliance, European integration, and Atlantic partnership.

There remains the alternative of a multilateral force which is genuinely integrated. Would it enable the sharing of nuclear control in a manner compatible with the wider political aims of Europe and the alliance? Such a force was proposed in 1960 by the Eisenhower Administration. It was reaffirmed in May, 1961, by President Kennedy at Ottawa and, more recently, by Secretaries Rusk and McNamara at the NATO meetings in December, 1961, and May, 1962. Since October, 1962, it has been under discussion among various NATO members.

A multilateral force could be constituted most readily by using ships, either surface or submarine, with Polaris missiles. In such a force, the ships and the missiles should be owned and controlled by the participants jointly, with no separate national ownership or control. They should be manned and operated by crews of mixed nationality in which no NATO member would predominate. Thus, no member could control the force or pull it apart. The task of organizing, training, and managing the force could be centralized in a joint executive agency.

The creation of crews composed of several nationalities would not be as difficult as some assume. Since the numbers are small, the members could be selected with great care. According to competent naval experts who have analyzed the problem, such crews could be trained and be fully effective for the operation of either surface ships or submarines.

Mixed manning is a crucial feature to assure that such a joint force could not be pulled apart. In a force composed of national units, the risk that one member may pull out its component makes for great uncertainty regarding planning or use. If the force is fully integrated, no one participant can withdraw any part of the ships. This is important for several reasons: the full force could be counted on for performing a specified strategic function. In the absence of national units, no member could threaten or undertake withdrawal as a lever or pressure on the others. Moreover, no one nationality would have unimpeded access to missiles or equipment aboard ship. Beyond this, unlike divisive national forces, the joint force with mixed manning would be a striking symbol of the cohesion of the alliance and of the mutual dependence of its members for their security.

The hardest problem regarding a multilateral force is control over its use. This issue also opens up questions as to which nations should participate in the force and how it should be related to other NATO or United States forces.

A multilateral force should clearly not be designed for a separate defense of Europe; it should be combined with American nuclear force in planning, targetting, and other ways. The defense of NATO is undoubtedly a single problem; strategic nuclear war could not be limited to Europe or the United States. But the Atlantic area is not a single political unit, and until it is, control will present an ultimate dilemma. In the long run Europeans are not likely to be satisfied with a solution which leaves all decisions to a President elected by only one portion of NATO. Yet, in practice the issue seems more theoretical than real. It is extremely hard to envisage a case where Europeans would wish to use strategic nuclear weapons when the United States would not be ready to do so. What is involved is more a matter of self-respect. Many Europeans want to feel that they have a genuine participation in the nuclear deterrent. And if they are to be treated as partners in the nuclear field, some way must be devised to provide for greater equality, at least for a unified Europe, in the matter of nuclear control.

If Europe moves toward unity, the United States should be willing to reorganize the force, if the Europeans desire, to permit its operation and use without the veto of the United States. In the Nassau Agreements, we accepted the right of Britain to withdraw and use its Polaris force in an extreme national emergency. We should be ready to concede to a multilateral force the same degree of ultimate autonomy as has already been granted the British national force. The final outcome might take the form of either an integrated NATO force in which the United States, without a veto, would be one member, or an integrated European force without the United States as a member, closely coordinated with United States forces but under ultimate European control. Either form has its disadvantages. But either would be far better than the continuance and spread of national nuclear forces, which involve serious problems in more intractable forms. Some have expressed concern that an eventual European force would split the alliance. But this would depend on whether Europe and the United States recognized the fact that their security was bound together by the facts of life. These perspectives are important, but they are in the future; the final form will depend greatly on the course of events, especially in Europe.

Admittedly, for the present, the issue of control is inevitably complex. It is manageable only if handled as an evolving factor. At the start, control can only be exercised by a committee of some or all of the participants. Under current proposals, the United States would be a member, and each major participant would retain a voice in control of the force, which in practice amounts to a veto. Any such force will take time to create. Even if surface ships are used, its formation will probably require five years or more. While the force is being developed, trained, and put into operation, the control issue will not have to be finally settled. And even in the first stage of operations, control could be handled by unanimity. The group could agree in advance to use the force to retaliate against large-scale nuclear attack on the NATO area; in other cases, the group would have some time to arrive at a joint decision, especially if NATO maintains adequate conventional forces. Thus, in the first instance, the need for unanimity would be solved by prior agreement; in the second, it would be possible to arrive at a method of meeting an attack through joint consultation.

During this decade, the shape of Europe will be evolving. Hopefully, it will be advancing toward greater political cohesion and ability to act as an entity. If that occurs, the control formula can be revised to provide for decision by less than unanimity, if the members wish.

Judging from comments in Germany and elsewhere, the leaders of those countries appear to view the proposal in these terms. For the initial period, they are ready to rely on some form of committee where each major nation has a voice. But, for the future, they expect to review this issue to decide whether or not the United States would give up its veto, especially in favor of a united Europe.

Thus, a multilateral force would provide a framework for meeting any demands for an integrated European force. It should therefore offer the chance for greater cohesion within the alliance. It should satisfy the German and Italian desire for equal treatment and a voice in nuclear defense without the creation of politically divisive national forces. Those Europeans who favor an integrated Europe can regard the multilateral force as a factor moving Europe in that direction.

What are the prospects for an integrated force ultimately absorbing the British and French national forces? The British might well join the multilateral force, even though retaining their national force for the present. As British opinion reappraises its national position, pressures to merge the British force into the joint force are likely to grow. France would certainly not take part in creating such a force under de Gaulle. But, as outlined by Messmer, the French force of three nuclear submarines will not be completed until 1973, even if the plans go forward as he hopes. Experience of that decade may well change the French attitude after de Gaulle. The objection that a multilateral force will tend to divide the alliance by isolating France is hardly valid. Actually, France has isolated herself by her insistence on a wholly independent national nuclear force. To refrain from action in which France may not join would give her a veto and paralyze the alliance.

In summary, a multilateral force offers a constructive method for handling the issue of nuclear control within the alliance. In its initial form, it is no final or perfect solution. As has already been stated, there is no perfect solution under existing conditions. The alternatives are clearly less constructive and offer less hope for the future.

An Anglo-French nuclear force would hamper real European integration. Assisting the national programs would solidify the commitment of France and Britain to national forces, encourage de Gaulle's concept of a Europe based on nation-states, push the Germans and Italians ultimately to a national nuclear effort, and fragment the alliance.

In contrast, a multilateral force avoids or resolves many of the problems posed by national forces in Europe, whether or not grouped together. Unlike national forces, a multilateral force would not fragment the alliance, but would tend to pull it together. Such a force would also enable West Germany and Italy to have a proper part in nuclear defense without raising the specter of a separate German strategic force. The question of discrimination against the Germans or other nations would not arise. The cost of such a force would be materially less for the members. By combining their efforts, they could create a respectable nuclear force without unduly diverting resources from more adequate conventional forces. The multilateral force should foster European integration by bringing together the "Five" and Britain into an integrated nuclear effort, open to France when she is ready to join. By initially involving the United States, the multilateral force would offer the best prospect. Even if it developed into a European force, it would still have close ties with the United States.

In short, among the alternative means for sharing nuclear control, the multilateral force seems to offer the route toward a solution most compatible with our basic goals of European unity and Atlantic partnership.

NATO MACHINERY

The tensions and disputes within Nato over strategy and nuclear control have arisen mainly from the inherent complexity of adapting strategy and forces to changing conditions; and differences in political purposes and priorities generated partly by the shifting political balance among its members. But the effort to overcome these obstacles has been badly handicapped by serious weaknesses in the Nato machinery for dealing with these matters.

The alliance has had no adequate focal point for analysis and discussion of the military and political issues involved. The Nato

Council cannot meet this need: its members are seldom highly qualified for strategic analysis and must depend mainly on instructions from their governments. The various statements and replies are, therefore, essentially methods of transmitting views formed in the capitals. Thus, discussions of the Council can hardly be expected to achieve real consensus. Nor is the NATO Secretariat staffed to provide studies or advice on strategic issues; the Secretary General has in practice had to rely on the Supreme Allied Commander, Europe (SACEUR) as his principal advisor on them.

The result has been to distort somewhat the role of SACEUR. During his tenure, General Lauris Norstad, who earned the respect and confidence of key European governments, was often a spokesman or conduit for their views within the alliance. While this service met a real need, the Supreme Headquarters of the Allied Powers in Europe (SHAPE) is not an ideal locus for planning and analyzing NATO strategy. Inevitably, its approach has serious limitations, with a tendency to pose the issues too narrowly in the terms of the European theatre, and with the bias any command has to favor having control over the requisite weapons and their use, as in the case of land-based medium-range ballistic missiles. A more serious handicap has been the failure to integrate political and military factors into the strategic analysis. SHAPE can hardly be expected to perform this function which national governments commit to their defense and foreign ministries.

With inadequate machinery, the efforts to revise NATO strategy and forces, which were bound to be controversial, have been marked by more acrimony and distrust than necessary. The initiative taken by the United States, often by statements at the semi-annual ministerial meetings, has generated resentment among many NATO members. Given the nature of such meetings and the absence of a suitable forum for follow-up, they have often felt that the United States was seeking to call the tune unilaterally. The fact that few of the other NATO members had the informed basis to judge the American conclusions has only heightened the sense of frustration. The resulting atmosphere of doubt and irritation has hardly been conducive to sober reappraisal or solid consensus.

NATO should act to correct this deficiency in machinery and shared knowledge. The steps taken at the Ottawa meeting in the spring of 1963 should be a start: the SHAPE nuclear planning and liaison at the Strategic Air Command in Omaha will at least expand the participation in the existing system of planning and targetting. But more is required.

NATO also needs a high official who could act as a sort of NATO defense minister charged with strategic analysis and planning for the alliance. He might be a deputy secretary-general but should have independent standing and authority. What is important is that he be the servant of the alliance as a whole, and that the various members respect his capacity and objectivity. To do his job, he would need a small, expert staff of qualified civilian and military planners. (The Standing Group should either be transferred to Paris to serve as part of his military staff or be replaced with other military advisors. At the same time, the Military Committee [which now includes all members] might also be moved to Paris, where its members could serve primarily as military advisors to the permanent representatives on the Council.) The task of the NATO defense minister would also be to keep in close contact with governments and to bring together key national officials for joint discussions.

Such a NATO defense minister, assisted by a proper staff, should be able to facilitate consensus on NATO strategy and on future revisions. By counteracting the existing imbalance in data, this agency would enable the Europeans to participate more effectively in the debate on, and analysis of, strategic issues. Hence, the result should be to dissipate some of the tensions and doubts which are now too widespread.

Even with such an agency, however, NATO will not easily and quickly reach agreed solutions for its problems of strategy or nuclear control. While the security interests on both sides of the Atlantic largely coincide, NATO members will inevitably view the strategic issues from differing slants resulting from their differences in size, power, geography, and other factors. Many of these can be ironed out by discussion or adjusted by sensible compromise. Some, however, especially on the question of nuclear control, are likely to be more intractable. Their source is not mainly misunderstanding about military factors but complications arising from a deeper divergence on purpose or priorities. Even such issues, however, should benefit from having a better alliance forum for airing and debating them. That will at least make it easier to disentangle the genuinely military aspects from the other factors and, perhaps, thereby put in clearer perspective the real reasons for positions taken.

But among the Atlantic nations, relations for some years seem certain to be marked by friction, dispute, and tension. In this period, Europe is trying to formulate its shape and purposes, and Europe and the United States are seeking to revise their relations and develop some new pattern which will be viable for the next stage. Obviously, both processes interact. And these processes and their interaction are bound to create turmoil and debate among the Atlantic nations on many different topics for some time to come. It is essential to keep their controversy in perspective. With the Communist world and the less developed nations in flux, the Atlantic nations have an historic role to help direct this change into orderly and constructive channels. In this crucial era, they must not permit divergence among themselves to sever the close working ties required to carry out these historic tasks.

THIRTEEN

ALASTAIR BUCHAN

The Multilateral Force:
An Historical Perspective

[*Editor's Note: Alastair Buchan, a distinguished British student of strategic affairs, has, as military correspondent for the influential* London Observer *and since 1958 as Director of the Institute for Strategic Studies, made major contributions to strategic thought. With respect to the Atlantic Alliance, Mr. Buchan has consistently called attention to the importance of defining priorities properly. In his view, the issue of nuclear control is primarily a political problem. Therefore, he has been extremely skeptical of efforts to solve it by primarily technical expedients, like the MLF. His constant concern has been to bring about closer political consultation and to recast the military command structure in order to harmonize political and military objectives.*

In this essay, Mr. Buchan traces the various forces and considerations that produced the proposal for a NATO *multilateral force. He demonstrates how a coalescence of frequently conflicting motives contributed to exacerbate the debate about nuclear control and why the underlying problems continue.*]

The control of nuclear strategy has presented a problem for the Western allies with which they have been attempting to grapple, by fits and starts, ever since the advent of the missile age made final nonsense of any simple policy of massive strategic action in response to any form of aggression in Europe. Many factors and arguments have been thrown into the debate as to whether and

AUTHOR'S NOTE: This paper is adapted from an article in *International Affairs* (XL, No. 4 [October 1964]), the quarterly journal of the Royal Institute of International Affairs in London, for whose permission to reprint it as an Adelphi Paper I am extremely grateful.

EDITOR'S NOTE: Reprinted with permission from the *Adelphi Papers*, No. 13, October, 1964, the Institute for Strategic Studies, London.

how the European allies should share with the United States the
responsibility for strategic decisions whose implementation still depends overwhelmingly on American-owned and -based weapons:
they have included the revived economic strength and potential
political strength of Western Europe; the danger that the nuclear
weapons programs of Britain and France may lead to imitation on
the part of the Federal Republic of Germany; the problem of the
credibility of the American response to a serious attack on Europe
in the light of the growing vulnerability of her own civilization;
the military requirement to offset by some means the growing Soviet MRBM threat to Europe; the need to share the burdens of strategic deterrence more equitably between the United States and her
European allies.

Out of these debates, official and unofficial, three possible
courses of action for the alliance began to emerge in the early
1960's. The first was to recognize that NATO is a coalition of sovereign states (even though it has a standby international command
system for certain kinds of forces) and to accept the fact that the
principal nations in it are not prepared to delegate major decisions
of policy, let alone of peace and war, to each other or to a central
system. This is the so-called multinational approach, and those who
have advocated it believe that the central problems of confidence
and coordination could be met by a reorganization of the machinery of NATO, both to give those responsible for civil policy a
greater control over military action and to give the European allies
a more constructive relationship to American planning. Certainly
a permanent solution involves bringing more and more national
nuclear forces within the scrutiny and authority of the alliance
itself, working towards a distant day when the whole of the American strategic force as well as the British and French forces are
within the system.

The second solution, which emerged from the acceleration of the
European Economic Community, and from the Kennedy Administration's encouragement of this development, would be to create
an analogous relationship in the strategic field to the unfolding
trans-Atlantic economic relationship, one of partnership between
units of roughly equal strength and importance. This would involve
the development of a European strategic nuclear force under the
control of an authority evolved by the Community itself. Though
the European force might not be as large as the American, it
would be of sufficient importance in both American and Soviet
eyes to enable Europe to develop its own strategic conceptions, and

to coordinate its force fully with the American forces on the basis of right rather than of grace. If it were to grow from European resources and internal European confidence it would require the participation of the United Kingdom.

The third alternative is to create within the framework of an alliance of sovereign states a new force owned, operated, and controlled jointly by the nuclear and non-nuclear powers—the so-called multilateral solution.

None of these solutions is foreclosed, but it is the third which holds the day at present, which has been most exhaustively explored by governments, and on which active negotiations will take place between the United States and the seven European countries interested in the proposal once the British and American elections are over. It is in many ways curious that this should be the case, since this third solution meets few of the anxieties that have found expression in the various allied countries since the control of nuclear strategy became a problem. Since France under President de Gaulle has expressed a lack of interest in the proposal, a multilateral force could not, in the foreseeable future, be considered a European Community force even if the American veto on its control were withdrawn. It does not, of itself, dispose of the British, let alone the French, nuclear force, and therefore, if European nuclear forces are prestige symbols, it does not eliminate the danger of a German national force, however remote in reality such a contingency may always have been.

As the proposal now stands, the multilateral force does not heighten the credibility of the American response to attack in Europe, since the United States, like all the other participating countries, will have a veto on its operational release: the problem of the credibility of the American response has in any case been less in the forefront of European anxieties since the Cuban missile crisis of October, 1962, and the end of the Soviet diplomatic offensive against Berlin. Nor can the force proposed, 200 Polaris missiles, be considered a strategic counterbalance (even if such a concept has any real validity) to the 800 Soviet MRBM's targeted on Western Europe. And a European share of 60 per cent of the finance of a force costing more than $400 million a year cannot alleviate more than about 1½ per cent of the cost of the American strategic nuclear forces, even if planned American force levels are reduced *pari passu* with the development of the MLF.

The reasons why the solution which most dispassionate students of the alliance problem would regard as the least satisfactory is now being pressed with such vigour are complex. The essential one is that the other two alternatives, the multinational system and the European-American strategic partnership, have become impossible to pursue—largely, but not entirely, as a result of French policy— at a time when the American desire to maintain a continuing private dialogue with the Soviet Union has made it essential for the United States to make a special effort to retain the confidence of the Federal German Republic. Though the MLF may be a left-handed means of doing this, many people in Europe and the United States have come to regard it as the best instrument available.

It is true that some progress has been made towards the development of NATO and the commitment of nuclear forces to enable it to function more successfully as a multinational coalition in the missile age. But the enormous task of reorganizing institutions and adjusting national habits to develop a better system of joint planning, force commitment and crisis management, has not only been inhibited by President de Gaulle's dislike of the degree of military integration which is involved. The will is still lacking in London and Washington, as well as in Paris, to confront the problems of giving allies a certain degree of control over a hitherto sovereign area of policy. As the brief historical sketch that follows suggests, such a transformation might have occurred, and the conclusion will suggest that it may yet have to come.

The concept of a European force has proved less attractive, and its difficulties more formidable, the more closely it has been studied, except to certain French spokesmen and writers and to the dogmatic European federalists. The idea has in any case been shelved as a matter of practical politics for the immediate future by the exclusion of Britain, the only European country with an existing military nuclear and thermonuclear potential, from the EEC; by the distaste of both parties in Britain for the idea; by the preference of the German Government for the MLF solution; and by increasing American doubts about the soundness of the concept or about the inevitable identity of European and American interests, now that the first euphoria about "the twin pillars" of European-American partnership has given way to longer thoughts. Although the situation has been complicated by the tendency of some American officials to talk of the multilateral force as the eventual nucleus of a European force, only the election of Senator Goldwater and a policy of old-fashioned American isolationism are likely to revive significant European enthusiasm for the idea in the immediate future.

II

The idea of creating a multilaterally owned and operational force of nuclear weapons within NATO has a mixed ancestry. It got its first impetus from certain studies conducted at SHAPE in the eighteen months after the meeting of the NATO heads of government which took place in December, 1957. These studies were conducted against the background of a still unresolved technological question of whether and when the United States could find a dependable long-range missile to match the apparent Soviet lead in this weapon. They suggested that there was a military requirement for a force of mobile *medium*-range missiles in Western Europe, mounted on trucks, railway cars or barges, and the conclusion was soon reached that a missile made relatively invulnerable by this means could not, by reason of its mobility, be operated under the bilateral agreements covering tactical nuclear weapons, but would require a genuine mixed-manned allied force to run it.[1]

These studies did not commend themselves to the American, British, or French governments, but they did lead those, especially in the State Department, who had begun to become sensitive to the political disadvantages of the American nuclear preponderance, to think that, if there were a serious military requirement for such mobile missiles, here was an opportunity to bring the non-nuclear powers within a more integrated system of allied planning and control than had been achieved thus far. The United States Government began the study of a "NATO Deterrent," as it was then called, in April, 1960. In October, a rudimentary plan was aired for a force of 300 Polaris missiles—some in submarines, some on mobile land mountings—under the control of the NATO Council. It was argued at that time that by thus making NATO into "the fourth atomic power" the danger of further national nuclear forces in Europe would be averted and faith in the credibility of Western nuclear weapons would be enhanced. The offer was formally made by Christian Herter, outgoing Secretary of State, at the NATO ministerial meeting in December, 1960.

The American proposal met with a cool reception in every country except Germany and Italy, and when the new Kennedy Ad-

---

[1] This possibility was first publicly explored, I believe, in the first edition of my book *NATO in the 1960's* (ISS Studies in International Security No. 1), published in March, 1960 (London: Chatto and Windus; New York: Frederick A. Praeger, 1960).

ministration took office, it looked as if it might be dropped altogether. One of the President-elect's first moves had been to set up
an informal commission of inquiry under Dean Acheson to examine the relative merits of schemes for strengthening NATO as a
multinational alliance or of introducing a new multilateral component within it, alternative approaches whose leading counsel
were Albert Wohlstetter, the distinguished strategic analyst from
the RAND Corporation, for the multinational solution, and
Robert R. Bowie, Director of the Harvard Center for International
Affairs, for the multilateralists. The evidence at that time told
against the multilateralists; the Pentagon had lost whatever interest it had earlier had in European-based missiles; Franz-Joseph
Strauss, the German Defense Minister, appeared more preoccupied
with a better German association with decisions affecting tactical
than with strategic nuclear weapons; President de Gaulle had not
yet begun to use the French nuclear force as a diplomatic instrument; and American strategic analysis was becoming increasingly
preoccupied with centralizing control over nuclear weapons in the
interests of a more flexible war strategy of controlled response.

This situation was reflected, not only in press reports that the
new President intended to bury the idea of a NATO deterrent,[2] but
also in the President's first major policy move—when he committed five American Polaris submarines to NATO "subject to any
agreed guide-lines on their control and use."[3] However, he did not
close the door on a NATO deterrent though he hedged it with the
formidable condition that the European allies should meet their
goals in conventional forces before "we look to the possibility of
eventually establishing a NATO seaborne missile force which would
be genuinely multilateral in ownership and control."[4]

Thereafter, the multilateral proposal simply dropped out of sight
for more than a year. There was little reaction in Europe to the
President's hint, certainly no united one, and it had little effect
upon the endemic arguments about the level of European conventional forces. The Berlin crisis of 1961 gave the leaders of the alliance other things to think about. At the same time there were
signs of an attempt in both London and Washington to withdraw
some of the veil of secrecy that surrounded nuclear targeting and
planning, and to operate the multinational system more success-

---

[2] E.g., article by Henry Brandon, in *The Sunday Times* (London), April 2,
1961.

[3] Speech in Ottawa, May 17, 1961. The figure was reduced to three in 1962.

[4] *Ibid.*

fully. However, there were certain pressures operating on the United States Government below the surface which became more evident and harder to resist during the second half of 1962.

One of these pressures was generated by the preoccupation of the Action Committee for a United Europe and its American supporters with finding a political role for the European Community that was not exclusively tied to French nuclear potential and that would provide an inducement for Britain to enter it: this had the effect of reviving the idea of a multilateral force as the foundation of a European one and of altering the American condition for launching it from the fulfilment of Europe's conventional force goals to the eventual achievement of a politically united Europe.

A second pressure was provided by the dismay of the German Government at realizing that the strategy of massive retaliation had been abandoned. (It had in fact been abandoned years earlier, if indeed it ever had been the real American strategy, but it was not publicly buried until McNamara's speech to the NATO Council in Athens in April, 1962.) This development revived doubts about the credibility of the American response and began to increase German enthusiasm for a multilaterally controlled NATO force (although German leaders continued to insist in private that they were more concerned with some sort of control over nuclear weapons on German soil than with long-range missiles).

A third pressure, in some American eyes at least, was the need to prevent the arguments used to justify the British, and still more the French, nuclear force from eroding the confidence of all the non-nuclear powers in the American sense of commitment to NATO and the integrity of Europe.

A fourth pressure was created by the fact that, as 1962 wore on, depressing evidence began to accumulate of the difficulties of improving the existing multinational machinery of NATO. There were unresolved arguments between governments about the move of the Standing Group from Washington to Paris, about the strengthening of the NATO Secretariat, and about the role of the Council. Though President de Gaulle was the most openly obstructive, neither McNamara nor the British Government appeared ready to take any significant step toward giving the other NATO allies greater control over American and British planning or decisions. As far as can be observed, the new Nuclear Committee of the NATO Council, created in April, 1962, in which the nuclear powers were to discuss their strategic policy with greater confidence and candor than hitherto, was stillborn.

Last, but by no means least, there was the pressure exerted by the presence in the State Department of a small number of senior officials who had early made up their minds that the multilateral solution was the correct one, and who have since displayed a degree of missionary zeal, not normally to be found in diplomatic offices, to convert—"lobby" is not too strong a word—others to their view.

In consequence, various American emissaries began to tour the West European capitals in the summer of 1962 to canvass the merits of a multilateral force. They came from the State Department, and their arguments were based partly on the need to provide a Europe that was surging towards unity with a worthy strategic role, partly on the need to prevent proliferation. The line of reasoning was based on President Kennedy's famous Declaration of Interdependence made at Philadelphia on July 4, and in contradiction of the major presentation of the new American strategy of controlled response which McNamara had made at Ann Arbor a month earlier. Judging from the impressions of those who talked to President Kennedy at this time, it would appear that he had made up his mind that one serious European nuclear force would be more easily reconciled in the long run with his Defense Secretary's insistence on centralized control than two small European national forces and the possibility of more.[5] He was not, however, prepared to try and force Britain out of the nuclear-weapons business.

One would have thought that the vindication of American firmness and decision in the Cuban missile crisis, and its beneficent effect on American prestige in Europe, might have set the question aside for a while. But, in fact, so strong was the American urge to make Europe strategically respectable and to find a formula that would enfold the British and French national nuclear forces within a larger framework, that, less than three weeks after the height of the Cuban crisis, George Ball was informing a European audience that:

[5] President Kennedy clearly had a private nightmare about nuclear proliferation which can have borne very little relation to the kind of scientific advice available to him. Consider this statement from his television interview of December 18, 1962: "If the French decide they want to become a nuclear power themselves, that is their decision. The question is whether the United States should join in helping to make France a nuclear power, then Italy, then West Germany, then Belgium. How does that produce security when you have ten, twenty, thirty nuclear powers who may fire their weapons off under different conditions?"

From a strictly military standpoint, we do not feel that the Alliance has an urgent need for a European nuclear contribution. But should other NATO nations so desire, we are ready to give serious consideration to the creation of a genuine multilateral medium-range ballisticmissile force fully coordinated with the other deterrent forces of the North Atlantic Treaty Organization. It is not for us—indeed, it would be out of keeping with the spirit of the Atlantic partnership— to dictate how such a force should be manned, financed, or organized. But it is a proper responsibility of the United States, which has had so much experience in the nuclear field, to make available to others our information and ideas with respect to the characteristics and capabilities of a multilateral force. And we are now in the process of doing so.[6]

In reality, Ball was being somewhat modest and disingenuous: the United States had by then a plan for a multilateral force that she was about to insist that her allies consider. This plan was unveiled just before the December meeting of the NATO Ministers in Paris in the form of a force that would consist partly of Polaris submarines and partly of a new medium-range, mobile, land-based missile known as Missile X, which the Pentagon had been somewhat reluctantly developing for the past two years.[7] The assumption behind Dean Rusk's exposition of this proposed force was that if it materialized, the British and French forces would become part of it but that its employment would remain subject to an overriding American veto for the time being.

III

At this point, a different issue became entangled in the discussion over a multilateral solution, which profoundly affected its later development and caused much of the confusion in which the question subsequently became enshrouded. The history of Anglo-American military relations and tensions caused by the decision to cancel the Skybolt missile belong to a different story. The point that is relevant here is that when Macmillan traveled to Nassau on December 18, 1962, to negotiate on a replacement, the United States Government had become too deeply committed to broadening the basis of cooperation on nuclear control to conclude a

[6] Speech to NATO Parliamentarians' Conference in Paris, November 16, 1962.

[7] Missile X was finally dropped from the American research-and-development in August, 1964.

straightforward bilateral arrangement with Britain. President Kennedy's formula (as he made clear in a background news conference a fortnight after Nassau[8]) was to pursue both the multilateral and multinational principles jointly and simultaneously, in order to see which would prove the most successful. The Prime Minister's thoughts appear to have been concentrated solely on the multinational solution.

Unfortunately, both delegations get their terminology muddled, and their final communiqué reflected two soliloquies rather than an understanding. Thus, Paragraphs 6 and 8 of the communiqué include the British offer to assign Bomber Command, British tactical nuclear forces in Europe, and the eventual British Polarises "as part of a NATO nuclear force targeted in accordance with NATO plans," *pari passu* with a similar American contribution. In subsequent months, the British Government elaborated this proposal to suggest that all NATO countries with tactical nuclear weapons should similarly be drawn into a new command and planning system within NATO. In Paragraph 8 of the Nassau communiqué, this was described as a *multilateral* force. The British impression was that the Americans agreed with them that the future structure of NATO should be organized around a closer commitment of existing national forces rather than on a new force, a view that was strengthened by the fact that an offer of American Polaris missiles was immediately made to President de Gaulle.

But State Department officials had a different concept of a multilateral force. In their view, it was to be a new force, consisting of submarines or surface ships, jointly financed, planned, owned and controlled by the participants, in which the non-nuclear allies would win their right to participate by their financial contribution. In Paragraph 7 of the communiqué, which spoke of joint support for the development "of a multilateral NATO nuclear force in the closest consultation with other NATO allies," they thought they had got British agreement to participate, but, in fact, the question of British participation was not settled at Nassau. The British, moreover, were led to think, by the tenor of the discussions there, that this was to be regarded only as a distant aspiration and a secondary American objective.

They were wrong. Less than three weeks after Nassau, President de Gaulle struck a heavy blow at the multinational solution when he rejected the American offer of Polaris and made it clear that

[8] *The Times* (London), January 2, 1963.

France would continue to develop a wholly independent nuclear force, as well as to exclude Britain from the Community. Macmillan, for reasons of British domestic politics, weakened his own position considerably when, in defending the Nassau Agreements in the House of Commons on January 31, 1963, he laid such stress on the continuing national command of British nuclear weapons as to rob their assignment to NATO of much of its significance, at least in European eyes. By the beginning of February, 1963, the American proposal for a new multilaterally owned and controlled nuclear force had become a prime objective of American policy: detailed plans were unwrapped, influential emissaries were dispatched to Europe, and any suggestions that the proposals for developing a better multinational command and planning system should first be studied and discussed, tended to be treated in Washington as irrelevant diversions from the main issue.

Why, one must ask, did the United States launch the MLF proposal with such vigor and haste, despite the fact that the "grand design" of a partnership between the United States and a United Europe was for the moment dead, that American prestige in Europe had seldom stood higher, and that Britain had just made an important *beau geste* to the solidarity of the alliance? The answer lies partly in the American view of German policy. It is true that the alarming Herr Strauss had fallen from office in November, 1962, and that Herr Erler, the widely respected deputy leader of the Social Democrats, and other German commentators, had expressed their preference for the multinational solution, though not condemning the MLF. But the Franco-German pact, signed in January, 1963, profoundly alarmed the United States and had aroused a specter of an eventual Franco-German nuclear cooperation. No time, it was argued in Washington, must be lost in offering Germany an alternative solution. There was no longer any question of waiting for a European request for participation in nuclear planning; the right solution must be sold to Europe before French influence spread.

There was a second reason why the British attempt to create a NATO nuclear force out of the assigned weapons of the nuclear powers, plus the nuclear-armed aircraft and other tactical weapons in Europe, received only nominal American support. Both President Kennedy and Secretary McNamara had become concerned about the drain of overseas military expenditure on the American balance of payments, and the latter had made clear that he equated an ally's right to influence NATO strategy with its readiness to make a special financial contribution to the costs of deterrence.[9] This the contribution of European allies to a multilateral force carried some promise of doing, while a re-grouping of the existing nuclear forces did not.

IV

It is a tribute to the amount of staff work on the MLF which had been quietly undertaken before it became a major premise of American policy that the proposal presented to the allies in March, 1963, is substantially that on which they are still negotiating a year and a half later. It called for a fleet of twenty-five mixed-manned surface ships to be jointly owned, financed, and controlled by those countries willing to participate, each armed with eight Polaris A-3 missiles. The cost was estimated at $5 billion spread over ten years (it has been slightly lowered since), and it early became established that the United States and Germany were prepared to pay 75 per cent of this sum between them. (The U.S. Congress' Joint Atomic Energy Committee had firmly refused to contemplate American nuclear submarines passing out of American hands. The new proposal was for a straightforward medium-range missile force but based on international waters, rather than the terrain of Western Europe, to avoid complications with both France and the Soviet Union.)

The first reaction in Europe to the MLF proposal was civil but not enthusiastic. The smaller nations that were approached (Canada, Norway, Denmark, and Portugal, as well as France, expressed no interest in participation) were worried about the cost of even a small share in such a force, especially if they were also to accede to American demands to strengthen their conventional forces; naval staffs were skeptical about the operational viability of such a fleet, and public opinion was skeptical or disinterested. And no one, except Kai Uwe van Hassel, the German Defense Minister, who early suggested a form of majority voting that was unacceptable to the United States, could see how the problem of control was going to be solved. The British Government first supported the proposal,[10] but it became increasingly tepid as Washington made

[9] Testimony to the U.S. Congress, House Armed Services Committee, January, 1963.

[10] "We shall certainly do our best, with the United States and Europe, to bring a NATO nuclear force into being, and as a first step we have offered to assign the whole of our V-bomber force to it. This has been widely welcomed

it clear that British participation was expected. When President Kennedy embarked on a "tour of exploration" in Europe in June, there were many, and not only in London, who thought that the MLF proposal would run into the sands, more especially as the President himself had never displayed the same enthusiasm for the idea as the ardent spirits in the State Department, particularly if it did not carry wholehearted British support. However, two developments had occurred which were about to give it a fresh lease on life.

One was the slow strangulation of the idea of strengthening the political machinery of NATO on the basis of multinational forces. The United States loyally supported such an idea at the Ottawa meeting of the NATO Ministers in May, 1963, where it was agreed that allied officers should be stationed at the headquarters of the Strategic Air Command in Omaha, Nebraska, and that a new Deputy Supreme Commander in Europe should be appointed to coordinate European nuclear planning (a Belgian general was appointed four months later). But this did not presage a serious reform of the alliance structure in the direction of giving the nonnuclear allies a significant share in strategic planning, and Couve de Murville's cold bearing made it clear that, while she did not object to tinkering with it, France was not prepared to see the alliance machinery recast in a more integrated design.

Moreover, from the spring of 1964, British ministers themselves began to demolish the foundations of their own position. As the British election began to loom on the horizon, and as they sensed that the future of the British deterrent might become an election issue, they began to lay increasing stress on the theoretic independence of British nuclear weapons rather than on the assignment of those weapons to the planning control of NATO. Even in Ottawa, where lay the best hope of convincing the non-nuclear powers of the significance of Britain's change of policy toward NATO, the then Foreign Secretary, Lord Home, found it necessary to make a speech stressing the national aspects of Britain's nuclear force.[11]

The other development was in Germany. There, for the previous two years increasing doubts about American policy had been accumulating, even in the hearts of the most judicious Germans. The

---

in Europe. We shall support, too, the efforts which the Americans are engaged upon to bring about a mixed-manned force as well."—Peter Thorneycroft, House of Commons, March 4, 1963.

[11] Speech to the Canadian Club, May 21, 1963.

McNamara strategy of controlled response, enunciated without any consultation with Bonn, hardly seemed to fit the security requirements of an exposed country like Germany. Operation "Big Lift" and talk of a limited American withdrawal from Europe exposed Germans to a drumfire of French propaganda that the United States would eventually pull out of Europe. Above all, the increasing American emphasis on arms control had made the German Government nervous, ever since the opening of bilateral Soviet-American discussions on Berlin, that the United States might, in order to meet her own security requirements, have to make agreements with the Soviet Union that conflicted with German interests. It was almost certainly the signature of the test ban treaty in July, 1963, handled by London and Washington with the minimum of consultation with Bonn, that convinced the German Government that the MLF proposal must be firmly embraced as the only modification in alliance arrangements that was available; partly to bind American military power inexorably and permanently to Europe; partly to ensure a stronger German voice in Washington; partly to compensate for the Pentagon's declining interest in a land-based European MRBM, despite the pleas of two successive SACEURS. In the depths of German thought the MLF had been, and still is, conceived as the German equivalent of the British and French independent deterrents. These additional stimuli meant that by the end of the summer of 1963 the German position on the MLF had changed from one of intelligent interest to something more closely resembling a demand.[12]

There was also a second reason for the interest of the new Erhard administration in the MLF. Since leaving office, Strauss, the leader of the Bavarian party affiliated to the Christian Democratic Union had become increasingly the spokesman of a form of German Gaullism that advocated a reorientation of German policy away from its Atlantic and American affiliations toward a Franco-German partnership, and that has offered increasingly vocal opposition to a policy of *détente* and movement in respect of the Soviet

[12] This judgment is based on my own observations and conversations in Germany. For a similar view, see Henry Brandon's appraisal in *The Sunday Times* (London), September 22, 1963. Just over a year later, the Bonn correspondent of *The Times* (London) noted that German enthusiasm for the MLF derived from the fact that "Although the Americans will retain a right of veto, the fact that their European partners will have a voice on the 'board of governors' will give them far more weight in forcing a decision in time of crisis than at present, through merely being able to ask for United States assistance."—*The Times*, October 6, 1964.

Union and Eastern Europe. The political future of Schroeder, the Foreign Minister, von Hassel, the Defense Minister, and even perhaps the new Chancellor himself, became entangled with the future of the MLF as a touchstone of Atlanticism. Consequently, when the United States began to re-exert pressure on the European countries in the autumn of 1963 to accelerate a decision on the MLF, the importance of retaining the confidence of Germany was more in the forefront of American arguments than before. The American arguments about the MLF as a device to arrest nuclear proliferation had by this time come to mean the arresting of Franco-German nuclear cooperation—not, as in 1958–62, the offer of an alternative to the French national force.

At the beginning of September, 1963, the only countries ready to enter into close negotiations with the United States were Germany, Italy, Greece, and Turkey. Throughout September, heavy American diplomatic pressure was applied to others to join the discussions on the MLF which were to begin the following month. This had the interesting and unusual effect of producing in Britain a public and endemic difference of opinion between two major departments of state—the Foreign Office and the Ministry of Defense. The former argued that Britain could not afford to stand aside from an important development in the relations between the United States and Germany, while the Ministry of Defense resolutely opposed the MLF as costly, vulnerable, unnecessary, destabilizing, and likely to encourage a German appetite for nuclear weapons. The consequence of this official schizophrenia was an announcement by the Prime Minister on October 1 that Britain would join the discussions but without commitment. It had by then become established that if Britain did join her share should be 10 per cent of the cost. Belgium had joined the group earlier; the Netherlands, taking her cue from Britain, joined with equal reluctance in January, 1964.

The following six months were spent mostly in official discussions, in Washington on the military problems, in Paris on the legal and political ones. A number of outline agreements—on the relative invulnerability of a seaborne force and on methods of financing it—were reached. The only practical action was the American offer of a ship to experiment with mixed manning, to which every country participating in the discussions, with the exception of Belgium, sent a contingent. Without doubt, the MLF began to gain official and political support during these months in all the countries concerned.

In April and May, 1964, a new note entered the United States Government's exposition of its MLF proposal. The day when Ball could suggest that this was an idea on which the Americans would lend advice only if the European countries wanted such a force belonged, of course, to the dim past. But what had been a proposal now became a demand. The driving enthusiasts in Washington had gotten a commitment to the MLF from President Johnson, who is essentially a man of action, which they had never got from his more analytic predecessor, and the word went out from there that all the relevant arguments had been thoroughly explored and that the time had now come for action. Once the American and British elections were over, it was essential to conclude an agreement, by December, 1964, at the latest, so that the necessary treaty legislation could be completed by next spring. Time was now of the essence, for the particular reason that the German legislative process is almost as complex, where treaty ratification is concerned, as the American, and that if the MLF treaty were not presented to the Bundestag early in 1965 it might not be completed before the following September's elections and would either become delayed into 1966 or become a prey to the growing dispute between the right and the moderate center in Germany, or both.

It was apparent by the spring of 1964 that the United States was now determined to go ahead with the MLF, if need be with Germany as the only major European member. It then became clear that Washington gave the demands of German internal politics priority over Britain's; for the effect of demanding an agreement in principle by December, 1964, would be to give the incoming British administration—a Labour government assuming office for the first time in thirteen years—ten, or, at the most twelve weeks, to reach a final decision. In view of the prevarications of British policy, there might well be some justice in this, were it not for the fact that Labour has certain proposals on NATO organization—akin to the multinational approach but not necessarily predicating a British nuclear force—that it has the right to ask the United States and its European allies to examine before committing itself to the MLF.

One further development occurred in July, 1964, before the opening of the campaign season in Britain and the United States temporarily becalmed the MLF. One source of opposition to the MLF, in the United States as well as in London, has been the American insistence since early 1963 that it must take the form of a force of surface ships. Two variants have been suggested. One is that the European allies should finance and control a part of the central American strategic force—namely, the Minuteman missiles in hardened silos in the Middle and Far West. Though just as logical as the seaborne force, and though commanding the support of late Secretary General of NATO Stikker and some influential Americans, the idea has never been popular in the Pentagon or in Congress. The other idea is to group part of the multilateral force around the longer-range interdiction aircraft and missiles already in service in Europe, or scheduled for the purpose. This idea has always appealed more to the British Government, partly because of naval objections to a large fleet of surface ships, partly from a belief that it is Europe-based weapons whose use or non-use would be of prime concern to the Europeans in the early stages of a nuclear crisis, and partly because Britain would play a larger part in such a mixed force than in a purely seaborne one.

In July, the British Government submitted to the other MLF powers a detailed plan for the mixed manning, joint finance, and control of the strike aircraft and missiles in Europe. (RAF Bomber Command in the last war is an example of the only mixed-manned strategic force in modern times.) The first American reaction to regard this plan as a diversionary tactic has given place to a decision to take the proposal seriously as a complement to, not as an alternative to, the seaborne force. There are no signs of any great enthusiasm for it in Europe partly from doubts about the role and importance of tactical aircraft in the long run, partly because they are not part of the strategic system of deterrence against the Soviet Union itself and therefore carry less deterrent weight and diplomatic prestige.

V

My reason for imposing this historical retrospect on the reader is my own conviction that it contains the clues to the five questions which will dominate discussion of the MLF proposal among the NATO allies over the coming months: Will the multilateral force in fact be launched? How will it be controlled? What sort of force will it be? To what developments in alliance relationships will it lead? What effect will it have on East-West relations?

If one examines the reasons why the United States decided to revive the MLF proposal at the beginning of 1963, on quite different grounds from those first used—namely, fear that Germany might succumb to French arguments about the desirability of a separate Franco-German diplomacy and strategy—there is no reason to feel that the argument is less valid almost two years later. It can reasonably be argued that American policy is itself responsible for building up France as an alternative pole of attraction in the alliance. It is also true that President de Gaulle seems now to be deeply disillusioned about the Franco-German alliance. But the United States has acquired a vested interest in the political future of the moderate center in Germany (she openly used her diplomatic influence on behalf of Adenauer in earlier German elections); and the collapse of the MLF would now be a setback to the Erhard government that the United States could not afford, since a strengthening of the German right wing might not only revive the Franco-German *entente* but might jeopardize the policy of *détente* with the Soviet Union and of "movement" in regard to Eastern Europe.

The assumption that Britain can kill the MLF, either by downright opposition or by proposing a different political solution for consultation and crisis management within NATO—views that are held in British service circles and in the Labour Party, respectively—is at best debatable. But the Macmillan government and its successor have failed in the past four years to put forward any proposals for the reorganization of planning and control in NATO which have captured the imagination of the smaller European allies, and those constructive steps that have been proposed remain stillborn by reason of the attitude of France. Whether a Labour government prepared to abandon British nuclear weapons (some $550 million is already committed in the British Polaris program) or to commit them to NATO as integrally as the multilaterally owned forces themselves can revitalize the political approach to NATO reform depends partly on France and partly on the willingness of Germany and the United States to turn aside from the MLF proposal for a complete reappraisal of all alternative solutions—something that is now not very probable. A Labour government, with its strong views about the importance of the Anglo-American relationship, cannot long stand outside a development to which the United States attaches the highest importance despite the hesitations of the Labour party in regard to Europe. To oppose the MLF categorically on grounds of its vulnerability, cost, incredibility, and effect on Soviet policy, as many service advisers would like, might risk exposing the relative weakening of the Anglo-American, as compared to the American-German, connection—a risk that any British government would be most unwilling to take.

However, the American handling of the multilateral proposal

has created an ambiguity about the control of the force which could still wreck it. This ambiguity has two sources, Washington and Bonn. As a study of the record has suggested, American support for a multilateral force was originally engendered by the passionate enthusiasts for European unity in the days before President de Gaulle put paid to the "grand design." And a number of senior American officials and their advisers have gone on talking about the MLF as a basis of an eventual European force even though the American motive for securing the MLF has altered.[13] This view is anachronistic in terms of American interests; it is a form of nuclear proliferation that the United States strongly condemns, and it also tends to undermine the position of von Hassel and the German enthusiasts for the MLF, who justify their attitude almost solely in terms of binding the United States indissolubly to Europe and disposing of any talk of a purely European force. This is true of every other European government concerned except Italy; there, the fear that the country is going neutralist, combined with the desire to keep on reasonably good terms with France, leads senior officials to argue that Europe must acquire collective nuclear responsibility as soon as possible. But Italian arguments aside, the readiness of European governments to translate the MLF proposal into treaty form (Germany for fear of France; Britain, Belgium, and Holland for fear of Germany) depends absolutely on the United States being a member and having a veto on its use for the indefinite future. Fortunately, the dogmatic "dumbbell" men now appear to be losing their influence in Washington and the President and the Secretary of State seem anxious, in their most recent statements, to eliminate this source of ambiguity. No doubt, the United States Congress will make the position even clearer.

[13] Thus: "The multilateral force would also inevitably make easier the eventual development of a European nuclear force." Robert Schaetzel, Deputy Assistant Secretary for Atlantic Affairs, at Ditchley, September 27, 1963.

"A united Europe may one day acquire control of the multilateral nuclear missile fleet." Vice President Johnson at Brussels, November 8, 1963.

"Such a force might evolve in either of two ways: it might become an integrated Atlantic force with the United States still a member but without a veto. Or it might develop into an integrated European force without the United States as a member." Robert Bowie at the Western European Union Assembly, December 3, 1963.

"We have wished to leave the structure of the MLF sufficiently flexible to adjust as Europe moves toward unity." Walt Rostow, Chairman of the Policy Planning Council, State Department, to the Western European Union Assembly, June 24, 1964.

The kind of ambiguity to be found in Bonn concerns suggestions that Germany would be prepared to accept an American veto on the use of the force but not that of any minor European subscriber—a position that conceals either the distaste of certain German officials at the prospect of Harold Wilson's finger on the safety-catch or a desire to make Britain buy a larger share of the MLF by scrapping her Polaris program. But any proposals for decision by majority voting in the MLF control group on operational issues, however ingeniously devised, cannot—in my view at least—survive the process of treaty ratification by national parliaments, including those of the small participants.

There is also a disturbing belief in the minds of some German officials that the MLF could somehow be used in a European crisis independently of the main American strategic forces. Such arguments play, of course, straight into the hands of the opponents of the MLF in London and elsewhere, but the fact that they are put forward suggests that, in their anxiety to retain German support for the project, American officials have been disingenuous in not confronting their German colleagues with the very stringent principles of control on which the administration will in fact insist—that it should be based on the unanimity principle if the smaller participants wish it and that it must be directly integrated with the American command-and-crisis control system. Since there is no dispute about this in Britain, it is possible that the closing phases of the MLF negotiations may require greater internal debate and clarification in Washington and Bonn and probably, Rome as well, than in London. For it can only emerge as a multi-veto, integrated, Atlantic force, though perhaps some very general provision for the revision of the arrangements by the consent of all concerned, if Europe should achieve political unity, could be written into the treaty.

The form of control has a direct bearing on the nature of the force. The 25-ship, 200-missile force proposed by the United States represents a compromise between the desire of the German government and the Supreme Commander, Europe, to have missiles with a strategic range directly committed to the defense of Europe, and the reluctance of the United States to base missiles of such range on the land in Western Europe. The British contentions are that the proposed force is too large and will be too long-range to put at the disposal of a regional commander and that, since it will have a fairly low credibility by reason of its control system, its size will constitute an unnecessary drain on the resources of the participants—hence, the proposal to extend the principle of multilateral control to the interdiction weapons that must be developed in any case and that are a central part of SACEUR's responsibility. The difficulty with the British proposal is that these interdiction weapons must have a high degree of credibility, which is somewhat harder to conceive under a system of multiple vetoes than under the present double-key arrangement. But since Britain is the most sophisticated military power in Europe, her entry into the MLF discussions has had the effect of challenging a number of American assertions about the manpower, finance, and training requirements of the seaborne force, and it is possible that the final discussions may well reduce the seaborne element to more modest proportions (ten or fifteen ships), extend the multilateral principle to certain interdiction weapons, and leave provision for the inclusion of others if the initial experiments satisfy the participants.

Fourth, what effect will the MLF have on the structure of the Atlantic relationships? Anyone who examines the record of gradually mounting support for the MLF in European foreign offices, or who talks to politicians and officials in Bonn, Brussels, the Hague, and even Rome, becomes aware that the real desire for this force does not arise out of any serious fear of nuclear proliferation in Europe nor from any overwhelming desire either to be associated with the firing control of nuclear weapons or to influence their targeting, or in any way to share the awesome responsibilities of the President of the United States. It reflects, rather, a wish to gain a more effective and influential role in the development of NATO's long-term strategic and diplomatic policy, especially as it affects relations with the third world and the Soviet Union as well as to play a more decisive role in crises—in other words, to achieve exactly the objectives for which the reform of NATO along multinational lines was first mooted several years ago.

The question which one must ask, therefore, is whether the United States Government understands where its own policy is leading. If it treats its MLF allies merely as technical collaborators and confines the discussions of the control group to such relatively uninteresting subjects as missile targeting or finance, it will cause grievous disappointment, particularly in Bonn, which might lead to the kind of German irredentism that the MLF is specifically designed to prevent. Nothing could be more fatal to American influence as the leading power in Europe if the MLF were seen in

Europe to be merely a military toy to keep the children quiet. Consequently, it seems to me that the United States will find herself speedily having to accord to the MLF powers a right of scrutiny into wider aspects of her policy which she has by and large refused to give to NATO—into strategic concepts, into force levels, into arms-control proposals, even into Far Eastern policy. But can the United States afford to place this "Little Entente" in such a favored position without drawing in Canada and the Scandinavian powers?[14] Can she indeed do so without France, unless she is prepared to face a virtual French withdrawal from the Western alliance which would overturn the whole of the defense of Europe and, indeed, the power structure of the Northern Hemisphere? Some Americans have seen the MLF as giving the United States greater autonomy in the Far East and in her relations with the Soviet Union: in fact, it is likely to have exactly the reverse effect.

It may well be, therefore, that the MLF will in the end prove to have been nothing but an expensive and time-consuming detour on the road to a more effective system of political and strategic planning among the Western allies, centered perhaps in Washington rather than Paris: a solution which became blocked by reason of French chauvinism, British hesitations, and a series of false American judgments about the nature of Europe and about the strength of her own position there, during the earlier years of this decade.

Finally, what effect will the decision on the MLF have on relations between the United States and the Soviet Union? To this question a study of its history provides no clear answer since the Soviet Union has only recently become a partner to the debate, and even now has not deployed its full diplomatic strength on the subject. There has been a noticeable tendency on the part of American officials to write off Soviet hostility to the MLF as merely captious or ritualistic. Some have even maintained that they have succeeded in convincing their Soviet opposite numbers that the MLF, by binding Germany even more closely into the NATO system, serves a Russian interest. Certainly, the whole American position on the MLF has rested on a calculation that the Soviet Union would prefer to see a moderate German government with

[14] Fear that the MLF may drive a wedge between the West European and the Scandinavian members of NATO was one of the principal reasons for the hesitation of the Netherlands in supporting the project. Norway is now as flatly opposed to the MLF as France.

a limited degree of control over some nuclear weapons than a more intransigent one, probably working closely with France, and no MLF.

But if this calculation is proved wrong, then a new situation arises, for the United States must give its relations with the Soviet Union as high a priority as those with any ally. Some who have talked to Soviet officials closely and privately on this question have derived the impression that the Soviet opposition to the MLF is not ritualistic and is based on a fear that important technical information on warheads and missile systems will pass gradually into German hands and will broaden the option of some nationalistic German government of the future, either for developing a national nuclear force or for some cooperative venture with France. This is what the Soviet Union means by proliferation.

This view may be wholly misguided, but if it is maintained, it must present the United States with several awkward choices. For one thing, the Soviet Union has made it quite clear in the Geneva negotiations that the abandonment of the MLF is her price for serious negotiations on a nuclear non-dissemination agreement. Such an agreement may be higher on the list of American than of Soviet priorities, and may rise still further if a nominal Chinese bomb is tested in the near future and it becomes important to prevent powers like India from shopping for a nuclear program of their own. Moreover, if a non-dissemination agreement falls by the wayside through dogged American adherence to the MLF this means alienating the more liberal and pro-American section of public opinion in the countries of NATO Europe which looks to the United States to maintain the momentum towards arms-control agreements initiated by the nuclear test ban. But the United States has placed so much emphasis on the MLF that to abandon it now would create a grave political crisis in Germany. It has been suggested that one possible way out of this dilemma would be to carry through the full provisions of the Irish resolution and initiate a treaty among the non-nuclear powers whereby they would agree not to manufacture or to acquire control of nuclear weapons. It is possible that if Germany were to take the lead in collecting signatures to such a treaty, it might prove successful, though again, the advent of the Chinese bomb makes this a difficult moment to ask India or Japan for their signatures without stringent security guarantees on the part of the United States (and perhaps the Soviet Union as well).

Alternatively, if the Soviet Union is adamant, the United States may have to regard the MLF more as a bargaining card than as fixed policy. The difficulty here is that the purpose of the MLF has been considered so much in German terms that the Soviet concession against which it is to be traded must be one that fully satisfies Germany. The displacement of Khrushchev by Kosygin and Brezhnev adds a new element of uncertainty to the Soviet reaction.

There is a danger that a diplomatic initiative undertaken originally to reconcile Germany to the existence of a Soviet-American dialogue may either endanger the dialogue itself or the influence of the United States with its allies. The coming crisis on the MLF is likely to illustrate once again that for the strengthening of allied cohesion and the pursuit of a stable relationship with the adversary cannot be separated, since they are two facets of the same problem.

At the beginning of November, 1964, the leaders who had been associated with the policies of the early 1960's had been replaced in every major country that is a partner to the old East-West confrontation except France. This can hardly be the appropriate moment to apply a plan that was evolved in quite different circumstances to those of today. If the MLF proves, after more profound discussion than has yet been attempted among the NATO powers (including France, whose unwise abstention from earlier debates has provided so much of the proposal's impetus), to be the soundest solution to the problem of allied confidence and control, then a year's delay will not diminish its soundness. If it gives way to proposals—emanating as much from Germany, Britain, and, one hopes, France as from the United States—that are more suited to the international climate of the late 1960's and the 1970's, then nothing—except a few diplomatic and academic reputations—will have been lost.

FOURTEEN

PIERRE M. GALLOIS

U.S. Strategy and the
Defense of Europe

[*Editor's Note: General Pierre Gallois, a high-ranking officer of the French Air Force and author of* Strategy in the Nuclear Age, *is perhaps the best-known advocate of independent nuclear forces within the Atlantic Alliance. In this role, he is also an active critic of American national security policy.*

The major thesis of his essay here is that little in the defense posture of the United States or in its attitude toward the Soviet Union inspires confidence among its allies. In his view, a nuclear stand-off exists between the United States and the Soviet Union, a condition that exposes allied countries to nuclear blackmail. No nation will commit suicide for another no matter how closely allied; to the extent that the nuclear stalemate demands this of the superpowers, their nuclear guarantees lose their credibility.

According to General Gallois, the United States' pressure for a build-up of conventional forces in Europe stems from its desire to avoid having to fight a nuclear war in defense of its allies. If the United States did use nuclear weapons, they would probably be tactical; fear of retaliation would keep the nuclear powers from attacking one another's homeland; and Europe would thus bear the burden of destruction.

General Gallois holds that these dangers can be avoided only by countries possessing independent nuclear strategic striking forces. He considers conventional armaments irrelevant to the defense of Europe. All this provides an interesting contrast to the views expressed by McNamara, Enthoven, Gilpatric, Wohlstetter, and Bowie (see above Chapters 5, 6, 7, 10, and 12). Though General Gallois draws extreme and one-sided conclusions which are by no means representative of European opinion, the uneasiness he expresses is fairly typical of the fears and attitudes that have produced the debate within the Atlantic Alliance.]

The foreign policy of the present United States Government has been deeply influenced by the revolution in weaponry. Studies of foreign policy and strategy conducted at Harvard University or at The RAND Corporation, which take into account the scientific and technical advances of the last few years, have gradually influenced the doctrine of the Kennedy Administration and inspired a repudiation of the ideas of such earlier policy-makers as Admiral Radford and John Foster Dulles. Thus, a U.S. foreign policy to which, not so long ago, many peoples had entrusted their security, has been reversed.

In 1958, the United States was still bound by treaties to help defend some forty-four countries in which 350 million people lived. Four years earlier, Secretary of State Dulles had offered an unlimited pledge to protect them. He specified that there could be no question of the U.S. facing the opponent's large armies with conventional weapons. Instead, aggression was to be discouraged by the threat of "massive retaliation." Since 1961, the U.S. administration has been saying exactly the opposite.

What has happened to the policy of total guarantee so generously extended to the allies of the United States? What reasons do U.S. leaders invoke as they abandon a policy which seemed to correspond to the power and purpose of America? The answer can be found in the area of science and weapons technology, where a formidable revolution has altered everything.

Indeed, by the time of Dulles' death, the U.S. had lost her unquestioned nuclear supremacy. The main advantage which the U.S. had possessed in the early years after the signing of the North Atlantic Treaty did not exist nine years later. But even after the passing of her nuclear monopoly, the U.S. retained the power to strike the U.S.S.R. while remaining outside its reach. All this changed within three years, 1959-62. In the course of forty months, the ratio of U.S. to Soviet forces, once believed to be a factor permanently favorable to the U.S., became a matter of speculation and concern.

Four developments, three of them technological in nature, were at the source of this radical strategic and political change.

SOVIET ACQUISITION OF THE ICBM

The first of these four developments was the Soviet acquisition of intercontinental missiles armed with thermonuclear warheads.

EDITOR'S NOTE: Reprinted with permission from *Orbis*, VII, No. 2 (Summer, 1963).

Today, the United States finds itself in the same strategic position as the European countries which have been for so long a time the battleground of the great conflicts. Because of the advent of ballistic missiles, there is no longer any significant difference between the six or seven minutes which are necessary for a missile launched from the U.S.S.R. to reach a target located in Western Europe, and the thirty or thirty-five minutes that another Soviet missile would need to travel to California or Texas.

The largest oceans as well as the highest mountains are no longer obstacles to the trajectory of missiles, and each country, almost independent of its geographical location, is equally vulnerable. The only difference would be the precision of the Soviets' firing and the relative remoteness of the New World, which compounds the problem of the accuracy of ballistic missiles. In order to destroy an American target, especially if it is as small as a missile located in a silo or even at an airport, the Soviets must launch a higher—perhaps four times higher for a very small target—number of missiles than if this target were located in Western Europe. Hence, the United States may still rely for a long time upon the threat of retaliation represented by more than 1,200 missiles buried, as are the Minutemen, in individual silos. In Western Europe, permanent mobility (airplanes carrying missiles similar to the Skybolt, or submarines armed with missiles similar to the Polaris) ensures the invulnerability of nuclear retaliatory forces.

What really matters is that yesterday, U.S. territory was out of reach, while today it lies in the front lines. Although two Soviet ballistic missiles are sufficient to destroy a town in Western Europe, perhaps three or four of them must be launched to level a large American city to the ground. Yesterday, participating in a worldwide conflict and playing a decisive role implied for the United States, at worst, the loss of an expeditionary force; today, it involves the risk of grave destruction to the continental United States.

Although World War II caused 55 million casualties, the United States, thanks to the quality of its weapons, its industrial power, its gift for organization, and, above all, the advantages of geographical location, lost only some 350,000 combatants. In recent years, civil-defense programs and literature on nuclear warfare have taught the American public that, in case a war should break out with the Soviet Union, more than one-half of the population and three-fourths of its cities might be destroyed within a few hours, even within a few minutes. The gradual realization of this new and terrible vulnerability is modifying the views of the American people as to their national security and safety. It has already upset United States policy toward Europe.

Yet, today, the American people, perhaps not yet fully aware of their vulnerability, seem ready to take greater risks than their government. At the time of the Cuban crisis, the average American urged stronger action upon the White House. In the years to come, however, public opinion will change. The situation is unprecedented. Traditionally, Americans have taken their might for granted; since 1812, their territory has never been invaded. They cannot believe that in these last few years everything has changed, and that world-wide conflict, which yesterday cost them only several hundred thousand combat casualties, could now kill tens of millions in their own cities. The civil-defense drills, the campaign for fall-out shelters, and the "literature of fear" which is sweeping book stores and newsstands, will give rise, gradually, to a far keener awareness of the dangers of the nuclear era.

Likewise, the United States will be led by prudent men who will be less inclined to take risks that are all the more uncertain because no nuclear war has ever been fought. The government fully realizes the immense destructiveness of the weapons now available. During the last two years, it has revised its foreign policy in order to take this basic factor into account.

THE CONTINUUM OF CONVENTIONAL AND ATOMIC WEAPONS

Ten years ago, the difference between the destructive power of the most dreadful conventional weapons and that of the least powerful nuclear weapons was enormous. For example, the type of bomb that was dropped by the hundreds of thousands on the factories of the Third Reich had a destructive radius of more than a hundred yards. At Hiroshima, everything was destroyed within a distance of approximately two miles from ground zero.

This difference of effects between conventional-weapons systems and nuclear-weapons systems helped to prolong the Korean conflict. If, at that time, "small-caliber" nuclear arms had been operational, and if General MacArthur, at the time his troops were thrown back behind the 38th Parallel, had used them, passing gradually from the most destructive conventional weapons to the least powerful atomic weapons, the conflict would have ceased abruptly, for neither the Chinese nor the North Koreans could have responded in the same manner. These weapons would have compelled the Communists to disperse their forces. Then, the Communists would have been unable to stop the American-led troops, who, immune from atomic attack, could have fought in close formation.

Today, provided both sides are equipped with the complete conventional and nuclear panoply,[1] armed conflict is rendered less probable. Neither knows beforehand which side would choose to capitulate rather than climb progressively the "steps" toward a conflict whose destructiveness would be out of all sensible proportion to the initial issue at stake. The Cuban crisis illustrated this new phenomenon. At the time Cuba was blockaded, the Soviets and Americans vied courteously with one another to avoid at any cost the incident which would have confronted both with this dilemma: capitulation or "escalation."

But the risk does exist that an incident will get out of hand, especially in Europe, where the two camps confront one another. In order to minimize the danger, the U.S. administration, taking advantage of the lack of understanding of the European public, has tried to remove the first "steps" of the nuclear staircase.

For more than a year, Washington has assiduously sought Allied acceptance of U.S. nuclear "disengagement." The recourse to submarines and now to surface ships cruising off European coasts, the refusal to deploy medium-range ballistic missiles on the soil of Western Europe, the withdrawal to the British Isles and even to the United States of the atomic-supported forces—are among the many disengagement formulas suggested. The aim of American policy-makers is, apparently, to place Western Europe in the same strategic category with other allies of the United States whose defense does not necessarily pose the risk of nuclear war.

Naturally, the European allies are worried about such arrangements. Yesterday, their territory, like that of the United States, was assimilated into a kind of "sanctuary" which no aggressor could violate without taking the same risks involved in attacking the American continent. Now, because of "escalation" and its dangers, Western Europe is to be "denuclearized"—that is to say, reduced to the level of those countries which may become host to local conflicts on the pattern of Korea, Indochina, and Malaya. Washington is now trying to design a strictly conventional defense of Western Europe, for the risk inherent in nuclear escalation in

[1] According to Alain Enthoven, there even exist nuclear explosives with a destructive power inferior to that of the most powerful TNT (*Aviation Week*, February 18, 1963).

Europe is, according to Washington, all the graver since American territory is now "under the enemy's guns."

Fact number two (the spread of small-caliber nuclear weapons) combined with fact number one (the vulnerability of the United States to Soviet ballistic missiles) leads Washington to oppose any conflict which, begun outside the United States, could lead to the destruction of American and Soviet territories. However important the stake of this conflict may be, it is no longer deemed proportionate to the cost. It is, therefore, important for the United States to try to avoid such a contingency. Thus, removing the "rungs" of the nuclear ladder leading to an exchange of blows between the U.S. and the U.S.S.R. becomes a matter of extreme urgency. Within the past two years, Henry Kissinger suggested that, in Western Europe, tactical nuclear weapons be grouped under one command and brought back to the "rear," so that their use would depend upon a calculated policy decision and not upon the vicissitudes of combat.[2] There are indications that the U.S. administration would like to go much farther and, if possible, withdraw all nuclear armament from the soil of Western Europe, which then would be protected only by strictly conventional forces.[3] Yet, most military authorities are convinced that a conventional defense of Europe is no longer feasible and that a nuclear withdrawal would seal Europe's fate.

Admittedly, many Europeans, unmindful of the imperatives of their own security, subscribe to the new doctrines of the White House. Through the voices of its leaders and the use of mass media, the United States exploits—just as the U.S.S.R. did for different reasons with the Stockholm Peace Appeal—the aversion that nuclear weapons inspire, in order to beguile the Europeans with the benefits of a purely conventional defense. Thus, progressively, Western Europe loses the advantage she once held—namely, of forming an integral part of the American security area. Europe is no longer an area of the world for the protection of which the United States would categorically assume the supreme risk.

[2] Henry A. Kissinger, The Necessity for Choice (New York, 1961), pp. 92–93; and "Problems of European Defense," Foreign Affairs, July, 1962, p. 540.

[3] Senator A. Willis Robertson (D., Va.), Chairman of the Joint Congressional Committee on Defense Production, declared that "we should take a careful look at the cost of defending Western Europe without the use of nuclear weapons." (New York Herald Tribune, March 9, 1963.) Such a statement indicates that a purely conventional defense of Western Europe has been studied and even considered favorably by the Congress.

President Kennedy said in his Berlin Crisis speech to the American people on July 25, 1961: "We intend to have a wider choice than humiliation or all-out nuclear action." It is the word "choice" that worries those Europeans who are aware of the logic of the nuclear era.

If American territory were seriously threatened, the U.S. Government would not "choose"; it would strike, and with all its might. From the very moment the President of the United States declares that he wants to be free to chose the way he would act to defend Europe and each of the states of Europe, the security of Europe is jeopardized. The American guarantee which only yesterday was unconditional is now conditional and, hence, under some circumstances, uncertain.

Such is the first consequence of the combination of the danger of escalation and the vulnerability of American territory to the destructive blows of an opponent.

INVULNERABLE RETALIATORY WEAPONS

The submarine and the Polaris ballistic missile constitute the third of the technological factors responsible for the present change in strategy.

As long as American and Soviet nuclear retaliatory weapons consisted of ballistic missiles on launching pads or buried in concrete silos, it was still possible to plan an act of aggression which would have been a rational gambit. Knowing the location of these missiles, the assailant could plan their destruction before they were launched upon him. If the assailant had previously developed the necessary and formidable arsenal,[4] he could, by a surprise volley-firing of missiles, destroy his opponent's means of counterattack and thus ensure the latter's defeat. Despite the formidable quantities of destructive energy required for the annihilation of each other's

[4] According to Dr. Ralph E. Lapp's calculations in *Kill and Overkill* (New York, 1962, p. 73), if Soviet missiles have a circular error probability (CEP) of two miles and carry ten-megaton warheads, the Soviet Union would have to fire a volley of 10,000–12,000 ICBM's in order to have a 90 per cent probability of knocking out 1,000 U.S. missiles in single silos. If the warheads were only one megaton, the Soviets would have to fire a volley of 40,000 to achieve the same results. The Soviets do not, at present, field as many as 200 intercontinental missiles. Of course, in the not too distant future, improvements in accuracy and reliability will considerably reduce the figures suggested by Dr. Lapp.

retaliatory forces, such an exchange of blows could have kept at least the appearance of rationality, since each belligerent could have hoped to launch the preventive blow which would destroy the forces of the other and thus eliminate or at least minimize a retaliatory attack. Furthermore, it might still have been possible to protect a friendly country or a group of allied countries, since the guaranteeing power could hope to destroy its opponent's missiles or bombers on their launching pads and airfields.

But, today, the submarine armed with Polaris missiles has deprived thermonuclear war of its last semblance of rationality. The United States possesses a fleet of submarines armed with missiles, which are now and will remain for many more years proof against simultaneous destruction. It is reasonable to assume that the Soviets, too, will build the same kind of fleet with a similar degree of invulnerability to American anti-submarine weapons. Because of this development, neither of these two countries will be able any longer to use a counter-force strategy against the other, and each will have to be content with "peaceful coexistence" with its main opponent, or otherwise risk national suicide.

The Soviet Union will still be able to destroy American urban centers, but its aggression would set off a counterattack led by submarines armed with Polaris missiles, which, in turn, would reduce the principal Soviet cities to ashes. Conversely, this reasoning applies to a U.S.-initiated attack. For the two great powers, equipped with nearly invulnerable retaliatory weapons, peaceful coexistence is the only solution, since resort to force would lead to the near extinction of both belligerents.

Everyone might rejoice at the stability resulting from this situation were the strategy of the mobile and nearly invulnerable retaliatory forces (Polaris) not marred by a serious shortcoming. If resort to force no longer merely implies risking the loss of an expeditionary army but hazards the very substance of national life, it is clear that such a risk can be taken only for oneself—and not for others, including even close allies. This conclusion signifies the complete collapse of the collective-defense systems upon which the security of the Western world has hitherto been based.

With soldier-like frankness, General Maxwell Taylor stated the dilemma of Western defense in a widely acclaimed book. It seems that the congruency of his views with those of President Kennedy's leading strategists prompted his recall from retirement and appointment to the position of Chairman of the Joint Chiefs of Staff. He wrote:

Under the conditions which we must anticipate in the coming years, it is incredible to ourselves, to our allies, and to our enemies that we would use such [nuclear] forces for any purpose other than to assure our national survival. When would our survival be at stake? Two clear cases would be an atomic attack on the continental United States or the discovery of indisputable evidence that such an attack was about to take place. A third possible case would be a major attack upon Western Europe, since the loss of that area to Communism would ultimately endanger our national survival. These seem the only situations imaginable in which our atomic retaliatory forces might be deliberately used. Hence, they are the only situations to which their deterrence applies.[5]

It will be noted that General Taylor envisages the use of American nuclear weapons in Europe only in the case of a major attack —i.e., the least likely military contingency in Europe. In the case of lesser threats, which are the only ones that Europe must dread, the American nuclear retaliatory forces will not be used. To meet these, General Taylor suggests conventional warfare:

Having recognized the limitations of our atomic deterrent forces, we should, in consistence, redefine general war as being synonymous with a nuclear exchange between the United States and the U.S.S.R. Limited war would then be left to cover all other forms of military operations. The question of using atomic weapons in limited wars would be met by accepting the fact that primary dependence must be placed on conventional weapons, while retaining readiness to use tactical atomic weapons in the comparatively rare cases where their use would be to our national interest.[6]

General Taylor's statement does not allow for any misunderstanding. The absolutely vital interests of the United States—i.e., the United States *itself*—will be protected with the help of nuclear weapons. As far as other nations are concerned, their defense will be left to the fortunes of conventional warfare. If one wins, so much the better. If one loses, one does not lose everything, for a war conducted with conventional means does not involve the defense of absolutely vital American interests. In good time, the essential stakes having been preserved, one will try—always with conventional means—to recover what has been lost.

Atomically, the U.S. can therefore guarantee only its own territory. Western Europe, having lost the status of an atomically pro-

[5] Maxwell D. Taylor, *The Uncertain Trumpet* (New York: Harper & Brothers, 1959), p. 145.
[6] *Ibid.*, pp. 145-46.

tected "sanctuary" which it had enjoyed until the end of the 1950's, is now viewed as a potential arena of limited conflicts. General Taylor's position is diametrically at variance with the statements made in 1953 and 1954, according to which any aggression against any NATO territory would be followed by nuclear retaliation.

With much stubbornness and great courage, President Kennedy has managed gradually to provide the means to realize General Taylor's ideas about the security of the free world. It has been suggested that, since the publication of his book four years ago, General Taylor has modified some of his stated views, especially regarding the security of Europe. Indeed, on August 9, 1962, in testimony before the Senate Armed Services Committee, General Taylor declared:

> I am known as the advocate of powerful strategic nuclear forces and also of tactical atomic weapons to support land operations. In order to have all the freedom of being able to choose [the best counterattack] at the time when it would be necessary to decide, it is important that the defense of Western Europe be secured by an abundant supply of nuclear weapons of various types, together with modernized and strong conventional forces. It seems to me that, faced with an attack aimed at Western Europe, we would have to use the necessary weapons and forces to triumph, whatever these weapons may be. Now, to face a massive attack, and because in the West we do not have at our disposal adequate conventional forces, it would be necessary, nearly at the starting point of the conflict, to resort to the use of atomic weapons.

INCOMPATIBILITY BETWEEN NUCLEAR AND CONVENTIONAL WEAPONS

The last sentence of the 1962 statement quoted above is ambiguous. General Taylor must know very well that no nation can establish a powerful military organization based upon the use of conventional weapons and then expect it, if the need arises, to fight a nuclear war.

More keenly than anyone else, U.S. Army generals are aware of the incompatibility of the two systems. As early as 1953, while observers began to think about the tremendous transformations brought about by atomic weapons, the U.S. Army initiated studies aimed at finding out how this new explosive could be used in land warfare. Every type of organization was considered and many schemes were tested. After several years of work, the obvious had to be acknowledged: it was impossible to reconcile nuclear weapons with the traditional forms of land combat. The new explosive not only was far more powerful than TNT, but it simply did not fit in with the historic curve representing the continuous increase of the destructive power per fire-unit. In fact, nuclear firepower rendered obsolete all the notions about military and combat organization to which centuries of warfare had given rise and which were deeply rooted in the military mind.

Organizational schemes such as the pentomic division, the "air cavalry," and the "atomic combat unit," advanced as solutions to the problem posed by atomic weapons for conventional armed forces, did not stand up either under analysis or in test maneuvers in the field. For these reasons, it is difficult to understand why General Taylor, going back on his former writings, should say that if Western Europe lacked "adequate conventional forces" to meet a massive attack, "it would be necessary, nearly at the starting point of the conflict, to resort to the use of atomic weapons."

What does General Taylor mean by "adequate conventional forces"? If, as he leads us to believe, and as all other NATO military commanders have declared, nuclear weapons would have to be used at a given time in the conflict (because the opponent is numerically superior and is himself armed with nuclear weapons), it is difficult to see why the Western world should resort to nuclear weapons only after it has sacrificed important conventional forces. The greater these forces and the longer their commitment to a conventional strategy, the more costly and absurd would be their sacrifice and the weaker NATO's capability to stand its ground in Europe when the conflict became nuclear.

The U.S. Government has been urging the European nations—excluding Britain which, despite its 52 million inhabitants, will not maintain 450,000 soldiers and has given up conscription—to increase their conventional forces. America's allies might well ask this question: What does the Alliance leader want? His present position lacks consistency, at least from a military point of view. No amount of subtle and sophisticated jargon on the part of American policy-makers will suffice to convince astute European observers that one can strengthen the military posture of the alliance by weakening it.

CONTRADICTIONS IN U.S. POLICY TOWARD NATO

Does Washington really believe in the military worth of its proposals? Or does the administration believe that the current leaders of the European allies are so ignorant of the state of military arts as to acquiesce in those solutions to the problem of the defense of Europe which appear less dangerous to Washington because they would fix limits to U.S. commitments? These are the questions raised by the new American policy toward the security of Europe.

Increase in Conventional Forces

Why does the American Government demand, with surprising insistence, an increase of conventional forces on the Central Sector? What magical virtues does it confer upon the number 30? This figure of thirty land divisions had been fixed in 1954. It represented the total number of divisions that the Allied nations proposed as their contribution to the defense of the Central European Sector in 1957. Why has President Kennedy fixed the raising of these thirty divisions as one of his prime objectives for the defense of Europe?

At the time the Allied countries were considering raising a force of thirty divisions, the Soviet Union was thought to have 175 land divisions and the satellite countries together about 50. Since then, American experts have estimated that the forces of the Soviet bloc are much smaller. At each session of NATO, representatives of the U.S. Government, anxious to make the increase of the Western conventional forces which they demand of the European countries appear less ridiculous, have produced smaller and smaller figures for the Soviet conventional forces. One wonders why, if the twenty-two Western divisions deployed in the Central European Sector were sufficient to hold the Soviets back when they were so powerful, it is now necessary to field at least thirty divisions to deter Soviet forces which have been reduced almost by half? If, as General Taylor wrote, it will be necessary at a certain time to resort to nuclear weapons, why, one may ask, would the American command use its nuclear weapons only when thirty Western divisions have been routed and not use them when only twenty-two divisions were beating a retreat?

According to the estimate supplied by American experts themselves, the Soviet Union, in order to launch an attack against the Allied forces holding the Central European Sector, would have to deploy at least twice as many forces.[7] If, for example, the Allies had

---

[7] American experts thus hope to convince their European allies that the imbalance of effectives is not as serious as it seems, because a defensive position can always be held with a number of forces smaller than that of the attacking ones. On occasion, Soviet forces and weapons have been evaluated differently

twenty-five divisions at their disposal, the Soviets would therefore have to send fifty against them—i.e., seventy-five would have to fight. Does the U.S. Government believe that if seventy-five divisions were fighting against each other in Europe, the European allies of the United States would consider this struggle a "limited conflict" in the sense General Taylor used this term in his book?

According to those Americans who demand an increase of conventional forces in the Central European Sector, the Western world would be properly defended only if thirty divisions were raised. By the above calculation, thirty NATO divisions would measure themselves against sixty Soviet divisions. It is only "above" such a conflict threshold that the U.S. would use nuclear weapons—at least, this is what U.S. officials, in calling for an increase in conventional forces, told the European allies.

There is undoubtedly a relationship between the Administration's desire to increase conventional forces and its desire, as reported by Stewart Alsop in his article on the President's "Grand Design,"[8] to have a choice between capitulation and nuclear war. The Europeans, mindful of the defense of their vital interests, regard this kind of choice with as much skepticism as would the Americans if it were a question of protecting *their* vital interests. For the sake of argument, imagine that the Soviet Union, having occupied Canada, threatens the United States from across a common border of some 2,800 miles. Would the American Government rely for the safety of the U.S. on raising the number of its divisions from fifteen to twenty, and then content itself with fighting a conventional war in which sixty American and Soviet divisions were engaged in Montana, North Dakota, and Minnesota? If the United States, its twenty divisions on the point of giving way under the pressure of Soviet forces, finally resorted to nuclear weapons, what benefit would have been derived from the deployment of conventional forces? Would not the initial preoccupation with a conventional deployment be blamed for having actually courted the aggression? By accepting the very idea of conventional war in defense of the "boundary states," by removing the ominous specter of a nuclear war, would not the U.S. Government have

---

according to time and the internal American situation (for example, the 1960 Presidential campaign "missile gap" which subsequently mysteriously disappeared).

[8] *Time and Tide*, March 29, 1962.

encouraged the Soviet Union to venture upon a "cheap" war of conquest?

The Pause Concept

Three years have passed since, at the request of Washington, General Norstad, Supreme Commander of the Allied Forces in Europe, began to talk of a "pause." The "pause" was one of the principal features of the circumspect policy the U.S. adopted toward the defense of Europe. Not only was the idea of a massive nuclear retaliation against any aggressor threatening NATO-controlled territory no longer mentioned, but an additional brake was placed on any Western reaction to the threat of Soviet aggression: nuclear weapons would not be used until after a suitable period of reflection which, it was hoped, would be sobering for the aggressor. In short, Moscow was assured that the Western powers would not reply with nuclear weapons to an attack against their forces. If they finally had to move up the nuclear ladder, it would be as a last resort, because the enemy had increased its pressure. Nuclear weapons would be employed because the delay granted to the enemy did not deter him from carrying out his design, presumably after consultations between the Allies or even tentative negotiations with the aggressor.

Though seemingly cautious, the "pause" is, in fact, an extremely dangerous gambit. Under the pretext of reducing hazards incurred in a premature use of nuclear weapons, it emasculates the deterrent and gives the enemy to understand that he runs much less risk than before in using force. Far from yielding any benefit, the "pause" provides the adversary with so great a maneuvering advantage as to allow him, by adhering to the rules laid down by his opponent, to attack at a lower order of risk. If NATO were to "pause," who would prevent the Soviets from occupying, let us say, Hamburg, or some other territory theoretically guaranteed by NATO? In such a case, what would be the reaction of the Allies? Would not all of them, except the one most directly affected, be prepared to act with the utmost discretion, thus weakening the restraining effect of the threat of eventual retaliation with nuclear weapons? Besides, the aggressor, if by any chance he found the going slow, could easily call for a peace conference in Geneva. Thither he would rush to negotiate a peace agreement on the basis of positions acquired just before the end of the "pause." After a few similar "pauses," Western Europe would cease to be free and independent.

Limiting Weapons Modernization

The idea of a "pause" having encountered some harsh criticism at home and abroad, the American experts looked for other means of limiting the risks of an American nuclear commitment in Europe. One method adopted was to refrain from modernizing the tactical atomic weapons used by the Army and the Air Force as devices intermediate between large-scale nuclear and conventional weapons. Short- and medium-range missiles, designed for the protection of the European theater and the destruction of the opposing tactical forces, gradually had to be replaced by more up-to-date weapons. When General Norstad himself asked that some of the tactical nuclear weapons then in service be replaced by mobile medium-range ballistic missiles (MRBM), his request was turned down by Washington. The retirement of the Supreme Commander of the Allied Forces in Europe was probably not unrelated to his unequivocal views on how best to carry out the mission entrusted to him in Europe.

Tactical Nuclear Support from Outside Europe

On the other hand, Thomas Finletter, U.S. Ambassador to NATO, proposed several times that the desired "tactical atomic support" be assured by earmarking weapons deployed outside continental Europe: one might, for instance, use the SAC bombers now partly relieved—because of the availability of operational intercontinental ballistic missiles—of their strategic mission.

It might also be possible, Finletter suggested, to resort to Polaris missiles carried either by submarines or by surface ships sailing in European waters. This scheme is, to say the least, ill advised. The European theater target list contains several hundred Soviet military objectives marked out for destruction (in fact, about one thousand). To accomplish this mission, approximately 2,000 Polaris missiles would have to be launched against hard Soviet targets. But could the necessary 125 submarines be placed at the disposal of the Supreme Allied Commander in Europe? Even if these missiles were available, it is not easy to understand why tactical objectives would justify the use of 500-kiloton explosives in instances when warheads 100 times less powerful would suffice. If one must compensate for the inaccuracy of a Polaris missile, launched from a distant craft, by its huge destructive power, why should the Europeans subscribe to it and thus acquiesce in the hurling of more than 1,000 megatons onto their own continent, when ten would suffice to destroy the tactical objectives?

NUCLEAR DISENGAGEMENT AND THE MULTILATERAL FORCE

The most serious of the contradictions in U.S. policy toward Europe arises from the Nassau accords. The Nassau Agreement provided an opportunity to reconsider the question of nuclear disengagement and present it in a new form acceptable to certain allies. Just as Soviet propaganda had stressed the danger inherent in the existence of nuclear weapons, so many American spokesmen and journalists had, as early as 1960, begun to underline the risks taken by European populations who accepted the nuclear protection of their territory. The deployment of these weapons in Europe was deemed a serious danger which could be easily averted by reliance on nuclear weapons kept at sea or even in the U.S. Thus, the fears inspired by the massive destructiveness of nuclear weapons has brought us, indirectly, to a "denuclearization" of Western Europe which bears a strong resemblance to the so-called Rapacki Plan.

A nuclear force at sea, whatever its multilateral aspects, would be under the strict control of the President of the United States and thus would have the advantage—for Washington—of avoiding a commitment of the Western forces—i.e., American forces. Moreover, it is well-nigh certain that such a nuclear force, if it were really multilateral and thus subject to the veto of several Allied nations, would be totally paralyzed. Thus paralyzed, it could not possibly take any action that would involve the United States against its will in a nuclear engagement. However, the planned nuclear force was not meant to be multilateral in terms of political controls. The Nassau plan had only the appearance of a certain degree of nuclear decentralization among the NATO powers and of concessions made to the national pride of those European nations which renounced the creation of independent nuclear deterrents; in reality, the Nassau proposals provided a solution only to the anxieties of Washington. Exposed to light, the offer shrank to a scheme for associating the Allies with the U.S. "nuclear operation plans" and for circumscribing the NATO nuclear force by placing it under strict American control. Thus, the U.S. would have another guarantee against the risk of escalation in Western Europe.

Here again, we are confronted by obvious contradictions between political-strategic realities and the position of the White House. Indeed, so obvious are these contradictions that Washington is very much perplexed as to how to gain acceptance for its proposal —an implausible proposal despite all the publicity given to it—as a gesture of American good will toward the other nations of the Alliance.

The first of these contradictions was startlingly revealed by Secretary of Defense McNamara. The Secretary, having declared in Athens in May, 1962, that it was dangerous for countries (other than the U.S. and the U.S.S.R.) to create small nuclear forces that could only pursue an anti-city strategy, subscribed nonetheless to a project of a multilateral nuclear force based exclusively on anti-city weapons.[9] The very size of the multilateral nuclear force which the Secretary now proposed was hardly larger than that of the national force which he had criticized so severely a few months earlier. The American press had ridiculed the British and French nuclear forces which, it was said, represented only 2 per cent of the American potential. But now Washington offered as a substitute for these national nuclear forces a multilateral force which would be numerically inferior to the British and French deterrent. One may wonder why this "2-per-cent" force would have no power of deterrence whatsoever in British and French hands, and why even a smaller nuclear force under complex Alliance controls now should be powerful enough to discourage aggression! Is it more unlikely that a government would use its anti-city weapons to defend its own country than that six members of the Alliance would risk committing collective suicide on behalf of a seventh member threatened by the aggressor?

Another contradiction arises from the incompatibility between the use of nuclear weapons, particularly when they are aimed at enemy cities, and the multi-government control systems. At the time of the Cuban crisis, President Kennedy declared in substance that, when the safety of the American people was at stake, he would act first and then consult his allies. This was good common sense. Why should not each of the Allied countries reason in the same manner as the United States, and why should it not declare that, in case of a serious threat against its national security, it would act first

---

[9] In a speech at Ann Arbor, Michigan, on June 16, 1962, Secretary McNamara stated: "There is, for example, the Polaris force, which we have been substantially increasing, and which, because of its specially invulnerable nature, is peculiarly well suited to serve as a strategic reserve force."

and consult its allies afterward? And why should it then subscribe to President Kennedy's proposal to participate in a multilateral nuclear force?

What is the real significance of this retreat to a "peripheral strategy" relying on Polaris missiles carried by nuclear submarines? And how can anyone plausibly assert that this strategy will spare Europe the destruction entailed by a nuclear war? Is it believable that, if the submarines launched their Polaris missiles toward Soviet cities, the Soviet Union would retaliate against the submarines rather than against the territories of the Allied countries, members of the multilateral force?

The United States did not content itself with submitting a proposal for a multilateral force to its allies. The United States proceeded to take unilateral action. The Cuban crisis and the Nassau meeting have resulted in an actual nuclear disengagement on the part of the United States in Turkey and Italy. The withdrawal from these two countries of land-based missiles was presented officially as a "modernization," and some ill-informed quarters in Europe accepted this interpretation. In reality, the Turks and Italians bartered a real deterrent weapon for the mere shadow of security.

Let us consider the case of Turkey. As long as fifteen Jupiter missiles, placed under the control of both Americans and Turks, were based on Turkish soil, no potential aggressor could take the risk of attacking Turkish territory with conventional forces without exposing himself to a possible retaliation with missiles. Granted, the missiles could not have been fired without the agreement of Washington. Even though no single Jupiter missile was powerful enough to raze a large city, the Soviets would have been foolish not to take the nuclear batteries into consideration. They could not be certain that, under all circumstances, these rockets would not be fired with or without the consent of Washington. In any plan of aggression against Turkish territory, the Soviets could not possibly ignore the existence of these rockets, however outmoded they might be. It is obvious that any attack against Turkey would have had to be preceded by the elimination of the fifteen Jupiter missiles. Their destruction might have been a relatively easy operation, for these rockets stood exposed on their "soft" launching pads and their locations were well known to the Soviets. But the aggressor would have had to run a double risk: First, he would have had not only to cross the border, but also to strike at the geographical center of Turkey. Secondly, and this would have been even more serious a matter, he would have had to take the nuclear initiative—not only destroying the rockets but also inflicting nuclear blows upon their American crews.

Washington announced that, by substituting Polaris missile submarines for the Jupiter rockets, it was modernizing the means of retaliation, and the Turkish Government, uninformed or complaisant, agreed to this peculiar transaction. In fact, by placing its retaliatory force on the high seas, Washington makes matters easier for the aggressor, who no longer has to be the first to fire nuclear weapons and run the risk of atomizing American military forces on station. On the other hand, the decision to strike first and to strike atomically now rests with the U.S. Government.

Since the Polaris missile is an anti-city missile, the United States would find itself in a most uncomfortable position: either not to retaliate at all, which decision the hypothetical Turkish crew members aboard the submarines would be unlikely to reverse, or to retaliate and destroy Soviet cities, knowing full well the heavy price which would have to be paid for this act as long as the United States remains exposed to Soviet ICBM's. As, in any case, the U.S. Government does not intend to strike first, it appears that by "modernizing" its retaliatory arrangements, the United States succeeds in neutralizing its own nuclear force when it is supposed to be providing Turkey with better protection.

The modernization of armament has always been costly. This particular attempt at weapons improvement might prove ruinous for the Turks. The Italians are not better off. Yet it cannot be argued convincingly that these two allies have proved more disloyal or feckless than the other members of NATO, or have pressed for "disengagement."

After promising the Allies the creation of a multilateral force consisting, in its first phase, of B-47 American bombers and British Vulcans (all of them subsonic aircraft designed some fifteen years ago) and, in its second phase, of Polaris missile submarines manned with international crews, the U.S. Government suggested that, upon further reflection, it might be preferable to arm surface ships, which are less expensive to build and technically better adapted to European capabilities. George Ball, Under Secretary of State, had secured the approval by Italy and Germany of a multilateral force based on Polaris missile submarines. Two weeks later, Ambassador Livingston Merchant arrived in Paris to discuss the conditions under which such a force could be created. All the capitals of the Alliance, save Paris, rejoiced in the new idea: the Western allies would use in common the most modern weapons created by the inventive genius of the Americans. France would be excluded and, no doubt, would soon regret it.

One month later, the Department of State revealed that the nuclear force proposed to the members of the Atlantic Alliance would be equipped with surface ships, rather than with submarines armed with Polaris missiles. The U.S. Navy appears to have been responsible for this reversal on the part of the State Department. Navy officials could not reconcile themselves to the idea that Polaris missile submarines, with their elaborate systems of navigation and communication and, especially, their highly sophisticated sonar, should harbor foreign specialists, even if they were allies. A search of the Pentagon files was rewarded with an old study proposal for a Polaris surface ship. A fleet composed of fast craft carrying Polaris missiles could escape destruction, or at least the simultaneous destruction of all of its units. But detection by orbiting satellites of surface movements makes the stationing of nuclear weapons at sea even more hazardous an undertaking than their stationing on the ground. Hence, long ago, the Pentagon had turned down the proposal for the Polaris surface ship as one of small benefit as far as the security of the United States was concerned. Resurrected from the files, the proposal was nonetheless submitted to the European allies who, since they had no better weapons of their own, would have to be content with this solution to their problems. Thus, the Polaris merchant-marine project, although condemned upon serious examination by American experts, was now adorned with new virtues and substituted for the Polaris of the depths.

But Livingston Merchant, before he had a chance to initiate talks with the Allies in order to persuade them to accept the transformation of the multilateral submarine into a trawler, was forestalled by untoward developments. The Atomic Energy Commission stated categorically that an amendment of the 1954 Atomic Energy Act was out of the question and that it was unthinkable to give nuclear weapons to non-U.S. forces. Thus, Merchant was deprived of his most telling arguments; President Kennedy's idea was opposed by an agency of his own Administration; and the multilateral force was transformed into a multilateral farce.

The story of the proposal for multilateral forces resembles uncannily that of the Anglo-American negotiations over the Skybolt missile, which terminated in the cancellation of the development of this weapon. In the beginning, the parties to the negotiation agreed to develop and use the Skybolt, to halt work on competing projects and to rely on a common policy. At the same time, bitter words were used to describe governments foolish enough not to take advantage of the opportunity for adhering to the agreement. Then, the agreement was rescinded by the party that had proposed it. It was asserted, in the wake of the Nassau Agreement, that the Skybolt was no longer essential to the security of the United States. A few months later, the Allies were given to understand that the Polaris missile submarine was too secret and too complex for their handling and that they must be content with more overt and simpler surface vessels.

A Conventional or Nuclear Defense?

The recapitulation of these complex diplomatic manipulations shows, once more, that the Western peoples still have much to learn about the characteristics of the nuclear era in which they must live and in which some of them must answer for the security of the world. Clearly, the responsibility for keeping a nuclear arsenal cannot be shared. The United States would be better advised to accept national deterrent forces instead of straining its diplomatic ingenuity to inhibit their creation. The present United States administration, had it better understood the problems of defending a European continent menaced by an adversary brandishing thousands of deadly weapons, would not have inaugurated its reign by asking for an increase in conventional forces.

Let us summarize the argument for more and better conventional forces: President Kennedy, like his predecessor, does not wish to be confronted in Europe with the dilemma of nuclear war or surrender. Understandably, he wishes to have the time to ponder the appropriate response to whatever might be the challenge. Yet, military specialists have known for years that it is impossible to switch suddenly from one strategy to another when one has to deal with arms as different as conventional and nuclear weapons. Two years ago, Henry Kissinger made it clear that once committed to a conventional defense system, the country that decided to switch to nuclear weapons would be lost.[10] Besides, there is no reason why a country should not resort from the start to nuclear weapons if it knew that it could thus gain a complete and immediate victory. Almost ten years ago, General Ailleret, the present Commander in Chief of French military forces, defined cogently

[10] Henry Kissinger, "Limited War: Conventional or Nuclear," *The Fifteen Nations*, March, 1961.

the differences between conventional and nuclear systems. More recent studies have merely confirmed his views.

In a lecture to the French Military Staff College in the fall of 1954, the then Colonel Ailleret stated:

> The extreme vulnerability to nuclear weapons of military personnel and vehicles in movement, of the means of communication, and of the strategic routes and port equipment will probably paralyze armies. Armed forces will have to spread out on very large areas and limit their actions to numerous infiltrations carried out by small units, for concentrations will be no longer possible. . . . Concentrations of large infantry and artillery units gathered around centers of resistance are now out of the question. They would be easily destroyed or neutralized. Large units now must be abandoned, just as close order formation had to be when the automatic rifle was adopted.

It is likely that, after many years spent on study and experiment, the U.S. Joint Chiefs of Staff have come to the same conclusion as the present French Commander in Chief. Hence, the contradiction between the views of the American Supreme Commanders in Chief in Europe, who insisted unwaveringly that Europe cannot be defended without resorting to nuclear weapons, and the arguments advanced by the U.S. Government in favor of an increase in conventional forces.

It is easy to demonstrate that the two systems—the conventional one and the nuclear one—have hardly anything in common and that, in a future contest, the latter must inevitably triumph over the former.

Clearly, the conventional system rests on the concentration of men and matériel, and its firepower is proportionate to troop concentration. It requires a complex logistics system capable of disposing of huge quantities of voluminous and heavy matériel. This form of war is dependent on time, for the "wearing out" of the belligerents is relatively slow. There is sufficient time to make use of mobilized reserves, to step up the production of armament, and to exploit industrial resources.

Nuclear weapons, unheard-of twenty years ago, have upset these calculations. Because of the extreme vulnerability of any surface target known to the enemy, concentrations of men and matériel are no longer possible. Traditional supply systems court destruction even before they can become operative. A long, organized conflict is no longer conceivable. Consequently, it is now out of the question to contemplate calling up reservists and increasing factory production. Neither the field of battle, nor the time, nor the men, nor the matériel, nor the doctrine are the same in the two systems. The mode of combat must be chosen before coming to blows. And this choice must be determined now by appropriate studies, research, armaments, recruiting and training of men, and physical preparation of the terrain. Any compromise in this matter would lead to disaster.

Once committed to the atom, it is impossible to draw back. What role could the 180 British bombers (compared to the tens of thousands of planes available in 1945) hope to play, if they could not carry at least one nuclear explosive? The same ratio holds for the United States, whose number of delivery vehicles is scarcely one-tenth what it was in the TNT era. The passage from one system to the other is all the less possible because the Western world remains on the defensive and, by definition, the adversary is given the initiative and the choice of means.

To make European countries believe that they must increase their conventional forces, and that only upon the defeat of these forces should recourse be had to nuclear weapons, is a fanciful endeavor. Great Britain understood long ago the uselessness of conventional armament in Europe. The more the European nations on the Continent equip themselves conventionally, the more vulnerable they will be to nuclear attack and therefore the stronger will be the temptation for the opponent to use nuclear weapons. Thus, the promoters of conventional rearmament in Europe are defeating their own aims. They strengthen the potential power of the adversary, who knows that he has no reason to fear a nuclear response. They offer to his nuclear cudgel unprotected and tempting targets, and thus encourage him to take the initiative.

The likely explanation for such dangerous advice must be sought elsewhere than in the canons of strategic logic. Is it given with an eye to preparing the way for Western Europe's "denuclearization?" By substituting for the nuclear system an enlarged conventional system, backed up by a dubious threat of strategic nuclear action, the lower rungs of the nuclear ladder on which many Europeans think that their safety hinges would be removed —and "escalation" would, hopefully, be halted at the bottom.

Many decisions taken unilaterally by Washington convey the idea that this indeed is the policy of the United States. Thus, we have gone a long way from the solutions put forward by the United States in 1957, when it proposed to extend nuclear weapons to all

NATO theaters and to make available to the Supreme Commander in Europe IRBM squadrons that would be manned by European personnel. The nuclear tide of the late 1950's is now receding. Reliance on conventional means, though diminishing the direct risks of the Americans, certainly increases those incurred by the Europeans.

It has been said that these risks will remain acceptable as long as American and British troops are stationed in Western Europe. But, according to the British "White Paper" on Defense (1962), the presence of British troops on the territory of West Germany depends on the balance of payments between that country and Great Britain. Following the visit to Bonn of Roswell Gilpatric, U.S. Under Secretary of Defense, the French daily Le Figaro reported on February 23, 1963: "If Bonn, in accordance with the Franco-German agreement, increases its imports from France to the prejudice of the United States, American troops stationed in Germany will be removed, or, at least, some of them." It is a strong alliance, indeed, where bilateral bargaining and unilateral decisions could mean a military disengagement and thus compromise the security of European countries.

The reason for the long-standing crisis of NATO is simple: the leader of the Western coalition tries to reconcile the irreconcilable. He refuses to accept for his country the formidable risks now inherent in all alliances. But, at the same time, he dares not face up to the logical consequences of the new situation and proposes alternative solutions that are inadequate and dangerous as well as unacceptable to any country other than the United States.

If it is not too late, it might be better to return to the policy of the previous administration, namely the unconditional guarantee of the security of Western Europe. Today, Khrushchev is not afraid to run the very same risks in Cuba that Kennedy would like to avoid in Western Europe. But if the United States deems it imprudent to go back to Dulles' forthright pledge, then it must accept a measure of proliferation of nuclear weapons, a proliferation which it cannot prevent—no more in Western Europe than it has been able to do in China. The United States, by coming to terms with the necessities of the age, might find a way out of the deadlock in which it has become entangled.

The tenor of official British pronouncements sounds as embarrassed as that of the official United States voice. In the House of Commons, Peter Thorneycroft, Minister of Defense, declared:

As an increasing number of more and more powerful missiles will be aimed at Washington and New York, can we be certain that a threat directed against our country would always be answered by an American counterthreat? And should we admit this certitude, would the Russians be equally persuaded? Is a deterrent under the exclusive control of America absolutely reliable?

Mr. Thorneycroft questioned, though his words were couched in the language of diplomatic discretion, the permanence of American guarantees—guarantees entailing enormous risks for the United States itself.

A few days after Mr. Thorneycroft revealed his gnawing doubts, Lord Home, Britain's Foreign Secretary, addressing the members of the North Atlantic Council in Paris on March 20, 1963, advised his colleagues against examining too closely the intentions of the United States regarding its commitments in Europe. Thus, when the independence of the instruments of *British* security is at issue, Her Majesty's Government is concerned about the uncertain character of the American guarantee. On the other side of the Channel, however, Lord Home declines to recognize the right of other peoples to question, when the security of the *Continent* is at stake, the intentions of the United States.

As long as Washington and London do not understand—or ignore—the imperatives of security in the nuclear age, the situation will remain confused and all the proposed solutions will prove ineffective or unacceptable. Powerful men do not find it easy to relinquish long-held and cherished, though fallacious, ideas. More than two years have already slipped by. The United States administration perhaps has not had sufficient time to adjust itself fully to the demands of the leadership it must exercise and on which, for better or for worse, the security of the West depends. In fairness, no one can deny that the problems are immensely difficult and the choices breathtakingly hazardous. But the problems grow every day more intractable, and the right choice will have to be made, lest policies of procrastination and ambiguity result not only in the discomfiture of this or that ally of the United States, but in collective Western disaster.

What Price Conventional Capabilities in Europe?

[Editor's Note: Dr. Bernard Brodie is one of the pioneers of the study of nuclear strategy in the United States. He was the first to attempt an assessment of the new technology shortly after the end of World War II, and he has been one of the leading strategic thinkers since. Since 1962, he has frequently criticized the views of Secretary McNamara and of his former colleagues at the RAND Corporation such as Wohlstetter, Hoag, and Enthoven, especially with respect to the feasibility of a conventional defense of Europe (see above, Chapters 5, 6, 10, and 11).

In this essay, Dr. Brodie argues that the emphasis on conventional defense in Europe is unrealistic for at least two reasons: (1) Europeans may find the level of destruction of a massive conventional war highly unattractive. They, therefore, see no reason to make major sacrifices for a strategy which may weaken deterrence for no significant advantage. (2) The existence of substantial nuclear establishments in Europe makes it probable that any massive attack would soon become nuclear. Mr. Brodie gently but brilliantly shows the extraordinary improbability of a massive Soviet conventional attack in Europe and the even greater improbability that it would remain conventional if it occurred.

In Dr. Brodie's view, emphasizing a remote contingency as the chief target of strategic planning undermines the cohesion of the Alliance. It uses up American prestige in the attainment of at best peripherally significant objectives. It emphasizes differences in perspective that a wise coalition policy would not make explicit.]

Just as the "massive-retaliation" doctrine characterized the main thrust of the Eisenhower administration's defense policies, so that

EDITOR'S NOTE: Reprinted with permission from *The Reporter*, May 23, 1963. Copyright 1963 by The Reporter Magazine Company.

of the Kennedy administration has been marked by persistent emphasis on very nearly the opposite theme. That theme is briefly stated as follows: although we will not voluntarily relinquish the nuclear ascendancy now enjoyed by the United States, prudent anticipation of the coming nuclear stalemate requires us to return to conventional forces for the tactical defense even of Europe.

The United States has acknowledged that it is prepared to use nuclear weapons "if necessary" for the defense of Berlin and other NATO territories, but the conception behind that "if necessary" has been responsible also for heavy pressure upon our NATO allies to make a larger contribution to the conventional capabilities of the alliance.

The new American school of thought, which exists in several variants on the part of advocates both in and out of government, possesses no label comparable in pithiness to the Dulles "massive-retaliation" tag, but we shall call it here the Conventional War in Europe philosophy (CWE).

The administration's authentic views on the subject of CWE have not been readily available to the public. There was some reference to them in Secretary of Defense Robert S. McNamara's Ann Arbor speech of June 16, 1962, but a later and much better source is his book-length statement before the House Armed Services Committee on January 30, 1963. The relevant comments are characteristically lean, but their significance is clear.

After pointing out that "we must continue to strengthen and modernize our tactical nuclear capabilities to deal with an attack where the opponent employs such weapons first, or any attack by conventional forces which puts Europe in danger of being overrun," McNamara went on to say, "But we must also substantially increase our non-nuclear capabilities to foreclose to our opponent the freedom of action he would otherwise have, or believe he would have, in lesser military provocations. We must be in position to confront him at any level of provocation with an appropriate military response. The decision to employ tactical nuclear weapons should not be forced upon us simply because we have no other way to cope with a particular situation."

These words are somewhat ambiguous concerning the maximum level of Soviet non-nuclear attack that McNamara would like to see us able to oppose successfully with non-nuclear means, but additional clarification is provided later in the statement:

Although we are still a long way from achieving the non-nuclear capabilities we hope to create in Europe, we are much better off in this regard than we were two years ago. Today, the NATO forces can deal with a much greater range of Soviet actions without resorting to the use of nuclear weapons. Certainly, they can deal with any major incursion or probe. But we must continue to do everything in our power to persuade our Allies to meet their NATO force goals, so that we will possess alternative capabilities for dealing with even larger Soviet attacks. And until these capabilities are achieved, the defense of Europe against an all-out Soviet attack, even if such an attack were limited to non-nuclear means, would require the use of tactical nuclear weapons on our part.

It is clear that McNamara would like to be able to meet even an "all-out" Soviet non-nuclear attack by non-nuclear means. Although in his opinion we already have the means for dealing conventionally "with any major incursion or probe," he feels that "we are still a long way from achieving the non-nuclear capabilities we hope to create in Europe." To achieve that end, he is willing "to do everything in our power to persuade our Allies" to make the required contributions.

However, on this issue as well as on several others, our major allies have for some time shown themselves markedly resistant to our persuasion. Following the French veto on Britain's admission to the Common Market, the NATO alliance has been in a state of shock. France's rejection of American leadership in military and other matters has been violent and extreme. In part, it is because President de Gaulle does not like to be led, but it is also in part a reaction against specific U.S. policies. And however much the French behavior is regretted by our other allies, the latter are not about to respond with a larger conventional effort.

In trying to understand this attitude, one must first remember that the view our government is now advancing as the only reasonable one is the reverse of the idea that our leaders were preaching only a few years ago. It is also well known abroad that the new view is by no means accepted by the majority of senior American military officers, including the recently retired Supreme Allied Commander in Europe, General Lauris Norstad.

Though official American emphasis is on meeting goals already agreed on, our allies are aware of the fervor behind the new concept in administration circles. The Germans especially distrust the future implications of that peculiarly intense conviction—as though we had achieved a "break-through" in thought—and they distrust also so extraordinary a goal as having a capability for stopping by conventional means any non-nuclear attack that could be mounted even by the full field strength of the Communist bloc.

The concept is usually coupled with talk about "accidental war," that is, of Soviet miscalculations or acts of repression that would set off hostilities on a large scale but, hopefully, leave us short of the final abyss. No answer is given to the question of how much territory in Europe we should be ready to give up before deciding that we can no longer withhold nuclear weapons.

The purposes of achieving a very large conventional capability are generally given as follows:

1. It should discourage the enemy from thinking that our unwillingness to be the first to use nuclear weapons, or to see nuclear general war visited upon the world, gives him opportunities to achieve limited but important victories by local non-nuclear aggression. He must not suppose that he can outbid us quickly and decisively in non-nuclear strength. Making it clear that he cannot will add materially to deterrence.

2. If he nevertheless becomes involved through "miscalculation" in an attack on us and finds that, because of our resistance, he has applied most or all of his non-nuclear strength, he will have a chance to pause and reconsider what he is risking. If he then continues his aggression, the onus for bringing in nuclear weapons will be on him.

3. It may be we who want to take the diplomatic and even military initiative, and it will make all the difference in our willingness to do so if we can make some meaningful move without nuclear weapons.

4. There is also the conviction that, by 1970 at least, there will be no such thing as a meaningful superiority in strategic nuclear capabilities. Thus, the threat of strategic nuclear war as the ultimate backstop to a diplomatic position will be unavailable.

In any case, the enemy is to receive the clearest warning that we will not accept a loss of territory or other comparable defeats. We remain committed to introducing nuclear weapons not only if the enemy does so but also if we find ourselves losing significantly. The aim of keeping war in Europe non-nuclear is considered terribly important, but nonetheless secondary to the aim of not losing.

We should distinguish this CWE philosophy from several other ideas which have become current of late and which I do not wish to challenge. At this date, few persons professionally involved in defense doubt the need for some conventional forces for the contingencies of limited war such as might easily occur outside Europe and conceivably inside Europe as well. Spelling out the specific requirements is difficult and controversial, but on the point of principle there is not much argument.

We should also distinguish various current doctrines of discriminate or controlled general war, especially that which not only stresses counter-force targets but adds special and positive emphasis to sparing cities. Avoidance of bombing cities, except in direct reprisal, probably has sufficient justification, apart from other obvious interests, in the elementary and familiar proposition that enemy cities have far more strategic significance as hostages than as ruins.

It is also true and important that our allies have made promises to NATO that they have not met and that, until the pertinent agreements are changed, we are justified in pressing them to fulfill. Although the commitments to these force levels were made under the explicit assumption that any outbreak of war in Europe between the Soviet bloc and the West would be almost immediately nuclear, there is no need to deprive available forces of all capability for fighting with conventional weapons.

What we shall be questioning, at least by implication, is, first, the image of the world reflected in the fervor and the zeal—and the excessive goals—behind what is up to a point a reasonable idea, and second, the evident impatience with the misgivings and contrary ideas of allies whose views are habitually dismissed on the ground that they just don't understand the basic facts of nuclear life.

CWE advocates feel, with some justice, that the United States is carrying a disproportionate share of the NATO defense burden. They argue also that American contributions to nuclear capabilities in a general war are more than adequate and should not be duplicated. They usually consider tactical nuclear capabilities in Europe dangerous and illusory. Therefore, according to them, obligations to the common defense by our European and Canadian allies can only and should only take the form of providing greater conventional capabilities.

This idea is hard to put across in Europe. The situation naturally varies from country to country. The smaller NATO nations seem content to go along with our views, but they also feel, as small countries have always felt, that what they can contribute is not going to make a critical difference in NATO strength anyway, so why exert themselves unduly? The British and French governments have different ideas from ours about the value to them of independent nuclear capabilities. The French especially have long been determined to go ahead with their program regardless of American objections—partly, perhaps, because they know the United States cannot withhold from France the protective covering accorded Europe, but mostly because they are bent on rejecting the status of a satellite.

The British seem to be less concerned about nuclear dependence on the United States, and among the many who have professed willingness to give up the independent nuclear deterrent is the new leader of the Labour Party, Harold Wilson. However, we should remember that many Britons who take that position do so for reasons that are not necessarily reassuring to the government of the United States. In Britain, rejection of the nuclear deterrent often goes with neutralism and certainly not often with any desire to see the reintroduction of conscription, without which Britain is not going to increase materially its contribution to conventional capabilities in Europe. The Germans, who are not yet avowedly nourishing aspirations to an independent nuclear capability, are nevertheless deeply alarmed by American emphasis on conventional-war strategies.

All these people share the view that we Americans have simply availed ourselves of our great wealth to build up the forces we thought necessary to our own defense. A good part of our defense budget has been absorbed by a large strategic nuclear capability that we have insisted on maintaining exclusively under our own national control, despite recent token gestures to the contrary. In providing protection for ourselves, we have created what in large measure protects also our European allies. They have not hitherto been asked to share the financial cost of the force that protects us all—though they have provided bases and thus shouldered some risks. It is a mistake to assume that we can now induce them to compensate us by raising additional forces which they feel they do not need and which in the French case would be at the expense of forces they insist on having.

Thus, appeals to our NATO allies to increase their military effort must be based on something more objective than the fact that we have shifted to a new strategic philosophy, especially one that must appear to them to cost more and at the same time diminish deterrence. Our insistence that it will increase deterrence is based on premises and assumptions which may be valid under some circumstances but which are certainly not unchallengeable. Our assumption that the new philosophy would demonstrate its superior merits *if* war breaks out will be weighed against the European presumption, however debatable, that the resulting stance could make it *easier* for war to break out—by appearing to push our nuclear strength into the background. Besides, our allies are deeply suspicious of alleged American efforts to get them to provide the "men-at-arms for the American nuclear knight"—to quote one German formulation for a thought that gets served up repeatedly in different verbal flavorings. In any case, their readiness to accept unquestioningly American tutelage in military and strategic matters is considerably less today than it was five or ten years ago.

Those CWE advocates who urge that we should put ourselves in a position to be able to stem at least for a time a full-scale nonnuclear attack by Soviet forces have in general advanced a startlingly modest view of the extra effort required.

Present promises to NATO would, if fulfilled, raise existing strength on the Central Front from something like twenty-four divisions to something like thirty. NATO may yet conceivably get those thirty divisions, but they are not likely to be well-equipped and full-strength divisions with adequate logistic backing. Thus, the first margin of extra effort is the difference between twenty-four lean divisions and thirty fat ones, and fat in the weaponry of conventional war.

Whatever serious studies have been made of requirements for any type of war, nuclear or non-nuclear, are naturally highly classified, but one well-informed CWE advocate offered me the probably optimistic offhand guess that the essential goals to be achieved for providing an "adequate" conventional force in Europe would require of our NATO allies about 1 per cent more of their respective gross national products than they are now contributing. And, after all, those GNP's are steadily rising.

Now, economists are accustomed to reckoning in percentages of GNP, but politicians are not. The latter think in terms of increases in existing budgets, and for a country already contributing, say, 5 per cent of its GNP to defense—which is not trivial by historical peacetime standards, and the larger allies contribute more—an increase of 1 per cent of GNP has more meaning as a 20-per-cent increase in the defense budget.

There is another point to be considered. If estimates of Soviet ground forces have been exaggerated, it is clearly desirable to cut them down to proper size. Obviously, we want to evaluate *any* forces correctly, whether they be enemy or allied. In pointing out inherent enemy weaknesses, however, we should be careful not to gloss over our own—for example, the inherent weakness of having a force structure stemming from fifteen different nations, with an allocation of commands designed as much to accomplish political as military ends. Whatever the number of divisions available to NATO, their effectiveness must surely fall short, perhaps markedly, of being comparable to a good single-nation army having the same number of divisions.

Anyway, the substantial reduction in Russian forces between 1955 and 1961 was a somewhat tardy adjustment to what the Soviets considered the requirements of the nuclear age (as well as, let us add, the absence of any strong urge to conquer a nuclearly defended Western Europe). They stopped further planned cuts in 1961, apparently in response to our build-up. Experience since then suggests their readiness to move up with us to maintain their relative advantage in ground forces in Europe. Their reasons for doing so may or may not be very sophisticated, but it is the one kind of tangible superiority they feel able to maintain.

As Sir Winston Churchill once wrote, concerning the planning for a particularly ill-starred offensive: "However absorbed a commander may be in the elaboration of his own thoughts, it is necessary sometimes to take the enemy into consideration." In the spinning of military theories, it is really remarkable how seldom that is done. In the present case, the "enemy" should be considered under both of two guises. First, there is the shrewd opponent familiar in war-gaming rooms, blessed with a free-ranging imagination and showing no biases other than those we share with him. He is shrewd, skillful, and aggressive; he has to be, or one cannot have a challenging and interesting game. The other is the real Soviet opponent, with whom we have had prolonged experience that is available for study but that only a few people do in fact study. He is the opponent who we know has very special ways of looking at things—in other words, who has strong biases, some of which are fundamentally different from ours. This is the opponent who not infrequently blunders but who always shows a deep respect for our strength.

Concerning the CWE school's argument that the enemy will be more deterred by a strong conventional force than he would by a somewhat lesser force committed to using nuclear weapons at a relatively early stage: this can only be the war-game opponent. Certainly, the argument requires some quite singular assumptions. One is that the Soviet Union will boldly make large forays against our nuclear power with non-nuclear arms. According to this line of reasoning, the determination of ourselves and our allies to resist clear aggression will collapse if there is any hint that tactical nuclear weapons may have to be used, and the Russians will know it. In fact, they will be so confident of our restraint that they will take what would otherwise be the most monumental risks! Actually, the question of "credibility" so effectively raised against the Dulles massive-retaliation doctrine hardly applies in Europe—and we are not talking about massive retaliation anyway, but tactical nuclear defense. It would probably take much persuasion on our part to shake the Soviet leaders from their apparent conviction that in the event of a substantial attack by them the nuclear weapons available to NATO forces in Europe would quickly be used. Why should we attempt to shake that conviction?

Another critical and dubious assumption is that the enemy will almost certainly refrain from using nuclear weapons if we refrain. Presumably it is "in his interest" to play the game that way—to make war locally but not to risk general war. But there is overwhelming evidence that he fears that *any* war in Europe is in great danger of escalating to general war, and that he rejects the notion that the introduction of nuclear weapons tactically makes all the difference.

Soviet military thinking continues to reject those refinements of military thought that have now become commonplace in this country—concerning, for example, distinctions between limited war and general war, between "controlled" and "uncontrolled" strategic targeting, and between nuclear and non-nuclear tactical operations. The kinds of civilian specialists who have given rise to most of the relevant ideas in this country do not even exist in the Soviet Union. The new Soviet manual of strategy written under the direction of former Chief of Staff Marshal Sokolovsky expresses scorn for the "modern school of American economists who consider that it is possible to juggle with nuclear warfare."

Perhaps the Soviet leaders are staging all this for our benefit, or perhaps they believe it now but will ultimately follow our lead. After all, the prospect of fighting a great land battle in Europe without nuclear weapons looked utterly bizarre to practically all Americans only a short time ago. However, the change in view in this country does not represent a mass conversion of the American defense community but rather the rise to political ascendancy of a minority view. The leading members of this minority have had close contact with and have thus exerted great influence upon each other. Can we achieve comparable communications with a similar (ascendant) minority in the Soviet Union?

Whether or not the logic is intrinsically sound, it obviously does not overwhelm all informed men in this country who are exposed to it. Is it bound to in time? Various factors are operating powerfully in the opposite direction, including the proliferation of all kinds of nuclear weapons with special uses, in all of which uses the nuclear tools show vastly higher efficiencies than their non-nuclear counterparts. Even the little Davy Crockett makes *large* conventional artillery forces not merely unnecessary but rather a joke, and it is difficult to live for a long time with an expensive joke.

Clearly, the proposed strategy offers no inducement to the Russians to stay non-nuclear in an all-out premeditated attack with their ground forces. Proponents of the CWE philosophy repeatedly assert that we will not allow ourselves to be beaten. Since, in tactical operations with nuclear weapons, first use is extremely important—for example, by accomplishing the quick destruction of the opponent's supporting air forces—our determination to introduce such weapons rather than accept defeat tells the enemy, if he believes us, that *he* must introduce them. It is one thing to propose an armaments restraint to which we promise to adhere, come what may, as long as the opponent does too; it is quite another to offer such restraint with the proviso that we will abandon it as soon as it clearly seems to interfere with the serious business of winning.

We are bemused, however, with the possibility of "accidental war." We feel that a conventional defense gives the opponent who lets himself slip into hostilities with us a chance to think it over. This is the concept of the "pause" for reassessment, which will enable the opponent (never ourselves, naturally) to remember the virtues of discretion. Anyway, if the enemy continues his aggression, he will proceed with it in a way calculated to win. If he refrains, it will be less our local conventional forces than our nuclear forces, strategic and tactical, that have obliged him to do so. That is exactly where we stand now and where we have stood since the beginning of NATO. What, then, will we have gained by a large conventional build-up?

The idea that the entire Russian field army could become involved in non-nuclear conflict as a result of an "accidental" outbreak of local violence is perhaps worth a place in the list of contingencies that a planner wishes to think about. But that we should consider the possibility strong enough to let it set a goal for our conventional build-up is fantastic. Anything that could properly be called "accidental war" has been extremely rare historically. What should make it more common in a nuclear age? The technical possibilities for nuclear accident are vastly outweighed by the enormous reluctance of national leaders, certainly including the Russians, to risk a war that might become nuclear.

A frequently cited scenario of accidental war has the Soviet troops putting down a major revolt in East Germany, which provokes West German troops to intervene. This implies, among other things, an ardor for intervention on the part of West German forces and a general lack of discipline all round that have yet to be demonstrated. Is the event conceivable? Of course! So are many other scenarios that follow quite different patterns. To say that something is conceivable may or may not mean that it is worth a second thought; it is hardly enough to establish that it warrants a basic shift in our strategic philosophy. In any case, why should our capacity to support an intervention, if we so desire, hinge upon our ability to fight a *large-scale* non-nuclear war? The raising of the initial level of violence is at least as much the enemy's option as ours, and it is hardly desirable to try to eliminate a consideration of our nuclear power from his reflections.

No doubt under some circumstances the Russians could not be made to feel the real determination behind our warning until they had done something to stir us to action. Something of that kind happened in Cuba. Probably too there is less chance that the demonstration will get out of control if nuclear weapons are meanwhile avoided. The idea of the "pause" is not altogether absurd. However, there is no good reason why the time for the pause should come when thirty divisions are involved rather than three, or even one. The risks may be smaller by choosing the lower threshold, because the discriminate use of small nuclear weapons can also be a powerful earnest of determination—which can have its effect *before* the opponent makes his commitment to a large-scale attack.

I see no basis in experience or logic for assuming that the increase in level of violence from one division to thirty is a less shocking and less dangerous form of escalation than the introduction of any kind of nuclear weapons. A galloping consensus has developed among some like-minded people around the entirely unfounded assumption that it is not size of conflict but use of nuclear weapons that would make all the difference. Our justified concern with the special emotions as well as the physical destruc-

tion provoked by the use of nuclear weapons has caused an unjustified depreciation of what it means to start fighting. Khrushchev
indicated quite clearly last fall that where he wanted the crisis
between the United States and the Soviet Union to stop was *before* one of our destroyers had fired a shot across the bows of a
Soviet transport ship.

In view of the lessons we must draw from the Cuban crisis of
1962 concerning our position in Berlin, it is a mischievous interpretation to hold that the outcome was determined *mostly* by our
local conventional superiority. If local superiority in conventional
arms made all the difference, why did not Khrushchev make some
face-saving retaliation in places where he was superior, as in Berlin? Many indeed predicted that he would. On the contrary,
Khrushchev and Ulbricht began, on top of the abject surrender in
Cuba, to be sweetly reasonable over Berlin. The significance of
this seems to have been completely missed by most observers, who
apparently accepted it simply as a bonus. And when the Chinese
Communists castigated Khrushchev for retreating from a "paper
tiger," his public reply was, "The paper tiger has nuclear teeth."

Surely all can agree that the Cuban episode demonstrated the
great aversion of the present Soviet leaders to *any* direct hostilities
with the United States. It indicated strongly that they fear even
small outbreaks of violence between them and us, no doubt because they consider such outbreaks too likely to proceed rapidly to
nuclear war. What surprised and sobered Khrushchev was our
readiness to confront him. Our previous behavior had apparently
led him to believe we would tolerate his installing the missiles;
when he found that we were not that tolerant, he rushed to get
them out—apparently unimpeded with any worries about "humiliation."

Still another assumption of the CWE school is that greater conventional strength would permit us occasionally to take the diplomatic and military initiative where we would not dare do so if we
had only nuclear weapons to work with. In the same speech at
West Point on December 5, 1962, that embroiled him with the
British, Dean Acheson offered the following view on "a sound
plan for military defense":

> A military plan and policy which would deprive the Soviet Union of
> conventional superiority on its front with Western Europe requires
> increased production by all the allied countries, including ourselves.
> Such economic and military developments, should they occur,
> would give reality to such political policies as the reunification of

Germany and more independent national lives for the East European countries. Finally, all these developments could bring such stability and balance in the relations between the Soviet Union and the Western allies that the control of armaments, including nuclear armaments, would become possible and practicable.

Later in the speech, he said, "Soviet domination of East Germany is largely based on the preponderance of Soviet conventional power on their western front. If this did not exist, Soviet intervention to support Ulbricht's authority might become increasingly impracticable."

One remembers in the 1952 elections the Republican talk of "roll-back," which only matched Acheson's earlier slogan about our need to build up our forces in order to be able to "negotiate from strength." No doubt we needed to build up our forces, but the fallacy in Acheson's slogan was the implication that he had an aggressive policy which only a lack of military support prevented him from implementing. What in fact he lacked, and what the build-up itself could not provide, was the kind of aggressive policy implied by his West Point remarks—which incidentally is to result in mutual arms control!

Since the end of World War II we have at no time taken or *seriously contemplated* any kind of military initiative that was not prompted by some external military aggression by the opponent. Concerning the uprisings in East Germany and in Hungary and the building of the Berlin Wall, we did nothing, and our reasons could hardly have hinged on a shortage of conventional forces. In Korea, we responded to a direct aggression against a protégé, and in Cuba we responded to a gambit aimed directly at ourselves.

There are many reasons why we are not more given to initiating crises where a clash of arms might be involved, but surely one is the same that caused Khrushchev to surrender in Cuba: violence between great opponents is inherently difficult to control, and it cannot be controlled unilaterally. We therefore save confrontations for the opponent's aggressions.

The most important ingredient in deterring Soviet aggression in Europe is our known readiness to oppose it. For support of this policy, our force structure has been in no important respect inappropriate. Stout hearts and a sense of Soviet methods have been and will surely continue to be more necessary than a conventional build-up.

But if war in Europe, however improbable, nevertheless does break out, what then? A future condition of stable mutual strategic deterrence (*i.e.*, where each side deems the second-strike retaliatory capability of the other to be extremely formidable) would no doubt inhibit escalation from a limited war to a general war. But surely such a barrier against general war will not act also to prevent the use of tactical nuclear weapons in limited war. It should have exactly the opposite effect.

It is probable that the tactical use of nuclear weapons would increase the danger of limited war. But who today considers any hostilities directly between the super-powers not to be anything but terribly dangerous? Who will take the first step toward war if he is so appalled at the thought of the second step, which is the use of nuclear weapons? At any rate, there seems to be no empirical reason for the belief that use or non-use of tactical nuclear weapons will make all the difference between what some seem to regard as a rather safe and sane use of large-scale violence and what would be an unutterably disastrous eruption.

There are other considerations. The Germans know that not much territory can be yielded before they have yielded all of theirs. The French have pointed to our CWE philosophy as evidence, among other things, of the beginning of American withdrawal from the commitment to defend Europe even at the risk of total nuclear war. To them, it confirms their foresight in aspiring for a national *force de frappe*. However wrong that deduction may be, we have needlessly given them much leverage for making it.

When charged that their philosophy looks toward making a new war in Europe resemble World War II, CWE advocates answer that it would be a lot better for Europeans than a tactical nuclear war—the implication being that they should jump at the chance. But most Europeans have a different way of looking at the present choice of alternatives. To contribute more men and money in order to make it possible to enjoy another World War II strikes them, at the very least, as too much relinquishment of the nuclear deterrent. They are abundantly convinced that our staunchness and readiness to use the kind of force we already have in Europe is quite enough to keep the Russians at bay. They seem to hold the same to be true of keeping our position in West Berlin—which makes them willing to follow our lead, though we should be clear that for our non-German allies Berlin is not the best issue for inspiring them to greater sacrifice.

The Europeans, in short, want to settle for deterrence on the tactical level as well as the strategic. It is not true that they eagerly accept tactical nuclear weapons out of ignorance of the terrible implications of their use. They accept them in the same way and for the same reasons that Americans accept nuclear strategic deterrence. In fact, deterrence on the tactical level means for them exactly what deterrence on the strategic level means for us.

The more sophisticated CWE advocates have argued that tactical nuclear war in Europe would be not only terribly destructive but also militarily infeasible, because troops simply could not live in a battle environment where nuclear weapons were liberally employed. The charge of greater destructiveness would depend on the stage of violence reached, and it is far from obvious that use of a few nuclear weapons—to demonstrate readiness to use more—will force the level of violence upward rather than down.

In any case, finding tactical nuclear operations infeasible does not make large-scale conventional war in Europe feasible. Where nuclear weapons are on stand-by availability to both sides, conventional war must proceed in an extraordinarily precarious environment. Besides, if one's own armies cannot live in a nuclear environment, the chances are that neither can the enemy's. A war is not fought in order to provide a suitable battle environment for troops.

The real issues are much more political than technical. Our experience with the Russians, crowned by the Cuban episode of last October, tells us that the Soviet opponent is not ten feet tall in the moral intangibles of power—as he would have to be to do some of the bold things he does in war games. Even in the Berlin "blockade" of 1948–49, when we failed altogether to test the Soviet resolve to deny us access on the ground, they did not attempt to interfere with our airlift, as they could easily have done simply by jamming our Ground Controlled Approach radar system. Why should we go on postulating a kind of behavior that is radically different from what they have demonstrated over a long time? After all, the Soviet leaders have now openly broken with the Marxist-Leninist philosophy of inevitable war, avowedly on the ground that nuclear weapons do matter.

Those weapons have vastly affected the expectation of major war in Europe, and it is absurd not to make the most of that change. It is illogical to propose that the NATO powers should add substantially to their defense burdens in order to exploit a probably slim chance for moderating a possible future European war—which, however, the present dispositions make highly improbable.

It is one thing to exhort our allies to see that their contributions of forces maintain reasonable standards of efficiency, which certainly ought not to exclude a capability for limited conventional operations. It is quite another to invoke fantasies of great modern armies locked in desperate combat in Europe with never a nuclear warhead going off between them. The one attitude invites credit for our political sense as well as for our strategic thinking; the other merely discredits us in both respects.

PART III

Neutrality and the Problem of Insurgency

Neutrality is not, of course, a new concept. However, its forms have changed in the modern period. Traditionally, states have been able to gain formal or legal recognition of their decision to remain nonbelligerents in war. Often, this decision has been an *ad hoc* one. Thus, despite her formal alliance with a belligerent, Italy remained neutral at the beginning of each of the world wars. Neutrality can also be a deliberate act of national policy. Some states have announced in advance that they would not join a conflict, regardless of the issues, unless their own territory was attacked. Sweden and Switzerland have made unilateral declarations of neutrality. Or else, as in the case of Belgium before the two world wars, neutrality may be given international status through a formal agreement of the major powers.

Whether a neutral country would be able to maintain its position depends both on the temptation it presents to an attacker and on the assistance other countries are willing to supply. The temptations in turn reflect the advantage to be gained by violating the neutrality. Since Belgium lies athwart the invasion routes into France, she has been less fortunate than Sweden in escaping war.

Countries aspiring to neutrality can rely for their defense on their own strength or on the implied assistance that other countries may furnish. If they aspire to self-sufficiency, they are likely to develop military forces far in excess of those required by a member of an alliance system. Even taking into account the difference in resources, Sweden's military power is much greater than that of Norway, which is a member of the Atlantic alliance.

On the other hand, when a neutral, because of either insufficient resources or deliberate policy, has made itself dependent on the assistance of other countries, it has often combined the disadvantages of alliance policy with those of neutrality. By itself, the neutral country was rarely strong enough to deter aggression, while, at the same time, its neutrality prevented it from making joint defensive preparations with a would-be protector. Belgium's position in the two world wars illustrates this point. But no matter what military policy is pursued, neutrality has implied the desire to abstain from close involvement in international diplomacy.

These traditional patterns of neutrality have been significantly modified by two contradictory tendencies in the current period. On the one hand, the advent of nuclear power casts in doubt the ability of any non-nuclear country to defend itself against a nuclear opponent. In other words, the neutral is deprived of the capacity to impose military risks out of proportion to the aggressor's objective, if the latter is prepared to use nuclear weapons and if the neutral cannot count on foreign nuclear protection.

At the same time, the bipolar nature of the international political order makes the probability of protection far greater than it was in the past. In contemporary international affairs, a country suffers fewer disadvantages from being neutral and may even gain some international stature through the competition of the major powers for its allegiance. In other words, the nuclear age has eroded the distinction between allies and neutrals.

This modification accounts for the emergence of a new type of neutral: a nation that deliberately exploits the great-power confrontation in order not so much to enhance its territorial security as to magnify its diplomatic importance. Far from standing apart in international conflicts, it becomes actively embroiled, by attempting to manipulate the great powers and to advance its own purposes in the process.

This type of diplomacy adds a destabilizing element to the international system. Though many neutrals have a stake in the avoidance of war, they also discover advantages in perpetuating the competition of the super-powers. For they consider that this conflict enhances their bargaining position and opens prospects of economic development to which they could not otherwise aspire.

In their turn, the major powers are handicapped by a paradox. Though their relative superiority over other nations has never been greater, it has also never been less relevant. The use of nuclear weapons against the uncommitted is for all practical purposes excluded. Other military forces have in the meantime become less and less suitable for the low-threshold warfare that is waged in uncommitted areas.

A diplomacy of weakness has been the result. When the uncommitted nations threaten the West: "If I go Communist it will be worse for you than for me," this creates a pattern for blackmail. It encourages local conflicts into which major powers are drawn, often against their wishes. As a corollary, it means that any major country determined to upset the equilibrium can do so at little cost. The sale of obsolescent military equipment to nations in a troubled area, like for example the Middle East, can undermine stability in a way that could not have been achieved by direct action.

If the uncommitted nations today have unprecedented scope for pursuing their self-interest, they are also subject to novel pressures. In the past, neutrality was usually the posture of very cohesive nations, certain of their identity and determined to defend it. But many newly independent nations are still in search of an identity. Often the sole link among their peoples is the common experience of colonial rule. Domestic cohesion is only precariously assured.

Thus, while the governments are relatively safe from the military pressures that have traditionally weighed on neutral nations, they are extraordinarily susceptible to domestic subversion. Those countries with a high capacity for fomenting domestic instability can achieve enormous influence. The lack of traditional forms of power, including nuclear power, may be more than counter-balanced by the possession of guerrilla training centers; capacities for subversion will be taken very seriously. Thus, Communist China can be a major factor in Africa, even though it lacks almost all forms of traditional long-range power.

The most frequent and likely kind of war is the one for which the West is least prepared—militarily, politically, and psychologically. In guerrilla war, superior fire-power loses its old relevance. Guerrillas need only join battle in places where they enjoy superiority, but the defenders must be strong everywhere, in anticipation of the unexpected. The ability to occupy territory is no longer decisive, for the real target has become the morale of the population and the system of the civil administration. If these can be undermined through protracted struggle, the insurgents will prevail no matter how many battles the defending forces have won.

What makes the situation particularly complex is that there is no purely military solution to guerrilla war. Pacification requires a government capable of enlisting the loyalty of the population. But such a government is difficult to establish because of the very nature of guerrilla war, whose chief targets are often civil administrators. Moreover, for a Western government aiding an Asian or

African ally, the criteria of stable government may prove elusive. Government can be stable by being oppressive. By contrast, a developing society inevitably creates dislocations. How does one achieve both development and stability, both progress and security? There is no more urgent task for analysis than to inquire into the nature of stable enlightened government in developing nations. The writers of the following chapters deal especially with this problem.

SIXTEEN

J. K. ZAWODNY

Unconventional Warfare

It is more than a knife in the enemy's back. . . .

[Editor's Note: In no other area of national security policy is the interrelationship between technology, strategy, and the political environment so obvious and so varied as in counterinsurgency warfare. Professor Zawodny shows how in counterinsurgency warfare, political and social conditions determine military strategy and tactics. His initial thesis is that purely military approaches intensify resistance, further alienate the population, and aggravate the condition they were designed to cure. There is a sense in which "wars are won and lost in the minds of men." The successful conduct of unconventional warfare requires constant awareness of the psychological and political element and systematic application of strategy and tactics toward influencing the attitudes and behavior of local populations.]

In the third century B.C., in the city of Argos, Pyrrhus of Epirus, known as the Red King, was killed by a chamber-pot thrown from a rooftop by an elderly lady. The basic elements of what is today known as "unconventional warfare" were embodied in her action: there was surprise, and an unusual—if not extraordinary—weapon; the object of attack was strategically important; the attack was successful; and it was performed by a nonprofessional warrior. The performer, not the technique, is the significant element of this episode.

The outstanding feature of unconventional warfare is that it is carried out by people of all ages and backgrounds and of both sexes. It is a "People's Warfare." A warfare of masses who have

EDITOR'S NOTE: Reprinted with permission from *The American Scholar*, XXXI, No. 3 (Summer, 1962). Copyright © 1962, by the United Chapters of Phi Beta Kappa.

lost patience, it is an unremittingly violent way of saying to the enemy by all possible means, "We hate you; we are everywhere; we will destroy you!" Unconventional warfare is the effective weapon of the weaker adversary; and, strange as it may sound, the United States is as vulnerable to this sort of warfare as Cuba. It is, furthermore, an extremely cheap weapon—at least, monetarily. It cost the United States taxpayers about $200,000 to kill one enemy soldier in a "conventional" manner during the Korean conflict; the Communist unconventional forces of Vietnam, spending only a tiny fraction of this sum, are inflicting losses variously estimated at 800 to 1,500 human lives a month.

Unconventional warfare is that part of "Special Warfare" that employs violence. It is offensive when one government promotes the overthrow of a foreign government or a change of its political elite. In these circumstances, organization, manipulation and assistance are carried into another territory; the recent invasion of Cuba at the Bay of Pigs is an example. It is defensive when a frustrated political group structures itself into a disciplined organization to apply violence against the government of its own nation or when a people fight the occupational forces of an invading army. This classification does not preclude both types from being (and they usually are) *strategically and tactically* offensive.

Communists have been and are using unconventional warfare. They have, in fact, developed a body of strategic doctrine and tactical theory for its application; the Chinese Communists, in particular, have reached a stage of considerable finesse and sophistication. Not counting the exploits of the Mescalero Apaches, of Mosby and Quantrill, America is relatively inexperienced in this kind of warfare, particularly in its offensive application. The organization of the invasion of Cuba, however, the present conflict in Vietnam, and the maintenance of several thousand specially trained "unconventional soldiers" in Germany, Okinawa, and Fort Bragg would seem to indicate that the government is seriously considering its use.

I

There seem to be three prerequisites for initiating unconventional warfare. First, an organization must be created to support those who will carry the violence directly to the enemy. Leadership, supplies and money are indispensable for the inception and survival of the underground. Guerrilla and saboteur units are only a small part of the structure; also included are headquarters, intelligence, communications, propaganda, cadres in reserve and training, and logistics.

In Poland under German occupation, it took about two years before systematically organized guerrillas emerged from the organization. People to provide leadership were needed first, and a basic skeleton of territorial organization had to be created. Simultaneously with the growth of the underground organization, leadership was solidified in the Polish government-in-exile. Contacts with allies were established to secure money and supplies. As the conflict escalated, six-men sections were combined into platoons, platoons into companies, and so on, until finally districts and areas were designated for unified command and the whole country was covered with an underground network. On each level of the structure, there was ideally but one human link between the immediate subordinates and a superior. A section leader knew his six subordinates and his platoon commander; the platoon commander knew his five section leaders and his company commander. A person's face and pseudonym were known only to about six others. (Communists prefer to hold this number to three, and wisely so.) Intuitively, a member does not want to know too much about the organization.

The second ingredient essential for the initiation of unconventional warfare is a culture that allows or promotes violence, and the effectiveness of the organization usually depends on the degree to which the cultural values and traditions of a people condition them to use violence. A Polish boy raised between World Wars I and II was encouraged by his teachers to sing over and over again the popular song:

> How beautiful it is when a lancer falls from his horse
>   during the war,
> His comrades do not feel sorry for him, they trample
>   over him in their charge.

The traditional Polish concept of manly virtue demanded a quick death on behalf of the country or in defense of a woman. The Polish belief in the grand gesture and redemption through suffering also contributed to produce good unconventional fighters. During World War II, the most bloody and intense unconventional fighting was done by those national undergrounds whose cultural values embraced suffering and self-sacrifice as part of their code of living. Suffering is here identified with virtue.

The third prerequisite for unconventional warfare is the volunteer, the guerrilla and saboteur, who carries violence to the enemy. Any movement aimed at using violence gathers to its ranks those who are threatened and/or dissatisfied. In the Polish underground movement between 1939 and 1945, the resentment against the cruelty and oppression of the German and Soviet occupation, the absence of formal channels for voicing grievances, and the lack of opportunities to change conditions caused the people to band together. Such, at least, were the usual explanations. Many men were unable to articulate the reasons why they fought. But they did believe that it was the only way they could "do something" about their problems. The messenger of a company in the Uprising of Warsaw (1944) was eight years old. No one knew why he was there, but the boy wanted to fight and was dependable. In one of the actions, a sergeant who had been a university professor was fighting because it was "his moral duty to uphold justice."

Women, following precedents in Polish history, were splendid unconventional fighters and did men's jobs, including manning street barricades and shooting. In fact, it appeared to this writer that when prolonged and steady physical effort was necessary, women, particularly peasant women, had more stamina and resilience than men. Like the men, they were of all ages and from all social classes. Women with high levels of intelligence worked themselves up into the policy-making levels of the underground (and of the enemy). Nor were they lacking in heroism. A beautiful Polish girl who was a superb linguist in the movement's intelligence was captured and tortured by the Gestapo in a most sadistic fashion. When she could no longer stand it, she asked for poison through a bribed guard. She revealed no information.

It should be emphasized, however, that not only the noblest are attracted by this kind of fighting. Because its participants spring from a very broad cross-section of the population, unconventional forces are also a cesspool of killers and people with aberrations looking for a formalized excuse to use violence. There was many a man ready and willing to kill a prisoner to get "even" for some real or imaginary reason known only to himself. Many kinds of men can be found, particularly among guerrillas. To idealize them is self-destructive.

Guerrillas and saboteurs are the true "unconventional fighters," for they carry violence directly to the enemy. It seems that, irrespective of culture and country, the people who are close to the soil and nature are the main stock of guerrilla units. These are not, on the whole, rich peasants; the well-to-do tend to stay out of the fighting. The guerrillas' pattern of living requires stamina, physical endurance, and a rather philosophical acceptance of hardship. The greatest hardship, other than physical, is the lack of women. Pleasures are scarce. This writer vividly remembers a seasoned fighter who always carried an old squeaky grind-organ playing two tunes: Sousa's "Stars and Stripes Forever" and "El Capitán." Mobility is one of the guerrilla's greatest assets; yet, the men tend to get over-equipped, particularly with heavy weapons when they are available. Such weapons provide them with some feeling of security. Another painful problem is the lack of identity. In many societies, it appears that men would rather fight in uniforms and be identified as a military unit rather than a guerrilla band.

Their lives are largely regulated by the degree of support given by the indigenous population, and also by the climatic conditions and the terrain. While valleys are avoided because they might become deadly traps, guerrillas can operate in literally any terrain so long as the distance between their hideouts and the targets is relatively short. When in danger of being encircled by the enemy, the guerrilla units will try to "evaporate" by disbanding and reassembling at a predetermined point. This is not a difficult task if the climate and terrain are favorable.

When possible, the members of the group try to live within communities among the peasants, and to assemble only when necessary for action. The Chinese Communist guerrillas during the revolutionary war tried to be self-sustaining and in some instances even operated cooperatives helping peasants produce food and the necessities of daily life; at the same time, they carried on very intense political indoctrination. This kind of approach has two direct gains: first, it conserves energy that can be utilized at the time of action; second, it cements the relationship between the guerrillas and the local population.

Guerrilla fighting has no rules. For security reasons, it might be necessary to shoot one's own wounded—an act practically unheard-of in conventional forces. Participants usually do not wear uniforms; thus, captives in many instances are treated as "bandits" and shot. Tactics are basically offensive in spirit. Hit-and-run fighting is practiced. Mobility, surprise, and dispersions are necessary. Ideally, guerrillas follow the principle of "Move while attacking; attack while moving." (Han Wu-ti, 140 B.C.) It would be this writer's axiom that if the enemy has a chance to reload his weapon, the guerrilla action was poorly planned or executed and should be abandoned.

The smaller the groups, the more active they seem to be in searching out and hitting the enemy. The greater the imagination of the leader, the more enterprising and unusual are the actions of the group. In July, 1950, four Koreans in a jeep rode into an American post and wanted their gas tank filled. After this was done they rode away, spraying the Americans with automatic fire. Successful action to some extent seems to depend upon determination and a cool head.

Guerrillas are not after territorial gains. Their effectiveness lies rather in binding the enemy forces, killing and spreading terror, destroying elements that are of strategic and tactical importance. Furthermore, they preserve and protect to a considerable degree the economic wealth and structure of a community.

According to Italian claims, guerrillas were tying down a few thousand German troops in the winter of 1943; in September–November, 1944, about half of the German army in Italy was engaged in chasing and combating the guerrillas; by April, 1945, at least two-thirds of the German forces in Italy were engaged in that task. It appears that the more guerrillas there are in a territory, the more enemy troops will be siphoned into it; however, fear of partisan attack will compel them to cluster and concentrate. This, of course, represents an exciting target for guerrilla attacks.

In regard to the destruction of tactically and militarily important objectives, one can point to the techniques of French guerrillas dealing with German transportation. The range of their activities was broad: faking, changing, and turning directional signs; felling roadside trees; spreading spikes on the roads; burning wooden bridges; mining roads; attacking telephone lines; blocking inland waterways. According to French sources, on June 22, 1944, 200 fully loaded barges (160 with food and 40 with lubricant for the German war effort) were immobilized by blowing up four locks. The next day, another three locks farther down the river were blown and yet another on August 13. Two hundred barges never reached their destination.

Needless to say, picking off a high-ranking officer or a member of the political elite is considered a coup by any guerrilla. Soviet partisans poisoned at least one German general and carried another out of his own headquarters wrapped in a carpet.

In many instances, guerrillas in Italy and the Soviet Union acted as protectors of the local industry, at the last moment preventing the German dismantling effort. One of the techniques by which guerrillas may preserve the integrity of the plants is to synchronize public riots and general strikes with their activities. Both these weapons were used in China, Italy, and the Soviet Union.

One final facet of guerrilla activities worth mentioning here is the organization of evasion. This term may encompass attempts to evacuate allied prisoners, airmen shot down, or sympathizers. It can also refer to the establishment of an underground railroad facilitating the escape of able-bodied men or specialists to join guerrillas or their supporters abroad. As many as 2,000 French volunteers to the Free French forces were entering England monthly in the late summer of 1940, in spite of the fact that the Vichy Government and the Germans were trying to stop them.

Troublesome as they may be to the enemy, guerrillas at certain times become as troublesome to their own political leadership. This happens when the country is liberated or when the political leadership feels obliged to set forth a concrete political program. Political leaders try to avoid specific pronouncements at the inception of the organization. By remaining vague, they are able to accommodate individual aspirations and thus increase their ranks. When the elite feels strong enough to seize power officially, however, or when, for one reason or another, they are compelled to state their political objectives, they prefer to do so when the guerrillas have been disarmed. Hence a gentle, and sometimes not so gentle, tug-of-war arises between the political leadership and the guerrillas. "Give us the weapons and we will give you the political program." "Give us the political program and we will give you the weapons." If the leaders have a label of legality and have the territory under control, the usual practice is to incorporate the guerrillas into the conventional military forces. Thus the guerrillas retain the weapons but they have little to say about the direction and content of political programs. Any successful guerrilla movement, however, carries within it the seeds of violent opposition to its own political leadership.

II

If guerrilla fighters are the artisans in violence, those who are engaged in sabotage are the artists. They are the "surgeons of violence" by profession; they deal with the nerves, heart, and brain of the enemy. They hit power stations, transformers, high-tension lines, and all possible centers of communication. They work themselves into the industrial network of the enemy, causing stoppages, faulty production, delays, and physical destruction of anything that might be of value.

The ingenuity with which sabotage men choose and attack their targets is boundless. There was one instance when even condoms produced for the German army were punctured. (How this was supposed to contribute to Allied victory is not clear.) They might put sugar in gas tanks, cause faulty execution of aircraft engine parts, spike oil wells and change the labels on freight cars. This latter procedure was used by the Polish underground in diverting precious metals used in the production of high-grade steel from Berlin to a small town in southern Greece. It took three months for this transport to reach Berlin, part of it having been blown up by Greek saboteurs.

Sabotage units are able to supplement even the air force. During bad weather in January and February, 1944, the French underground damaged 570 locomotives; in the same span of time, Allied attacks from the air damaged only twenty-four locomotives in occupied France.

If these groups really want to get a man, there is practically no chance for him to survive. The German general who commanded the security police in Warsaw rode to and from his office by different routes every day with an escort of armored cars. Nonetheless he was ambushed and killed.

There is no logistics problem with the members of sabotage units as there is in the case of guerrillas. They live "ordinary" lives and maintain themselves. The Polish experience showed that to pass information to the members of the group took about ten hours in a large city; to get them ready and assembled at the point of action took an additional six to ten hours. Outside of their time in action, they are responsible for their own maintenance and their own lives.

III

It must be emphasized that as effective as is the guerrilla and sabotage units' tactical and strategic contribution to defeating the enemy, this does not adequately explain their value in the struggle for political power. Here, *the greatest contribution of guerrillas and saboteurs lies in catalyzing and intensifying counter-terror which further alienates the enemy from the local population.* The

enemy as a rule will relegate the responsibility for dealing with unconventional fighters to military forces or security agencies. These
groups deal with the fighters by using the only methods available
to them—those involving force. Because the guerrillas are elusive
and the saboteurs even more so, the frustration of the pursuers results in counter-violence, which falls on the lifeline and source of
manpower of these units—the local population. Reprisals begin.

This is what sophisticated political leaders of guerrillas may
expect. There is no better way to alienate a regime in power from
the population than to incite it to apply nonselective terror. Guerrillas and saboteurs serve this purpose eminently. The ebb and
flow of membership in these units is not related to the number of
tactical victories, to their losses or even to their prospects for success. The rate of recruitment is directly related to the intensity of
terror applied by the enemy in suppressing the movement. Any
counter-terror by the enemy brings to the ranks of the unconventional fighters new recruits who are escaping from the reprisals or
who wish revenge. In this way, the movement perpetuates itself.
Unless the guerrillas are also using terror against the population,
the more terror the enemy applies, the more fighters he produces,
provided, of course, that the cultural values permit violence. (Certainly, Quakers would react to counter-terror differently from
Catholic Poles.)

The existence of an underground and its result—unconventional warfare—is evidence of the breakdown of social order.
When this occurs, there is a considerable alteration of the operational values and social mores of the society. What was a crime
before the struggle can become exemplary behavior during strife.
Killing, destroying property that may be of use to the enemy and
slowing production become not only respectable, but also moral
obligations. This modification of values affects the process of so-
cialization of the generation growing up while the underground
activities are in progress. Violence becomes an acceptable means
and part of solving problems for that generation. Polish underground authorities were aware of this and established a special
"Pedagogical Council" to see that the boys would not become
one-track killers, but would continue with the acquisition of education and the development of moral values necessary for existence
in a normal democratic society. A man who grows up in the Judaic-
Christian tradition of compassion and love has to go through intellectual calisthenics to rationalize his participation in the ruth-
less operation of unconventional warfare. This is not the case with

the Communists, where all activities of this kind can be explained and justified in terms of class struggle.

In terms of American cultural values, it seems that to engage in unconventional warfare we would have to abandon two rules in our code of manly conduct—waiting for the enemy to reach for his gun first, and face-to-face combat. These two ideals are the very antithesis of unconventional fighting.

IV

Mass movements using unconventional warfare exist at this time in at least eleven countries: Algeria, South Africa, Angola, Burma, China, Vietnam, South Korea, Kenya, Laos, Venezuela, and Guatemala. There are also "dormant" underground movements in at least ten countries in East Central Europe now within the sphere of Soviet influence. In the years since the end of World War II, the political elites and forms of governments in six countries have been changed through the application or with the assistance of the techniques of unconventional warfare: China, Israel, Vietnam, Iraq, Cuba, and Laos. Such techniques for gaining political power will be used frequently by technologically backward people because they are cheap and effective.

Our political leadership ought to face this question squarely: Is unconventional warfare an instrument of foreign policy to be applied in international relations as an element of power and pressure, or is it merely an infantry combat technique to be used in wartime? If the latter is what we have in mind, then we are really using "unconventional warfare" in the most "conventional" fashion. On the other hand, *if* we intend to enter the game of systematically initiating, manipulating and fostering political mass movements in order to help peoples realize their political objectives through violence, then we must understand and clearly distinguish between the prerequisites, the techniques and the objectives of unconventional warfare.

If such a definition takes place, then the aspirations and expectations of the indigenous people with whom we plan to work ought to be given paramount attention and faced squarely and honestly! Otherwise we shall fail, as we did in Cuba.

This is even more important when we try to fight guerrillas, as we are doing now in Southeast Asia. True, in some situations it is necessary to deal with guerrillas in the most stern and unyielding manner. (Seek them out and put such pressure on them that the guerrilla will not have a chance to stop behind a bush to relieve himself. . . .) But this is a short-term tactical answer; the final solution should not rest at this. For a long-range consideration, it is necessary that a basic question be asked: "Why did guerrillas emerge and what are their values, goals and grievances?"

You cannot expect a starved peasant in an underdeveloped country to fight on behalf of "free enterprise"—he has experienced it already from his landlord. Neither does the word "freedom" mean much to him—freedom to do what? Behind a guerrilla's gun is a man; that man shoots in the direction from which there is no hope. He shoots because he does not believe that for him justice and satisfaction can be achieved in any other way. In the long run, therefore, he should be met on the level of his expectations and hopes, and not with a rifle. "For a partisan may be completely wrong on what he is fighting *for*, but is not likely to be nearly so wrong on what he is fighting *against*."

SEVENTEEN

FRANKLIN A. LINDSAY

Unconventional Warfare

[Editor's Note: This article—though its title is identical with the preceding one—is much more specific in subject matter. It deals in detail with one particular problem: that of organizing effective counter-measures to the tactics of guerrilla insurrection perfected and employed by the Communists since the end of World War II. Like Professor Zawodny, Mr. Lindsay contends that, though the instruments are military, the problem is essentially political. The key to success is the establishment of a set of political goals that the average person can both understand and accept.

Mr. Lindsay does not belittle the military aspect of the problem, but he insists that it becomes decisive only in terms of a political framework. He emphasizes that attracting and supporting skillful and dedicated local partisans is a complex and arduous business. It is, unfortunately, an activity for which the West has, up to now, shown little aptitude. Nevertheless, he stresses that along with the development of military skills, a systematic effort must be made to work out techniques and train experts in the political aspects of village warfare.]

I

Unconventional war is the war that is being fought today in Laos and South Vietnam; it is the war that the French fought in Indochina and are now fighting in Algeria. It is a form of warfare the Communists have learned to employ with great effectiveness and one they will continue to exploit to the maximum in furthering their long-range objectives.

Unconventional warfare differs profoundly from warfare in which regular armies are openly engaged in combat. The objective of such conventional combat is to win control of a state by

EDITOR'S NOTE: Reprinted with permission from Foreign Affairs, XL, No. 2 (January, 1962). Copyright © 1962 by the Council on Foreign Relations, Inc., New York.

defeating the enemy's military forces in the field. In contrast, the strategy of unconventional forces must be to win control of the state by first winning control of the civil population. For without the disciplined support of the civil population, militarily inferior guerrilla forces can have no hope of success.

As yet, the West has not developed a form of defense that is adequate against this form of warfare. And even where the defense has been effective, the costs to the West of suppressing such attacks have been many times the costs to the Communists of mounting them. In Greece between 1945 and 1948, for example, Communist guerrilla forces, numbering less than 20,000 armed men, successfully cut the country in two so that the only communication between north and south was by sea and air. A Greek army of several hundred thousand men, heavily supported by the United States, was required to contain the very much smaller guerrilla force. The total cost of military and political pacification, and of economic reconstruction, was about $2 billion—or somewhere between 100 and 1,000 times what the Communists had spent. The fortuitous defection of Yugoslavia from the Soviet bloc, and the consequent loss of guerrilla bases in Macedonia, caused the Communists to call off their attack. Had this not occurred, the costs in men, money, and matériel needed finally to subdue the Communist rebels would have been many times greater. And the outcome would not have been certain.

The essential reasons the Communists have been able to do so much with so little in many areas of the world are four:

1. They have learned thoroughly the techniques of gaining control of the civil population by combining effectively the positive incentives of a political doctrine, applied meticulously from the grass roots up, and the negative pressures of a terrorism applied against those who refuse to accept their leadership voluntarily.

2. They have mastered the principles and techniques of guerrilla warfare, a form of warfare quite apart from regular or frontal warfare.

3. They have directed their most determined attacks against countries whose territory is contiguous to the Communist empire so that safe haven and training areas can be provided for guerrillas and so that supplies can be provided clandestinely.

4. They have also been able to exploit effectively the pent-up hatreds against former colonial powers and pent-up frustrations with the slow pace of economic advancement.

In most cases these have proven to be unbeatable combinations.

To gain control of a key part of the civilian population is an absolute prerequisite for further action. Having gained this control, the Communist leadership is then in a position to use its guerrilla force with great advantage against equal or superior forces supporting the government in power.

A guerrilla force is like the top of an iceberg; the supporting civilian organization, without which it cannot survive, is the much larger part that can't be seen. Just as control of the air has become a prerequisite for successful frontal warfare, so control of the population is a prerequisite for successful unconventional warfare. From the outset of conflict, a major struggle for control over the civilian population will take place and it will continue throughout the entire course of the war. Each side must try to organize the civil population into a tightly disciplined force, and, through propaganda and police activities, try to break the grip exercised by its adversary.

In Vietnam, for example, the defeat of the French was due primarily to the Communists' success in this regard. It made it possible to trap French forces in one bloody ambush after another until the French were so weakened they could no longer keep open supply lines to their fortified outposts. Once the fortified outposts were isolated and could no longer be supplied, except in driblets by air, the Communists were in a position to complete the establishment of political and military control over the rest of the country. With their base of operations thus secured, they could safely convert their guerrilla forces to regular assault forces equipped with heavy artillery and a supply system to back it. The final phase was to launch massive frontal assaults against these weakened fortresses. Thus the French and their local supporters were progressively driven from the country into the villages, and from the villages into the cities until, at the end, they held in the north of Indochina only the heavily fortified perimeter immediately surrounding Hanoi. In the areas from which they had withdrawn, the Communists erected a political structure that exacted the positive loyalty of every peasant and his family by the stark example of violence to some and the threat of heavy punishment or death to others.

The key to the successes of the Communist guerrillas in Vietnam and elsewhere is found in the fact that they had established control over the rural population as a first step. For every man in a guerrilla force carrying a rifle, there must be a large number of civilians who provide the support he must have to survive and fight. They are the source of food, clothing, and recruits. Even more important, the civilian organization must supply the guerrilla force with constant operational intelligence on every movement of the enemy. Only with such information can a militarily inferior guerrilla force be forewarned of an encircling trap, a planned offensive, or an ambush. This intelligence net embraces not only the peasants who observe military movements but also spies in enemy headquarters who provide advance warning of intended offensives.

The cause of the French defeat in Vietnam can be traced to their loss of the support of the civilian population. Here, as elsewhere, the Communists had been able to capitalize upon a basic anti-colonial feeling and to harness this antagonism into an effective tool for political indoctrination of the population. But in order to obtain effective control, the Communists go far beyond political indoctrination. Once they have a fanatically dedicated minority, they begin the application of systematic terror to ensure that the masses of the people will be brought under, and kept under, complete Communist control. Their objective is to build in each village—even though it may be under nominal control of the legitimate government—a shadow government completely controlled by the local Communist representative. It has often happened that in a single village two governments exist simultaneously, one the official and open government representing the anti-Communist central government, the other the secret government that in fact exercises complete control over the actions of every member of the village.

The use of terror to form a secret government under the nose of the enemy has long been a Communist technique. In some of the worst German concentration camps, a secret Communist government was often sufficiently powerful to bring about the execution, through clandestine manipulation of Gestapo records, of those prisoners who failed to accept its control.

The French were defeated in Vietnam because they were fighting blind. They never knew where the enemy was. They were repeatedly caught on the march in the most indefensible positions where, without warning, they were subjected to murderous rifle, machine-gun, and mortar fire from concealed positions on both sides of the track. The surviving remnants of one ambush lived only to be cut down the next day by the same Viet Minh force, which held them constantly under surveillance and moved through the jungles on foot to prepare the next ambush on the expected line of march. When the French undertook mop-up operations in areas known to be harboring guerrilla forces, the Communist-controlled civil population collaborated in warning the guerrillas and in helping them to hide or escape.

The pattern of, first, political organization, second, guerrilla warfare and, finally, frontal assault was followed in Yugoslavia during World War II, in China from the 1930's until the Communist victory in 1950, and in Vietnam prior to the partition of the country in 1954. Now it is being followed in South Vietnam, where Communist organizers have been increasingly active in building clandestine organizations in the rural areas. During the last year, guerrilla activities were stepped up with the objective of forcing government troops to withdraw from the villages into the larger towns and into fortified positions. Now it appears from reports from Saigon that the Communist leaders have decided that their control of many areas outside the cities is sufficiently firm to permit the use of regular military units trained in North Vietnam. If their judgment is correct, the war for South Vietnam has entered the third, or final, assault stage.

Because the Communists have been permitted to consolidate their hold over most of the country, the forces of the government, supported by the United States, find themselves in a very precarious position. They can be extricated from the situation only by an extraordinary military effort coupled with a major effort to free the rural areas from the pressures of Communist terror.

In Malaya and in the Philippines are found two examples of the successful suppression and ultimate defeat of Communist guerrilla forces. In both cases, the heart of the Western strategy was twofold: (1) a vigorous and aggressive pursuit of the Communist guerrillas into their own territory, while maintaining constant pressure on them so that they were denied the initiative and the ability to launch attacks on their own terms; (2) a major political program undertaken to win back the population, to protect it against the violence and reprisals of the Communists, and to match force with force.

The second of these represents one of the West's most difficult problems, for it is obvious that when two forces are contending for the loyalty of, and control over, the civilian population, the side that uses violent reprisals most aggressively will dominate most of the people, even though their sympathies may lie in the other direction. Communist efforts to dominate the population must be frustrated before their control has become strong enough to support guerrilla operations. If the Communists are unopposed in their initial application of force against the civilian population, and thereby gain control, the counter-force which must be applied finally to break that control will be far greater and the population will suffer far more than if action had been taken resolutely at the outset.

In 1945 in Rumania, for example, a broad popular feeling of support for the monarchy had spontaneously developed. As evidence of this loyalty, people wore badges with the royal coat of arms. Communist thugs began systematically beating up people wearing the monarchist symbol whom they were able to catch alone in back streets after dark. There was no reaction from the population other than to stop wearing these pins when they were alone at night. Thus emboldened, the Communists became more aggressive until they beat up, in broad daylight and in the open streets, those who still wore the monarchist pins. Finally the pins were driven completely from the streets; the will of the people had been broken, and the first step in the Communist takeover had been accomplished.

The way in which force is applied to combat Communist terror is nevertheless all-important. The strategy of the Communists may be to use acts of terror and sabotage to goad the government into repressive counter-measures and thereby widen the split between the population and the government. Thus, when the government and its security forces use force to meet the Communist terror, they must do so resolutely but with great selectivity and only against those who are directly responsible.

II

The first step in mobilizing a civilian population against Communist subversion and guerrilla attack is to establish a set of political goals expressed in terms that the average person can understand. They must be goals that strike a sympathetic response and that aim to remove the inequities in the existing society and the grievances which they have caused. Through mass communications, these reform programs must be communicated effectively, and repeatedly, to the population.

But this is only the beginning of the task. Political organizers must be recruited and trained in sufficient numbers to reach by direct contact nearly every family in the land. They must be as thorough as the best of ward or district leaders in American politics. The organizer must know everyone in his village. He must know who are the Communist sympathizers and who are the secret Communist organizers. He must know who comes and goes in the village and what their business is. He must build a core of persons loyal to himself and to the government. Through these people, he must be constantly informed of the activities of the Communists and the pressures they are placing on villagers to gain their secret help. Above all, he must be able to provide effective protection to those who, against their will, are being forced into Communist collaboration by threats of violence against themselves and their families. To accomplish this, he must have the support of his own government and of the West; he must be able not only to provide physical protection but to alleviate the legitimate economic and political grievances of this village. More than anyone else, the local political organizer holds the key to success or failure. If he is successful in his task, he will hold the loyalty of his village and will be able to integrate its people and resources into the effort to defeat the Communists.

If he is not successful, the shadow of Communist control will gradually be extended and consolidated until the village is organized entirely in support of the Communist forces. Food and money will regularly be collected for that purpose. The entire village will become part of the Communist intelligence network, reporting to the guerrilla commanders every movement of the government security forces. At the same time, the government will be totally cut off from information about the guerrillas—their strength, their movements and their intentions.

The organization of the civilian population will require months, if not years. But where control by the Communists has already progressed to the point where they are able to launch guerrilla war, military operations must be conducted aggresively against them, regardless of the disadvantage at which government forces will be operating. Government patrols must push vigorously into Communist-dominated territory, try to contact the guerrillas and force them into open combat. Lacking the intelligence that the civilian population might have provided, the defending forces must employ to the fullest all other means, such as air reconnaissance. The United States has effectively applied its advanced scientific skills to the solution of major problems in the missile and space fields. There is now the opportunity, as yet largely untried, to apply these same scientific capabilities to the development of modern equipment designed to help meet the special problems of guerrilla and counter-guerrilla warfare.

The basic principle of counter-guerrilla military operations is to maintain the offensive and thereby deny the guerrillas the initiative. The Communist guerrilla strategy, in turn, will be to attempt to seize and hold the initiative by mounting a variety of attacks against fixed installations so that large government forces are pinned down defending towns and villages, rail lines, power lines, ports and other vital installations. A counter-guerrilla offensive, then, will have these objectives:

1. To keep guerrilla units off balance at all times, to force them to flee continuously from attacking government units, and, thereby, to minimize their opportunities to mount attacks on vital communication lines and military installations or to lay ambushes.

2. By maintaining the initiative, to force guerrilla units to overrun their intelligence screens, and thereby to deny them the protective cover they need to survive against superior military forces.

3. To prevent guerrilla forces from grouping for strong attacks against isolated points.

4. To tire them out, and keep them tired out, through constant offensive action against them; to force them into more isolated hinterlands where food supplies are less and less available; to force them through constant offensive action to expend their limited ammunition.

Whatever the means used to carry out this offensive strategy, the basic and overriding necessity is that counter-guerrilla forces be organized early enough and strongly enough so that they are able to meet and contain, at the outset, the attacks of guerrilla forces. *Too little and too late* has been the normal reaction of governments to the development of such forces.

The core of the counter-guerrilla troops must be a highly mobile attacking force. Normally, it need not be substantially larger than the guerrilla elements opposed to it. It should be able to meet and defeat guerrilla forces essentially on their own terms, that is, with small mobile units capable of moving in patrols over extended periods in enemy territory. As soon as one patrol is withdrawn for rest, another should take its place.

Mobile counter-guerrilla units should operate without fixed plans, and with the ability to modify their operations quickly, in order to take advantage of unforeseen targets and to concentrate superior forces against guerrilla units that have ben located and brought to combat. In contrast, the government force that relies on "set piece" offensives, based on plans drawn up days in advance, will always be at a disadvantage. Even before the operation is launched, such plans may find their way into the hands of the guerrillas, who will have moved meanwhile to another area. Periodic offensives of limited duration have the further disadvantage of permitting the guerrillas to hold the initiative between offensives. A strategy of constant offensive can effectively deprive the guerrillas of the opportunity to conduct the war on terms favorable to themselves.

It will also be necessary to provide defensive forces to guard key installations. Care must be exercised, however, that these forces are not spread out beyond all reasonable bounds in the attempt to defend an increasingly large number of fixed installations. A French military commentator has written, "There should be no fortified posts except those necessary for promoting mobility."

III

In a broader sense, the dilemma of the West is that, even if we can develop a more effective strategy for defending countries against unconventional Communist warfare, it can at best only limit further losses. When one considers a strategy for liberating areas over which the Communists have gained control, the difficulties are seen to be very great. The organization of clandestine activities in a Communist state faces extraordinary obstacles. It is, for example, common practice for the Communists to undertake provocative activities designed to test the loyalty of each individual in the regime. A person may at any time be contacted by someone purporting to represent a clandestine organization. Even though the sympathies of the person approached may be strongly anti-Communist and his fondest hopes that the Communists be overthrown, he must assume that this is not a genuine resistance movement but rather one conducted under the control, and at the direction, of the secret police. To prove his loyalty he must not only refuse to join the purported clandestine organization, but must also inform the police. If he does not, he will have failed to demonstrate his positive loyalty to the regime and will be subject to reprisals and imprisonment. Thus, a clandestinely organized resistance within a consolidated Communist regime is not likely to get very far before someone has, out of fear, reported its existence to the police.

A second device used by the Communists is to form a clandestine anti-Communist organization under their own secret control, to encourage its growth by recruiting unwitting members, and to permit them to conduct actual operations against the regime until finally, having attracted a large number of the most aggressive anti-Communists, its entire membership is arrested.

The communes and collective farms provide other means of containing potential resistance operations, by centralizing food supplies, rather than allowing them to remain under the control of individual peasants. It is thus extremely difficult to obtain locally the food needed to support a guerrilla force. Similarly, the Communist practice of issuing new currency from time to time minimizes the opportunities to build up currency reserves to finance resistance operations.

Because of these techniques, a Communist dictatorship probably can be overthrown from within only in an area in which the Communists have not yet consolidated their control or in which their control has been seriously weakened by other events. It is therefore of the utmost importance to move quickly to prevent the total consolidation of a nation into a completely controlled police state. This struggle will take place at a very personal level, and the final outcome will depend on whether the individual, faced by the Communist instruments of terrorist control, can, in the face of this force, be given a viable alternative to complete surrender.

Where the effective political control of the country has passed to the Communists, it will not be enough to conduct long-distance propaganda activities or to make plans on the assumption that the very real and very considerable dissatisfactions with the Communist regime will automatically result in a popular uprising as soon as the guerrilla forces appear. Clandestine support of at least a part of the villages and the countryside is an absolute prerequisite of the employment of guerrilla forces, for they must have local intelligence support and supplies if they are to survive in areas in which superior enemy forces are openly in control. In Yugoslavia, for example, in World War II, the Communist partisans had in many ways as favorable a situation for guerrilla warfare as might be expected anywhere. The main German forces were engaged by powerful allies on other fronts. Tito's partisan forces had as overt allies not only the Soviet Union but the United States and Britain. And from the latter two they received massive air support. In Slovenia, where there were no Cêtnik forces of Mihailovich to contend with, the political commissars of the Communist-established National Liberation Front could represent themselves to the people as the only force fighting the invader and as having the complete support of all the major powers fighting the Germans. Yet, they still found it necessary, in the words of one commissar, to "prepare the area intensively by the introduction of clandestine political organizers for a period of several months before we dared to introduce guerrilla forces."

It is not merely with benefit of hindsight that one can say it would have been a better strategy in Cuba to have built organized support in the villages and rural areas of Cuba and to have organized widespread guerrilla activities rather than to have risked all on a spontaneous uprising following a single assault landing. By far the largest part of any population will not voluntarily risk reprisals even though their sympathies may be strong. Instead, they will sit on the sidelines while others battle it out, joining in only when the outcome becomes a foregone conclusion. The political organization of each village must be undertaken under the nose of vigilant Communist political and security services. This is not easy. It requires unusual men possessing great personal courage and high motivation as well as superior political organizing skills. They must be thoroughly trained and then supported to the fullest extent possible under the circumstances. Guerrilla operations can be initiated only as the Communist control at the village level is loosened so that clandestine support to guerrillas can be provided.

The West needs to acquire the ability to conduct unconventional warfare successfully, and it must do so quickly. The Communists have evolved a highly effective strategy combining grass-roots political organization and guerrilla warfare which they are employing against the non-Communist world. They have devised a totalitarian political structure that is highly resistant to counterattack. The creation by the West of an adequate defensive and offensive capability for political and guerrilla warfare will require time and effort. It must be pursued vigorously and without further delay.

The United States has expanded significantly its military capabilities and, in the Army's Special Forces units, is creating a highly competent corps of guerrilla and counter-guerrilla fighters. This capability must be quickly matched with the political skills to conduct unconventional warfare at the village level. This will require training in depth and an extraordinarily high level of individual aptitude and competence. Specifically, we require a system of training—both of our own personnel and for those we are aiding—comparable to that for an army officer, a physician, or an engineer. A national institute or staff college comparable to those of the Army, Air Force, and Navy is needed to provide a center for training of United States and possibly foreign personnel and for elaborating strategic concepts of unconventional warfare and developing practical and effective tactics to meet the operational problems we now face in many parts of the world. Similar institutes should be established jointly with our NATO partners and in the countries lying across the Communist lines of attack.

The Communists have allowed themselves lead times of as much as nineteen to twenty years in training revolutionary leaders. One can only hope that the free world yet has time to build the political leadership, both abroad and at home, to meet their threat successfully.

PART IV

The Control of Modern Weapons

Though proposals for disarmament have been made in the past, particularly after World War I, there was an air of unreality about them. In the era of what we now call conventional weapons, the force-in-being was not nearly so significant as the industrial potential and the mobilization base. A nation planning to attack had to engage in extended preparations, which were difficult to hide; technology was much more stable; travel was relatively free. Since surprise was not so crucial and since victory could generally be achieved only through a prolonged mobilization of resources *after* a war had started, the contribution that arms control could make to stability seemed marginal. Armaments, it was then correctly said, were the symptom and not the cause of tension. The best method of achieving a stable peace was to remove the causes of political conflict.

Although this remains true today, conditions have basically altered. The forces-in-being are almost surely decisive—at least in all-out war; the advantage of surprise can be overwhelming. Technology is extremely volatile—indeed, a major cause of instability is the very rate of technological change. Every nation lives with the nightmare that even if it puts forth its best effort, its survival may be jeopardized by a technological breakthrough achieved by its opponent. It knows also that every invention opens up the prospect of many others. No country can protect itself against *all* the technological possibilities that become available to its opponents. Conversely, an advantage once achieved will produce a powerful incentive to exploit it, for the scientific revolution that made it possible also ensures that it will be transitory.

There exists, therefore, an unprecedented incentive to stabilize the arms race. All countries have an interest in preventing a war that might break out simply because of the automatism of retaliatory forces. At the very least, they have an interest in making certain that if war does start, it is the result of a deliberate decision and is not produced because the opponents, in taking measures they deem to be defensive, push each other into an attack in self-defense—so-called pre-emptive war. In short, with modern technology, arms (at least, certain types of them) are themselves a factor of tension. As a result, arms control acquires new significance. This is the theme of the essays, reproduced below, by Thomas Schelling and Leo Szilard. Schelling deals with the problem of achieving stability through tacit understandings; Szilard, with stability by means of formal agreements. (See below, Chapters 18 and 19, pp. 361 ff. and 376 ff.)

No single aspect of the arms race contributes more to insecurity than the fear of surprise attack. The power of modern weapons and the speed of their delivery make it possible for a country to be destroyed in a matter of hours. The measures it takes in what it conceives to be self-defense may increase instability—for they may be interpreted by the opponent as a prelude to attack. Where the advantages of a first blow are so great—perhaps even decisive—the temptation to launch a pre-emptive war may be overwhelming. Any consideration of arms control almost inevitably returns to the problem of surprise attack.

Almost equally serious is the problem posed by conflicts that break out among the minor powers. The emergence of so many new states and their integration into the international system would produce difficulties even if the Communist countries did not actively promote chaos. There is always the possibility that local disputes may spread and engulf the nuclear powers. It may be to their interest to reduce the likelihood of the outbreak of war, or, if that is impossible, to provide safeguards so that it does not automatically spread into a general conflagration.

There is also the problem of the diffusion of nuclear weapons to still more countries. The greater the number of countries able to launch nuclear war, the greater is the risk of accident. Though some consequences of nuclear diffusion have been exaggerated and though not all of them are inevitably destabilizing, there is no doubt that this issue requires the most urgent attention. A serious effort to think through the implications of what has been called the "nth-country" problem is all the more essential because the 1960's represent perhaps the last decade during which it can still be dealt with. The Nuclear Test Ban Treaty represents a small initial step in this direction. Statements by President Kennedy and

Secretary of State Dean Rusk (see below, Chapters 20 and 21, pp. 392 ff. and 402 ff.) supply the rationale for this effort.

At the same time, the factors that make negotiations on arms control so important also set its limits. While schemes for arms control could prove highly useful in reducing the tensions caused by weapons themselves, they should not be considered a substitute for dealing with the political causes of the Cold War. Until progress is made toward solving these more fundamental problems, measures for arms control can ameliorate but not remove the climate of distrust. Edward Teller has consistently emphasized the dangers and ambiguities inherent in arms-control schemes in a climate of international tension.

EIGHTEEN

THOMAS C. SCHELLING

Managing the Arms Race

[Editor's Note: Two occasionally contradictory considerations must shape national security policy in the nuclear age: the consequences of a decision for the society making it; and the effects of the same decision on the behavior of possible opponents. On one level, national security policy involves mobilization of national resources. On another, it is a form of tacit bargaining by which potentially hostile nations adjust their relations. Professor Schelling's concern is to transform this bargaining from a haphazard into a deliberate and rational process. He is interested in determining how unilateral programs can be transformed into a coordinated system of maximum stability.

This article complements another essay by Professor Schelling, "Nuclears, NATO and the 'New Strategy' " (see above, Chapter 9), in which he was concerned with harmonizing strategic doctrines among friends—specifically, the United States and its NATO partners. In this essay, Professor Schelling deals with the even more complicated problem of how potential enemies can concert their strategic doctrines and programs in order to achieve maximum stability. According to Professor Schelling, what appears as an arms race contains elements of arms control. A relationship of conflict at the same time includes complicated forms of international negotiation. And the reverse is also true. Any form of arms reduction must be seen in relation to the sanctions against violation and the risks of evasion.]

In earlier eras, American armed forces in peacetime were maintained on a stand-by basis. Except for minor interventions, as in Cuba and Nicaragua, the peacetime function of the armed forces

EDITOR'S NOTE: Reprinted with permission from *National Security: Political, Military, and Economic Strategies in the Decade Ahead*, edited by David M. Abshire and Richard V. Allen and published for the Hoover Institution on War, Revolution, and Peace by Frederick A. Praeger, Publishers (New York, 1963).

was to stay alive. Their purpose was to maintain a capacity for mobilization in the event of war. The enemy was the budget. The participation of our armed forces in foreign policy was modest until war broke out or was imminent, at which point war policy virtually dominated foreign policy.

The present is different. American armed forces are the principal instrument for diplomacy with an important set of countries —the countries we recognize as potential enemies. Military deployment, the defense budget, and weapon decisions are not just preparations for war: they are a means of communication to the Soviet bloc. The stationing of troops in Europe, the pre-emptive landing of troops in Lebanon, the call-up of reserves, the alert status of the Strategic Air Command, the dispatch of a battle group to Berlin, and even the blockade of Cuba are at least as important in what they do to Soviet expectations as in what they do to Western capabilities.

In other words, military policy in this era is concerned with enemy intentions, not just capabilities. The idea of "deterrence" assumes that we can not only estimate enemy intentions but influence them. And we do it by conveying to the Soviet Union an appreciation of how the Western nations will react. Our military policy is continually concerned with manipulating enemy expectations. For that purpose, we confront potential enemies with threats of resistance and punishment for misbehavior and with assurances that they will not receive gratuitous punishment if they stay within bounds.

Much of our policy is concerned with making believable to the Russians a pattern of American response. In cases where they might doubt we are sufficiently resolute (or foolhardy) to react violently to their intrusions, we often try to get ourselves into a position that leaves no doubt—a position where the choice is made for us, or where the costs in leadership, reputation, and prestige in failing to respond as promised would be so intolerably high that we could not but react as we had threatened.

The Soviet Union engages in the same process of military diplomacy. Each of us, furthermore, tries to erode or to undermine the other's threats and to detach each other's military force from political commitments, in order that the other's threatened response, not being obligatory, may not be forthcoming. This is a continuous bargaining process between potential enemies, each having substantial capacity to damage the other but only at substantial cost to itself. Each continually tests and probes; each

tries to burn its bridges to show that it cannot be expected to retreat. Each tries at times to help the other to discover a bridge
by which it can gracefully retreat in the hope that, if graceful retreat by the other is possible, graceful retreat may occur.[1]

With respect to what we call "aggression"—overt penetration
of political boundaries with military force—this process of deterrence and brinkmanship is taken for granted. But the bargaining process is less explicit and less self-conscious where domestic
arms preparations are concerned. We threaten the Soviets that if
they seek strategic advantage by invading Turkey or Iran we shall
react with military violence. We do not so explicitly threaten that
we shall react with military violence if the Soviets seek military
advantage through procurement of a large missile and bomber
force or if they seek to deny us an effective force by building missile and bomber defenses. On the whole, we consider war, even a
very limited war, an overt act calling for a military response; we
do not consider arms preparations, even when directed against us,
an overt provocation requiring or justifying hostilities.

Nevertheless, in principle, an arms build-up with hostile intent
might be met with a military response. The concept of preemp-
tion suggests that "hostilities" can be initiated by an enemy country within its own borders, entailing quick military response.
Mobilization of armed forces has typically been considered nearly
equivalent to a declaration of war. At the outbreak of World War
I, "deterrent threats," unfortunately unsuccessful, were aimed at
domestic acts of mobilization as well as against overt aggression.
And preventive war against an arming opponent has been a lurk-
ing possibility at least since the early Greek city-states.[2]

[1] Alfred Vagts' discussion of European "armed demonstrations," though
less inclusive than the arms-race phenomena discussed here, is highly suggestive. "Since the seventeenth century, governments have not maintained armies
and navies merely for the purposes of making war and maintaining order at
home. The existence of armed forces in peacetime was also designed to have
a continuous or occasional diplomatic effect. . . . As bodies charged with
potential violence, a number of their actions could be made highly demonstra-
tive, pointing to an application of the force presented, with more to come if
necessary." *Defense and Diplomacy* (New York: 1956), p. 231.

[2] "The Corinthian delegates: 'You Spartans are the only people in Hellas
who wait calmly on events relying for your defense not on action but on making people think that you will act. You alone do nothing in the early stages to
prevent an enemy's expansion; you wait until your enemy has doubled his
strength. Certainly you used to have the reputation of being safe and sure
enough; now one wonders whether this reputation was deserved. The Persians,
as we know ourselves, came from the ends of the earth and got as far as the

More recently, the United States has engaged in directly coercive military threats to deny the Soviet Union the military advantage of advance deployment of missiles. While Cuba is probably best viewed as a political and geographical Soviet move, it can also usefully be viewed as a Soviet effort to achieve quickly and cheaply an offensive military advantage. An interesting question is whether a comparable crash program within the Soviet Union to acquire a first-strike offensive force might be eligible for comparable sanctions.

As a matter of fact, arms-build-up bargaining does seem to take place, though in a less explicit fashion than the overt territorial bargaining that takes the form of alliances, declarations of commitment, and expressions of retaliatory policy. During most of the Eisenhower administration, the American defense budget was a self-imposed restraint on the Western arms build-up. The motivation may well have been mainly economic, but it is a fair judgment that part of the motivation was a desire not to aggravate an arms race. Even when the assumed "missile gap" created grave concern about the vulnerability of American retaliatory forces in 1959 and the Strategic Air Command displayed a lively interest in the rapid enlargement of an airborne alert, the administration was reluctant to embark on crash military programs, and there was some evidence that its reluctance was a preference not suddenly to rock the arms-race boat. Moreover, among the many inhibitions on civil defense in this country over the last several years, one was a desire not to add a dimension to the arms race, not to appear frantically concerned about general war, and not to destabilize the defense budget.

There have also been direct efforts to negotiate understandings about the relation of armed forces on both sides. With the exception of the test ban, these have come to nothing; and the test ban, whatever combination of good and harm it may have done so far, pertinently illustrates the combination of threats and reassurances that, at least implicitly, go with any bargaining process. In addi-

---

Peloponnese before you were able to put a proper force into the field to meet them. The Athenians, unlike the Persians, live close to you, yet still you do not appear to notice them; instead of going out to meet them, you prefer to stand still and wait till you are attacked, thus hazarding everything by fighting with opponents who have grown far stronger than they were originally.' " Thucydides, *The Peloponnesian War*, tr. Rex Warner (Penguin Books, 1954), p. 50.

tion to the argument, "We won't if you don't," there has been the argument, "And we will if you do."

But the bargaining goes further than that. In the early summer of 1961, in response to provocative Soviet statements about Berlin, President Kennedy deliberately called up reserves and raised the defense budget. The evident purpose was not only to increase quickly our preparation for a military emergency in Berlin, but also to impress on the Soviets the costs and dangers of aggravating the arms race by provocative action, an arms race that was not yet nearly as furious as it might be. Khrushchev's "retaliatory" announcement of Soviet increases is surely better interpreted as "negotiation" than as just military preparation.

And when the summit conference in Paris collapsed in May, 1960, in the wake of the U-2 incident, Khrushchev showed his sensitivity to this bargaining process. In response to a reporter's question why American forces had gone on some kind of alert the night before, he remarked that it was probably the American administration's attempt to soften up American taxpayers for a defense budget increase. In that remark, he showed himself perceptive of the arms-build-up bargaining that goes on between us and alert to the early symptoms of an aggravated arms race.

In a less articulate way, we surely do relate our arms programs to Soviet programs, and they relate theirs to ours. Our estimated "requirements" for bombers, missiles, submarines, and ground forces are related to what we believe will be the forces opposing them. Our bomber build-up in the 1950's was a reflection of the expected Soviet bomber forces and air defenses. The "missile gap" of the late 1950's spurred not only our research and development but also our weapon procurement. The most recent appropriations for Minuteman, Polaris, and other strategic forces must relate to U.S. intelligence on what the Soviet Union may confront us with in the years to come.

Presumably the Soviets, too, have to make their long-range military plans with a view to the expected capabilities of the United States and other countries in future years. Whether the Soviets aim at superiority, equality, or some acceptable ratio of inferiority, they have to have some idea of whether American missiles year by year throughout this decade will be numbered in the scores, hundreds, or thousands.

Implicitly, then, if not explicitly, each of us in his own program must influence the other in some fashion. The influence is surely complicated and uneven, indirect and occasionally irrational, and undoubtedly based often on inaccurate projections of each other's programs. But the influence is there. The Soviet Union may not have realized when it lofted its first Sputnik into orbit that it was doing for American strategic forces what the Korean invasion had done earlier to Western military programs. They might have guessed it; and even if they did not, in retrospect they must be aware that their early achievements in rocketry were a shot in the arm to American strategic-weapon development. Whether the Soviet Union got a net gain from making the West believe in the missile gap in the late 1950's may be questionable, but it is beyond question that both our bomber and our missile forces were enhanced in qualitative performance, and some of them in quantity, by our beliefs.

The Korean War was undoubtedly the most dramatic postwar demonstration of how much Western military programs are a response to a perceived threat. The Greek civil war and the more recent Berlin crises had a similar effect. Overt aggression appears to be more provocative than domestic military programs in this respect, but some interaction between both sides' long-term military programs is always evident. Recently, Soviet boasts about an anti-ICBM capability have probably spurred greater American interest in problems of penetration and interception. Boasts, of course, are different from the real thing. But the same principle is involved; the difference is only one of evidence.

Here it becomes clear that the so-called "inspection" problem, widely argued in relation to disarmament, is really no more relevant to disarmament than to armament. We always have our "inspection" problem. With or without disarmament agreements we have a serious and urgent need to know as accurately as possible what military preparations the other side is making. Not only for overt political and military responses around the world, but even for our own military programming, we have to know something about the quantity or quality of military forces that oppose us. In deciding whether to plan for 20 or 200 Polaris submarines, for 500 or 5,000 Minutemen, in deciding whether the RS-70 will have special capabilities against particular targets, in reaching decisions on the value and the performance of defenses against ICBM's, in deciding what to include in the payload of a missile we build and how to configure our missile sites, we have to estimate the likely military forces that will confront us year after year throughout the planning period.

We have to use what information we can get, whether from unilateral intelligence or from other sources. If we decide unilaterally to be just as strong, twice as strong, or ten times as strong as the Soviet Union over the next decade, our need to know what it is doing is as important as if we had a negotiated agreement that we should be just as strong, twice as strong, or ten times as strong over the decade.

The difference is, apparently, that, under disarmament agreements, it is acknowledged (at least in the West) that each side needs information about what the other is doing. It is even acknowledged that each ought to have an interest in displaying its program to the other in the interest of maintaining the agreement. But this should be equally true without any agreement: the Soviets in the end may actually have suffered from our belief in the missile gap, much in the way they would suffer under a disarmament agreement that provided us insufficient assurance about the pace of their own program. If we insist on a given ratio of superiority and drastically overestimate what the Soviets have, not only do we spend more money but *they* must, too. They have to try to keep up with us; and in so doing may "justify" *ex post facto* the program that we had set afoot on the basis of our original exaggerated estimates.

Once this interaction between armed forces of both sides is recognized and acknowledged, it is hard to see that "arms control" adds anything new in principle. Acknowledging "arms control" as a legitimate and almost inevitable part of the interaction process may help to increase both sides' consciousness of the bargaining relation between them. It may help to improve communications between both sides (although it may, as it often seems to at Geneva, just add noise to the channel). The role of information in the arms race may become better understood, and we may become more aware of the possibility of "deterring" Soviet military preparations as well as deterring overt military acts.

But, at least unconsciously, each side surely is aware of the "feedback" of its program on the other's future program, both qualitative and quantitative. It is doubtful that a country as hard-pressed economically as the Soviet Union would maintain, year after year, a military program without regard to the size and character of Western military programs. They could undoubtedly do more; they unquestionably would save valuable resources by doing less. In the short run, there is great inertia in defense budgets, probably in the Soviet Union as well as here; in the longer run, it can hardly be supposed that Soviet military forces, both in the aggregate and in detailed composition, will be derived from Marxist-Leninist principles that do not take enemy strength and intentions into account.

In the short run, we can presumably base our military plans on decisions the Soviet Union has already taken and programs it has already set afoot. There is substantial lead time in the procurement and deployment of weapons, and for some period, measured in years rather than months, it is probably safe to *estimate* enemy programs rather than to think about *influencing* them. At least, it is probably safe to estimate them rather than to try to influence them in the downward direction. We could probably boost Soviet military production within a year or two, just as they could boost ours by their actions; it is unlikely that either of us would slack off drastically on account of any short-run events—short of a change in regime or the discovery that one's information has been wholly wrong for several years. (The fading of the "missile gap" did not reverse the decisions it had earlier provoked.)

But in thinking about the whole decade ahead—in viewing "the arms race" as an interaction between two sides (actually, among several sides)—we have to take some account of the "feedback" in our military planning. That is, we must suppose that over an appreciable period of years Soviet programs respond to what they perceive to be the "threat" to them, and in turn our programs reflect what we perceive to be that "threat" to us. Then, by the end of the decade, we may be reacting to Soviet decisions that in turn were reactions to our decisions early in the decade; and vice versa. The Soviets should have realized in 1957 that their military requirements in the middle 1960's would be, to an appreciable extent, a result of their own military programs and military public relations in the late 1950's.

This is the feed-back process in principle, but its operation depends on the fidelity of perception and information, biases in the estimating process, lead time in military procurement decisions, and all of the political and bureaucratic influences that are brought to bear by inter-service disputes, budgetary disputes, alliance negotiations, and so forth.

An important question is just how sensitive either of us actually is to the other's program. To approach that question, we ought to inquire into the processes by which either of us reacts to the other. These reactions are surely not just the result of a coolly calculated and shrewd projection of the other side's behavior and a coolly calculated response. Nor do the military decisions of either side result simply from rational calculations of an appropriate strategy based on some agreed evaluation of the enemy. Partly they do, but partly they reflect other things.

First, there may be a certain amount of pure imitation and power of suggestion. There is usually a widespread notion that, to excel over an enemy, one has to excel in every dimension. There seems to be a presumption that, if the enemy makes progress in a particular direction, he must know what he is doing; we should make at least equal progress in that direction. This seems to be the case whether in economic warfare, nuclear-powered aircraft, foreign aid, ballistic-missile defenses, or disarmament proposals. This particular reaction seems to be based on hunch; it may be a good one, but it is a hunch.

Second, enemy actions may simply remind us of things we have overlooked, or emphasize developments to which we have given too little attention.

Third, enemy performance may have some genuine "intelligence value" in providing information about what can be done. The Soviet Sputnik and some other Soviet space performances may have had some genuine value in persuading Americans that certain capabilities were within reach. The U.S. detonation of nuclear weapons in 1945 must have been comparably important in making clear to the Soviet Union, as to everyone else, that nuclear weapons were more than a theoretical possibility and that it was perfectly feasible to build a weapon that could be transported by airplane.

Fourth, many decisions in government result from bargaining among services or among commands. Soviet performance or Soviet emphasis on a particular development may provide a powerful argument to one party or another in a dispute over weapons or budget allocations.

Fifth, many military decisions are politically motivated, inspired by the interests of particular congressmen or provoked by press comment. Soviet achievements that appear to be a challenge or that put American performance in a poor light may have, beneficially or not, some influence on the political-decision process.

And in all of these influential processes, it is not the true fact but beliefs and opinions based on incomplete evidence that provide the motivating force.

I see no reason to suppose that the Soviet Union reacts in a more rational, more coolly deliberate way, than the West. Russians surely suffer from budgetary inertia, interservice disputes, ideological touchstones, and the intellectual limitations of a political bureaucracy, as well as from plain bad information. Furthermore, both we and the Soviet Union play to an audience of third countries. Prestige of some sort is often at stake in weapon-development competition; and a third-area public exercises some unorganized influence in determining the particular lines of development that we and the Soviets are motivated to pursue.

On the whole, the evidence does not show that the Soviet Union understands this interaction process and manipulates it shrewdly. The Korean War, in retrospect, can hardly have served the Soviet interest; it did more than anything else to get the United States engaged in the arms race and to have NATO taken seriously. The Soviets may have been under strong temptation to get short-run prestige gains out of their initial space successes; perhaps they lamented the necessity to appeal to a public audience in a fashion that was bound to stimulate the United States. Whatever political gains they got out of the short-lived missile gap which they either created or acquiesced in, it not only stimulated Western strategic programs but possibly gave rise to a reaction that causes the Soviets to be viewed more skeptically at the present time than their accomplishments may actually warrant. Maybe the Soviets were just slow to appreciate the way Americans react; or maybe they, too, are subject to internal pressures that keep them from pursuing an optimal strategy in the arms race. But if on their own they do not understand the extent to which Western programs are a reaction to theirs, perhaps we can teach them. Do we want to teach them? How would we go about teaching them?

One possibility is that we do not want to teach them. We are economically superior to the Soviets and will hold that advantage for some time if not indefinitely. Perhaps we want to maximize the strain on the Soviet economy by our influence on the Soviet defense budget. Making them try to keep up with us in an expensive arms race may be a way to retard them economically. Alternatively, making them try to keep up with us in some other expensive race—for the moon or for the underdeveloped countries—may be a way to limit what they can channel into the arms race. In a sense, those who want to maximize the tempo of the arms race to strain the Soviet economy and those who would like to divert resources to a "peace race," with emphasis on economic aid and all that, are both proposing that we use our economic advantage to strain the Soviets' defense budget.

A quite different policy would be to persuade the Soviets that the arms race is something they just cannot win. This would involve two parts: first, to persuade them that *if* we choose to outmatch them in military assets, we have the economic strength to do so; second, to persuade them that we have determined to pursue that goal, outdoing whatever they do.

Historically, this kind of thing has happened. Samuel P. Huntington examined a number of qualitative and quantitative arms races during the century since about 1840, and he does find instances in which one power eventually gave up challenging the supremacy of another: "Thus, a twenty-five year sporadic naval race between France and England ended in the middle 1860's when France gave up any serious effort to challenge the 3:2 ratio which England had demonstrated the will and the capacity to maintain. Similarly, the Anglo-German naval race slackened after 1912, when, despite failure to reach formal agreement, relations improved between the two countries and even Tirpitz acquiesced in the British 16:10 ratio in capital ships." He points out, though, that "in nine out of ten races the slogan of the challenging state is either 'parity' or 'superiority.' Only in rare cases does the challenger aim for less than this, for unless equality or superiority is achieved, the arms race is hardly likely to be worth while."[3] The latter statement might, however, be more relevant to a pre-nuclear period in which military force was for active defense rather than for a deterrent based on retaliation potential. "Minimum deterrence" or something like it may not have had a good counterpart in the nineteenth century.

Our question, then, is whether it might be possible and worth while to attempt to make clear to the Soviet Union that any effort to achieve strategic superiority over the United States—or even any substantial parity—is too unlikely of success to be worth the cost.

Consider a missile race for purposes of illustration. Suppose that we have solved the complex problem of comparing Soviet forces in the aggregate with our own and that one can speak in very crude terms of a numerical ratio. Suppose that we design and present to Congress our long-term defense-budget plans not in terms of a given size of force to confront a foreseeable threat, but as a functional relationship between the Soviet force expected

[3] Samuel P. Huntington, "Arms Races: Prerequisites and Results," *Public Policy*, ed. Carl J. Friedrich and Seymour E. Harris (Cambridge, Mass.: Harvard University Press, 1958), pp. 57, 64.

at any given point in time and the appropriate U.S. force.[4] Suppose, just for illustration, that we decide to have a force equal to three times the Soviet force, no matter what. Then, the defense budget is presented only as an estimate of what would be required by this ratio, with the understanding that we would actually do whatever the facts determined under this ratio. Suppose this policy were bolstered with congressional resolutions or with new defense-budget legislation prescribing that some specified ratio vis-à-vis the Soviets be maintained. Could this be done and communicated in such a way as to leave the Soviet Union under no doubt about American resolution to maintain a stipulated ratio of superiority? And what might be the Soviet response, once they appreciated it?

Alternatively, without being quite so arrogant or patronizing as to legislate some specified superiority in perpetuity, we might use our behavior or private and subtle communications to inform the Soviets that we had every intention of staying ahead in the arms race—that we would continually glance back to see how they were doing and would accommodate our speed accordingly. What alternatives would then confront them?

It is hard to believe that the Soviets could openly acknowledge that they were reconciled to perpetual inferiority. It may even be extremely difficult for them to acknowledge it to themselves. It might, however, be possible to discourage very substantially their genuine expectations about what they could accomplish in the arms race. In particular, we might demonstrate to them—if, in fact, it is demonstrable—that a good first-strike capability was not in the cards for them, at least not sufficiently likely to make it a wise gamble of the resources invested in the attempt. It might be possible to ease them into some kind of "minimum-deterrence" posture.

It still has to be decided whether we want to discourage them in this way. It may be wiser to let them spend futilely on a losing race rather than to show them where it will all end so they can cut back and use the money elsewhere. It might be even wiser, if we can get away with it, to tantalize them with the prospect of strategic parity, so that they continually slight their ground forces, their foreign aid programs, and domestic investment in the vain hope of overtaking us strategically.

Essentially, this process of discouraging the Soviets in the arms

---

[4] Relative, not absolute, force goals were not uncommonly legislated by the British and German governments prior to World War I. See Winston S. Churchill, *The World Crisis: 1911–18* (London: 1943), pp. 75–81.

race is no different from trying to persuade them that they are getting nowhere by pushing us around in Berlin. In Berlin, as in Cuba, we are trying to teach them a lesson about what might have been called "peaceful coexistence," if the term had not been discredited by Soviet use already. We did, in the Cuba event, engage in a process intended to teach the Soviets something about what to expect of us and to discourage them from making future miscalculations that might be costly for both of us. In the vicinity of Berlin we have been trying, not without success, to persuade them that certain courses of action are doomed to futility.

I am suggesting that we might want to consider teaching them similar lessons with respect to the arms build-up itself. We might not use the same techniques of education—direct military confrontation and threats of military hostilities—but the principle is much the same. We would instead seek an equivalent of a Formosa Resolution in the arms-race arena.

It does seem worth while to have some design for managing the arms race over the next decade or two. It is prematurely defeatist to suppose that we could never persuade the Soviets, at least tentatively, that this was a race they could not win. The principle of containment ought to be applicable to Soviet military preparation. However constrained they are by an ideology that makes it difficult for them to acknowledge that they are bested or contained, they must have some capacity for acceptance of the facts of life. But it would be up to us to make our response appear to be a fact of life.

I cannot suggest that the Soviets could be taught, once and for all, that crime does not pay. To tame a beast so that it no longer has any interest in consuming its keeper is an ambitious prospect; to teach it that a vigilant keeper cannot be overcome, and will make the attempt painful, may be feasible. And while one may hope that sustained discouragement may eventually lead to tameness, the urge to relax vigilance would have to be resisted.

This is a kind of "arms-control" objective. But it differs from the usual formulation of arms control in several respects. First, it does not begin with the premise that arms agreements with potential enemies are intrinsically obliged to acknowledge some kind of parity. (But since there are many different ways of measuring military potency, it might be possible to permit an inferior power to claim—possibly even to believe in—parity according to certain measures.) Second, it explicitly rests on the notion that arms bargaining involves threats as well as offers.

It may be impolite in disarmament negotiations explicitly to threaten an aggravated arms race as the cost of disagreement. But, of course, the inducement to agree to any reciprocated modification of armaments must be some implicit threat of the consequences of failure to agree. The first step towards inducing a potential enemy to moderate his arms build-up is to persuade him that he has more to lose than to gain by failing to take our reaction into account. Perhaps it is not altogether unwise deliberately to plan and to communicate a somewhat excessive military build-up ratio relative to the Soviet force in order to enhance their inducements to moderate their own program. (This sort of thing is not unknown in tariff bargaining.)

Finally, this discussion has raised the question whether we might not profitably be more explicit about the kind of arms build-up bargaining that takes place in any case between the Soviets and ourselves. We always have an implicit threat, whether we intend it or not, that an intensified Soviet arms build-up will lead to an intensification here. We might make the explicit threat stronger, and we might articulate the kind of power relationship that we would demand and settle for.

This discussion has for the most part assumed that the arms race is a matter of "more" or "less," a matter of quantity. Of course, it is not. There is a difference between a first-strike force and a second-strike force, even though it is not as clear-cut as theoretical discussions assume. There is a difference between weapons systems designed for counterforce tasks and systems mainly designed for the destruction of cities. There is a difference between good and poor facilities for command and control. There is a difference between weapons so co-located with cities as to oblige the destruction of cities in a counterforce war and weapons substantially separated from cities.

Some dimensions of the arms build-up are not of the character suggested by the term "arms race." There are facilities that are not competitive: facilities to minimize false alarm, facilities to prevent accidental and unauthorized acts that might lead to war, and many other improvements in reliability. That is to say, it may be no disadvantage to one side that the other make progress on those particular capabilities. Furthermore, some developments are more purely defensive or deterrent than others, some more offensive or pre-emptive. A missile-hardening race is not the same as a missile-numbers race. Getting across to the Soviets the kind of reaction they can expect from us therefore involves more than quantitative planning; it may involve getting across the kinds of weapons programs that would appear less provocative and those that would appear more so. The Cuban affair is a reminder that there can be a difference.

If, in our attempts to plan a decade or more ahead, we take seriously the problem of arms-race management and consider the interaction between our programs and the Soviets', we have to engage in quite a new exercise: thinking about the kind of military-force posture that we would like the Soviets to adopt. Typically in discussions of military policy we treat the Soviet posture either as given or as something to be determined by factors outside our control, to which we must respond in some adequate way. As a result, nothing appears to be gained by thinking about *our* preferences among alternative *Soviet* postures, doctrines, and programs. But if we begin to examine how we might influence the Soviet posture, we have to consider which alternative Soviet developments we prefer and which we would deplore.

Quantitatively, this requires us to decide whether we want a maximal or a minimal Soviet effort. Qualitatively, it requires us to consider alternative Soviet weapons systems and force configurations. The kinds of arguments we occasionally have in this country about first-strike versus second-strike forces, the merits of active and passive defenses of the homeland, a counterforce or a city-busting general-war doctrine, and a mix of forces between intercontinental and limited-war capability—all of these arguments we can also imagine taking place within the Soviet Union, too. If we are to have any influence on the outcome of those arguments, diffuse and indirect though it may be, we have to decide in what direction we want to exert it.

A main difference, then, between military policy for the longer run and military policy for the shorter run is this: the longer the run considered, the more the arms race takes on the character of a two-sided adaptive system rather than a pair of unilateral programs. Actually, of course, there are more than two sides; neither the Western Alliance nor the Soviet Bloc is single-minded in its interests and policies. If we look a decade or more ahead, the world may become less polarized than it is now. By the time that we have learned to think of the process as a two-sided interaction, rather than as a pair of unilateral programs, it may have ceased to be just two-sided.

NINETEEN

LEO SZILARD

"Minimal Deterrent" vs.
Saturation Parity

[*Editor's Note: Thomas Schelling's article on "Managing the Arms Race" (Chapter 18) explored how even unilateral arms policy can produce incentives for an opponent to act in a way to enhance stability. In the following essay, the late Professor Leo Szilard discussed how some areas of mutual interest could form the basis for explicit agreements to reduce the level of arms.*

According to Professor Szilard, only one valid objective exists for national security policy: a level of nuclear armaments sufficient to inflict unacceptable damage in a counterblow. This is called minimum deterrence and is in sharp contrast to Secretary McNamara's concept of multiple options, according to which the United States should retain the capability to conduct many kinds of nuclear operations, including some confined to purely military objectives. Professor Szilard insists that a choice between these two approaches is crucial, particularly since both of the major nuclear powers are on the verge of achieving "saturation parity," that is, the capability to destroy the entire urban population of the opponent. Once that stage is reached, a new and more intensive arms race is likely to begin. Professor Szilard argues that the Soviet Union might be prepared to enter into an agreement for a step-by-step reduction of nuclear armaments to a minimum deterrent level. He believes that effective inspection procedures are possible and urges measures against the proliferation of nuclear weapons.]

THE "MINIMAL DETERRENT"

We are close to the point where America and Russia could destroy each other in any degree, and, therefore, one would perhaps

EDITOR'S NOTE: Reprinted with permission from the *Bulletin of the Atomic Scientists*, March, 1964. Copyright 1964 by the Educational Foundation for Nuclear Science, Inc., 935 East 60th Street, Chicago, Illinois 60637.

think that the arms race is about to come to an end. In fact, a new arms race may be just around the corner.

Russia may before long deploy antimissile-missiles in defense of her rocket-launching sites. For such a defense to be effective, it is only necessary to prevent a ground-burst of the incoming rockets, and this is, quite possibly, an attainable goal. Thus, the administration might find itself under Congressional pressure to double, or triple, the number of Minutemen scheduled to be built in order to overcome Russia's defense of her bases.

Russia may go further and also deploy antimissile-missiles for the defense of some of her larger cities. If she does, we would be forced to do likewise. There is this difference, however: Russia could deploy antimissile-missiles around a few of her largest cities and stop there, but if we deployed antimissile-missiles around any of our cities, the administration would be under pressure to deploy such missiles around every one of our cities.

Because fallout can kill most people in a city if Russia were to explode suitably constructed bombs at some distance from the city, it would make little sense for us to deploy antimissile-missiles around our cities without also embarking on a program of building fallout shelters for the protection of the population of these cities.

Economic considerations might slow Russia's build-up of her antimissile defenses sufficiently to make it still possible for us to avoid such a new arms race by reaching an agreement with Russia on a cut-off in the production of bombs and rockets.

Russia would perhaps agree to such a cut-off—as a first step—if America and Russia were to reach a meeting of the minds on reducing their strategic striking forces, step by step, to a level *just sufficient* to inflict "unacceptable" damage in a counterblow in case of a strategic strike directed against their territory.

An agreement providing for a reduction of America's and Russia's strategic striking forces to such a "minimal" level would also have to provide for adequate measures of inspection. It would take very stringent measures of inspection indeed to make sure that no bombs and rockets whatever remain hidden in Russia, but as long as we retained a striking force large enough to inflict unacceptable damage on Russia in a counter-blow, we could be satisfied with rather limited measures of inspection, we would need to have just enough inspection to make sure that Russia would not secretly retain a strategic striking force large enough to be capable of destroying a significant portion of the "minimal" striking forces we retained. The same considerations also hold true, of course, in the reverse for Russia.

Many of those who joined the Kennedy Administration in 1961 have come to believe that we would be much more secure in the years to come if we concluded with Russia an agreement based on the concept of the minimal deterrent. In the course of the last year, Russia has accepted the notion that America as well as Russia may retain a small strategic striking force until the "end of the third stage" of the "disarmament agreement," and that inspection shall not be limited to equipment which is to be destroyed, but be extended also to equipment which is being retained.

We shall have to explore whether the Russians mean the same thing as we do when they appear to accept the principle of the "minimal deterrent." We shall be able to discover this, however, only if we first find out what we mean ourselves when we speak of this principle.

We may as well start out by asking ourselves how large the strategic forces retained would need to be in order to fulfill their function.

If Russia retained twelve rockets and bombs of one to three megatons each that could reach their target, then her counter-blow could demolish twelve of our largest cities, totaling more than 25 million inhabitants. Clearly, this would be unacceptable damage, since in none of the conflicts which may be expected to arise in the foreseeable future would we be willing to pay such a price for the sake of attaining the political objectives involved.

Because Russia has fewer large cities, we might have to retain about forty bombs if our retaliatory counter-blow is to demolish Russian cities housing more than 25 million people.

Both America and Russia could maximize their immunity to undetected violations of the agreement by maintaining a certain balance between land-based long-range rockets and submarine-based rockets, within the limitations set by the agreement.

The warheads carried by antimissile-missiles may have to be limited to perhaps twenty kilotons each and to a total of, say, three megatons for Russia and for America alike. The deployment of antimissile-missiles around cities may have to be prohibited.

It is my contention that we need to reduce the strategic striking forces down to the level of the "minimal deterrent" as soon as possible, because of the perils we face when we reach the end of the current transitional period.

Had a conflict between Russia and America led to an armed clash a few years ago and had, at some point along the line of escalation, Russia made a sudden attack against America's strategic air bases and rocket bases, then America's "residual striking capacity" would have been sufficient to demolish, in a counter-blow, all of Russia's sizable cities. But if, conversely, America had made such an attack against Russia's air bases and rocket bases of *known location*, Russia's residual counter-blow could not have caused any comparable destruction.

Today, America's strategic atomic striking forces are presumably still superior to those of Russia, perhaps by a factor of between three and ten, in the number of hydrogen bombs that they could deliver; presumably, America could maintain this kind of numerical superiority in the years to come. She could not, however, by doing so, keep Russia from steadily increasing her "residual striking capacity." In recent years, Russia has steadily proceeded to harden her rocket-launching sites and build additional submarines capable of launching long-range rockets. Today, she has reached the point where her "residual counter-blow" would be sufficient to demolish most of America's major cities on the eastern seaboard and some of her cities in the west. This is a higher price than America would be willing to pay for reaching her political objectives in any of the conflicts that might be expected to occur in the predictable future. In other words, Russia's "residual striking capacity" today would be sufficient to inflict "unacceptable damage" on America. Conversely, America's residual striking capacity would be sufficient today to *demolish all of Russia's cities of more than 100,000.*

It might be true that America today would still be able to recover from an all-out atomic war, whereas Russia would lose all of her cities of more than 100,000 and thus suffer a destruction of her society from which she would not recover.

In the situation in which we find ourselves at present, we no longer try to "deter" Russia with threatening a massive strategic strike against her cities. We realize that such a threat would come very close to being a threat of murder and suicide, and clearly not believable in any conflict in which major American interests might be at stake, but not America's existence as a nation. Instead, we are currently maintaining a military posture that threatens to lead step by step to an escalation of the war and ultimately to our accepting "unacceptable" damage, in return for the virtually complete destruction of Russia's society. We maintain this military posture in order to discourage Russia from embarking on any military conquest.

Right after World War II, the security of Western Europe was threatened by the combination of Communist pressure from the inside and the possibility of a Russian military intervention from the outside. Today, the Russians would be exceedingly unlikely to embark on a conquest of Western Europe, whether or not we maintained our current military posture, but—because of the military posture we maintain—if a war broke out, as the result of a border incident or an uprising in East Germany, it would be likely to escalate and to end up with an exchange of strategic atomic strikes between America and Russia.

Presumably, only conventional weapons would be used at the outset of such a war. At some point during the see-saw of fighting, Russia might be tempted, however, to send her troops in hot pursuit across the prewar boundary, and they might penetrate deep into Western territory. In case of a deep penetration of Western Europe by Russian troops, our plans call for the use of tactical weapons, not only in combat against troops which have penetrated the pre-war boundary, but also against the lines of communications of the Russians in East Germany, Poland, and Russia herself. If, conversely, certain NATO units were to penetrate into East Germany, the Russians would presumably bomb communication lines in Western Europe, including the ports where American troops disembark. Because the size of tactical bombs ranges all the way from one to several hundred kilotons, there is no substantial gap between where tactical bombings end and where strategic bombings begin. Thus, a war that neither America nor Russia wanted could easily end up in an all-out atomic war between them.

The risk that such a war in Europe might end up in an all-out atomic war is the price we pay for maintaining our present military posture. To my mind, this is far too high a price to pay for deterring Russia from something that she wouldn't be likely to do anyway.

A meaningful agreement on arms control based on the concept of the minimal deterrent would limit not only the number of the strategic bombs retained, but also the number, as well as the size, of the tactical bombs retained. The size of these bombs might be limited to one kiloton; America, as well as Russia, might each be limited to 300 such bombs.

The total tonnage of the tactical bombs retained by either side would thus amount to only a few per cent of the total tonnage of the strategic bombs retained by them but still it would amount to about ten per cent of the tonnage of high explosives dropped during the last world war.

By establishing a wide gap between the size of the tactical bombs retained, one kiloton, and the size of the strategic bombs retained, presumably about one megaton or larger, one may establish a clear distinction between bombs which might be used against troops in combat and bombs which have been retained only to be used in a counterblow, in retaliation for a strategic strike.

America ought to resolve and to proclaim that she will not resort to the use of tactical bombs if there is a war in Europe, except in case of a 100-mile penetration of Western Europe by Russian troops and would then use them only within the Western side of the prewar boundary—as long as Russia imposes similar limitations upon herself. Then, if a war were to start in Europe which neither America nor Russia wanted, it would be less likely to end up with an exchange of strategic strikes between America and Russia.

Even the limited numbers of tactical bombs retained could have an important effect on the course of such a war, and their effect could be to slow it down and stabilize a front across Europe, provided that America and Russia imposed upon themselves the restraints spelled out above. For if Russian troops were to cross the prewar boundary in hot pursuit and penetrate 100 miles into Western Europe, with America in possession of tactical bombs the Russians could not very well mass troops and conventional armor at any point in front of the American defense line in sufficient strength to break through that line. Conversely, Russia would gain the same advantage from her possession of tactical bombs if certain NATO units were to cross the pre-war boundary and were to penetrate one hundred miles deep into Eastern Europe. The fear that atomic bombs might be dropped on troops massed for a breakthrough would thus tend to stabilize a front across Europe, giving time for tempers to cool and for ending the war by a settlement. However, no agreement providing for arms control would be likely to withstand the strain of a *protracted* war in Europe.

SATURATION PARITY

In the last few years, Russia has steadily proceeded with the building of submarines capable of launching rockets and with the hardening of her long-range rocket bases, located on Russian territory. It is clear that, in time, Russia must reach the point where her "residual striking capacity" would be large enough to demolish all of America's sizable cities. *At that point, Russia will have achieved parity of saturation.* Russia may reach saturation parity, at a modest economic sacrifice, within a very few years.

General Curtis LeMay said, in a major speech of December 17, 1963, that those who argue that the United States has an extensive "over-kill" favor cutting American strategic striking forces so they would only be capable of hitting cities. He said that such a reduced force would leave the United States too weak "to destroy the enemy's nuclear forces before they destroy us," and that America's maintenance of "superior counter-force strength" gives American policy-makers the widest range of credible options for controlled responses to aggression at any level. According to General LeMay, this paid off during the Berlin and Cuban crises, in which the United States forced Russia to back down and won her political objectives because the Russians knew that the United States had a clear margin of strategic nuclear strength.

I do not propose to take issue with General LeMay at this point, except to say that the "deterrent effect" of America's margin of strategic nuclear strength obviously comes to an end when the striking forces of the Soviet Union reach saturation parity with those of the United States. If our "margin" was in fact responsible for Russia's yielding in the Berlin and Cuban crises, then if another similar crisis were to occur after Russia reaches saturation parity, we would no longer have any reason to expect that Russia would yield.

Had Russia not yielded in the Cuban crisis of October, 1962, and had her ships continued on their course to Cuba in defiance of America's proclamation of a partial naval blockade of that island, American warships would have sunk Russian ships. No one can say how far escalation would have gone and whether Russia, being unable to resist America in the Caribbean, would have retaliated elsewhere, perhaps in Europe.

General LeMay believes that, if it had come to an armed clash in the Cuban crisis, the Russians would have put an end to escalation at some point along the line. But even if one were to accept this view, one could still not predict which of the two countries would take the first step to halt escalation if a similar clash were to occur a few years hence in the symmetrical situation of saturation parity. And, if it is no longer possible to say who would put an end to escalation, then also one cannot predict just how far escalation might go. In saturation parity, escalation might go to the point where all of America's and all of Russia's cities of more than 100,000 are demolished.

Manifestly, saturation parity presents a threat to the survival of our society.

Let us now consider how saturation parity may be expected to affect our allies in general and Western Germany in particular.

Let us ask ourselves, for example, what would have happened if there had occurred a few years ago a major uprising in East Germany against the established government and if substantial units of armed West German volunteers had moved into East Germany to assist the insurgents. Presumably, at first one would not have known with certainty whether these volunteers were acting with the tacit approval and active participation of the West German government or whether they were acting against its wishes and in disregard of its orders. Had such a contingency occurred a few years ago, the odds are that America would have extended protection to West Germany against the strategic striking forces of Russia on the ground that America must prevent the destruction of West German military power. America would have been likely to extend such protection to West Germany whether Germany was or was not the aggressor, and if there had been any doubt on this score, Germany would have been given the benefit of the doubt.

If a contingency of this sort were to occur in the years to come and if the Russians were to fear that the clash might escalate into all-out atomic war, they might decide to knock West Germany out of the war by dropping, all at once, five to ten hydrogen bombs on West German cities. Having done this, Russia would then be in a position to speak to America as follows: "German aggression forced us to do what we did, lest the clash on arms escalate into an all-out atomic war, which neither Russia nor America wants. We realize that America could now respond by demolishing one Russian city after another, but for every Russian city that America may demolish, Russia would demolish one American city. Let's be rational about this. What has happened, has happened; let's see now where we go from here. Russia does not intend to occupy any West German territory and she is willing to put up a few per cent of her industrial output to help rebuild the cities of West Germany, provided her contribution is matched, dollar-for-dollar, by America."

The Russians would hardly assume that the Americans would respond in a rational fashion if they were to drop bombs on American cities but, in the contingency described above, they might, rightly or wrongly, expect a rational response if they demolished German cities only and refrained from extending their attack to America's own territory.

The nations of Europe are becoming gradually aware of the situation they will face in saturation parity and they are beginning to ask themselves whether each may not have to maintain a strategic striking force under its own control in order to safeguard its own security.

Few people contemplate with equanimity the possibility that Germany may acquire a substantial atomic striking force. There are those in America who believe that we might keep Germany from wanting to have such a striking force under her own control by setting up a strategic striking force under the joint control of America and Germany, with perhaps a few other nations joining in. The multilateral strategic striking force under discussion would be equipped with 200 Polaris missiles, enough to demolish 200 cities if all of them were to reach their target, yet it would not give the Germans what they need in saturation parity so long as America can veto the use of this force. There is reason to believe that the Germans propose to participate in it only because they assume that it may be possible for them to get rid of the veto.

The creation of such a strategic striking force would make it possible to endow West Germany, by the mere stroke of a pen, with a striking force of her own, a force corresponding in size perhaps to the financial stake that Germany would have in the joint force. Those Americans who advocate the setting up of such a joint force in order to keep the Germans from having a force under their own control follow the principle of the lesser evil. Following this same principle could lead to transferring to Germany control of a part of the joint force later on if the Germans should proclaim that they would otherwise build a substantial striking force of their own.

It is doubtful whether control over atomic bombs can be kept from the Germans by a gadget like the multilateral nuclear striking force, or for that matter by any gadget, *and it is probably true that in the long run it would be impossible to prevent the proliferation of atomic bombs if saturation parity were to prevail.*

Under an agreement based on the concept of the "minimal deterrent" that would leave Russia in possession of, say, twelve bombs and rockets, Russia would put herself at a disadvantage if, in the contingency discussed above, she were to use up five to ten of her twelve bombs and rockets in a "first strike" against German cities. If she were to do this, she would have only two to seven bombs and rockets left in comparison to the forty bombs and rockets retained by America, and she would therefore put herself at a disadvantage in the crisis that would follow her attack. In this sense, an agreement limiting Russia to twelve bombs and rockets would provide protection to the cities of our allies in Western Europe, but this would be true only if we could be certain that Russia would not secretly retain, say, another twelve strategic bombs and rockets which are operational or could be made operational on short notice. The measures of inspection instituted at the outset of the agreement would not be likely to give any certainty in this regard, because initially we might have to be satisfied with measures of inspection which give us assurance that *Russia cannot secretly retain a striking force large enough to be capable of destroying a significant fraction of our minimal striking forces.*

It is therefore necessary to explore what additional measures of inspection would provide our allies with the protection they need, and whether such measures would be acceptable to Russia.

In an extended conversation I had with Chairman Khrushchev in October, 1960, I said that, even if Russia were willing to admit international inspectors in unlimited numbers, it would not be possible for us to be sure that there would not remain a few bombs and rockets hidden somewhere in Russia which were operational or could be made operational very quickly. I told Khrushchev that I believed that the Soviet Government could reassure the world in this regard only if they were to create conditions in which we could rely on a Soviet citizen reporting secret violations of the agreement to an international authority. He got the point, got it fully, and his answer was very gratifying.

I would not attach as much significance to this as I do if I had not accidentally discovered in December of the same year, when I attended the Pugwash meeting in Moscow, that some of our colleagues of the Soviet Academy of Sciences scheduled to attend this meeting had been given a detailed report of my conversation with Chairman Khrushchev. In this report, Khrushchev was quoted to have said to me that, for the sake of making general disarmament acceptable to the United States, the Soviet Government would give serious consideration to creating conditions that would make it possible for the world to rely on a Soviet citizen reporting violations of the disarmament agreement to an international authority.

After the Pugwash meeting, I stayed on in Moscow for about a month and had numerous private conversations with our Russian colleagues. I wanted to discover, most of all, whether the Soviet Government could, if it wanted to, create conditions in which the world could rely on Russian citizens reporting violations of the disarmament agreement. I finally concluded that this would not be easy but that it would be done, provided the arms control agreement offered Russia a substantial increase in her security and permitted the Soviet Government to divert substantial funds from armament to other uses.

I believe that it would be much easier to get the Soviet government to accept very far-reaching measures of inspection for the sake of obtaining an objective that makes sense to them than to get them to accept quite limited measures of inspection for the sake of any "first steps" which would not offer any major direct benefits to Russia.

Speaking before the Economic Club of New York on November 18, 1963, Secretary McNamara stated that we have now more than 500 operational long-range ballistic missiles and are planning to increase their number to more than 1,700 by 1966. In addition, we have today more than 500 bombers on quick-reaction ground alert. In his speech, McNamara refers to the "damage-limiting capability of our numerically superior forces," which I take to mean our capability of making massive attacks against Russia's strategic air bases and rocket bases.

It is my contention that we will not be able to negotiate a meaningful agreement on arms control until we are willing to give up what General LeMay calls our "capability to destroy the enemy's forces before they destroy us," and that by giving it up we will gain more than we would lose.

If I were given an opportunity to cross-examine General Lemay, I would ask him what contingencies he has in mind when he speaks of "destroying the enemy's nuclear forces before they destroy us." It would then turn out that, while we could invoke the "damage-finding capability of our numerically superior forces" by making a massive attack against Russia's strategic air fields and rocket-launching sites of known location in certain conceivable contingencies, these contingencies are very contrived and most unlikely to occur.

The "damage-limiting capability of our numerically superior forces" might have a certain marginal value in the least probable contingencies, but in the most probable contingency, if a war were to break out which neither Russia nor America wanted, then our capability of making a sudden massive attack against Russia's rocket-launching sites of known location would render an escalation of the war more likely than less likely. For if the superiority of our strategic striking forces is anywhere as great as General LeMay claims, the Russians might fear at some point that our next move in the pursuit of war would be the waging of a massive strike against their rocket bases of known location, and at that point they might be driven to launch rockets against our cities and the cities of our allies from all of their bases that are vulnerable to an attack.

There is no need to belabor this point, however, because the "superiority of our strategic striking forces" of which General LeMay speaks is at best a vanishing asset. Within a few years, we shall have saturation parity, and in that situation Russia will no longer have to fear a massive strike against her rocket bases of known location.

In saturation parity—as far as the strategic striking forces are concerned—America and Russia will find themselves in a fully symmetrical situation, and at this time the only meaningful choice before us is between the symmetrical situation of saturation parity, in which both America and Russia maintain strategic striking forces at a high level, and another symmetrical situation in which they both maintain strategic striking forces at a "minimal level."

More and more people within the administration realize that it would be futile and increasingly dangerous to continue to use our strategic striking forces as a deterrent the way we used them in the past, and that *these forces must be used only for the purpose of threatening a counterblow in case of an atomic attack directed against our territory.* Those who take this position inevitably arrive in time at realizing that both America and Russia would gain, rather than lose, in security by reducing their strategic striking forces from the level of saturation parity to the level of the minimal deterrent.

We must ask ourselves at this point under what conditions would Russia want to have an agreement based on this concept, and want it strongly enough to be prepared to pay the price in terms of the measures of inspection needed.

I think that Russia would have no desire to enter into such an agreement unless she could be sure that it would not be necessary for her later on to abrogate the agreement and to rebuild her atomic striking forces, so to speak, from scratch. Thus, Russia would have to be convinced that Germany is not going to have under her own control an atomic striking force, and also that China would not build a substantial atomic striking force of her own.

I do not know what it would take to induce China to forgo having atomic bombs, but it is conceivable that China might be willing to go along with an agreement on arms control that would leave America and Russia in possession of minimal strategic striking forces, provided that in return America would agree not to resort to the use of either strategic or tactical atomic bombs in the Far East and Southeast Asia, and to set up an atom-free zone that would include these areas.

There are those who say that America could not agree to forgo the use of atomic bombs in the Pacific because it might be necessary to use atomic bombs in the defense of Formosa.

Quite similar views were voiced at the Disarmament Conference of the League of Nations which was held in Geneva in the 1930's. At issue at this conference was the elimination of the bomber plane from the national arsenals and the outlawing of bombing from the air. At one point during the negotiations, Anthony Eden, who was at that time a civil servant, told the conference that His Majesty's Government could not be a party to the outlawing of bombing from the air. He said that, from time to time, the Royal Air Force engaged in bombing the mud huts of the unruly tribes of the northern frontier of India and that this was the only effective way to keep these tribes from making periodic incursions into Indian territory. Some people have no sense of proportion.

It is probably true that we cannot have general disarmament without also having a far-reaching political settlement. The conclusion of an agreement providing for arms based on the concept of the minimal deterrent need not, however, await a political settlement in Europe or elsewhere. Moreover, in view of our current estimates of Russia's military manpower and resources, we need no longer insist that the reduction of the number of bombs and rockets to a minimal level must be accompanied by the reduction of the conventionally armed forces. Rather, we may rely on economic considerations to limit the armies maintained by the nations of Europe, including Russia.

The reduction of the strategic striking forces to the "minimal" level spelled out above need not take place at the very outset of the agreement, all at once, but there would have to be substantial step-by-step reductions to intermediate levels soon after the agreement goes into force. What matters is not so much in what steps and just how fast a reduction of the strategic striking force takes place, but rather whether America and Russia are in full agreement on the level of the "minimal" striking forces which would be retained under the agreement.

In these circumstances, Russia and America could enter into conversations aimed at reaching a meeting of the minds on the reduction of the number of atomic bombs and rockets to a minimal level and could thereafter seek the concurrence of the other nations, including Germany and China.

If these conversations were carried far enough to convince the Russians that an agreement could be negotiated without running into any major hitches, then the Russians might accept a product cut-off in bombs and rockets even before an agreement based on the minimal deterrent is fully spelled out with the i's dotted and t's crossed, and for the purposes of a production cutoff the United States would presumably be satisfied with inspection limited to production facilities of known locations.

POSTSCRIPT

I do not know anyone in the Department of Defense who would not on the whole agree with the analysis, given above, of the perils of saturation parity and the security to be gained from the "minimal deterrent." Some people in the Defense Department might say that I am overstating my case, that it would not be sufficient for us to retain forty large bombs and rockets because only a certain fraction of the Polaris and Minutemen launched would reach their target, the rest being duds. They might say therefore that, instead of forty bombs and rockets, we ought to retain perhaps 100 or 150 of them. These are not essential differences because, as the reliability rating of our rockets increases, their numbers could be more or less automatically reduced.

Others in the Defense Department might say, not publicly but privately, that I am understating my case when I say that Russia may achieve saturation parity within a few years, and that Russia has achieved saturation parity already. This is not an essential difference either.

I should perhaps add that I am not personally acquainted with any of those in the Defense Department who are part of the "military-industrial complex" of which President Eisenhower spoke in his Presidential farewell address, and who have a vested interest, emotional or otherwise, in maintaining large strategic striking forces. Even though these people do not occupy top positions in the administration, they must be reckoned with because they have considerable influence in Congress.

While the "military-industrial complex" might well attempt to block any significant reduction of our strategic striking forces, when such a reduction becomes a "clear and present danger" our current failure to make any decisive progress on arms control must not be attributed to them. Rather, this failure is mainly due to our method of negotiating with the Russians.

We have not made, thus far, and are not likely to make in the predictable future, a formal proposal on arms control which the Russians could accept as it stands, for fear that the proposal would become the starting point of "horse trading" and that we would end up with an agreement that might endanger our security.

Each time we introduce a new feature into our proposals which we hope could create a basis for negotiations, it takes the Russians about six months to respond. This sluggishness of the Russian response is not surprising because there are few people concerned with the problem of arms control working within the Russian government who are capable of coping with the unprecedented problems involved. These few men have their hands full taking care of the day-to-day problems and cannot devote much time to long-term planning. This may well be the reason why the Russians take so long to respond, even if we propose something that clearly would be in their interest to accept.

The number of those working within our administration who can cope with these problems is larger, but it is not large. These men are plagued by being uncertain as to what the Russians would be likely to accept and also what Congress would be likely to accept.

What the Russians would accept and what Congress would accept depends on whether the administration can make them understand the need to avoid a new arms race, the perils which we face in the current situation, and the advantages that an agreement based on the concept of the minimal deterrent would hold for all concerned. Unless it becomes somehow possible to arrange for greatly improved communication between the administration and the Soviet Government, on the one hand, and between the administration and Congress, on the other hand, no decisive progress toward a meaningful agreement on arms control is going to be made. Instead, we might be taking a number of little steps, like the test ban, for instance. These little steps improve the international climate, but if nothing decisive is done before long, the climate may keep on improving and improving until there is a new crisis, and then we shall be back where we started from. To make progress is not enough, for if the progress is not fast enough, something is going to overtake us.

TWENTY

JOHN F. KENNEDY

Nuclear Testing and Disarmament

[Editor's Note: In 1958, the United States and the Soviet Union voluntarily ceased nuclear testing pending the negotiations of a test ban treaty. On September 1, 1961, the Soviet Union ended this moratorium and conducted a series of tests lasting two months. On September 5, 1961, President Kennedy authorized a resumption of United States tests, and on March 2, 1962, he announced that the United States would resume atmospheric testing in the latter part of April.

Later in 1962, the Cuban missile crisis brought the two major nuclear powers into direct confrontation. Whether as a result of this clash or for other reasons, the United States, Great Britain, and the Soviet Union, in July, 1963, concluded a treaty banning nuclear tests in the atmosphere, outer space, and under water.

This speech by President Kennedy was delivered from the White House and transmitted by television and radio on March 2, 1962. It provides the President's full explanation of the reasons for the United States' resumption of testing at that time, and of the President's hope for the eventual agreement to a test ban treaty.

In the following selection (Chapter 21), Secretary of State Dean Rusk provides a more detailed discussion of the issues concerning the Nuclear Test Ban Treaty.]

Seventeen years ago, man unleashed the power of the atom. He thereby took into his mortal hands the power of self-extinction. Throughout the years that have followed, under three successive Presidents, the United States has sought to banish this weapon from the arsenals of individual nations. For of all the awesome responsibilities entrusted to this office, none is more somber to contemplate than the special statutory authority to employ nuclear arms in the defense of our people and freedom.

But until mankind has banished both war and its instruments of destruction, the United States must maintain an effective quantity and quality of nuclear weapons, so deployed and protected as to be capable of surviving any surprise attack and devastating the attacker. Only through such strength can we be certain of deterring a nuclear strike, or an overwhelming ground attack, upon our forces and allies. Only through such strength can we in the free world—should that deterrent fail—face the tragedy of another war with any hope of survival. And that deterrent strength, if it is to be effective and credible when compared with that of any other nation, must embody the most modern, the most reliable, and the most versatile nuclear weapons our research and development can produce.

The testing of new weapons and their effects is necessarily a part of that research and development process. Without tests—to experiment and verify—progress is limited. A nation which is refraining from tests obviously cannot match the gains of a nation conducting tests. And when all nuclear powers refrain from testing, the nuclear arms race is held in check.

That is why this nation has long urged an effective world-wide end to nuclear tests. And that is why in 1958 we voluntarily subscribed, as did the Soviet Union, to a nuclear-test moratorium during which neither side would conduct new nuclear tests and both East and West would seek concrete plans for their control.

But on September 1 of last year, while the United States and the United Kingdom were negotiating in good faith at Geneva, the Soviet Union callously broke its moratorium with a two-month series of more than forty nuclear tests. Preparations for these tests had been secretly under way for many months. Accompanied by new threats and new tactics of terror, these tests—conducted mostly in the atmosphere—represented a major Soviet effort to put nuclear weapons back into the arms race.

Once it was apparent that new appeals and proposals were to no avail, I authorized on September 5 a resumption of U.S. nuclear tests underground, and I announced on November 2—before the close of the Soviet series—that preparations were being ordered for a resumption of atmospheric tests and that we would make whatever tests our security required in the light of Soviet gains.

This week, the National Security Council has completed its review of this subject. The scope of the Soviet tests has been carefully reviewed by the most competent scientists in the country. The scope and justification of proposed American tests have been carefully reviewed, determining which experiments can be safely deferred, which can be deleted, which can be combined or conducted underground, and which are essential to our military and scientific progress. Careful attention has been given to the limiting of radioactive fallout, to the future course of arms-control diplomacy, and to our obligations to other nations.

Every alternative was examined. Every avenue of obtaining Soviet agreement was explored. We were determined not to rush into imitating their tests. And we were equally determined to do only what our own security required us to do. Although the complex preparations have continued at full speed while these facts were being uncovered, no single decision of this administration has been more thoroughly or more thoughtfully weighed.

Having carefully considered these findings, having received the unanimous recommendations of the pertinent department and agency heads, and having observed the Soviet Union's refusal to accept any agreement which would inhibit its freedom to test extensively after preparing secretly, I have today authorized the Atomic Energy Commission and the Department of Defense to conduct a series of nuclear tests—beginning when our preparations are completed, in the latter part of April, and to be concluded as quickly as possible (within two or three months)—such series, involving only those tests which cannot be held underground, to take place in the atmosphere over the Pacific Ocean.

These tests are to be conducted under conditions that restrict the radioactive fallout to an absolute minimum, far less than the contamination created by last fall's Soviet series. By paying careful attention to location, wind, and weather conditions, and by holding these tests over the open sea, we intend to rule out any problem of fallout in the immediate area of testing. Moreover, we will hold the increase in radiation in the Northern Hemisphere, where nearly all such fallout will occur, to a very low level.

Natural radioactivity, as everyone knows, has always been part of the air around us, with certain long-range biological effects. By conservative estimate, the total effects from this test series will be roughly equal to only 1 per cent of those due to this natural background. It has been estimated, in fact, that the exposure due to radioactivity from these tests will be less than one-fiftieth of the difference that can be experienced, due to variations in natural radioactivity, simply by living in different locations in this country. This will obviously be well within the guides for general population health and safety, as set by the Federal Radiation Council, and considerably less than one-tenth of 1 per cent of the exposure guides set for adults who work with industrial radioactivity.

Nevertheless, I find it deeply regrettable that any radioactive material must be added to the atmosphere—that even one additional individual's health may be risked in the foreseeable future. And however remote and infinitesimal those hazards are judged to be, I still exceedingly regret the necessity of balancing these hazards against the hazards to hundreds of millions of lives which would be created by any relative decline in our nuclear strength.

In the absence of a major shift in Soviet policies, no American President—responsible for the freedom and safety of so many people—could in good faith make any other decision. But because our nuclear posture affects the security of all Americans and all free men—because this issue has aroused such widespread concern—I want to share with you and all the world, to the fullest extent our security permits, all of the facts and thoughts which have gone into my decision.

Many of these facts are hard to explain in simple terms—many are hard to face in a peaceful world—but these are facts which must be faced and must be understood.

Had the Soviet tests of last fall reflected merely a new effort in intimidation and bluff, our security would not have been affected. But in fact they also reflected a highly sophisticated technology, the trial of novel designs and techniques, and some substantial gains in weaponry. Many of their tests were aimed at improving their defenses against missiles—others were proof tests, trying out existing weapons systems—but over one-half emphasized the development of new weapons, particularly those of greater explosive power.

A primary purpose of these tests was the development of warheads which weigh very little compared to the destructive efficiency of their thermonuclear yield. One Soviet test weapon exploded with the force of 58 megatons—the equivalent of 58 million tons of TNT. This was a reduced-yield version of their much-publicized 100-megaton bomb. Today, Soviet missiles do not appear able to carry so heavy a warhead. But there is no avoiding the fact that other Soviet tests, in the one-to-five megaton range and up, were aimed at unleashing increased destructive power in warheads actually capable of delivery by existing missiles.

Much has also been said about Soviet claims for an antimissile missile. Some of the Soviet tests that measured the effects of high-altitude nuclear explosions—in one case more than 100 miles high —were related to this problem. While apparently seeking information (on the effects of nuclear blasts on radar and communication) which is important in developing an antimissile defense system, these tests did not, in our judgment, reflect a developed system.

In short, last fall's tests, in and by themselves, did not give the Soviet Union superiority in nuclear power. They did, however, provide the Soviet laboratories with a mass of data and experience on which, over the next two or three years, they can base significant analyses, experiments, and extrapolations, preparing for the next test series which would confirm and advance their findings.

And I must report to you in all candor that further Soviet series, in the absence of further Western progress, could well provide the Soviet Union with a nuclear attack and defense capability so powerful as to encourage aggressive designs. Were we to stand still while the Soviets surpassed us—or even appeared to surpass us— the free world's ability to deter, to survive, and to respond to an all-out attack would be seriously weakened.

The fact of the matter is that we cannot make similar strides without testing in the atmosphere as well as underground. For, in many areas of nuclear-weapons research, we have reached the point where our progress is stifled without experiments in every environment. The information from our last series of atmospheric tests in 1958 has all been analyzed and re-analyzed. It can tell us no more without new data. And it is in these very areas of research —missile penetration and missile defense, for example—that further major Soviet tests, in the absence of further Western tests, might endanger our deterrent.

In addition to proof tests of existing systems, two different types of tests have therefore been decided upon. The first and most important are called "effects tests"—determining what effect an enemy's nuclear explosions would have upon our ability to survive and respond. We are spending great sums of money on radar to alert our defenses and to develop possible antimissile systems—on the communications which enable our command and control centers to direct a response—on hardening our missile sites, shielding our missiles and their warheads from defensive action, and providing them with electronic guidance systems to find their targets. But we cannot be certain how much of this preparation will turn out to be useless; blacked out, paralyzed, or destroyed by the complex effects of a nuclear explosion.

We know enough from earlier tests to be concerned about such phenomena. We know that the Soviet Union conducted such tests last fall. But until we measure the effects of actual explosions in the atmosphere under realistic conditions, we will not know precisely how to prepare our future defenses, how best to equip our missiles for penetration of an antimissile system, and whether it is possible to achieve such a system for ourselves.

Secondly, we must test in the atmosphere to permit the development of those more advanced concepts and more effective, efficient weapons which, in the light of Soviet tests, are deemed essential to our security. Nuclear-weapon technology is still a constantly changing field. If our weapons are to be more secure, more flexible in their use, and more selective in their impact—if we are to be alert to new breakthroughs, to experiment with new designs—if we are to maintain our scientific momentum and leadership—then our weapons progress must not be limited to theory or to the confines of laboratories and caves.

This series is designed to lead to many important, if not always dramatic, results. Improving the nuclear yield per pound of weight in our weapons will make them easier to move, protect, and fire— more likely to survive a surprise attack and more adequate for effective retaliation. It will also, even more importantly, enable us to add to our missiles certain penetration aids and decoys and to make those missiles effective at higher-altitude detonations, in order to render ineffective any antimissile or interceptor system an enemy might some day develop.

Whenever possible, these development tests will be held underground. But the larger explosions can only be tested in the atmosphere. And while our technology in smaller weapons is unmatched, we know now that the Soviets have made major gains in developing larger weapons of low weight and high explosive content—of one to five megatons and upward. Fourteen of their tests last fall were in this category, for a total of thirty such tests over the years. The United States, on the other hand, had conducted, prior to the moratorium, a total of only twenty tests within this megaton range.

While we will be conducting far fewer tests than the Soviet Union, with far less fallout, there will still be those in other countries who will urge us to refrain from testing at all. Perhaps they forget that this country long refrained from testing, and sought to ban all tests, while the Soviets were secretly preparing new explosions. Perhaps they forget the Soviet threats of last autumn and their arbitrary rejection of all appeals and proposals, from both the U.S. and the U.N. But those free peoples who value their freedom and security, and look to our relative strength to shield them from danger—those who know of our good faith in seeking an end to testing and an end to the arms race—will, I am confident, want the United States to do whatever it must do to deter the threat of aggression.

If they felt we could be swayed by threats or intimidation—if they thought we could permit a repetition of last summer's deception—then surely they would lose faith in our will and our wisdom as well as our weaponry. I have no doubt that most of our friends around the world have shared my own hope that we would never find it necessary to test again—and my own belief that, in the long run, the only real security in this age of nuclear peril rests not in armament but in disarmament. But I am equally certain that they would insist on our testing, once that is deemed necessary to protect free-world security. They know we are not deciding to test for political or psychological reasons—and they also know that we cannot avoid such tests for political or psychological reasons.

The leaders of the Soviet Union are also watching this decision. Should we fail to follow the dictates of our own security, they will chalk it up, not to good will but to a failure of will—not to our confidence in Western superiority but to our fear of world opinion, the very world opinion for which they showed such contempt. They could well be encouraged by such signs of weakness to seek another period of no testing without controls—another opportunity for stifling our progress while secretly preparing, on the basis of last fall's experiments, for the new test series which might alter the balance of power. With such a one-sided advantage, why would they change their strategy, or refrain from testing, merely because we refrained? Why would they want to halt their drive to surpass us in nuclear technology? And why would they ever consider accepting a true test ban or mutual disarmament?

Our reasons for testing and our peaceful intentions are clear—so clear that even the Soviets could not objectively regard our resumption of tests, following their resumption of tests, as provocative or preparatory for war. On the contrary, it is my hope that the prospects for peace may actually be strengthened by this decision—once the Soviet leaders realize that the West will no longer stand still, negotiating in good faith, while they reject inspection and are free to prepare further tests. As new disarmament talks approach, the basic lesson of some three years and 353 negotiating sessions at Geneva is this: the Soviets will not agree to an effective ban on nuclear tests so long as a new series of offers and prolonged negotiations, or a new uninspected moratorium, or a new agreement without controls, would enable them once again to prevent the West from testing while they prepare in secret.

But inasmuch as this choice is now no longer open to them, let us hope that they will take a different attitude on banning nuclear tests—that they will prefer to see the nuclear arms race checked instead of intensified, with all the dangers that intensification is likely to bring: the spread of nuclear weapons to other nations; the constant increase in world tensions; the steady decrease in all prospects for disarmament; and, with it, a steady decrease in the security of us all.

If the Soviets should change their position, we will have an opportunity to learn it immediately. On March 14, in Geneva, Switzerland, a new eighteen-power conference on disarmament will begin. A statement of agreed principles has been worked out with the Soviet Union and endorsed by the U.N. In the long run, it is the constructive possibilities of that conference—and not the testing of new destructive weapons—on which rest the hopes of all mankind. However dim those hopes may sometimes seem, they can never be abandoned. And however far off most steps toward disarmament appear, there are some that can be taken at once.

The United States will offer at the Geneva conference—not in the advance expectation they will be rejected, and not merely for purposes of propaganda—a series of concrete plans for a major "breakthrough to peace." We hope and believe that they will appeal to all nations opposed to war. They will include specific proposals for fair and enforcible agreements: to halt the production of fissionable materials and nuclear weapons and their transfer to other nations; to convert them from weapon stockpiles to peaceable uses; to destroy the warheads and the delivery systems that threaten man's existence; to check the dangers of surprise and accidental attack; to reserve outer spaace for peaceful use; and progressively to reduce all armed forces in such a way as ultimately to remove forever all threats and thoughts of war.

And of greatest importance to our discussion tonight, we shall, in association with the United Kingdom, present once again our proposals for a separate comprehensive treaty—with appropriate arrangements for detection and verification—to halt permanently the testing of all nuclear weapons, in every environment: in the air, in outer space, under ground, or under water. New modifications will also be offered in the light of new experience.

The essential arguments and facts relating to such a treaty are well known to the Soviet Union. There is no need for further repetition, propaganda, or delay. The fact that both sides have decided to resume testing only emphasizes the need for new agreement, not new argument. And before charging that this decision shatters all hopes for agreement, the Soviets should recall that we were willing to work out with them, for joint submission to the U.N., an agreed statement of disarmament principles at the very time their autumn tests were being conducted. And Mr. Khrushchev knows, as he said in 1960, that any nation which broke the moratorium could expect other nations to be "forced to take the same road."

Our negotiators will be ready to talk about this treaty even before the conference begins on March 14—and they will be ready to sign well before the date on which our tests are ready to begin. That date is still nearly two months away. If the Soviet Union should now be willing to accept such a treaty, sign it before the latter part of April, and apply it immediately—if all testing can thus be actually halted—then the nuclear arms race would be slowed down at last, the security of the United States and its ability to meet its commitments would be safeguarded, and there would be no need for our tests to begin.

But this must be a fully effective treaty. We know enough now about broken negotiations, secret preparations, and the advantages gained from a long test series never to offer again an uninspected moratorium. Some may urge us to try it again, keeping our preparations to test in a constant state of readiness. But in actual practice, particularly in a society of free choice, we cannot keep topflight scientists concentrating on the preparation of an experiment which may or may not take place on an uncertain date in the future. Nor can large technical laboratories be kept fully alert on a standby basis waiting for some other nation to break an agreement. This is not merely difficult or inconvenient —we have explored this alternative thoroughly and found it impossible of execution.

In short, in the absence of a firm agreement that would halt nuclear tests by the latter part of April, we shall go ahead with our talks—striving for some new avenue of agreement—but we shall also go ahead with our tests. If, on the other hand, the Soviet Union should accept such a treaty in the opening months of talks, that single step would be a monumental step toward peace—and both Prime Minister Macmillan and I would think it fitting to meet Chairman Khrushchev at Geneva to sign the final pact.

For our ultimate objective is not to test for the sake of testing. Our real objective is to make our own tests unnecessary, to prevent others from testing, to prevent the nuclear arms race from mush-rooming out of control, to take the first steps toward general and complete disarmament. And that is why, in the last analysis, it is the leaders of the Soviet Union who must bear the heavy respon-sibility of choosing, in the weeks that lie ahead, whether we pro-ceed with these steps—or proceed with new tests.

If they are convinced that their interests can no longer be served by the present course of events, it is my fervent hope that they will agree to an effective treaty. But if they persist in rejecting all means of true inspection, then we shall be left no choice but to keep our own defensive arsenal adequate for the security of all free men.

It is our hope and prayer that these grim, unwelcome tests will never have to be made—that these deadly weapons will never have to be fired—and that our preparations for war will bring us the preservation of peace. Our foremost aim is the control of force, not the pursuit of force, in a world made safe for mankind. But whatever the future brings, I am sworn to uphold and defend the freedom of the American people, and I intend to do whatever must be done to fulfill that solemn obligation.

The Nuclear Test Ban Treaty: Symbol of a New Course

I appear here this morning to support the Treaty Banning Nuclear Weapon Tests in the Atmosphere, in Outer Space, and Under Water. Last week in Moscow, the treaty was signed on behalf of the United States and the other original parties—the United Kingdom and the U.S.S.R. The Senate of the United States now has the Constitutional responsibility to examine this treaty with care so that it may give the President its advice and, I earnestly hope, its consent to a prompt ratification.

The President has given the treaty before you this morning an apt characterization. It is, he has said, "not the millennium. . . . But it is an important first step—a step toward peace—a step toward reason—a step away from war." Since 1789, the Senate has given its consent without reservation to the ratification of 943 treaties. I believe this may well prove one of the most significant occasions for the exercise of that constitutional prerogative.

U. S. Efforts for International Controls

The United States, as the first nation to unleash the power of the atom, recognized from the beginning its awesome potentialities for good and evil. In the less than two decades since the first use of a nuclear weapon, the United States has worked continuously to achieve effective international controls so that the power of the atom might be committed to the improvement, rather than the destruction, of mankind. Disarmament and the control of both nuclear and conventional weapons have been concerns of the highest priority for the three administrations that have borne re-

EDITOR's NOTE: Statement made before the Committee on Foreign Relations, U.S. Senate, August 12, 1963. Representatives of the Senate Armed Services Committee and the Joint Atomic Energy Committee also attended the hearing.

sponsibility for the great issues of peace and war during the atomic era.

Less than a year after the explosions at Hiroshima and Nagasaki, the United States presented its first comprehensive proposal for international control of the atom. As offered by Bernard Baruch at the first meeting of the United Nations Atomic Energy Commission on June 14, 1946, the plan called for the creation of an International Atomic Development Authority with responsibility for control of all atomic-energy activities potentially dangerous to our security, with the power to control, inspect, and license all other atomic activities, and with the duty of fostering the beneficial uses of atomic energy.

During the remainder of the Truman administration, the United States continued to press these proposals in the United Nations and elsewhere. Though the great majority of the countries accepted the basic principles of the plan, the Soviet Union, unfortunately, did not.

President Eisenhower was in office less than three months when he renewed the United States offer for "international control of atomic energy to promote its use for peaceful purposes only and to insure the prohibition of atomic weapons." Two years later, at the summit meeting in Geneva, he personally launched the "open-skies" proposal. Throughout the ensuing years, no matter what the temperature of the cold war, the United States has pursued in every available forum its search for peace through effective and verified disarmament.

These efforts disclosed a wide gap between the approach of this country and that of the Soviet Union to disarmament problems, mainly on the question of inspection and control. In the mid-1950's, therefore, the United States undertook to explore more limited measures. The most promising of these was control of nuclear-weapons testing. There were good reasons for this. All mankind had what might even be described as an instinctive impulse to end the pollution of the air and earth that was a consequence of unrestricted testing. And, while arrangements banning bomb tests could not be wholly self-enforcing, the problem of detection and control seemed manageable. An agreement to stop testing—or not to begin—would not strip a nation of its defenses or carry it too far into the unknown. Here, many felt, was a good point from which to start.

The first Western proposal for control of nuclear tests was submitted to the Disarmament Subcommittee of the United Nations

General Assembly on August 21, 1957. Sponsored by the United States, the United Kingdom, Canada, and France, it called for a comprehensive twelve-month ban on testing. This proposal, however, again encountered the reluctance of Communist states, with closed societies, to accept the international inspection and control required for effective enforcement of a comprehensive ban. On April 13, 1959, after months of inconclusive debate on this issue of inspection and control, President Eisenhower and Prime Minister Macmillan advanced a proposal for a ban on tests in the atmosphere up to an altitude of fifty kilometers. This proposal did not require on-site inspection, since significant tests of this kind could be detected and identified by national systems. Even this, however, was not accepted by the Soviet Union.

When the present administration assumed office, President Kennedy immediately undertook further explorations of the possibility of banning nuclear weapons tests. In 1961, President Kennedy, again with Prime Minister Macmillan, proposed a ban on tests in the atmosphere that would produce radioactive fallout. It was rejected by the U.S.S.R. The full text of a treaty embodying a ban on nuclear tests in the atmosphere, in outer space, and under water was tabled by the United States and United Kingdom delegations at Geneva on August 27, 1962. At the same time, they tabled the text of a comprehensive treaty which provided for on-site inspections for detecting and identifying underground tests.

Before these texts were tabled, there were consultations both with appropriate committees of Congress and with our allies and associates. For the past year, the text of a three-environment test ban has been before the world for comment and discussion. The treaty we have just signed in Moscow and which is now before you is based in its essential elements on the draft tabled in Geneva a year ago. Throughout this period, the concept has remained the same—to take a first step toward the control of nuclear weapons by prohibiting testing in those environments where our national systems are capable of detecting significant violations, leaving for subsequent steps the elimination of those tests that can be detected and identified only with an adequate system of inspection.

Limiting the Risk of Nuclear War

Some may ask why three administrations representing both of our great political parties have devoted so much effort in attempting to make progress toward disarmament and, in particular, toward a ban on nuclear tests when those same administrations were also building a nuclear arsenal of increasing and massive destructive power. The answer lies at the heart of the dilemma which troubles our world.

The values that are the heritage of a free society have been menaced by a Communist bloc armed with the most modern weapons and intent on world domination.

For our nation, this poses a special problem. We must, for our own security and as the leader of the free world, maintain a mastery of the most advanced weapons while technology moves forward at a breathtaking pace. At the same time, we must use all our resources of will and intellect in an effort to halt the burdensome and dangerous competition in weapons that is the somber characteristic of the present world situation.

I recall the comment of a fellow officer in 1945, when we heard about the explosion of the first atom bomb. "War," he said, "has devoured itself." Today, the United States has operational weapons in its arsenal hundreds of times as destructive as that first atom bomb. The Polaris and Minuteman missiles are armed with warheads tens of times as powerful. The Soviet Union also has weapons of great destructive power.

The hard fact is that a full-scale nuclear exchange could erase all that man has built over the centuries. War has devoured itself because it can devour the world.

If our nation is to survive today, we must be able at all times in the absence of the far-reaching disarmament which still eludes us to endure a nuclear attack and deliver counter-blows of vast devastation. As Secretary McNamara will make clear, we have the ability to do so. We intend to keep it that way, lest others be tempted by ambition to abandon reason.

Yet the facts must be faced. No one can realistically think of "victory" in a full-scale nuclear exchange. Last October, during the Cuban crisis, men confronted decisions that might have moved to a nuclear war. That experience has been sobering for all.

No responsible man will deny that we live in a world of vast and incalculable risks. Where decisions may be required in minutes, we must be constantly on guard against the accident or miscalculation that can lead where no one wants to go. A local conflict anywhere around the globe in which the interests of the great powers are engaged might suddenly pose the prospect of nuclear war.

Nor can any responsible person say that we can improve our security by an unlimited arms race extending without relief into the future. On the contrary, great as the risks now are, they would rapidly increase. Arsenals will grow larger, weapons more destructive, the frustrations of stalemate and fear more intense. The risks will increase unpredictably as nuclear weapons become available to more and more countries.

It is against this prospect, which the world must frankly face, that the Senate is asked to consider the present treaty. If there may be marginal risks in it, they are far less in my opinion than the risks that will result if we accept the thought that rational man must pursue an unlimited competition in nuclear weapons.

All three of our Presidents who have borne supreme responsibility for our national security during the nuclear age have found the risks of an unlimited nuclear race far greater than those inherent in safeguarded progress toward arms control.

Provisions of the Treaty

Let me review with you the provisions of this treaty.

The treaty before you is a self-contained document, and it embodies the whole of the agreement. As the President said in his message of transmittal, there are no side arrangements, understandings, or conditions of any kind.

The fundamental obligation is set forth in Article I. That article prohibits nuclear-weapon tests as well as all other nuclear explosions in peacetime in three environments: the atmosphere, under water, and outer space. Underground explosions are permitted as long as the radioactive debris remains within the country where the explosion takes place. Each party also undertakes not to assist any other country, whether or not a party, in conducting nuclear explosions of a kind prohibited under the treaty.

This treaty does not affect the use of nuclear weapons in war. It has to do with nuclear weapon testing in time of peace. Nuclear explosions for peaceful purposes are, however, subject to the same limitations as nuclear weapons tests. This restriction is necessary because it is difficult to distinguish between the two without on-site inspection. It will not mean the end of our Plowshare program. Many of the peaceful experiments and uses in which we are interested can be conducted underground within the limits of the treaty. Dr. Glenn T. Seaborg, Chairman of the U.S. Atomic Energy Commission, will discuss this with you in detail.

Article II provides a procedure for amending the treaty. Amendments may be proposed by any party and are approved by a majority vote. The majority must include the United States, the

United Kingdom, and the U.S.S.R. Amendments do not enter into force until instruments of ratification have been deposited by a majority of the parties, "including the instruments of ratification of all the Original Parties." Thus, no amendment to the treaty can enter into force until it has been considered and approved by the Senate.

It has been said that this amendment process involves a veto. It does. I regard such a veto as essential to the security interests of the United States. Without it, the ban could be extended on terms and conditions that would be unacceptable—as, for example, to underground testing without on-site inspection.

Article II also provides that, if one-third of the parties so desires, a conference may be called to consider amendments, but a conference is not a necessary part of the amending process.

Article III prescribes the procedures for ratification and accession. We hope the treaty will have the widest possible application.

It has been suggested that, by the act of subscribing to the treaty, a regime might gain recognition by parties to the treaty that do not now recognize it. No such effect can occur. In international law the governing criterion of recognition is intent. We do not recognize, and we do not intend to recognize, the Soviet occupation zone of East Germany as a state or as an entity possessing national sovereignty, or to recognize the local authorities as a government. Those authorities cannot alter these facts by the act of subscribing to the test ban treaty. The President made this clear in his press conference of August 1. On August 2, the Department of State issued a formal statement to the same effect. Copies of both should be a part of the record of this hearing.

All this would necessarily follow from the general rule of international law that participation in a multilateral treaty does not affect the recognition status of any authority or regime. But this treaty contains additional safeguards. Treaties typically provide for a single depositary. Article III, however, provides that each of the three original parties will be a depositary of the treaty. No depositary need accept a signature or an instrument of accession from authorities in a territory it does not recognize as a state.

The East German authorities will subscribe to the treaty in Moscow. The Soviet Union may notify us of that act. We are under no obligation to accept that notification, and we have no intention of doing so, but the East German regime would have committed itself to abide by the provisions of the treaty.

By this arrangement we not only assure that no implication of recognition may arise, but we reserve our right to object if later the East German regime should seek to assert privileges under the treaty, such as voting or participating in a conference called under Article II.

Article IV gives any party the right to withdraw from the treaty "if it decides that extraordinary events, related to the subject matter of this Treaty, have jeopardized the supreme interests of its country." A party must give three months' notice of its decision to withdraw. This provision is in our interest. If and when events occur that make testing in any of the three environments necessary for the security of the United States, we will be able to resume. Under the treaty we alone will decide whether extraordinary events have occurred and whether they jeopardize our supreme national interests. We need answer to no tribunal and to no authority other than our own conscience and requirements. We hope that the treaty will last and will grow in strength, but certainly no President of the United States would hesitate to exercise the right of withdrawal if the national security interest requires it.

If the Soviet Union itself were to test in violation of the treaty, the fundamental obligation that is the consideration for our adherence would disappear. In that case the United States could, if it chose, consider itself released from its reciprocal obligation and could resume testing without delay.

U.S. Security Maintained

Under this treaty, the national security of the United States can and will be fully maintained.

This country has learned much from the experience of the last eighteen years. We do not propose to forget those lessons. We have no basis yet for assuming a fundamental change in Soviet objectives. We are still engaged in a contest between free choice and coercion. The President made this clear, and I want to reiterate it here today.

But there is nothing inconsistent between this treaty, or other effectively enforcible arms control agreements, and a policy of vigilance. The same three administrations that have sought disarmament over the past eighteen years have effectively met Communist threats of aggression—in Iran, in Greece and Turkey, in Berlin and Western Europe, in Korea, in Southeast Asia, in Cuba. But whatever may be the fundamental antagonisms between us and the Soviet Union, we have a mutual interest in avoiding mutual destruction.

We shall remain ready to meet further challenges. The treaty permits underground testing. The policy of the United States is to continue to test underground as necessary to our security. Moreover, although we hope for compliance, we cannot discount the possibility that the Soviet Union may violate the treaty. We shall be on the alert for any violations, and we have a high degree of confidence in our ability to detect them. The Secretary of Defense and the Director of the Central Intelligence Agency will discuss this capability in detail. But I am confident that, if significant testing in violation of the treaty takes place, we will know about it. And we will be ready at all times to resume testing in all environments, and promptly, if that should become necessary. Dr. Seaborg will be prepared to deal with these matters in detail.

Concrete Gains

This is a limited treaty. The President listed the things it does not do, and we must keep them in mind in judging its significance. At the same time, if—as seems likely—most of the nations of the world adhere to the treaty, and if they observe its obligations, this will in itself bring concrete gains.

First, the United States and the Soviet Union already have enough nuclear power to inflict enormous destruction on each other. Still, the search for bigger, more destructive weapons goes on. Each generation of major weapons has been more expensive than the last. Each has involved an increasing burden, an increasing diversion of resources from the great unfinished business of mankind. Yet greater armament has not demonstrably brought greater security. The treaty, if observed, should slow this spiral, without damage to our relative strength.

Second, the treaty will help contain the spread of nuclear weapons. Most of the countries with the capacity and the incentive to develop nuclear weapons over the next decade or so have already announced that they will accept the self-denying ordinance of the treaty. While this does not guarantee that they will never become nuclear powers, their renunciation of atmospheric testing will act as a deterrent by making it much more difficult and expensive for them to develop nuclear weapons.

Third, the treaty will reduce the radioactive pollution of the planet. The increased radioactivity from nuclear testing has thus far stayed within tolerable limits, in a statistical sense. But, as the President said, "this is not a natural health hazard, and it is not a statistical issue." Moreover, if testing were not restricted, more and more countries would conduct tests. Many of them would lack either the incentive or the means to minimize the fallout. We have a high obligation to safeguard life and health and the genetic integrity of the human race. Today, no one can say for certain how much fallout is too much. But if this treaty is observed, it will go a long way to assure that we do not transgress the limits.

"A Choice Between the Quick and the Dead"

For eighteen years, we have held the Communist drive in check largely by the deterrent force of our massive military strength. We shall maintain that overwhelming strength until we are certain that freedom can be assured by other means.

But, throughout, we have known that a lasting peace could not be founded upon armed might alone. It can be secured only by durable international institutions and by a respect for law and its procedures. The problem has been to convince the Communist world that its interest also lay in that direction.

The most important thing about the treaty is, therefore, what it may symbolize and what new paths it may open. That, no one can now foretell.

But, as the Senate undertakes its appraisal of this treaty, it is well to recall the vivid statement that Bernard Baruch made to the United Nations when the nuclear age was first upon us: "We are here to make a choice between the quick and the dead. . . . Behind the black portent of the new atomic age lies a hope which, seized upon with faith, can work our salvation. If we fail, then we have damned every man to be the slave of Fear."

For seventeen years, all men have lived in that shadow of that fear. But if the promise of this treaty can be realized, if we can now take even this one step along a new course, then frail and fearful mankind may find another step and another until confidence replaces terror and hope takes over from despair.

TWENTY-TWO

EDWARD TELLER

The Nuclear Test Ban Treaty

[Editor's Note: Ever since the debate over whether or not to build the hydrogen bomb in 1951, the noted physicist Professor Edward Teller has been perhaps the most prominent scientific advocate of continuous and intense research on problems of weapons development. His basic argument has been that the advance of scientific knowledge cannot be halted by international agreement, especially when the agreement is with the Soviet Union. He believes that most arms-control schemes—and certainly the Nuclear Test Ban Treaty— jeopardize the security of the free world. His position has been supported by many senior military officers and by a portion of the United States Senate.]

The President of the United States has asked for a full discussion of the test ban treaty, this most important treaty, which is before you.

Those of us who are worried about this treaty have a clear and strong obligation to put before you our worries. I intend to do this, and I intend to try and do it with complete frankness, and with the proper kind of moderation which the importance of the occasion demands.

I have already told you that I am worried about the treaty, and I want to make it clear at the very outset what the basis of this worry is in general terms.

The purpose of the treaty is to safeguard peace, to make a step toward peace. There cannot be and there is not any difference of opinion on this basic point. Peace has been of the greatest importance at all times, but today, when I know very well how sudden and how devastating war can be, peace is more important than it has been ever before.

EDITOR'S NOTE: Statement made before the Committee on Foreign Relations, U.S. Senate, August 20, 1963.

The reason that I am worried about this treaty is because I believe that this treaty is not a step toward peace but rather a step away from safety, possibly a step toward war.

In January, it will be twenty-five years since I heard, together with quite a few other scientists, at a conference which we organized here in Washington, about nuclear fission. Within a few days, the grave consequences of this discovery had become clear to most of us. This worry has not left me in this past quarter of a century. I want to start out by telling you something about this long period, and by emphasizing one particular point.

This has been a time of extremely rapid development, and it has been a time full of surprises. At no turn did we know what the next step would bring. At no time could most of us predict the future. Yet what we are now trying to do is, essentially, to predict the future, and when some of the best and most outstanding people contradict each other, they do so because the future is necessarily uncertain.

I beg you to have patience with me, to tell you a little of the past in order to put the future into perspective.

During the war, many of us labored diligently and with success on the first nuclear explosion. Even then, the result was a surprise. You may not know it, but on the day when the first nuclear explosive was fired, no serious prediction had succeeded in guessing at the real size of the explosion. All of us underestimated it. After four years of strenuous effort, of theoretical calculations, of careful design, we did not succeed in predicting what was going to happen. We succeeded in making something that was effective, but experiment could not have been replaced by any prediction.

Right after the explosion, shortly after, the director of the laboratory made a statement to me which I will never forget. He said, "We have done an excellent job, and very many years will pass before anybody will be able to improve it in any important detail."

This is an old story now and the point is gone. You know that only six years later another step was taken. That step was taken under the stimulus of another surprise. Most of us believed, and the U.S. intelligence firmly and unequivocably predicted, that the Russians would not have a nuclear explosion for many years. The first Russian test in 1949 was a complete surprise. Some of us got worried. I got very worried about the next surprise that might be in store for us, and we started out on the next step, which the majority of the scientists said could not be done—the thermonuclear explosion.

You know that within a short time that succeeded, with an effect almost a thousand times as great as the first explosion, and that, in turn, was followed within a few months with the Russians producing something that looked very much like a thermonuclear explosion—again, in contradiction to all expectations, to all predictions, to the explicit statements of the intelligence community.

In time, these big explosions triggered another development in the United States, the development of missiles.

Right after the war, the judgment was that accuracy of these missiles could not be great enough to justify carrying the relatively small nuclear explosives available at that time.

With the thermonuclear explosives, there was no longer any possibility to avoid the knowledge. Missiles, very important, could have a deadly significance. Yet while we were getting started on missiles, while General Schreiver* has done the most excellent and the most fantastic job in developing our own missile systems, we still did not realize the great potentialities that rockets would have in space exploration. The 1957 sputnik took us by surprise once again. Intelligence did not alert our government about that important step, and we went into the missile age with deficient preparation.

During our last, big, well-planned test series in 1958, the missile age was still young, and the experiments which we then performed did not have as much relation to our preparation for the missile age as they should have.

Let me explain this. We had succeeded in making big explosions. We had succeeded in making these big explosives light, and while we succeeded we knew we could develop further. I do not claim that the further developments will be of very great additional significance. There is another point which we have neglected.

In 1958, none of us believed in any serious way that missile defense was a realistic possibility. We have not studied the effects, or most of the effects, which are of primary importance in trying to stop a missile, and which are of great importance in defending our own missile sites, which at that time hardly existed, against the attack of incoming missiles.

You all know that in 1958 we went into a prolonged moratorium. Here again, even during the moratorium, while we tried

* EDITOR'S NOTE: General Bernard A. Schreiver, Commander, Air Force Research and Development Command from 1959 to 1961, is presently Commander of the Air Force Systems Command.

hard to foresee what is going to happen, we did not foresee.

In some little respect we succeeded to make an extremely important step.

In 1957, we made our first underground nuclear explosion. It was a small one. I argued long for it and strongly, mostly on the basis that this is an unknown area which we should explore. We explored it in the scientific field, we learned a lot from it, and we learned something else that we did not really expect to learn. We learned something about the possibility of clandestine testing. This was not in my mind when I proposed the 1957 explosion, but when we sat down to the conference table in 1958, as the months went by, it became clearer and clearer that big atmospheric explosions can be policed, that there is real doubt about small atmospheric explosions, and that there is most serious doubt about explosions underground, and also in space; that underground explosions cannot be policed, that this point had to be taken seriously because it became known to us only because of the accident that for other reasons—for reasons of scientific curiosity—we happened to make a test of an underground explosion in 1957.

How important this fact has become later, I don't need to tell you.

You all know what the next surprise is, because surprises in the past are not surprising. In the late summer of 1961, the Russians resumed testing.

We know now that this test series was by far the most powerful—we have reason to believe that it was the most powerful—in the whole history of Russian preparations, and it was the most plentiful, the most repetitious, the most solid ever carried out by any nation.

I don't think that any expert will disagree with me when I say that this test series had to be prepared for many months in advance, and that the preparations had to be expensive, widespread, and should have been open to intelligence information. It is possible, I would even say that it is probable, that the planning of this abrogation took a time longer than a year. Yet, on the day before Khrushchev made his announcement, our government still did not know that a test series was impending.

Here is another surprise, another failure of ours to predict what the future will bring and what the Russians intend to do.

As a result of this test series, the Russians made a big explosion. For one, I can tell you this was no surprise. I wish I could talk about it more: it is interesting, it is slightly relevant, it is classified. But the Russians did have a surprise in store for us, and that surprise was their announcement (and evidence supporting that announcement) that they did make great strides toward missile defense.

In 1961, and in the similarly impressive test series in 1962, the Russians had every chance in the world to make the observations in the atmosphere which are the firm basis of any plan for an effective or half-way effective missile defense, and I say half-way effective in the most serious way.

A few years ago, I firmly believed that missile defense was hopeless. I am now convinced that I was wrong. Stimulated by the Russian statements, we have looked into the matter very thoroughly and I now believe, I am now convinced, that we can put up a missile defense that can stop the attack of any weaker power, such as China, for the next two decades.

In a time when we rightly worry about proliferation we must not neglect our defenses against an attack from a quarter other than Russia. In addition, I also believe that our defense can be partially effective against the Russians. We may not be able to save our cities, we may be able to save our retaliatory capacity, and thereby we may lend force to the argument that we can hit back and that the Russians, therefore, will not hit first. We can make a missile defense, in all probability, that will safeguard at least reasonably strongly built shelters which one can build in great numbers and which we should build.

No matter what we do in missile defense, I still believe that the nuclear war will be very terrible, but missile defense may make the difference between the end of our national existence and our survival as a nation. And, perhaps even more important, missile defense, by deterring the Russians, may make the difference between peace and war.

Excuse me, that I have made this introduction. As you will see, what I have said is relevant in several respects. I have now arrived at the point of the present test treaty. This test treaty is to be viewed in our past experience. I will try to be brief. I hope that the many and complex questions connected with this treaty will be brought out by your questions. I want to concentrate on the main argument for the treaty, and on the main argument against the treaty.

These arguments are extremely important, and I would not like to obscure the issue by trying to give you a bag full of arguments —some important, some not.

The strongest argument, in my mind, for the treaty is to stop the spread of nuclear weapons. We have been worried about such a spread for many years, and rightfully so. We know, today, that it is easy to make nuclear explosions, and that any country that can acquire nuclear materials can make an explosion within a year. Yet it has been claimed that this treaty will stop proliferation. Why?

Secretary Rusk and Secretary McNamara, in their testimony, have spelled out the answer very simply and very clearly. Any nation which signs this treaty will have to test, if it tests at all, underground, and underground testing is more expensive.

On this point, however, there is a simple statement I can make, a simple statement connected with dollars about which there is no doubt. An underground test of a magnitude that has been traditional for the first test of any nation will cost approximately $1 million. This cost, I want to make very clear, is the cost of testing. It does not include the cost of the weapon. It certainly does not include the much bigger cost of the whole development of nuclear reactors or whatever else had to be done to make the material, of the research that went into putting the material together.

This million-dollar figure that I mentioned to you is, I think, slightly higher, not very much higher, than the cost that would be incurred if the test were performed in the atmosphere. But no matter how these two costs compare, once a nation has gone to the expense of developing a nuclear explosive, the additional single million dollars that is needed for underground testing will certainly not be a financial deterrent.

I had an opportunity, a few days ago, to make the statement to Secretary McNamara. He answered that he did not mean the cost in dollars. He meant the psychological and political cost. I am not an expert in psychological and political costs. I am glad to concede that, under this test treaty, the Swedes and the Swiss may refrain from underground testing in order to be as completely in agreement with world opinion as they can be. I doubt whether more dangerous nations will be so deterred. This, as far as I can see, is the argument, and the only argument, against proliferation.

Let me now turn to the main argument against the treaty. This treaty will permit the Russians and us, and anybody else, to develop nuclear explosives underground. This will permit us to perfect not every kind of an aggressive weapon, but very important kinds of aggressive weapons. This treaty, therefore, will not have the direct effect of slowing down the development of aggressive weapons. What it will do is to prohibit us from acquiring the knowledge about effects of weapons—those effects which are of vital importance in ballistic-missile defense.

In the early 1950's, we made plenty of observations on the effects of nuclear explosives on houses, on ships. But in those days, we were not talking about missile silos. In those days, we did not investigate the way how nuclear explosives can be used. We did not investigate the way how nuclear explosives can be used to stop a missile attack.

In the missile age, we have performed only one test series in the atmosphere in 1962. This we have performed with little planning, in a great hurry, and I would like to state that we ended with the conviction that the amount of knowledge that we still desperately need vastly exceeds the knowledge that we already possess. In the same missile age, the Russians have tested in an essentially unrestricted manner.

Secretary McNamara has told you that on missile defense the Russians have probably no more information than we do. How does he know? There are some experiments which are unmistakably designed for missile defense. These are few, but, in very many other experiments, apparatus may have been around, probably was around, that looked at effects relevant to missile defense.

Our information about nuclear explosions in Russia is very limited. What we know firmly is only the great extent of our ignorance. What, in these more than 100 atmospheric explosions, the Russians may have learned about atmospheric tests, about missile defense, we have no better way of knowing than we had a way of knowing whether they prepared a test series in 1961.

On the basis of the past performance of our intelligence, we cannot be comfortable and we cannot say that we know what the Russians know. What we must say is that they had three or perhaps four times more opportunity to find out the relevant facts on missile defense than we had.

I am going to continue to talk to you for a short time about this question of missile defense, and I will do it by referring to a connected important topic.

Secretary McNamara has told you that we are stronger than the Russians, that we have many more missiles, that when they build more missiles, we will know it, and we will outbuild them any time.

Perhaps our intelligence has now improved sufficiently that we can rely upon it. I hope so, although I must also say that of all things where it is difficult to compete with a police state, intelligence is likely to be the most difficult.

But this test ban has nothing at all to do with how many missiles either side builds. This test ban has something to do with knowledge, and it does not have to do so much with knowledge concerning aggressive potentials. It has something vitally important to do with knowledge concerning missile defense, concerning the vulnerability of our retaliatory forces. I believe that the Russians have acquired this knowledge. I believe that, because they have acquired this knowledge, they don't need any more atmospheric tests, and I believe that is why Khrushchev is willing to sign the treaty at present.

In 1960, he wasn't willing to sign, but now he had these magnificent test series of 1961 and 1962. He now knows how to defend himself. He now knows, probably, where the weaknesses lie in our defense. He has the knowledge, and he is now willing to stop and prevent us from obtaining similar knowledge.

If the Russians want to build a big missile force with which to attack us, they can do so legally under the present testing. What they need is knowledge, and that is what they have. What we need is knowledge, and that is what we don't have.

Secretary McNamara has told you that if you don't have enough knowledge about the hardening of our missile sites we will make up for it by building more missiles, by spacing these missiles farther apart, by making them harder. All this costs money. All this costs billions of dollars. What Secretary McNamara is telling you is that he is willing to substitute brawn for brain, and to spend more and more money for defense. This is what has been rightly called an arms race. To acquire more knowledge, to acquire more knowledge in order to know how to defend ourselves, this, I would suggest, is not quite properly called an arms race.

This treaty will not prevent the arms race. It will stimulate it. This treaty is not directed against the arms race. This treaty is directed against knowledge, our knowledge.

Why do we need this knowledge?

Secretary McNamara has told you, and he is right, that we can do a lot about missile defense. We can study the incoming missiles, we can study the decoys, and we can try to see the difference between them. We can perfect our radars, make them harder, more versatile, faster. By underground testing we can develop the best kind of nuclear explosives with which to kill an incoming missile, because when you are shooting at such a fast and uncertain target as an incoming missile, you cannot hit it with a bull's-eye. You need a powerful counter-force, a small nuclear explosion.

Secretary McNamara has said rightly that we can do all that.

But there is one thing, one circumstance he did not explain. He did not explain to you that we must expect not one missile to come against us but five, and not to come alone but to come accompanied by twenty-five decoys. We have to discriminate between these, find out which are the dangerous objects and shoot them down, not some of them but all of them. The first shot that we fire will blind us, and will make us less prepared to shoot against the second missile that comes hard on the heels of the first.

To do that is easy. It is very easy for a powerful country like the Soviet Union. That there is this difficulty we know. To know how big the difficulty, how to circumvent it, what to do about it, needs experimentation and more experimentation. Missile defense is the most complex military operation that I have ever been in touch with. To try to build up our missile defense forces without proper and complete experimentation, experimentation that can be performed faithfully and in a relevant way only in the atmosphere, to do without this experimentation is most hazardous.

No underground tests can take the place of the actual tryout.

The Russians had an opportunity. They had also a motive. Some of you may have read, all of you will have heard, of the recent book by Marshal Sokolovsky (he did not actually write it), which has been translated from the Russian and is now available to us. The title of the book is *Military Strategy*. And if you read that book you cannot be left in doubt about the great importance that the Russians, who had been hurt so badly at the beginning of World War II—the great importance that they place upon air defense and missile defense.

We are still hesitating whether to put in a missile defense. The Russians are working on it. With all the uncertainty that will continue to be with us in this test ban, we may never put in our missile defense.

This test ban has given the Russians the knowledge on the basis of which they can now proceed and spend money in a reasonable way. We do not have the corresponding knowledge.

This is the main argument against the test ban treaty. It weakens our defense, and as long as we have reason to distrust Soviet intentions, the weakness of our defense will invite attack. This is why I say that this treaty is a step, not more than a step, but a step, in the wrong direction.

There are some additional points. Will we know, as Secretary McNamara has said, when the Russians begin to deploy more missiles, more radar? I certainly hope so. I believe it, but I do not believe it with complete assurance, not after the many disappointments we had in predicting what the Russians will do. There is an additional way of no less importance. We should and we may deploy a missile defense which might not be as good as it could be if we had more knowledge but which might be satisfactory anyway—the best we can do, perhaps enough to deter the Russian aggression. But will we help our allies, will we give, as we should give to our allies, defensive missiles, thousands of them, as we should?

If we don't, if we defend ourselves, and leave our allies undefended, our allies who are closer to Russia, who are menaced by the cheaper and more numerous intermediate range missiles, if we do that, I think it will be a clear and strong psychological force that will drive the alliance apart.

But I am sure you are raising the question in your minds: could we, would we, in any case, in giving these missiles to our allies, giving them thousands of nuclear warheads, would that not have the same effect as proliferation? Would it not invite war by accident? Would it not risk misuse? I am saying to you that we can do it without any of these risks. We can tie missiles to their sites, nuclear warheads to the missiles. We can put into the whole system an electronic program such that the missile will not explode before it has reached an altitude where it can do no damage on the ground. We can make sure that the missile will explode or otherwise be destroyed before it leaves the territory of the country that had fired the missile. These missiles cannot be used for anything except to shoot down flying objects. It can be used for only one purpose, for a justified self-defense.

I believe that at least in the spirit of our present laws, we could do this, and I think we should do this if we ever get a reasonably satisfactory missile defense, and this is the way how together with our allies, with common work and common results we could strengthen our alliance.

But, as far as I read the text of this treaty, this treaty prevents any such measure. The treaty says that we must not help, aid, encourage, or in any way participate in somebody else's nuclear test explosion or in any other nuclear explosion carried out by somebody else.

If we give the Belgians a defensive missile, and a button to push, and they only have to push the button and the missile goes off and explodes over Belgium harmlessly, if we make sure, as we must make sure that they can push the button in self-defense any time without calling Washington, because these missiles are flying only for minutes and if the emergency arises you must push the button and make no phone calls.

If we do that, have we not aided, encouraged, and participated in potential explosion?

If the Russians would claim to have installed such defensive missiles in Cuba, would we take it?

We have no other possibility in order to save our alliance, to make the defenses common. Yet to me it seems that this treaty, unless very thoroughly amended, will erect a big barrier between our allies and ourselves in a most important area of defense.

I could add that the treaty calls into question our ability to come to the aid of a country in Asia in case this country could be invaded.

What if the Chinese march over the Himalayan passes and we have reason to believe that India will be conquered in six weeks— long before we had time to send over men or supplies. We still could close the Himalayan passes by nuclear explosives. But the treaty says we must not perform a nuclear test explosion or any other nuclear explosion.

I know very well that Secretary Rusk has stated that in case of war we can use these explosions. Still, I am uneasy. I do not know what the precise legal situation is, and I know that even if legally the treaty says the opposite of what it appears to say, the psychological impact will be enormous, and the treaty will perhaps even rightly hold our hand if we try to help in the defense of freedom anywhere on the globe. More than that, other nations reading this treaty will question our will to support them if the case should seriously arise.

I certainly would have wished that if this treaty had to be drafted it should have excluded nuclear test explosions and not any other explosions. We must maintain our right to use nuclear explosions in our defense, in the defense of our allies, and in the defense of any country against massive aggression.

I have talked about the past, and I have talked about the present. I would like to say a few words about the future. There is another surprise around the corner, and the surprise is not so great because some of us have foreseen it, and worked for it for years.

When it comes, the surprise still will be great, because people barely begin to believe us. During this very year of 1963, we claim, and we are convinced, that we can use nuclear explosions for peaceful purposes. We can move great amounts of earth for one-tenth the amount of money that it used to cost us to move earth.

We can make harbors, we can make sea-level canals, we can deflect rivers, we can throw off overburden from deep deposits, deep mineral deposits, and increase our wealth and the wealth of other nations. We can do it in a very clean way. We can do it in such a way, I believe, two years from now it will be possible to make an explosion that will have made a crater and have land in this crater as soon as the dust has settled, in fifteen minutes, without exposing ourselves to more radiation than we have taken year in and year out in our laboratories. All this can be done. But there will be some measurable radioactivity, and this treaty prohibits the deposition of any radioactivity outside the territory of the United States.

Can we build a sea-level canal? Can we help a backward country in making a harbor or getting at its mineral deposits? Can we do so legally by a simple agreement between us and that country or do we have to go for permission from case to case to the Soviet Union?

The Chairman of the Atomic Energy Commission, Glenn Seaborg, has rightly emphasized the great importance of Plowshare. He has rightly stated that the treaty does not prohibit our developing Plowshare inside the United States as long as no radioactivity is deposited elsewhere, and he also said that when we have fully developed this capability, then we will go back to the Russians and ask for a change in the treaty.

I hope, and I am not completely convinced, that the Russians will observe the treaty, and will not break it in a clandestine way. I certainly am a little doubtful whether the Russians will be willing to change the treaty in the future in order to please us, whether they will be willing to give up a hold that this treaty gives them over our negotiations with friends and other countries.

The treaty explicitly prohibits nuclear explosions in space; yet many of the possible futuristic and as yet unproven applications of Plowshare, of the peaceful uses of atomic energy, lie in space exploration.

Even space propulsion may become possible using nuclear explosions. This treaty is a treaty whose main point is to bar knowledge, to prohibit knowledge, the acquiring of knowledge that we need now for our defense. It also interferes with knowledge which we may acquire otherwise in the future, and which we may want for scientific purposes, for the purpose of a big and expensive space adventure.

I am at the end of my statement. I want to summarize. I know that this treaty has been signed by now by more than sixty nations. I know that it will be a very difficult thing not to ratify it. Because of the terrific setback this will give to American diplomacy, I am prepared to say, although this is not my field, that it would be a mistake not to ratify the treaty.

Senator PASTORE. Would you say that again, please?

Dr. TELLER. I say, that, as an inexpert witness in diplomacy, I am willing to admit that not to ratify the treaty would be a mistake. But I want to say that this treaty prohibits future science, future progress, the kind of thing on which the greatness of this country has been based. I say that this treaty erects barriers between our allies and ourselves, and may lead to the disintegration of NATO, and I say that this treaty makes it very hard and very dubious whether we can defend our own country as well as we otherwise might defend it.

These, to my mind, are overriding considerations. I, therefore, say to have signed the treaty was a mistake. Having made this mistake, no matter what you do next will be a mistake. To ratify it will be a small mistake.

Senator HUMPHREY. Would you repeat that again, Doctor?

Dr. TELLER. I am sorry, I didn't mean to say that. If you reject the treaty this will be a small mistake. It will be a painful mistake to reject the treaty but it will not endanger the future of the United States.

If you ratify this treaty, I think you will have committed an enormously bigger mistake. You will have given away the future safety of this country. You will have increased the chances of war, and, therefore, no matter what the embarrassment may be in rejecting the treaty, I earnestly urge you to do so and not to ratify the treaty which is before you.

PART V

National Security Policy and Governmental Organization

One of the key problems of contemporary national security policy is the ever-widening gap that has opened up between the sophistication of technical studies and the capacity of an already overworked leadership group to absorb their intricacy. It is unlikely that even the most conscientious President can devote as many hours to a given problem as the analyst has had years to study it. He will have to work with approximations, and his decisions must be made under stress. Even if he perfectly comprehends the logical symmetry of a strategic theory, he must also weigh the consequences of its failure. In other words, there is a danger that doctrines of too great a complexity could bring about the kind of psychological failure that I noted in connection with the Schlieffen Plan in 1914 (see above, p. 10).

Inevitable problems of confidence and competence between the technical and political levels of domestic decision-making may make it difficult to implement a strategic doctrine. Architects of strategy need to be continually aware that their audience is not a group of colleagues of similar technical competence but of hard-pressed individuals for whom strategy is but one of many concerns. Thus, excessive complexity may lead to paralysis. The strategists must at every stage ask of the decision-maker: Does he understand the doctrine? Does he believe in it? Will the doctrines meet emergencies or provide an excuse for inaction. Does it instill a sense of mastery or produce a feeling of impotence? What does the decision-maker really mean when he accepts a strategy? Does he accept it with the notion—"In prescribed circumstances, this is what I will do, I will do nothing"?

Thus, national security policy mirrors a social and political problem: where to strike the balance between the requirements of organization and the need for inspiration. Organization expresses the importance of continuity; the routine by which it operates represents a recognition that a society must be able to assimilate and utilize mediocrity. Inspiration, on the other hand, is the mechanism of growth; it is the ability to transcend a framework that has come to be taken for granted. The stability of a society depends on its skill in organization, which enables it to react mechanically to "ordinary" problems and to utilize its resources to best effect. The greatness of a society derives from its willingness to chart new ground beyond the confines of routine. Without organization, every problem becomes a special case. Without inspiration, a society will stagnate; it will lose the ability to adapt to new circumstances or to generate new goals.

There is a temptation to confuse this with smoothly running administration. But efficient administration, though necessary, is not enough. A smoothly working bureaucracy creates the illusion of running by itself; it seeks to reduce all problems to administrative terms. The basic motivation of a bureaucracy is its quest for safety; its preferences favor a policy of minimum risk. A bureaucracy, therefore, tends to exaggerate the technical complexities of its problems and to seek to reduce questions of judgment to a minimum. Technical problems are susceptible to "objective" analysis, whereas questions of judgment contain too many uncertain elements. An administrative mechanism has a bias in favor of the *status quo*, however arrived at. Short of an unambiguous catastrophe, the *status quo* has the advantage of familiarity. No "objective" criteria can prove that a change of course will yield superior results. The inclination of a bureaucracy is to deny the possibility of great conception by classifying it as "unsound," "risky," or according to other terms that show a preference for equilibrium over exceptional performance. It is no accident that most great statesmen were opposed by the "experts" in their foreign offices, for the very greatness of the statesman's conception tends to make it inaccessible to those whose primary concern is with safety and minimum risk.

A society owes its vitality to its ability to strike a balance between the requirement of organization and the need for inspiration. Too much stress on organization leads to bureaucratization and the withering of imagination. Excessive emphasis on inspiration produces a *tour de force* without continuity or organizational stability. The best solution is a bureaucracy that runs smoothly enough to take care of ordinary problems as a matter of routine, but not so pervasive as to inhibit the creative thought that is inseparable from true leadership.

The test of any organization is twofold: (a) whether it brings its members to think spontaneously about the problems that are in fact of deepest concern, and (b) whether the qualities that are encouraged in its participants' rise to eminence are those required in key positions. All discussions about organization return to these issues; the selections listed in this volume are no exception. The difference in the approaches taken by Roswell Gilpatric and Samuel Huntington illustrates the problem. (See below, Chapters 24 and 25, pp. 443 ff. and 451 ff.)

TWENTY-THREE

A STAFF REPORT OF THE SENATE
SUBCOMMITTEE ON NATIONAL
POLICY MACHINERY

The National Security Council

[Editor's Note: The work of this Subcommittee, of which this report is one expression, has been well described by its distinguished
Chairman, Senator Jackson, as follows:

"One of the major purposes of this Congressional consideration
of executive activities is an educational one. As long as we govern
with the democratic system, the ultimate test of a government
policy is its acceptance by the people. In the final analysis, the
people must be persuaded of the effectiveness of the policy process
and the wisdom of the policies and programs they are asked to
support—and pay for. Congressional study and debate can be a
vital element in this educational task.

"With such considerations in mind, in 1959 I initiated a Senate
study of the national security policy process. Authorized by resolution of the Senate, it was the first full-scale review since the discussion and debate preceding the creation of the National Security
Council by Act of Congress in 1947.

"The inquiry of the Subcommittee on National Policy Machinery was not directed to the substance of policy decisions.
Rather, it was concerned with how the processes of government
help or hamper prompt and effective action in national security
affairs. The Subcommittee assumed that this was a national problem, transcending either political party or any particular administration.

"President Eisenhower, and then President Kennedy, assured the
cooperation of their staffs with the Subcommittee's work. Throughout, the study was conducted on a professional and non-partisan
basis. . . .

"The Subcommittee solicited the views of present and former
government officials and students of the policy process. It held
extensive hearings over a period of two years, during which time

eminent witnesses gave generously of their counsel. The Subcommittee also issued a series of staff reports with detailed findings and suggestions for improvement. The studies found a wide audience in official Washington, in the academic community, and among private citizens. Upon the conclusion of the inquiry in 1962, successor Subcommittees, which I have had the honor to chair, have continued to monitor the operations of the Executive Branch in national security affairs. . . .

"Trends in administrative philosophy influenced by the Subcommittee's study include: support of the principle that each President needs freedom to adapt his Executive Office and policy procedures to suit his own style; resistance to proposals for super-Cabinet officers and super-staffs that clog the established line of authority from the President to executive department heads; emphasis on the authority of the individual executive who takes the oath of office—giving him responsibility, expecting him to use it, and holding him accountable for the use of it; upholding the Secretary of State's right and responsibility to be the President's chief adviser on national security affairs; acceptance of the principle that no government is better than the men and women it can develop through career service or attract from private occupations; and recognition that the criterion for appointment to a top national security post should be ability to do the job—regardless of party. . . .

"Actual reforms carried out in government operations that were sparked by the Subcommittee's study include: a simplification of the operations of the National Security Council and elimination of many interdepartmental coordinating committees; removal of certain nonessential staff activities from the immediate White House office; devolution to individual department heads, and to identifiable subordinates, of the responsibility for recommending policy and for overseeing the execution of decisions; improved coordination between the State and Defense Departments, including the successful State-Defense Officer Exchange Program; the deliberate use of the Budget Bureau as a prime management tool of the President; reducing the rate of turnover of ranking executive officers by adopting the practice that candidates for national security posts give advance assurances that they intend to serve at the pleasure of the President and their department chiefs; renewal of the fight against overstaffing in the national security departments and agencies; and long overdue federal pay-raise legislation."]

INTRODUCTION

By law and practice, the President has the prime role in guarding the nation's safety. He is responsible for the conduct of foreign relations; he commands the armed forces; he has the initiative in budget-making. He, and he alone, must finally weigh all the factors —domestic, foreign, military—that affect our position in the world and by which we seek to influence the world environment.

The National Security Council was created by statute in 1947 to assist the President in fulfilling his responsibilities. The Council is charged with advising the President "with respect to the integration of domestic, foreign, and military policies relating to the national security so as to enable the military services and the other departments and agencies of the Government to cooperate more effectively in matters involving the national security."

The Council was one of the answers to the frustrations met by World War II policy-makers in trying to coordinate military and foreign policy. It is a descendant of such wartime groups as the State-War-Navy Coordinating Committee.

The Council is not a decision-making body; it does not itself make policy. It serves only in an *advisory* capacity to the President, helping him arrive at decisions that he alone may make.

Although the National Security Council was created by statute, each successive President has great latitude in deciding how he will employ it to meet his particular needs. He can use the Council as little, or as much, as he wishes. He is solely responsible for determining what policy matters will be handled within its framework, and how they will be handled. An important question facing a new President, therefore, is how he will use the Council to suit his own style of decision and action.

This study, drawing upon the experience of recent years, places at the service of the incoming administration certain observations concerning the role of the Council in the formulation and execution of national security policy.

EDITOR'S NOTE: A *Staff Report of the Subcommittee on National Policy Machinery*, Committee on Government Operations, U.S. Senate, December 12, 1960. Reprinted with permission from Henry M. Jackson, ed., *The National Security Council: Jackson Subcommittee Papers on Policy-Making at the Presidential Level* (New York: Frederick A. Praeger, 1965).

The Council and the System

When he takes office in January, the new President will find in being a *National Security Council* and an *NSC system.*

The Council itself is a forum where the President and his chief lieutenants can discuss and resolve problems of national security. It brings together as statutory members the President, the Vice President, the Secretaries of State and Defense, the Director of the Office of Civil and Defense Mobilization, and as statutory advisers the Director of Central Intelligence and the Chairman of the Joint Chiefs of Staff. The President can also ask other key aides to take part in Council deliberations. The Secretary of the Treasury, for example, has attended regularly by Presidential invitation.

But there is also today an NSC system, which has evolved since 1947. This system consists of highly institutionalized procedures and staff arrangements and a complex interdepartmental committee substructure intended to undergird the activities of the Council. Two interagency committees—the Planning Board and the Operations Coordinating Board—comprise the major pieces of this substructure. The former prepares so-called "policy papers" for consideration by the Council; the latter is expected to help follow through on the execution of Presidentially approved Council papers.

The new President will have to decide how he wishes to use the Council and the NSC system. His approach to the first meetings of the Council under his administration will be important, for these early sessions will set precedents. Action taken or not taken, assignments given or not given, invitations to attend extended or not extended, will make it subsequently easier or harder for the President to shape the Council and the system to his needs and work habits.

He faces questions like these: Which principals and advisers should be invited to attend the first Council meetings? What part should Presidential staff assistants play? What should the participants be told about the planned role and use of the NSC system? Who will prepare the agenda? What items will be placed on the agenda? Should the Council meet regularly or as need arises?

The New President's Choice

The new President can choose one of two broad approaches to the National Security Council:

1. He can use the Council as an intimate forum where he joins with his chief advisers in searching discussion and debate of a limited number of critical problems involving major long-term strategic choices or demanding immediate action. Robert Lovett has described this concept of the Council in terms of "a kind of 'Court of Domestic and Foreign Relations'":

> The National Security Council process, as originally envisaged—perhaps "dreamed of" is more accurate—contemplated the devotion of whatever number of hours were necessary in order to exhaust a subject and not just exhaust the listeners. . . . The purpose was to insure that the President was in possession of all the available facts, that he got first-hand a chance to evaluate an alternative course of action disclosed by the dissenting views, and that all implications in either course of action were explored before he was asked to take the heavy responsibility of the final decision.

2. The President can view the Council as the apex of a comprehensive and highly institutionalized system for generating policy proposals and following through on Presidentially approved decisions. Seen in this light, the Council itself sits at the top of what has been called "Policy Hill." Policy papers are supposed to travel through interdepartmental committees up one side of the hill. They are considered in the Council. If approved by the President, they travel down the opposite side of the hill, through other interdepartmental mechanisms, to the operating departments and agencies.

THE COUNCIL'S SPAN OF CONCERN

The voluminous record of meetings held and papers produced makes it clear that the Council and its subordinate machinery are now very busy and active. A long list of questions always awaits entry on the NSC agenda. Presidential orders now in force provide that all decisions on national security policy, except for special emergencies, will be made within the Council framework. In theory, the embrace of the NSC over such matters is total. Yet many of the most critical questions affecting national security are not really handled within the NSC framework.

The main work of the NSC has centered largely around the consideration of *foreign-policy* questions, rather than *national security* problems in their full contemporary sense. A high proportion of the Council's time has been devoted to the production and study of so-called "country papers"—statements of our national position toward this or that foreign nation.

The Council, indeed, appears to be only marginally involved in helping to resolve many of the most important problems that affect the future course of national security policy. For example, the Council seems to have only a peripheral or *pro forma* concern with such matters as the key decisions on the size and composition of the total national security budget, the strength and make-up of the armed services, the scale and scope of many major agency programs in such fields as foreign economic policy or atomic energy, the translation of policy goals into concrete plans and programs through the budgetary process, and many critical operational decisions with great long-term policy consequences.

The fact is that the departments and agencies often work actively and successfully to keep critical policy issues outside the NSC system. When the policy stakes are high and departmental differences deep, agency heads are loath to submit problems to the scrutiny of coordinating committees or councils. They aim in such cases to bypass the committees while keeping them occupied with less important matters. They try to settle important questions in dispute through "out of court" informal interagency negotiations, when they are doubtful of the President's position. Or else they try "end runs" to the President himself when they think this might be advantageous.

Despite the vigorous activity of the NSC system, it is not at all clear that the system now concerns itself with many of the most important questions determining our long-term national strategy or with many of the critical operational decisions that have fateful and enduring impact on future policy.

THE PLANNING BOARD

As the NSC system operates today, most of the matters that appear on the Council agenda are the product of a highly formalized and complex "policy paper production" system. The heart of this system is the NSC Planning Board, an interagency committee whose membership parallels that of the Council at the Assistant Secretary level. Initial drafts of policy papers are normally written by the departments and agencies, acting individually or in concert. But the Planning Board is responsible for the final content and language of most papers that reach the Council table. As Governor Rockefeller told the Subcommittee, "I think the public does not recognize the degree to which the Planning Board really does 95 per cent of the work. It is not very often that a paper is changed by the National Security Council."

The Planning Board is an interdepartmental committee, chaired by the Special Assistant to the President for National Security Affairs. Although formally appointed by the President, who has admonished them to act in their individual capacities in seeking "statesmanlike" solutions, the departmental members are oriented to the problems and perspectives of their own agencies. They can be expected to try to guard departmental interests.

From the outset, the drafting of a Planning Board paper is an involved process of negotiation, barter, offer, and counteroffer among the many departments involved. Governor Rockefeller has described the Planning Board process in these words:

> A major question is presented to the Planning Board, and the various interested parties—namely, the departments, each with its own role in relation to the area under discussion—work carefully with highly skilled representatives to get language into the position paper that, while it does not violate the objective, protects their own position and their own special responsibility—I don't say interest—in this field. . . . You get a watered-down version before it comes to the NSC and . . . permissive language that is not too obvious in the phraseology. This is quite an art, this business.

Many papers going from the Planning Board to the Council do indeed contain "splits"—statements of different departmental viewpoints.

But it is not at all clear that the "splits" actually help the Council understand the real policy alternatives and the true policy options available on some issue under debate. They may crystallize minor points of difference between competing agency views. The alternatives the "splits" normally reflect, in any case, represent differences in departmental or agency viewpoints. Such differences do not necessarily define or illuminate the real policy choices available. Moreover, "splits" are themselves a product of interagency bargaining. Their phrasing is adjusted to what the traffic can bear and shaped in the interest of winning allies for particular points of view.

Furthermore, the Planning Board papers are not "costed" except in the most general way. The budgetary consequences of proposed courses of action are set forth only in order-of-magnitude terms. As a result, Council members are little assisted in weighing the benefits of alternative policy courses against the costs.

Finally, by its very nature, the Planning Board is not a creative instrument for developing and bringing forward imaginative and sharply defined choices, particularly in uncharted areas of policy. Interagency committees of this kind have a built-in drive toward lowest-common-denominator solutions. They can comment, review, and adjust, but they are not good instruments of innovation.

The limitation of the Planning Board itself in developing new responses to new problems is in part demonstrated by the employment for this purpose of outside consultants and "distinguished citizens committees," such as the Killian and Gaither Committees on defense and the Draper Committee on military and economic assistance.

The main source of policy innovations is the contribution of an individual. He may be found outside, or anywhere within, the government. But normally he will be found working in a government department or agency, grappling day in and day out with some pressing national security problem. Given imaginative proposals from such individuals, interagency committees like the Planning Board can be helpful in criticizing and commenting. But if, in the interest of "agreed solutions," such committees blur the edges and destroy the coherence of these proposals, they do the President a disservice. There is strong reason to believe that this is now the case.

THE COUNCIL ITSELF

The National Security Council now holds regular weekly meetings, which vary in size. Sometimes, the President meets with only a handful of principals in conducting important business. On other occasions, thirty or forty people may attend. A typical session may have two dozen people present; some fifteen may sit at the Council table, with perhaps another ten looking on as observers and aides.

James Perkins has made this comment on the size of Council meetings:

> I think that the more one uses the NSC as a system of interagency coordination and the legitimatizing of decisions already arrived at, the growth in numbers is inevitable, because people left out of it and not at the meetings whose concurrence is required have a *prima facie* case for attending.

But if one views the Council primarily as a Presidential advisory body, the point quickly comes when the sheer numbers of participants and observers limits the depth and dilutes the quality of the discussion. The present size of most Council meetings appears to have reached and passed this point.

There are different kinds of Council meetings. Some are briefing sessions designed to acquaint the participants with, for example, an important advance in weapons technology. Other meetings center around so-called "discussion papers," which aim not at proposing a solution to some policy problem but at clarifying its nature and outlining possible alternative courses of action.

The more typical Council session, however, follows a precise agenda and focuses upon the consideration of Planning Board policy papers. Robert Cutler has described them:

> For convenience, a routine format for policy statements was developed. Thus, the busy reader would always know where to find the covering letter, the general considerations, the objectives, the courses of action to carry out the objectives, the financial appendixes, the supporting staff study; for they invariably appeared in this sequence in the final document. . . . The standardization of these techniques made it possible for the Council to transact, week in and week out, an enormously heavy load of work.

The main work of the Council, thus, now consists of discussion and a search for consensus, centering around Planning Board papers.

The normal end product of Council discussion is a Presidentially approved paper setting forth the recommendations of the Planning Board paper, with amendments, if any, adopted after Council deliberations. This paper is transmitted through the Operations Coordinating Board to the operating departments and agencies.

But one point is fundamental: policy *papers* and actual *policy* are not necessarily the same. Pieces of paper are important only as steps in a process leading to action—as minutes of decisions to do or not to do certain things.

Papers that do not affect the course of governmental action are not policy: they are mere statements of aspiration. NSC papers are policy only if they result in *action*. They are policy only if they cause the government to adopt one course of conduct and to reject another, with one group of advocates "winning" and the other "losing."

It appears that many of the papers now emerging from the Council do not meet the test of policy in this sense.

The Operations Coordinating Board

The job of helping to follow through on policies emerging from the Council and approved by the President is entrusted to the Council's Operations Coordinating Board. In terms of the NSC system, the OCB is to policy follow-up what the Planning Board is to policy development. It is an interdepartmental committee at the Under Secretary level, chaired, like the Planning Board, by the Special Assistant to the President for National Security Affairs.

The OCB, assisted by an elaborate system of interagency working groups, prepares plans for carrying out the intent of NSC policies, transmits them to the departments and agencies, secures information on the status of programs under way, and reports back through the NSC to the President on progress.

In theory, the OCB does not *make* policy. Its mandate extends only to helping to *carry out* policy. But this limitation is not and cannot be observed in practice.

When it receives an NSC policy paper, the initial job of the OCB is to determine the real meaning of the document in hand. It must often translate general statements, susceptible of varying interpretations, into tangible objectives together with plans for achieving them.

Departmental aims and interests are at stake in this determination. The process of translating an NSC paper into an action-oriented program therefore involves the same kind of interagency bartering and negotiating that takes place earlier in the Planning Board.

The OCB is an interagency committee that lacks command authority. It can advise, but not direct, the operating agencies.

Many of the most important decisions affecting the course of programs under OCB surveillance are made outside the framework of the Board. Programmatic budgetary decisions are a notable example. Also, the departments often bypass the OCB, pursuing their own interpretations of policy or engaging in "bootleg" coordination through extramural means.

The formal machinery of the OCB includes a large number of working groups that turn out detailed follow-up studies and papers. The significance of much of this work has been strongly questioned. Secretary of State Christian A. Herter made this comment before the Subcommittee:

I was Chairman of OCB for two years. The feeling of utility varied an awful lot. At times, you felt that you were being very useful. At other times, you felt you were fanning the air or spending a lot of time reviewing minutiae. . . . When you get into the formal sessions, you again apply yourself to paper-work. Sometimes you get yourself so bogged down in the editing of a word or a sentence that you say, "My God, why am I spending so much time on this?"

The nature of the danger seems clear. Actually, the OCB has little impact on the real coordination of policy execution. Yet, at the same time, the existence of this elaborate machinery creates a false sense of security by inviting the conclusion that the problem of teamwork in the execution of policy is well in hand.

Recently, the OCB has abandoned or relaxed many of the rigid reporting requirements that governed its work when it was established, and has focused its attention upon a smaller number of important problems rather than spreading its efforts across the board. These steps have reportedly been helpful. But there is a more fundamental question at issue: Can an interdepartmental committee like the OCB be counted on to discharge effectively major responsibilities for follow-through? The evidence points to the contrary.

New Directions

Two main conclusions about the National Security Council emerge:

1. The real worth of the Council to a President lies in its being an accustomed forum where he and a small number of his top advisers can gain that intellectual intimacy and mutual understanding on which true coordination depends. Viewed thus, the Council is a place where the President can receive from his department and agency heads a full exposition of policy alternatives available to him, and, in turn, give them clear-cut guidance for action.

2. The effectiveness of the Council in this primary role has been diminished by the working of the NSC system. The root causes of difficulty are found in over-crowded agenda, overly elaborate and stylized procedures, excessive reliance on subordinate interdepartmental mechanisms, and the use of the NSC system for comprehensive coordinating and follow-through responsibilities it is ill suited to discharge.

The philosophy of the suggestions that follow can be summed up in this way—to "deinstitutionalize" and to "humanize" the NSC process.

The President's Instrument. The Council exists only to serve the President. It should meet when he wishes advice on some matter, or when his chief foreign and defense policy advisers require Presidential guidance on an issue that cannot be resolved without his intervention. There are disadvantages in regularly scheduled meetings. The necessity of having to present and to discuss something at such meetings may generate business not really demanding Presidential consideration. Council meetings and the Council agenda should never become ritualistic.

The Purpose of Council Discussion. The true goal of "completed staff work" is not to spare the President the necessity of choice. It is to make his choices more meaningful by defining the essential issues that he alone must decide and by sharpening the precise positions on the opposing sides. Meetings of the Council should be regarded as vehicles for clarifying the differences of view on major policy departures or new courses of action advocated by department heads or contemplated by the President himself. The aim of the discussion should be a full airing of divergent views, so that all the implications of possible courses of action stand out in bold relief. Even a major issue may not belong on the Council agenda if it is not yet ripe for sharp and informed discussion.

Attendance at Council Meetings. The Secretaries of State and Defense share the main responsibility of advising the President on national security problems. They are the key members of the Council. Whom the President invites to Council sessions will, of course, depend on the issue under discussion. However, mere "need to know," or marginal involvement with the matter at hand, should not justify attendance. Council meetings should be kept small. When the President turns for advice to his top foreign-policy and defense officials, he is concerned with what *they themselves* think. The meetings should, therefore, be considered gatherings of principals, not staff aides. Staff attendance should be tightly controlled. As a corollary to the strict limitation of attendance, a written record of decisions should be maintained and given necessary distribution.

The Planning Board. The NSC Planning Board now tends to overshadow in importance, though not in prestige, the Council itself. However, some group akin to the present Board, playing a rather different role than it now does, can be of continuing help to the Council in the future.

Such a Board would be used mainly to criticize and comment on policy initiatives developed by the departments or stimulated by the President. It would not be used as an instrument for negotiating "agreed positions" and securing departmental concurrences.

More reliance could also be placed on informal working groups. They could be profitably employed both to prepare matters for Council discussion and to study problems that the Council decides need further examination. The make-up and life of these groups would depend on the problem involved. So, too, intermittent outside consultants or "distinguished citizens committees," such as the Gaither Committee, could on occasion be highly useful in introducing fresh perspectives on critical problems.

The Secretary of State. The Secretary of State is crucial to the successful operation of the Council. Other officials, particularly the Secretary of Defense, play important parts. But the President must rely mainly upon the Secretary of State for the initial synthesis of the political, military, economic, and other elements that go into the making of a coherent national strategy. The Secretary must also be mainly responsible for bringing to the President proposals for major new departures in national policy. To do his job properly, he must draw upon the resources of a State Department staffed broadly and competently enough with generalists, economists, and military and scientific experts to assist him in all areas falling within his full concern. He and the President need unhurried opportunities to consider the basic directions of American policy.

The Operations Coordinating Board. The case for abolishing the OCB is strong. An interdepartmental committee like the OCB has inherent limitations as an instrument for assisting with the problems of policy follow-through. If formal interagency machinery is subsequently found to be needed, it can be established later.

Responsibility for implementation of policies cutting across departmental lines should, wherever possible, be assigned to a particular department or to a particular action officer, possibly assisted by an informal interdepartmental group. In addition, the President must continue to rely heavily on the budgetary process and on his own personal assistants in performance auditing.

Problems of Staff. The President should at all times have the help and protection of a small personal staff whose members work "outside the system," who are sensitive to the President's own information needs, and who can assist him in asking relevant questions of his departmental chiefs, in making suggestions for policy initiatives not emerging from the operating departments and agencies, and in spotting gaps in policy execution.

The Council will continue to require a staff of its own, including a key official in charge. This staff should consist of a limited number of able aides who can help to prepare the work of the Council, record its decisions, and troubleshoot on spot assignments.

The NSC system now contains several staff components. These might well be more closely integrated. Also, various special project staffs on foreign policy matters have been established in recent years at the White House. Consideration could be given to bringing them within the NSC framework.

A Special Problem. The National Security Act intended that one Council member regularly bring to the NSC perspectives on our domestic economy and domestic resources. The Director of the Office of Civil and Defense Mobilization is the present heir of that role. But the concern of the OCDM focuses on civil defense and mobilization problems of wartime emergencies. The Council of Economic Advisers, among other agencies, is now much more concerned than the OCDM with the kind of domestic perspectives relevant to the problems of a protracted conflict that stops short of major war. The new President and the Congress may therefore wish to ask whether the Director of OCDM should have continued statutory membership on the Council.

The NSC and the Budgetary Process. Today, there is often little resemblance between a policy statement emerging from the NSC and the programs finally carried out by the operating departments and agencies. The actual scale and scope of these programs is determined largely by budgetary decisions made outside the Council.

An attempt to use the Council for the details of resource allocation would be no more feasible than trying to use the Cabinet for this purpose. Yet the search for ways and means of relating the Council's advice more closely to the budget process must be pursued. The problem is not to make the Council the manager or czar of budget preparation. Rather it is to insure that the perspectives of the Secretaries of State and Defense are brought to bear on an ordering of national priorities at the target-setting stage of the annual budget preparation. The National Security Council is the appropriate body for helping the President define such priorities.

TWENTY-FOUR

ROSWELL L. GILPATRIC

The Joint Chiefs of Staff and
Military Unification

[*Editor's Note: When the system of the Joint Chiefs of Staff was created in the Pentagon in 1948, some feared that it would lead to a sort of Prussian General Staff, operating independently of the civilian branch. Others have expressed a contrary concern: that the creation of a single Secretary of Defense would reduce the service chiefs to rubber stamps and hamper the application of professional military expertise to the management of the armed forces.*

The long debate about the relation of civil to military authority within the Department of Defense appears to have been settled. The Secretary of Defense is now in undisputed control. The major victims have been the Joint Chiefs of Staff, whose claims to policy-making powers have been radically diminished since the advent of the Kennedy Administration.

In his capacity as Deputy Secretary of Defense, Mr. Gilpatric assisted in shaping the existing structure. He argues in this article that the management of organizations as complex as the Department of Defense requires a special set of skills, which are inherently neither military nor civilian. Though over-all civilian control is essential, professional military advice is crucial also. Mr. Gilpatric believes that the Joint Chiefs of Staff are most effective when divorced from the details of administering their respective services, partly because existing missions overlap traditional service boundaries, partly because this frees them to concentrate on acting as a highest-level strategic advisory group to the President and the Secretary of Defense. Many professional officers disagree with this view and contend that responsible strategic advice must flow from a command position within the existing services.]

The question of how far the United States military should be unified is still as controversial and divisive as it was when the National Security Act was adopted in 1947. Yet, during the intervening seventeen years, many of the original issues have become academic. Every Secretary of Defense, with the possible exception of General Marshall, backed by the President in office at the time, has favored moving toward more centralization of authority in the Defense establishment. Even the first Defense Secretary, James Forrestal, who agreed with the original unification concept of merely a loose confederation of the armed services, came around before his death to the view that has since prevailed among his successors.

Why, then, do feelings run high when the subject of military unification is brought up? That the issue remains a touchy one was brought out only recently when the chairmen of the two Armed Services Committees of the Congress thought they detected, in the promotion of a certain officer, an effort to strengthen the position of the chairman of the Joint Chiefs of Staff.

In consequence, every President has moved rather warily, if at all, in asking the Congress to approve further steps to unify the armed services. It took President Eisenhower five years to ask for the defense-streamlining legislation that he had promised in his 1952 campaign speeches. President Kennedy never even approached Capitol Hill on the subject of unification legislation during his nearly three years in the White House. If President Johnson has any plans for such moves, they have not as yet been revealed.

Since the arguments for and against military unification began after World War II, there has been little changing of sides. The Navy has always been against unification. The Army was originally very much for it, and among the military the most effective leadership toward unification was furnished by top Army generals such as Eisenhower and Taylor. In recent years, the strongest service support for unification has come from the Air Force.

On the civilian side, as has been noted, most Defense Secretaries have tended, with varying amounts of enthusiasm and in differing degrees, to move in the direction of more centralized control. In Congress, on the other hand, the dominant attitude has been one of skepticism, and at times downright resistance, toward

EDITOR'S NOTE: Reprinted from *The New York Times Magazine*, "An Expert Looks at the Joint Chiefs," March 29, 1963, pp. 11, 71, 72. Copyright © 1964 by The New York Times Company.

any change that might facilitate centralization and ultimately unification.

Notwithstanding this relatively fixed pattern of support and opposition, much progress toward unification has occurred. To be sure, the National Security Act still preserves the different service entities and requires that the service departments be separately organized and administered under their respective service Secretaries. Yet the authority of the Secretary of Defense, under the President, is paramount, and his ability to control and direct the activities of the services is unconditional and unquestioned.

The one area through which separate service influence can still be significantly brought to bear is the Joint Chiefs of Staff. The service Chiefs, as principal military advisers to both the President and the Secretary of Defense and in their capacities as members of the Joint Chiefs of Staff, play two major roles in the military establishment: (1) they originate all strategic planning, and (2) they direct and supervise all military operations carried out by the principal combat commands.

True, they can be overruled by the Secretary of Defense and the President. But the force of a military position taken by a majority of the service Chiefs, even if not joined in by the chairman of the Joint Chiefs, carries such weight that even the most senior civilian official hesitates to disregard it. The status of the chairman is still only that of first among equals. He can reason with and try to persuade his fellow Chiefs, but in the final analysis his vote counts for no more than one of theirs.

Given the present structure of the U.S. military establishment, in what respects might there be further moves toward unification that would be in the national interest? One—the ultimate step— may be dismissed as currently lacking any considerable support. That would be the complete obliteration of service lines, with all of the armed forces in one uniform. Short of such a monolithic form of organization, there are, however, some changes that could bring about benefits, at the expense—so say those who oppose them—or relinquishing certain values inherent in the existing system. Possible further steps toward unification may be grouped in two categories.

One has to do with separate departmental organization of the Army, Navy and Air Force, each of which has its own civilian Secretary and military Chief. The need for these departments within a larger department seems open to legitimate question under current conditions. Since the enactment of the original unification legislation, the Marines have functioned as a separate service under their own leadership within the Navy Department but without being a separate department. Why then should not the three other services be similarly organized; that is, without constituting separate departments but yet preserving their autonomy within the Defense Departments?

Doing away with the three service departments would, of course, eliminate the service Secretaries. That is to say, the titles and the offices would no longer exist, but there would still be a need for most of the functions now performed by the individuals who occupy those offices.

Although the service departments are no longer in the chain of command for military operations—which runs directly from the President and the Secretary of Defense through the Joint Chiefs to the combat commands—they carry out essential support functions. They enlist and train the military personnel and develop and procure the weapons and other equipment on which the effectiveness of our fighting forces depends. The service Secretaries are now responsible for supplying this support, subject to the control of the Secretary of Defense. Without separate service departments and service Secretaries, there would still have to be Defense Department officials, probably Under Secretaries of Defense, to see to the performance of these vital support roles.

The elaborate coordinating mechanism now required to insure standardized procedures within the separate service departments could be greatly reduced. More important, the compulsion to represent his own service, and if possible to see that a particular service point of view prevails, would not rest as heavily on an individual serving as a Defense Under Secretary as it now does on the service Secretary.

But there is another side to each of these coins. Undoubtedly, to the extent that the separate identities of the services were subordinated to or submerged within the Defense Department, certain values would be lost. Intangible though they may be, pride of service, tradition and esprit de corps are significant in maintaining the quality of the uniformed elements in the U.S. military establishment.

Moreover, in the eyes of many, the conversion of the service Secretaries to Defense Under Secretaries would be taken as downgrading the offices, even though the change would be less in substance than in form. This could be detrimental; it is difficult enough now to find individuals with the qualifications and motivation called for if the Secretary of Defense is to have the assistance on which he must rely to be effective.

Persuasive as are these considerations for retaining the existing service department structure, there is, I now believe, a further compelling reason for retaining the present organizational pattern. With strong Defense Department leadership, such as Secretary McNamara has provided, and the full exercise of the powers both explicit and inherent in his office, the existence of the separate service departments need not impede centralized management and efficient administration.

Indeed, by using the service departments as executive agents of the Defense Department as a whole—as Secretary McNamara has done on occasion—a convenient and effective management tool can be provided. On balance, therefore, it no longer seems wise to me to press unification to the point of eliminating the separate service departments.

There remains a second area where the present system leaves much to be desired—what is sometimes called the "two-hatted" role of the service Chiefs and the manner in which they function collectively as the Joint Chiefs. Before considering possible changes in this highly sensitive area, let us note how the work of U.S. military leadership has multiplied during the last decade.

Weapons-system development has become vastly more complicated as the pace of technological change has quickened. The training and retention of qualified military manpower is more difficult, by several orders of magnitude, than it was before the days of Polaris submarines and space satellites. The prospect ahead is for more, not fewer, skills and talents to keep U.S. military power an effective instrument of national policy.

With no diminution in their duties as heads of their services, the military Chiefs in recent times have had to assume greatly increased responsibilities in their capacity as members of the Joint Chiefs of Staff. They now direct, through the combat commands, U.S. military operations worldwide. In every crisis situation the Chiefs must consider, and recommend to the President and the Secretary of Defense, the forces needed to meet U.S. commitments, how they should be equipped and employed, and so on.

Another major responsibility of the Joint Chiefs of Staff is strategic planning. All contingency plans—what used to be termed war plans—originate with the Joint Chiefs, who must constantly revise and update concepts for military operations in a myriad of differing situations, including the ever-growing wave of subversive insurgency that the Communist powers stir up.

But this is only part of the work of the service Chiefs. As principal military advisers to the President and the Secretary of Defense, they are increasingly being drawn into arms-control and disarmament matters. When the limited test ban was under consideration last summer, weeks of the Joint Chiefs' time had to be set aside for their part in it. Their participation in military-alliance problems and United Nations peace-keeping assignments promises to become greater, not less, in the years ahead.

Small wonder then that the Joint Chiefs' organization now puts in longer hours than ever before in peacetime and that it takes weeks and months, rather than days, for a JCS paper to work its way through that overburdened organization. There are reasons other than work load, however, why it might be well to recast the functions of the Joint Chiefs.

Each military Chief inevitably brings to the deliberations of the Joint Chiefs the position or point of view of his particular service. This is only natural, because he spends much of his time surrounded by his own service colleagues. A Chief does not always vote in the Joint Chiefs as his service desires, but it would be too much to expect the head of a service as a rule not to be loyal to the concepts and doctrines espoused by his service.

The defenders of the present set-up see nothing wrong in this. In their eyes, splits among the Joint Chiefs reflect underlying diversity in military views of which the President and Secretary of Defense, as well as the National Security Council, should be made aware. Moreover, they say, such splits can always be resolved by higher authority after the differing opinions of the military advisers have been weighed. They add that, in the case of a split among the Joint Chiefs, the Secretary of Defense can always follow—though he is not compelled to—the views of the Chairman of the Joint Chiefs.

The principal shortcoming of the present system, as I see it, is that it tends to promote needless fragmentation of military thinking. Too often, in critical conflict situations, the President and his other policy advisers are confronted with a fractured military position reflecting divergent service views rather than differing military judgments. I remember one situation in recent years when, at a meeting of the National Security Council, the five members of the Joint Chiefs of Staff expressed five different viewpoints.

One way to minimize this would be to create a set of conditions whereby the Joint Chiefs could exercise more self-discipline in arriving at a military position before passing it to their civilian superiors. In short, the Joint Chiefs should be enabled to do their own work better as well as to accomplish it faster.

To help to achieve this end, it would be desirable to relieve the Joint Chiefs of part of their growing and at times well-nigh overwhelming work load. Their corporate duties might be redefined so as to consist principally of strategic planning and studies on which their advice is requested by the President, the Secretary of Defense or the National Security Council. It is in the planning area that all points of view, however divergent, should be taken into account.

This change would take the Joint Chiefs as a body out of the chain of command over military operations, which would then extend down from the President as Commander in Chief through the Secretary of Defense and the Chairman of the Joint Chiefs to the heads of the combat commands. There is nothing in existing law which requires that the Joint Chiefs in their corporate capacity be brought into the line of authority over tactical operations.

The services, of course, would retain a major voice in all such operations since service support is indispensable for those operations and each commander and JCS staff assistant comes from one or another service. Moreover, all military operations would be conducted pursuant to plans developed by the Joint Chiefs.

But the Joint Chiefs as a separate echelon in the command chain would no longer need to concern themselves with every operational move within one of the commands or with resolving differences between commands on tactical matters. Among other benefits from such a change would be a clearer and quicker line of command and control from the President on down.

Any reduction in the JCS role to a planning and advisory body is bound to raise a hue and cry with those, particularly in the Congress and among retired military personnel, who profess to see in any aggrandizement of the position of the Chairman of the Joint Chiefs the much feared vision of a "man on horseback." Shades of the pre-World War II Prussian general staff system will be evoked by those who are opposed to any further unifying of control over the military. In fact, some of those so minded would favor turning the clock back and undoing certain of the consolidating and centralizing changes that have already occurred.

These standpatters must accept responsibility, if their views against further change prevail, for perpetuating a system of mili-

tary planning and command which cannot function as effectively
as it should and as the national interest demands. Not long ago,
an authority on the military profession, Dr. Samuel P. Huntington,
of Columbia University, summed up the effect of continued divisions among the U.S. military in this fashion:

> Inter-service controversy, intra-service divisions, inter-program rival-
> ries—all helped to weaken the voice of the military. On few, if any,
> major issues did the military professionals develop a coherent mili-
> tary viewpoint. Split among themselves, they invited civilian inter-
> vention into military affairs. When they were able to compromise
> their differences and agree on a common program, the result was
> often so obviously a political compromise that civilian leaders were
> justified in tearing it apart on grounds of sound military logic.

If the United States is to hold or regain initiative in international security affairs, and if its military establishment is to be
responsive to the need for almost split-second reaction in crisis
situations, the President and his assistants must be able to receive,
clearly and speedily, military advice of a range and depth that
will not always be forthcoming under the present JCS system.
Capable and dedicated as the service chiefs may be individually,
more is expected of them in time of trouble than they can fulfill
through the system as constituted today.

TWENTY-FIVE

SAMUEL P. HUNTINGTON

Inter-Service Competition and the Political Roles of the Armed Services

[Editor's Note: The post–World War II history of the Defense Department has been enlivened by violent public inter-service disputes as the Air Force–Navy B-36 Carrier argument of 1947–49 and the Army–Air Force Thor-Jupiter dispute of 1955–57. There has been a tendency to interpret such events as evidence of service disunity and inefficiency, and much of the impetus for Secretary McNamara's reforms of the Pentagon stems from this conviction. Professor Huntington argues the opposite point of view. He holds that service rivalries tend to serve the public interest. They provide the mechanism whereby the public in general and the Congress in particular is kept informed of the issues while national security policy is still in a formative stage, and they guarantee the active participation of the civilian branches in the decision-making process.

Professor Huntington fears that growing centralization will create doctrinal uniformity and the stifling of debate. The resulting decline of controversy could well destroy the cohesion and weaken the interaction of the various components of our military establishment. This would, in his view, undermine our security and radically alter the established principles of civilian control.]

"Conventional wisdom" (to purloin a phrase from Galbraith) holds that inter-service competition necessarily undermines economy, efficiency, and effective central control in the military establishment. The remedy is further unification, possibly even the merger of the services into a single uniform. Conventional wisdom

AUTHOR'S NOTE: This article is adapted from my contribution to the volume *Total War and Cold War*, edited by Harry L. Coles (Columbus, Ohio: Ohio State University Press, 1962). I am indebted to William T. R. Fox, Louis Morton, Robert E. Osgood, and David B. Truman for criticisms and suggestions.

EDITOR'S NOTE: Reprinted with permission from *The American Political Science Review*, LV, No. 1 (March, 1961).

also holds that political action by military groups necessarily threatens civilian control. The remedy is to "keep the military out of politics." The pattern of American military politics and inter-service rivalry since World War II, however, suggests that conventional wisdom may err in its analysis of their results and falter in its prescription of remedies.

I. The Roots of Inter-Service Rivalry

Service political controversy between the world wars had two distinguishing characteristics. First, on most issues, a military service, supported, perhaps, by a few satellite groups, struggled against civilian isolationists, pacifists, and economizers. The Navy and the shipbuilding industry fought a lonely battle with the dominant forces in both political parties over naval disarmament. The Army lost its fight for universal service after World War I, and throughout the 1920's clashed with educational, labor, and religious groups over ROTC and with other groups over industrial mobilization preparation. In the annual budget encounters the issue usually was clearly drawn between service supporters who stressed preparedness and their opponents who decried the necessity and the legitimacy of substantial military expenditures. To the extent that the services were in politics, they were involved in conflicts with civilian groups. Behind each specific opponent of the moment was that broad and deeply ingrained anti-military sentiment which had characterized American society since the eighteenth century. By the end of the Coolidge administration, this sentiment was so far in the ascendancy that the appropriations for the Army and the Navy together had been whittled to about $750 million in a total annual budget of just under $4 billion.

Second, each service waged its own political battles independently of the other. Throughout the 1920's and 1930's, the services cooperated in strategic planning through the Joint Board and in a few other enterprises. Strategic planning, however, involved no immediate claims upon scarce resources. It produced some disagreement but no real political conflict. The most significant intramilitary controversies involved the efforts of the two semi-services, the Air Corps and, to a lesser extent, the Marine Corps, to achieve greater autonomy and *de jure* recognition as services. The two major services, however, seldom fought each other politically and virtually never helped each other. They were distinct departments. Separate legislation, handled by separate Military and Naval Affairs Committees in both houses of Congress, established and organized them, authorized their strengths and prescribed their systems of promotion and recruitment. Separate appropriations subcommittees provided their funds in separate supply bills. The political successes and failures of one service had little implication for the other: the National Defense Act of 1920 boded neither good nor ill for the Navy; the Vinson Acts of the 1930's neither assumed nor precluded an increase in the Army. Each service struggled along in its own world with its peculiarities and preoccupations, its own friends and enemies.

In some respects, this interwar pattern of relationships persisted into the postwar period. The traditional service-civilian conflict reappeared in the struggles between the Navy and the State Department over the Japanese mandates, the military and the scientists over the control of atomic energy, and the Army and a number of civilian groups over universal military training. These conflicts, however, were holdovers from a previous era. The primary locus of service political activity shifted drastically. World War II destroyed the separate political universes of the services. The development of new weapons and the emergence of a new role for the United States in world affairs meant a change in their old functions and activities. Service futures were now interdependent. The concerns which each service felt for the future tended to focus into a concern over the effect of the other services on that future. A unified defense organization meant competition over organizational position and strategic doctrine. A unified appropriations process meant competition for funds. The inter-service battle over unification between 1944 and 1947 was not only a model of battles to come but it also shaped the nature of those battles. Inter-service rivalry was the child of unification. Both reflected the unity and complexity of modern war, and without the one, the other would never have come into existence.

The transition from civilian-service controversy to inter-service controversy as the main focus of service political activity was graphically illustrated in the struggle over Universal Military Training between 1945 and 1948. The lines of battle were initially drawn between the Army and certain patriotic and veterans groups on the one hand, and various civilian educational, religious, pacifist, and farm groups on the other. The opposition, one War Department consultant declared, included "subversive groups and a large section of the public which does not think."[1] The opponents replied with dire warnings of the dangers of militarization. Here was a conflict in the classic pattern of the 1920's and 1930's with all the familiar arguments, clichés, and symbolism. The resolution of the issue in 1948, however, reflected not so much the relative strength or persuasiveness of the two coalitions as it did the relative appeals of the Army and Air Force strategic doctrines. The issue was redefined from "UMT *vs.* no-UMT" to "UMT *vs.* a seventy-group Air Force." "The effect of the Finletter report and of the Brewster-Hinshaw Board," Forrestal noted in his diary for March 8, 1948, "has been to convince the country that by a substantial increase in appropriations for Air, there would be no necessity for UMT."[2] Congress added $822 million to Air Force appropriations, and the UMT legislation died in committee. The conflict of the Army and its affiliated groups against an extensive coalition of civilian groups became a conflict of one service against another.

The rise of inter-service rivalry had a direct impact on civil-military relations. Potential conflict between civil and military institutions was sublimated and deflected into conflict among the services. Inter-service controversy substituted for civil-military controversy. Two crucial focuses of civil-military relations in modern states have been between the Foreign Office and the military on the one hand, and between the military and the budgetary agencies on the other. American civil-military relations in the postwar decade, however, were characterized by the relative lack of sharp conflict between a united military establishment and either the State Department or Budget Bureau. Service rivalry permitted the civilian agencies to pick and choose. When the State Department wanted to reinforce Europe in 1950, elements in the Air Force took a skeptical attitude, but the Army moved in to help develop and merchandise the policy. Conversely, when the Secretary of State later spoke of massive retaliation, the Army dissented, but the now-favored Air Force congratulated the diplomats on their military common sense. When the budget was reduced in fiscal-year 1954, Vandenberg made his futile protests while the Army and Navy sat on the sidelines. When it was reduced in fiscal-year 1955, the Air Force was pleased with the new emphasis, and the Army fought alone against the cuts. Civil-military relations before

---

[1] Hearings, *War Department Publicity and Propaganda Relating to Universal Military Training*, House Committee on Expenditures in Executive Departments, 80th Cong., 1st sess., pp. 31, 38.

[2] Walter Millis, ed., *The Forrestal Diaries* (New York: 1951), p. 388.

and after the Korean War would have been far different if the frustrations generated by the budgets under Secretaries of Defense Johnson and Wilson had not in part been dissipated in decrying other services and other strategic doctrines. Indeed, at no point after World War II were the President and his Budget Bureau confronted with a truly joint, integrated military program, publicly announced and supported by all military men as the indispensable minimum for national security. The *imprimatur* which the Joint Chiefs bestowed upon force-level recommendations was seldom more than *pro forma*. The "minimum" programs were service minimum programs for 70, 143, or 137 wings; for one *United States*, ten *Forrestals*, or a series of nuclear carriers; for twelve, twenty-four, or twenty-seven divisions. Each service chief tended to attack not the over-all ceiling on the military budget but rather the allocation of the budget among the services.[3] The oft-commented-on failure of the American military to have a distinctive "military viewpoint" on national policy after World War II was not unrelated to the presence of distinctive service viewpoints.

In almost every modern state, the division of the military forces into two or more separate groups has been used to bolster civilian control. Totalitarian states create SS or MVD troops to check their regular forces. The Founding Fathers provided for both a militia and a regular army. After World War II, inter-service rivalry played a similar role. "I want competition," Representative Carl Vinson is quoted as declaring.[4] Inter-service rivalry not only strengthened civilian agencies but also furnished them with a whipping boy upon whom to blame deficiencies in the military establishment for which just possibly they could be held responsible.

Inter-service controversy rendered unlikely any military rejection of the civilian world and its values, such as occurred in the late nineteenth century and between the two world wars. Civilian agencies were now more frequently arbiters than opponents, and each service was impelled to adjust its values and interests to those of influential civilians or to risk falling behind its rivals. Inter-service conflict stimulated a politicization of the military which meant both a less military attitude in dealing with civilians and more sophisticated political techniques in dealing with other mili-

---

[3] E.g., Maxwell D. Taylor, *The Uncertain Trumpet* (New York: 1960), pp. 63–64, 74.

[4] J. L. McConaughy, Jr., "Congressmen and the Pentagon," *Fortune*, LVII (April, 1958), 162.

tary groups. Implicitly, service activity directed at other services was more acceptable than service activity directed at civilians. The services themselves found it easier and more virtuous to tangle with each other than to challenge civilian groups and arouse the hallowed shibboleths of civilian control.

Despite these functions which it apparently served, inter-service rivalry nevertheless was often denounced by civilians as the source of many evils in the Department of Defense. Inter-service harmony, the elimination of duplication (rational organization), reduced costs, and greater unification were often seen as directly related; and the achievement of inter-service harmony, it was argued, was a step toward the achievement of the others.[5] If this were the case, however, it is indeed strange that political and military leaders so persistently refused to realize these values. Why wallow along with inter-service bickering, duplication, needless expenditure, and administrative disunity, if they could all be eliminated or reduced together by taking a few simple steps? The relations among these goals were considerably more complex than they superficially appeared to be.

Inter-service competition was not so much a cause of decentralization, duplication, and increased expenditures as it was the result of the desire to eliminate these supposed evils. More harmony among the services could be bought at the price of disunity, duplication, higher costs. It is generally conceded, for instance, that the less money there was in the military budget, the more intense and bitter was the competition of the services for it. Similarly, inter-service competition in the postwar decade originated in unification, and efforts to increase unification usually tended to produce greater inter-service competition. "If you try to put on the heat too much right now," Admiral Radford observed in 1958 with respect to the authority of the Secretary of Defense over the services, "they all take refuge in the law and you actually drive them apart."[6] On the other hand, the less unification there was, the greater the freedom of the services to go their own way, the less they feared control by a central organ dominated by a hostile service, and the less the likelihood of serious inter-service rivalry. In

---

[5] E.g., Congressman Mahon, *The New York Times*, April 28, 1957, p. 1.

[6] Hearings, *Defense Department Reorganization Act of 1958*, Senate Armed Services Committee, 85th Cong., 2d sess., p. 418. Admiral Radford used this point to urge statutory strengthening of the Secretaryship. Both the 1949 and 1953 reorganizations, however, had purported to establish his full authority over the Department.

comparable fashion, duplicating ambitions were a cause of inter-service rivalry; duplicating programs and functions a means of reducing that rivalry. Both the Army and the Air Force wanted to develop, produce, and operate intermediate range ballistic missiles. This conflict of ambitions was, in part, mediated by allowing both services to produce their respective missiles. In one sense, duplication was a result of inter-service rivalry, but it was a result which tended to reduce its cause, and efforts to decrease duplication tended to increase inter-service tension.

Inter-service harmony could thus be achieved at the sacrifice of reduced expenditures, rationalized organization, and greater unification. In addition, inter-service peace would probably have certain costs in decreased civil-military harmony. Conversely, the achievement of these other values was only possible by accepting a considerable degree of inter-service competition. One suspects that the real cause of the sustained deprecation of inter-service competition was not its direct association with other evils in Defense Department management, but rather because it was a discomfort which had to be endured if these other evils were to be reduced. What people identified as the consequences of inter-service competition were in reality the alternatives to it. Inter-service competition became an ubiquitous, inherent, and permanent feature of the defense establishment because it would simply cost too much to eliminate.

For the services, inter-service competition was a justification for, as well as a cause of, service political activities. Traditionally, and again immediately after World War II, service appeals to their officers to be public-relations–conscious stressed the close interrelation of political and military affairs and the general responsibility of military officers to enlighten the public on the needs of national security. Increasingly, however, the stress on the public relations responsibility of the officer assumed a service-oriented approach. Exhortations to political action were couched in terms of putting the service view across—informing the public of the indispensability of sea, air, or land power to national security.[7] Competitive emulation thus provided the impetus for the multiplication of service political activities. "The Jupiter," as Wernher von Braun

---

[7] E.g., Gen. J. L. Collins, "The War Department Spreads the News," *Military Review*, XXVII (September, 1947), 15; Lt. Cmdr. J. L. Howard, "The Navy and National Security," *U. S. Naval Institute Proceedings*, LXXVII (July, 1951), 753; Col. T. M. Smith, "Air Force Information at the Grass Roots," *Air University Quarterly Review*, V (Spring, 1952), 83.

explained, "involves several hundred million dollars of the taxpayers' money. One hundred per cent security would mean no information for the public, no money for the Army, no Jupiter. . . . The Army has got to play the same game as the Air Force and the Navy."[8]

Each service, with the notable exception of the Marine Corps, developed an image of itself as the "silent service," politically underprivileged, misunderstood by the public, incapable of competing equally in the public arena with its more articulate and dramatic rivals. Each service's feeling of inadequacy was undoubtedly real, and the ritualistic deploring of its inferiority furnished a perfect rationale for, and incentive to, political action. Contrary to what one might expect, however, the stronger a service was, the more it tended to deplore its inferiority. Perhaps the greater its power and the more extensive its activities, the more the service felt the need to justify them by stressing how weak it was. Conceivably, too, feelings of inadequacy derive more from the gap between a service's power and its aspirations than from its power relative to its rivals. Or, it may be that bemoaning the state of one's public relations is itself an inherent part of public relations activity and increases as the latter increases. In any event, by almost any standard, the Air Force was the strongest service politically during the postwar decade. It consistently outscored its rivals, for instance, in public-opinion polls, and after 1951 it regularly received the lion's share of the Defense Department budget. Yet the Air Force undoubtedly complained the most about its political weakness. The Air Force, one of its generals declared, had "a special problem in public relations" because most Americans did not understand the basic concepts of strategic air power and believed air power to be too expensive. "The Vice Chief of Staff," an Air Force journal reported in 1954, "is convinced that the Air Force has failed to keep the public properly informed."[9] A distinguished lawyer and brigadier general in the Air Force Reserve compiled an imposing list of obstacles to the development of American air power:

Air power is the victim of cultural lag. . . . The military commentators were brought up in the older services. . . . The Air Force

[8] *The New York Times*, June 27, 1957, p. 8, quoted in Douglass Cater, *The Fourth Branch of Government* (Boston: 1959), pp. 10–11.

[9] Lt. Gen. E. W. Rawlings, "Public Opinion and Air Force Dollars," *Army Information Digest*, VIII (April, 1953), 58; "The Big Look," *Air University Quarterly Review*, VI (Winter, 1953–54), 133.

lacks representation in the Office of the Secretary of Defense. . . . The Congressional relations of the Air Force are inferior to those of the other services. . . . The Air Force is really the silent service. Its senior commanders do not write books and articles. . . . Those responsible for the development of national air power have not made use of the basic instrumentalities of information and enlightenment to get the public behind them.[10]

The *Air University Quarterly Review* endorsed these conclusions and pointed out other deficiencies. Both the Army and the Navy had regular TV programs; the Air Force had none. Fewer movies were made about the Air Force than about the other services. The *Review* found just one area of Air Force superiority. "Only in the mass medium of the comics does the Air Force come out ahead, with 'Steve Canyon' and 'Terry and the Pirates' far out-stripping any competition in that field of communication and public relations."[11] The complaints of the other services differed only in quantity, not in quality, from those of the Air Force.

II. THE POLITICAL CASTELLATION OF THE SERVICES

Inter-service competition tended to weaken the military as a whole but to strengthen the military services. Challenging the services, the rivalry also toughened them and forced them to develop the mechanisms and support necessary for survival in the pluralistic world of American politics. The expansion of their political activities tended to resemble a process of castellation. Building out from its inner keep, each service slowly constructed political, institutional, and legal defenses, after the fashion of an elaborate medieval castle with inner and outer walls, ramparts and barbicans, watchtowers and moats. The services, in short, entrenched themselves on the American political scene, as countless other interest groups, private and public, had done before them.

Expansion of Public and Congressional Relations[12]

Service emphasis upon reaching the public and Congress was concretely reflected in the elevation of these activities in the for-

[10] W. Barton Leach, "Obstacles to the Development of American Air Power," *Annals of the American Academy*, CCXCIX (May, 1955), 71–74.

[11] "Approaches to Air-Age Education in American Schools and Communities," *Air University Quarterly Review*, VIII (Summer, 1956), 116.

[12] For perceptive discussions of service public-relations activities, see Hanson W. Baldwin, "When the Big Guns Speak," in Lester Markel, ed., *Public Opinion and Foreign Policy* (New York: 1949), pp. 97–120; W. S. Fairfield, "PR

mal administrative hierarchy. During the 1920's and the 1930's, the Army and Navy public-information sections occupied subordinate positions in the Intelligence branches of the services. Inevitably, the outlook and values associated with the collection and interpretation of intelligence were not those which encouraged the collection and dissemination of news to mass media of communication.[13] Congressional-liaison responsibilities were dispersed among a number of bureaus in the Navy and assigned to the information offices in the Army and Air Force. By 1956, however, all three major services had similar organizational arrangements for public information and legislative liaison: two distinct offices at the highest level directly responsible to the service secretary.

The elevation of these offices was accompanied by an expansion and diversification of their activities. The Army Chief of Information, for instance, opened a branch office in Los Angeles in 1952 to improve relations between the Army and the movie industry, and another in 1956 in New York, designed, in the words of the Chief of Staff, to "assist in getting its story across to the public" through all the available news media. At the same time, the Chief of Staff pointed with pride to the award by the American Public Relations Association of three citations to Army organizations for outstanding public relations. Public relations was included in the Army Program System. Public information objectives were established quarterly, covering "those critical areas for which the Department of the Army particularly desires emphasis during the period." The parallel between the military services and the large industrial corporations was pointed out, and the military were urged to adopt the public-relations philosophy of industry. General Ridgway's call in 1954 for the "creation of a public-relations-conscious Army" had its counterparts in similar exhortations by the other services.[14] Increased activities meant increased funds,

---

for the Services—In Uniform and in Mufti," *The Reporter*, XVIII (May 15, 1958), 20–23; Morris Janowitz, *The Professional Soldier: A Social and Political Portrait* (Chicago: The Free Press of Glencoe, 1960), chap. 19; Gene M. Lyons, "PR and the Pentagon," *The New Leader*, XLIII (October 17, 1960), 10–12.

[13] Significantly, perhaps, the Marine Corps never subordinated public information to Intelligence. The Marines established a Publicity Office in 1925 and a full-blown Public Relations Section in 1933. Robert Lindsay, *This High Name: Public Relations and the United States Marine Corps* (Madison, Wis.: University of Wisconsin Press, 1956), p. 46.

[14] Matthew B. Ridgway, "Army Troop and Public Relations," *Army Information Digest*, IX (August, 1954), 5; Maxwell D. Taylor, "Biennial Report of the Chief of Staff," *ibid.*, XII (September, 1957), 61.

and, reportedly, total military expenditures for legislative liaison doubled between 1953 and 1958.[15]

"Backstop" Associations and the Articulation of Service Interests

A second aspect of the growth of service political activities in the postwar decade was the increased number, membership, and activities of service "backstop" organizations, private associations concerned with the support of the services and the articulation of their programs. The Navy League, oldest of the major associations, was formed by a group of civilians in 1902 to counterbalance the reaction against the Navy in the years after the Spanish-American War. Prior to World War II, the League was an active and devoted advocate of the Navy, but never a very large, affluent, or influential one.[16] The unification controversy of 1945–47, however, gave the League a new role to play, not in fighting anti-Navy midwesterners, but in fighting anti-Navy soldiers and airmen. The Air Force Association was organized in 1946 and the following year it took over the publication of the monthly *Air Force* magazine, previously published by the Army Air Force. In 1959, it had 55,000 members. The Association of the U.S. Army was formed in 1950 by the merger of the Infantry and Field Artillery Associations. In 1955, it assimilated the Antiaircraft Association, and by 1958 it had a membership of 50,000 and almost a hundred chapters.

The development and vitality of the "backstop" associations was particularly relevant to one major problem of service behavior in the postwar period: the definition and articulation of service interests. Normally, the leaders of a group are its natural advocates and defenders. With the services, however, this is not necessarily true. To be sure, the role of the service Secretary differs little from that of the secretary in a civilian department. In most civilian agencies, however, the definition, articulation, and promotion of the agency's interests are also a function of the top career leaders of the agency, those whose work-lives are continuously identified with it. The freedom of the military leaders to perform this function, however, is restricted by their presumably instrumental char-

[15] McConaughy, *op. cit.*, p. 166.
[16] Armin Rappaport, "The Navy League of the United States," *South Atlantic Quarterly*, LIII (April, 1954), 203–12. On the "backstop" association in general, see Janowitz, *op. cit.*, pp. 383–87, and Hearings, *Employment of Retired Military and Civilian Personnel by Defense Industries*, House Armed Services Committee, 86th Cong., 1st sess., pp. 390–476.

acter. The Department of Agriculture, for example, has a responsibility for and to the farmers of the country as well as a responsibility to the President and Congress. The military, on the other hand, are responsible only to the higher political authorities of government: their representative role is minimal; this is the essence of "civilian control." Thus, the top military leaders of a service—those who might be presumed to be most active and influential in the defense of its interests—are normally among those who must act with the greatest circumspection in this area. The "backstop" association, however, is uniquely able to perform this function. As a private group, it can openly criticize the Administration while service leaders limit themselves to oblique suggestions under the prodding of sympathetic congressmen. The Chief of Staff speaks for his service but also for the Administration and the Department of Defense. The service association speaks only for the service.

In addition, the association can engage in political tactics and methods which are denied to the service. The Regular Army, for example, in its struggles with the National Guard Association and the Reserve Officers Association, is, as one scholar has pointed out, handicapped "by its inability to throw charges—either reckless or responsible charges—into the headlines as its opponents frequently do."[17] Service associations are under no such restraints, and the less directly they are associated with the service, the greater their freedom. On the other hand, they cannot become completely detached; if they are too distant from the service, they decrease their authority and responsibility and may misjudge the service's interests.

Preserving the balance poses problems with respect to membership. From the start, the Navy League protected its freedom of action by barring from membership military men on active duty. The Air Force Association permitted active personnel to be members only in a non-voting, non-office-holding capacity. In contrast, the Army Association was originally composed largely of active officers. In 1956, however, it was reorganized, and the leadership was transferred to individuals not on active duty "so that the Association may exercise its right to express its own independent opinions."[18] While they may in consequence have the freedom to do so, the service associations rarely, if ever, take stands opposed by

---

[17] Charles D. Story, "The Formulation of Army Reserve Forces Policy: Its Setting Amidst Pressure Group Activity" (Ph.D. Dissertation, University of Oklahoma, 1958), p. 257.

[18] Secretary of the Army, *Army*, VII (December, 1956), 79.

the leaders of their service.[19] The resolutions and programs adopted by the service associations at their annual conventions represent approximately what the leaders of the services would ask for if they were freed from Administration restraints. In 1959, for instance, the Administration advocated an Army of 870,000 men, the Chief of Staff one of 925,000 men, and the Army Association one of 1 million men.

Usually the service recognizes the unique position of the service association and the special relations which exist between them. At the same time, it also stresses the independence of the association. The Navy League, the Secretary of the Navy declared in 1958, is "the civilian arm of the service." Two months later, however, Admiral Burke told a Navy League audience that the Navy "has absolutely no control over your fine organization." Air Force sources have informally referred to the AFA as "our lobby," and in 1949, General H. H. Arnold even described the Association as "Air Force–controlled." Yet its private character is also emphasized. The Secretary of the Army has declared that the relationship between the Department and the Association "although unofficial, must be close and cooperative." The "success of the Association," he said, "is a matter of vital interest to the Department of the Army."[20]

Cultivation of the "Grass Roots"

The postwar period was also marked by increased service activities designed specifically to reach public opinion at the "grass roots." Service installations and activities, of course, were spread across the face of the land. A clear distinction existed, however, between the interest of a community in a particular installation and its interest in the service as a whole. The congressman from Charleston is an ardent supporter of the Navy—until the Navy proposes to cut its operations at the Charleston Navy Yard. Unlike many private associations and a fair number of governmental agencies, the services could not easily mobilize sentiment across

[19] Rappaport, op. cit., p. 208. See the rather strained efforts of the Air Force Association leaders to differentiate their viewpoint from that of the Air Force, Hearings, Employment of Retired Military and Civilian Personnel, p. 407.

[20] Congressional Record, CIV (May 1, 1958), A4026; Army-Navy-Air Force Journal, XCV (July 5, 1958), 1312; The New York Times, December 29, 1956, p. 2; Hearings, National Defense Program—Unification and Strategy, House Armed Services Committee, 81st Cong., 1st sess., p. 70; Army, VII (December, 1956), 79.

the country in support of a national program. The problem which they faced was not dissimilar from that confronted by the large industrial corporations. Both the corporation and the service are national and highly centralized institutions. Political power in America, however, is to a large extent channeled through local organs. Individual political influence depends upon prolonged local residence and participation: the employees of the corporation and the service are continually on the move. On the one hand, the economic health of the local community may depend upon decisions by a General Staff in Washington or a board of directors in New York. On the other hand, the small community normally possesses direct access to state and local governing bodies, and frequently to Congress, in a way which is denied to the national organization.

Corporations have attempted to adjust to the decentralization of political power by supplementing their general public relations activities with other efforts specifically designed to reach local publics. The armed services have done likewise. Among them, the Army has been most active; more than the other services, it is apt to be concerned with issues where grass-roots support is important. Shortly after World War II, for instance, when confronted with the need to stimulate recruiting and to arouse support for universal military training, the Army sponsored the creation of Army Advisory Committees in numerous communities, each committee made up of leading local figures in business, religion, education, the press and radio, and civic organizations. "Information on our actual policies and actual plans," the Army's Chief of Information declared in 1947, "can be disseminated down through these advisory committees to all the various agencies that affect public opinion right out in the 'grass roots.' That is very important."[21] Antedating the Committees, but subsequently closely associated with them, were the civilian aides to the Secretary of the Army. Their duties included advising the Secretary on matters relating to the public standing of the Army, investigating specific problems at his request, and cooperating with the local Army commanders in furthering their programs. The Navy's counterpart to the Army Advisory Committees was the Advisory Council on Naval Affairs, sponsored by the Navy League. The members of the Advisory Council were appointed by the commandants of the various naval districts and furnished the Navy with a means of reaching local

[21] Collins, *op. cit.*, pp. 11–12.

opinion groups.[22] In addition to these broadly purposed programs, all the services emphasized the importance of "community relations" to the commanders of their posts and installations and urged them to carry on an active program of visits, support of local charities and projects, and sympathetic consideration of local interests.

The reserve structure was another means of reaching local public opinion. The reserve organization and, to an even greater extent, the National Guard were influential with Congress simply because they were organized locally. As more than one congressman has noted, in contrast to the service "backstop" associations, the reserve organizations "have the votes." "Because the National Guard Association represents the fifty-one states and territories," as one National Guard leader put it, "and is able through its membership to bring considerable pressure to bear on Congress, it has consistently enjoyed a high respect from Congress." The strength of the Guard, he continued, lies both "in the state representation" and in "the potential vote represented by the 500,000 and their families."[23] Army spokesmen and supporters frequently urged that efforts be made to utilize the reserves to put across the Army viewpoint.[24] The very power of the reserve organizations, however, made them less susceptible to use by the service leadership and more likely to have interests different from those of the service. The Guard, for instance, was politically stronger than the Army reserve, but also more independent of the Regular Army.

Industrial Bulwarks

The high level of military spending required by the cold war and the heavy concentration of that spending on complex weapons brought into existence a significant peacetime munitions industry for the first time in American history. In their search for support in civil society the services could hardly overlook their contractors.

[22] Lt. Col. T. J. Cleary, "Civilian Aides to the Secretary of the Army," *Army Information Digest*, VII (November, 1952), 13–18; Hearings, *Employment of Retired Military and Civilian Personnel*, p. 439; *The New York Times*, April 13, 1958, p. 12; *New York Herald Tribune*, April 15, 1958, p. 9.

[23] Maj. Gen. James F. Cantwell, Chief of Staff, New York National Guard, July 23, 1957, quoted in Story, *op. cit.*, pp. 210–11.

[24] E.g., Major Gen. E. S. Bres, "The ORC, Too, Can Tell the Army's Story," *Army Information Digest*, I (October, 1946), 3–5; "Representatives of National Security," *Infantry Journal*, LIX (July, 1946), 54–55; Col. S. Legree, "We Must Get Together," *ibid.*, LX (May, 1947), 25–29.

In mobilizing industry, the Navy and the Air Force started with two advantages over the Army. Both the Navy and the Air Force furnished a substantial portion of the total demand for the products of two distinct industries. The ship-building industry would always encourage a larger Navy and the aircraft industry a substantial Air Force. The Army, in contrast, had no such concentrated source of industrial support. Secondly, the research, development, and, in some cases, the production of Army weapons was traditionally handled in government arsenals. The Navy made greater use of private industry, and the Air Force came into existence with little organized experience in research and development and hence depended very heavily upon the private aircraft companies. Army arsenals could generate support from the congressmen of their districts, but the aircraft companies could do this and also engage in all the public relations and propagandizing activities which their private status and funds permitted. "The aircraft industry," Senator Goldwater observed, "has probably done more to promote the Air Force than the Air Force has done itself."[25]

Inter-service rivalry stimulated industrial competition, and industrial competition, in turn, fanned the flames of inter-service rivalry. In 1959, as the conflict between the Army Nike and the Air Force Bomarc missiles came to a head, Boeing took newspaper and magazine ads to counter the "misinformation" spread about Bomarc, and Army officials urged Western Electric to increase its advertising on behalf of Nike.[26] On the other hand, as General Gavin said, "What appears to be intense inter-service rivalry . . . in most cases . . . is fundamentally industrial rivalry."[27] Trade journals, Wernher von Braun declared, engage in "active instigation of inter-service rivalry." They "often seem to feel that they owe it to their advertisers to go to bat for them" and to "publish quite frequently some rather vitriolic articles, taking a very one-sided stand in favor of one of the services."[28] In nation-wide advertisements, Chrysler proudly heralded the Army's successful Jupiter C space shot. Two weeks later, Douglas retaliated with ads declaring that the Air Force Thor was "already in mass production." The

[25] Quoted in Fairfield, *loc. cit.,* p. 22.
[26] Hearings, *Employment of Retired Military and Civilian Personnel,* pp. 570 ff., 739–44, 752, 910–11.
[27] Lt. Gen. James M. Gavin, *War and Peace in the Space Age* (New York: 1958), pp. 256–57.
[28] Hearings, *Inquiry into Satellite and Missile Programs,* Senate Armed Services Committee, 85th Cong., 1st sess., p. 615.

Army Director of Special Weapons replied by referring caustically to a missile with "an apogee of four feet." The Air Force struck back by leaking information concerning its new solid-fuel Minuteman missile and at the same time deprecating the expense of the Navy's solid-fuel Polaris missile. The Navy replied that Polaris was less vulnerable and much closer to operation than Minuteman. "Thus a publicity contest between two corporations," as William S. Fairfield observed "now involved the uniformed personnel of all three services."[29]

The Thor-Jupiter controversy was perhaps a classic example of how inter-service rivalry initially can open a choice to the top civilian leaders of the defense establishment and then, in effect, shut off that choice through the competitive castellation of services. Thor and Jupiter were, as one general said, "about as alike as the Ford and the Chevrolet."[30] The Secretary of Defense repeatedly asserted that only one or the other would be put into production. He delayed his decision, however, and in the end, choice was impossible. "If the Defense Department suggested canceling the Air Force's Thor program," a former Pentagon official declared, "a Congressional delegation from California would be down our necks. And elimination of the Army Jupiter program would have half the Alabama delegation plus a couple of representatives from the Detroit area fighting us."[31]

The shift from aircraft to missiles tended to broaden the ties of the aircraft industry with the services. The Navy, of course, had always been a significant purchaser of aircraft, and increasingly in the 1950's the Army also turned to the aircraft companies for its missiles. "The aircraft industry," one Air Force legislative liaison officer is quoted as saying in 1958, "just isn't likely to be as good a source for lobbying as it was two years ago."[32] In the conflict between Jupiter (Chrysler) and Thor (Douglas), Douglas Aircraft was on the side of the Air Force. In the conflict between the Air Force Bomarc (Boeing) and the Army Nike (Douglas), however, Douglas was presumably on the side of the Army. As the major defense contractors in missiles and electronics increasingly held contracts with two or more services, the lines of industrial competition did not always coincide with and sometimes perhaps blurred those of inter-service competition.

[29] Fairfield, op. cit., p. 23.
[30] Hearings, Satellite and Missile Programs, p. 959.
[31] Quoted in Fairfield, op. cit., p. 21.
[32] Ibid., p. 23.

The Proliferation of Doctrine

After World War II, inter-service competition contributed to increased service concern with, and output of, doctrine. Every bureaucratic agency, military and civilian, tends to develop a "bureau philosophy" or "ideology."[33] The armed services differ from most civilian groups, however, in the extent to which the bureau philosophy becomes formal, self-conscious, and explicit. The philosophies of civilian agencies may be just as real as those of the military, but they are seldom codified into written statements of "doctrine." The importance of doctrine stems from the extent to which the military groups are perceived to be and perceive themselves to be simply the instruments of a higher national policy. The armed services explicitly rationalize their existence in terms of a higher national end, and each activity and unit is justified only by its contribution to the realization of the prescribed hierarchy of values and purposes. This instrumentalism is reflected in the emphasis, peculiar to the military, on the concept of "mission,"[34] and it manifests itself most concretely in the elaboration of doctrine.

Prior to the 1930's, doctrine was reasonably well developed in the Navy, somewhat less so in the Army. The rise of airpower, however, was a powerful stimulant to the military quest for ideology. Lacking secure organizational existence, or general acceptance during the 1920's and 1930's, the supporters of airpower, like any new, crusading group, were tremendously concerned with the development of an intellectual rationale. The existence of the surface forces might be taken for granted; the need for an air force had to be demonstrated. Moreover, no longer was it possible for a service to elaborate a doctrine defining its importance to the nation and its relation to national policy without explicitly—and not just inferentially—defining the position of the other services also. Mahan had constructed a doctrine of seapower without specifically denigrating landpower. For the supporters of airpower, however, the attack on the surface forces was unavoidable. Once the Air

[33] See Herbert A. Simon, Donald W. Smithburg, Victor A. Thompson, *Public Administration* (New York: 1950), pp. 543–44.

[34] "Military officers, perhaps more than members of other professions, are accustomed to thinking of their duties in terms of specific missions. . . . The mission concept is common to all command and staff duties and functions. It is one of the constants of our profession." Department of the Army, *The Role of the Army* (Pamphlet 21–70, June 29, 1955), pp. 3–4.

Force was established, the intensity of its doctrinal concern perhaps moderated somewhat, but by this time the other services had felt compelled to reply in kind. Just as unification led to inter-service political conflict, so it also stimulated inter-service doctrinal conflict, and with the same power goals in view: jurisdiction, appropriations, and influence.

The historical output of political theory, it has been suggested, correlates rather well with the presence of political crisis, turmoil, and conflict. So also, when vital controversies arise, military doctrine flourishes. After 1945, it proliferated in a variety of forms in manuals, speeches, journals, regulations, War College theses, and staff studies. The competitive spur to its formulation was concretely reflected in the creation of special staff units specifically designed to develop doctrine and arguments for use in the inter-service debates, such as the Navy's "Op-23," headed by Captain Arleigh Burke during the B-36 hearings, and the Army's Policy Coordinating Group, the head of which retired shortly after the inter-service blow-up in the spring of 1956. Each service also attempted to formulate concise statements of doctrinal guidance for its members and persuasion for its potential supporters.[35]

III. THE CHANGING CONTEXT OF INTER-SERVICE COMPETITION

Inter-service competition and the castellation of the services continued throughout the fifteen years after World War II. The content and the significance of the competition, however, changed markedly. In the immediate postwar period, fundamental issues of service existence and strategy were at stake. After a major war, military policy is in a state of flux. The cake of custom, bureaucratic routine, and sustained habits of behavior—executive, congressional, and popular—are broken. Change is not only possible, but expected. In such periods, existing organizational units have the most to fear from major threats to their existence, and new organizational units have the best prospects for an easy birth or growth.

After World War II, each service and hoped-for service was anxious to carve out a role for itself suitable to its ambitions and self-conceptions before a postwar equilibrium was established and the patterns of organization and behavior jelled into enduring

[35] E.g., the nineteen-page Air Force Manual 1-2, *United States Air Force Basic Doctrine*, and the sixty-five-page *A Guide to Army Philosophy* (Pamphlet 20-1, January 22, 1958).

form. The unification battle involved the general pattern of postwar organizational relationships for all the services and, specifically, the formal recognition of the separate existence of the Air Force. Closely linked with this were the legitimate fears of the Navy and Marine Corps for their future being. "Why should we have a Navy at all?" asked the commanding general of the Army Air Forces, and answered himself by declaring that, "There are no enemies for it to fight except apparently the Army Air Force." Similarly, the then Chief of Staff of the Army, Dwight D. Eisenhower, made it quite clear that the Marines ought to be maintained as only a minor landing force.[36] The uneasiness these views inspired in the sea-going services was not allayed until their functions were carefully defined in the National Security Act and the Key West roles-and-missions paper, the Forrestals floated forth on the flood of Korean War appropriations, and the Marine position was sanctified in the Marine Corps Act of 1952. By 1952, the United States had four recognized services instead of the two it had had in 1940. After 1952, whatever the vicissitudes of budgets and strategy, the existence of no service was in serious danger from another. An equilibrium had been reached.

The strategic debates of the late 1940's seemed equally momentous for the services. All agreed that the next war would be a total war. They did not agree how that war should be fought. In the Air Force image, the war consisted of an initially decisive—or airpower—stage in which victory would be irretrievably won or lost, and then a second mopping-up stage in which the other services might be of some use. The Army view (and essentially the Navy view, too) was that the initial air exchange would be indecisive until the surface forces had been built up to the point where they could move forward to seize bases and territories close to the enemy. After they had done their work, the air attack might play a somewhat more important role. But the final *coup de grâce* would still be administered by ground forces moving in, defeating the enemy's land armies, and occupying enemy territory. Between these two concepts of a future war and the way in which it should be fought, no compromise seemed possible.

The debate, however, soon became obsolete. The war whose strategy the services were debating never occurred. Instead, the

---

[36] Quoted in Hearings, *The National Security Act of 1947*, House Committee on Expenditures in Executive Departments, 80th Cong., 1st sess., p. 506; *National Security Act of 1947*, H. Rep. 961, 80th Cong., 1st sess., pp. 12–14.

Korean War and the development of thermonuclear weapons changed the framework of strategic thought. It became less and less likely that another war would be World War II plus nuclear weapons. The Air Force no longer stressed the decisive aspect of airpower, but rather its deterrent quality. The experience of the other services in Korea was codified into a doctrine of limited war. Previously, the Air Force concept and the surface forces' concept of how to fight a general war had been completely incompatible. Deterrence and limited war, on the other hand, were complementary and competitive but not incompatible. Previously, any increase in the effectiveness of strategic airpower meant a decrease in the probable roles of the other services. Now, the more effective the massive deterrent became, the greater the probability of the smaller-scale disturbances with which the other services were primarily concerned. To be sure, the debates still continued over how much of the effort should be devoted to one purpose and how much to the other. All the services, however, accepted the necessity of devoting some resources to each. What had been conflicting images of a single-contingency future were replaced by general agreement on a multiple-contingency future, although the priorities and probabilities of the various contingencies remained in dispute.

In the mid-1950's, inter-service debate was just as prevalent and intense as it had been previously. Strategic questions, however, had become less important and proprietary issues more important. The question was less what should be done than how it should be done and who should do it. Neither the fundamental existence of the services nor fundamental alternatives of national strategy were main issues, but rather marginal gains and losses of weapons and functions. Major strategic issues were still debated, but the debate was not so strictly along service lines. In 1949, the Navy attacked the entire theory and practice of strategic air warfare: "the threat of instant retaliation," Admiral Radford had declared, "will not prevent [war] and may even invite it."[37] In 1956, the Army and the Air Force tangled over neither the doctrine of retaliation nor the need to develop strategic missiles to implement that doctrine, but rather over who would build the missiles, who would operate them, and how much would be spent on one missile against another. Service enthusiasts might be as passionate as ever, but their

---

[37] Hearings, *Unification and Strategy*, p. 52.

disputes involved proprietorship, not principle. The cause of Colonel Nickerson's martyrdom was hardly in the same class with that of John Crommelin, much less that of Billy Mitchell.

The lines of strategic cleavage thus diverged from the lines of inter-service competition. The strategic functions of the cold war —massive deterrence, defense of Western Europe, continental defense, preparation for limited wars, construction of a general war mobilization base—fell within the domain of no single service. One service might be more interested in one strategic mission than another, but the differences were differences in degree rather than kind. The Army played a major role in the defense of Western Europe and in the maintenance of a general war mobilization base. It also, however, had the three-division Strategic Army Corps for limited war, and devoted perhaps fifteen percent of its budget to continental defense. During the mid-1950's, also, the Army developed Redstone and Jupiter missiles for strategic deterrence and the exploration of space. Similarly, the Navy contributed to a variety of missions: naval forces in the Atlantic and Mediterranean to the defense of Europe; naval aviation and Polaris submarines to strategic deterrence; warning aircraft, radar ships, and, increasingly, anti-submarine warfare to continental defense; carrier task forces and the Marine Corps to limited war needs. The major combat commands of the Air Force, in turn, were concerned with strategic deterrence, continental defense, and the tactical support of limited war forces.

The diversification of service functions had several important consequences. First, it tended to foster intraservice conflict. In the late 1950's, a continuing debate went on within the Army over the extent to which it should aspire to a role in strategic deterrence. "For $5 billion worth of troop equipment," one division commander remarked in 1959, "I'd trade Huntsville away in a minute."[38] Similarly, the Army commitment to the defense of Europe necessarily limited its effort to develop the Strategic Army Corps. Within the Air Force, officers of the Strategic Air Command openly attacked the recommendations of the Air Force–sponsored Project Vista on tactical nuclear weapons and of Project Lincoln on continental defense. In 1949, Air Force fighter pilots reportedly stimulated press leaks unfavorable to the B-36,[39]

---

[38] "Forces on the Ground," *Time*, LXXIII (May 11, 1959), 23.

[39] Paul Y. Hammond, "Super-Carriers and B-36 Bombers: Appropriations, Strategy, and Politics" (Twentieth Century Fund Project on Civil-Military Relations; mimeo.), p. 59.

and junior officers of the Air Defense and Tactical Air Commands later repeatedly warned of the dangers of giving overriding priority to strategic retaliation. On retiring in 1959, General Weyland, commander of the Tactical Air Command, "warned that the Pentagon's preoccupation with strategic bombing and long-range missiles may soon leave us unprepared to fight a limited war."[40] Within the Navy, intra-service struggle was muted because of the variety of functions to which individual naval weapons might contribute. Nonetheless, like the Army, in the mid-1950's, the Navy in the early 1960's was tending to divide between those who favored increased emphasis upon strategic deterrence and those favoring greater attention to the naval weapons and forces useful in limited and conventional warfare.

Intra-service rivalry, however, never rivaled inter-service rivalry. The services were like nation-states: loyalties to them tended to override sectional or class affiliations and also to be stronger than transnational loyalties. Normally, it is easier to change sectional or class affiliations within a nation-state than to change citizenship from one state to another. Changes in the former, moreover, can be partial and gradual, while changes in the latter are usually abrupt and clearcut. Similarly, within the military, the lines between functional groupings within a service were seldom as clearcut as the lines between services. If the Navy withered away, naval officers could not easily become citizens of the Air Force. On the other hand, if one naval function declined, no insuperable barriers prevented the transfer of officers associated with that function to other functions. The officers of a service were united in a common hierarchy, advancement through a common promotion list, identification with common symbols, allegiance to a common high command, and, to an increasing extent, attendance at a common undergraduate academy. The institutional ties probably precluded intra-service controversy from becoming as intense as inter-service controversy.

The relation of the services to fundamental issues of strategy in a sense tended to resemble the relation of the political parties to fundamental issues of national policy. The two parties have different centers of gravity with respect to policy, and yet each includes groups representing almost all viewpoints on the political spectrum. Similarly, while the outlook and doctrine of each service differs somewhat from that of the others, each service also has

[40] Jim G. Lucas, *Washington Daily News*, July 29, 1959, quoted in Hearings, *Employment of Retired Military and Civilian Personnel*, p. 473.

interests all across the strategic spectrum. At times, of course, there may be party votes on major issues of policy, and at times, also differences over strategy may coincide with differences between the services. Moreover, just as the parties exist independently of the issues of the moment, so also the existence of the service is independent of the strategy of the moment. The resolution of any particular set of issues, whether political or military, does not end the competition among the groups, whether parties or services. The competition continues, rising to peaks fixed by the calendar of biennial elections and annual budgets. Partisan debate and inter-service debate are often carried on in clichés, slogans, and appeals, with little operational significance for governmental action. A member of a service is loyal to the service irrespective of its strategic function, just as a good organization Democrat or Republican is loyal to the party irrespective of its stand on policy. The existence of the services, moreover, like the existence of the parties, tends to obscure the issues of debate. The argument that the United States is well off to have nonideological parties and that it would be unfortunate if the division between left and right coincided exactly with the division between Democrat and Republican may also hold true with respect to the services and strategy. Strategic issues are blurred by the overlay of service competition, and the proprietary issues at stake in the latter are inherently easier to compromise than basic issues of strategic principle.

The cold war thus replaced the simple pattern of service-*vs.*-service rivalry by a complex matrix of rivalry between service and service, service and function, function and function. The multiplication of the lines of conflict also tended to minimize its intensity. In this, the evolution of military politics followed a classic American path. Overlapping memberships in interest groups moderate group conflicts. The conflict of interest groups within and across party lines moderates the party struggle. Party conflict across institutional boundaries moderates executive-legislative conflict. Similarly, in the military area, just as inter-service rivalry moderated the potential conflict between military services and civilian agencies, the emergence of conflicting functional programs tends to moderate inter-service rivalry. A society, as E. A. Ross said, "which is riven by a dozen oppositions along lines running in every direction, may actually be in less danger of . . . falling to pieces than one split along just one line. For each new cleavage contributes to narrow the cross clefts, so that one might say that society *is sewn together* by its inner conflicts."[41] Experts in military organization often argue that "unification" requires either the merger of the four services into a single uniform or the abolition of the services and organization of the Pentagon purely on a functional basis. The former proposal, however, is blindly utopian in rejecting the inevitability of pluralism, and the latter could intensify conflict to the point where it would be unbearable. "Unification" is more likely to come not from the reduction or elimination of intramilitary controversy but from its multiplication.

Diversification of function also gave the services organizational flexibility and balance by freeing them from identification with and dependence upon any single strategic concept or functional mission. "The Army," its Secretary declared in 1957, "cannot—and indeed assiduously seeks not to—commit itself to any particular doctrine, strategy, or tactic."[42] Noncommitment was the means of self-preservation. Shifts in emphasis in national policy from massive retaliation to limited war to continental defense would affect the relative standing of the services, but it was unlikely that they could threaten the existence of any service. The new role of the services was formally recognized in the Reorganization Act of 1958: the inter-service and functional commands became clearly responsible for combat, the services for personnel, training, and logistics. By reducing the combat functions of the services, the act insured their continued existence.

If this tendency continued, eventually the services would end up as English regiments on a grand scale—administrative organizations rather than fighting organizations. Thus, at the very time when inter-service competition was forcing the services to develop doctrinal justifications, the evolution of strategy was depriving them of their traditional source of doctrine. As a result, the doctrinal issues debated among the services often seemed to have but minor relevance outside the locus of inter-service competition. Not infrequently, they assumed a certain metaphysical quality, in arguments over whether landpower or airpower was the dominant force in modern war and whether guided missiles were aviation or artillery. Such issues had little practical consequence for policy,

---

[41] Edward A. Ross, *The Principles of Sociology* (New York: 1920), p. 165. See also Lewis A. Coser, *The Functions of Social Conflict* (Chicago: The Free Press of Glencoe, 1956), pp. 76–81.

[42] W. M. Brucker, "A Year of Progress," *Army Information Digest*, XII (February, 1957), 2.

except—and it is a vital exception—so far as the future of the service was concerned.

The value of the services thus stemmed precisely from their incomplete commitment to any single doctrine. An organization such as SAC or the Continental Defense Command, which exists for only one strategic purpose, cannot be receptive to changes in its purpose or to the creation of new organizations embodying competing purposes. The functional commands of today are the vested interests of tomorrow. So long as the existence of no service, however, depends upon any single strategic purpose, no service has reason to oppose intransigently changes in strategic purposes. Organizational permanence is the partner of strategic flexibility. Thus the unified and specified commands may become the instruments of strategy, and yet the political castles of the services may also continue to stand, with their storied keeps of service loyalty and tradition, their inner and outer walls in the executive and Congress, their towers and barbicans in industry, their moats flowing with the currents of public opinion. Perhaps, at some point, a major political or military innovation may, like gunpowder, bring these political structures down in a heap of broken masonry. The experience of other established organizations in American politics, however, suggests a different fate: that the castles of the services, like many of their medieval counterparts, will remain in existence, battered but untaken, long after the decisive battles —both political and military—have shifted to other fields.

Editor's Conclusion

The traditional mode of military analysis, which saw in war a continuation of politics but with its own appropriate means, is no longer applicable. Policy and strategy merge at every point. No statesman can overlook the cataclysmic alternatives before him. No problem can be left solely to the arbitrament of arms. Communication in the nuclear age is particularly important among adversaries. Arms control requires the same sense or urgency as does the study of strategy and of diplomacy.

When strategy first attracted the attention of academic analysts, the inconsistency between traditional modes of thought and the nature of modern weapons was obvious. As long as an analysis was systematic, it was likely to uncover discrepancies and weaknesses that needed correction.

Today, the situation is more complicated. A great degree of sophistication in technical studies has been achieved—so much, in fact, that the danger today is precisely the opposite of what it was a decade ago. Skill in quantitative analysis may downgrade those factors that cannot be quantified. A complex strategic theory may be so intellectually satisfying that the difficulties of human beings employing it in moments of great tension and confusion may be overlooked. It may be tempting to treat allies as factors of a security arrangement and to forget that their ultimate contribution depends on intangibles of political will. In the day-to-day press of events, we may lose sight of the fact that we need sound general criteria for measuring political progress in the developing countries. This is another way of saying that national security policy is not primarily a technical problem, but a challenge to political understanding and, ultimately, to philosophical insight.